Training minds for the war of ideas

MANCHESTER
1824

Manchester University Press

Training minds for the war of ideas

*Ashridge College, the Conservative Party
and the cultural politics of Britain, 1929–54*

Clarisse Berthezène

Manchester University Press

Published by Manchester University Press
Altrincham Street, Manchester M1 7JA
www.manchesteruniversitypress.co.uk

British Library Cataloguing-in-Publication Data
A catalogue record for this book is available from the British Library

Library of Congress Cataloging-in-Publication Data applied for

ISBN   978 0 7190 8649 6   hardback

First published 2015

Typeset
by Carnegie Book Production, Lancaster
Printed in Great Britain
by CPI Group (UK) Ltd, Croydon, CR0 4YY

In memory of Ewen Henry Harvey Green
(16 October 1958–16 September 2006)

Contents

Acknowledgements

This book has been under way for an embarrassing number of years. At no point did the research or the writing resemble what the Conservatives identified as the triumphant march of progress at play within the Whig interpretation of history. It was never a linear process, but rather a constant meandering and groping towards an uncertain end. Throughout this long journey, many people have helped me.

Ewen Green first told me about the *Ashridge Journal* when I was a doctoral student in 1999, so that's how far back we're going. The Journal mentioned a College of which there seemed to be few traces left. Intrigued by the snippets I found in the Conservative party archive, I decided to visit Ashridge College in Hertfordshire, whose 13th century beauty was legendary. On a cold winter day in 2001, I met Mick Thompson, the gardener of the estate, who had just been appointed archivist – just like in a play by Jean Giraudoux, except it wasn't set in Bellac – and was in charge of an uncatalogued archive, which I expected to be fragmentary, but which turned out to be an extraordinary source of great historical significance. By placing it alongside other archives, I saw the story of Ashridge College unfold. This book is first and foremost a story, a forgotten story. I thank Mick Thompson for his time and his help and Leslie Hannah, the Chief Executive of Ashridge Business School at the time, for his generosity in hosting me at Ashridge. I am grateful to the Bonar Law Memorial Trust for permission to use photographs and quotations from their collections.

I would like to acknowledge the generous financial support of LARCA at Paris Diderot University, which subsidised most of my trips to Britain over the years, as well as the GDR 'mondes britanniques' (Paris Sorbonne), and thank my colleagues at Paris Diderot University for their support and encouragement.

Special thanks are due to the indispensable staff at archives and libraries I visited, in particular Colin Harris at the modern papers reading room at the Bodleian Library, Helen Langley, also at the Bodleian, and the current archivist at the Conservative party archive, Jeremy McIlwaine whose unfailing assistance in responding to my always urgent requests and emails and whose extraordinary professionalism deserve a special mention. The Conservative Party Trust kindly permitted me to quote from their collections. Extracts from two letters written by Winston Churchill are reproduced with permission of Curtis Brown, London on behalf of the Estate of Sir Winston Churchill. Copyright © Winston S. Churchill. I am grateful to the Syndics of Cambridge University Library, to The Master and Fellows of Trinity College, Cambridge, Churchill Archives Centre, Churchill College, Cambridge, the Parliamentary Archives, House of Lords Record Office, King's College, London, the Cadbury Research Library: Special Collections, University of Birmingham and the British Library Board in London for making the obtaining of permissions to quote an easy process.

An earlier, somewhat different, version of this book was published in French by the Presses de Sciences po in 2011. In attempting to translate myself, I rewrote the book differently. In this process, I was helped by Vanessa Bloor and Robert Boyce.

I am very grateful to my friends and colleagues from the PRI 'Iles britan-niques' who provided a stimulating environment and dialogue over the years. I am glad to have the opportunity to thank my friend Laura Downs, who is also part of the 'Transnational history of conservatism' seminar organised at the EHESS with Marc Olivier Baruch and Jean-Christian Vinel. All three have been both challenging and fun interlocutors and friends.

I am deeply grateful to my much-valued tutor at the LSE and friend Robert Boyce, who, with the greatest generosity, worked his way carefully through the complete draft of this book weeding out my mistakes. Jose Harris read earlier drafts of the manuscript and offered sharp and perceptive comments and suggestions. Stefan Collini bolstered my courage when it faltered and very kindly read and commented on several chapters of the manuscript. After such expert advice, any remaining errors are entirely mine! My greatest intellectual and personal debt is to the late Ewen Green, who was the inspiration for this book. His extensive knowledge and body of work on the history of British Conservatism, as well as his sparkling sense of humour and constant encouragement, were inspiring and nurturing. He is greatly missed and this book is dedicated to his memory.

I owe special thanks to all those who have given me a convivial home in London and Oxford, sometimes for months on end, for my research trips when I was no longer living in Britain. Robert Boyce and Gudrun Sveinbjarnardottir, Tanya Seghatchian and her family and the 'Southmoor

Road network' in Oxford: Alison Light and John O'Halloran; Caroline and Dermot Roaf.

My warmest thanks also go to those friends who have listened patiently to my ramblings about British Conservatives over the years and tolerated my obsession with Conservatism, in particular Ninon Vinsonneau, Jonathan Magidoff, Pauline Lavagne and Benoît Rossel. They have all been there when I needed them most.

To my family, Cédric, Cassandre, Hector, Balthazar and Coriolan, and my parents, Claire and Michel Berthezène, who are an unfailing source of love and support, I owe much gratitude.

Abbreviations

ACPPE	Advisory Committee on Policy and Political Education
BBC	British Broadcasting Corporation
BLMC	Bonar Law Memorial College
BLMT	Bonar Law Memorial Trust
BUF	British Union of Fascists
CCO	Conservative Central Office
CPA	Conservative Party Archive
CPC	Conservative Political Centre
CPRE	Council for the Preservation of Rural England
CRD	Conservative Research Department
ICI	Imperial Chemical Industries
JIL	Junior Imperial League
LRC	Labour Representation Committee
LSE	London School of Economics
NBA	National Book Association
NUCA	National Union of Conservative and Unionist Associations
RBC	Right Book Club
SDF	Social Democratic Federation
TUC	Trade Union Congress
WEA	Workers' Educational Association

Introduction

In 1928, the chairman of the British Conservative party, J. C. C. Davidson, raised almost £250,000 to acquire the estate of Ashridge, a historic manor house and its park, near Berkhamsted in Hertfordshire. The following year, he transferred the property of the estate to the 'Bonar Law Memorial Trust', the goals of which were the following:

(a) To honour the memory of a Great Statesman.

(b) To preserve a great and beautiful historical building from destruction.

(c) To cause the said Mansion House and Gardens and Park to be used for the purposes of an Educational Centre or College ... for educating persons in Economics in Political and Social Science in Political History with special reference to the development of the British Constitution and growth and expansion of the British Empire ...

(d) To trains [sic] persons to become Lecturers Speakers Writers and Workers with the view of furthering the object set forth in paragraph (c).

(e) To provide from time to time lectures and discussions either at the College or at any other place or places in the British Empire to which the General Public may (if thought fit) be admitted either gratis or on payment of such a fee or fees as may be prescribed.

(f) To provide such a staff both administrative domestic educational protective or otherwise ...

(g) To allow the College to be used as a Hostel (including the furnishing of board and lodging) for students either gratis (in the case of poor and deserving students) or for ... payment.[1]

On 21 November 1929, the Bonar Law Memorial College was founded at Ashridge. Until 1954, it acted as a 'College in citizenship' to provide, both through teaching and publications, adult political education. Although founded by the Conservative party, the College did not belong to the party and it functioned autonomously, claiming its political independence. Yet, the Trust Deed stated clearly that the Leader and the Chairman of the Party, as well as two representatives of the National Union of Conservative and Unionist Associations (NUCA), were to be ex-officio members of the Governing Body of Ashridge. The Conservative party, as an institution, was not mentioned in the Trust Deed, but the main contributor to the purchase of the estate, Urban H. Broughton, was described as being 'deeply concerned at the danger of ... "Bolshevism" and he believed that the best way to preserve liberty under a constitutional government was by educating the electorate in the responsibilities of citizenship'. Broughton had been a Conservative MP for Preston: he considered the Conservative party the best guarantor of 'responsible citizenship'[2] and wished to ensure that eminent members of the Party sat on the Council of Governors of the College.

For the next twenty years the College, the full title of which was the Bonar Law Memorial College, Ashridge (hereafter referred to as Ashridge) was to act as a school for Conservative intellectuals, creating, in their own words, 'Conservative Fabians', and as a 'College of Citizenship' for 'the general education of the electorate'.[3] In 1954 its Deed of Foundation was changed by Act of Parliament, and Ashridge was 'refounded' as an educational charity. In 1959 it became a Management College, which it remains today.

Ashridge's archive is an extraordinarily rich, largely untapped source of considerable historical importance in terms not only of Conservative party history, but also of the history of adult education, the intellectual and social history of political education and the cultural history of 'middlebrow' thought in inter-war Britain.[4] The Ashridge archive is divided into departmental holdings related to various aspects of the administrative structure and functioning of the Bonar Law Memorial Trust (BLMT) and Ashridge. It was transferred from Ashridge College in Hertfordshire to the Conservative party archive at the Bodleian Library, Oxford on 13 January 2011 and is in the process of being catalogued and scanned. Placed alongside material contained in Arthur Bryant and J. C. C. Davidson's archives, this material provides rich insights into the political and intellectual history of Conservatism and the Conservative party. Stanley Baldwin's and R. A. Butler's archives are also valuable sources and show the frequently conflictual relationship between the College and the party, a perspective that can be further supported by drawing on material from the Conservative party archives. The attempt to create a residential 'College in Citizenship', which would act as an adult education community, is an interesting institutional history in its own right. Furthermore, it sheds new light on debates and tensions within the Conservative party in the period 1929–54. Finally, it throws into relief the question of the 'anti-intellectualism' of the Conservative party, which in turn has often acted as synecdoche for the anti-intellectualism of British public and political life. Ashridge was explicitly designed to reflect on the nature and the role of Conservative intellectuals and to assist in shaping them.[5]

This book aims to make a contribution at the point of intersection of three historiographical traditions. The first is the political history of the Conservative party. Ashridge College was a staff college as well as a centre for political education and its aim was to contribute to the electoral dominance of the Conservative party. After the 1935 general election, the *Ashridge Journal* stated that

> The new Cabinet is almost entirely composed of Ashridge lecturers – Mr. Baldwin, Mr. Ernest Brown, Mr. Neville Chamberlain, Mr. Duff Cooper, Sir Philip Cunliffe-Lister, Mr. Anthony Eden, Mr. Walter Elliot, Sir Bolton Eyres-Monsell, Lord Hailsham, Lord Halifax, Sir Samuel Hoare, Mr. Ormsby-Gore, Lord Eustace Percy, Mr. Runciman, Sir John Simon, Mr. Oliver Stanley, Mr. J. H. Thomas, and Lord Zetland. This is just as it should be. Indeed, association with Ashridge seems to be the surest stepping-stone to Cabinet rank.[6]

Ashridge was at the centre of a number of networks within the Conservative party. This fact cannot be gainsaid, and in this respect the study of Ashridge is a contribution to the institutional history of the Conservative party.[7] Yet, by exploring Ashridge's role in creating and diffusing a distinctively Tory body of ideas about history, culture and citizenship, this study seeks to make a further contribution to the history of Conservative thought. Since the 1990s, several historians have taken an interest in Conservative thought, opposing the simplistic stereotype that the Conservative party was the most 'stupid party'. E. H. H. Green, David Jarvis, Philip Williamson, and more recently David Thackeray, focused on the Conservatives' *ideas*.[8] The story of Ashridge is part and parcel of this renewed political history.

The second historiographical tradition is articulated to the first, in so far as it has been concerned with the alleged 'anti-intellectualism' of the Conservative party. The study of Ashridge College plays a part in a broader intellectual history centred on what Stefan Collini called the 'absence thesis' – the supposed absence of intellectuals as a significant category in British public life – and the general cultural valorisation of 'common sense' over reason. The emphasis on a Conservative 'middlebrow' ideal and on specifically 'middlebrow' thinkers as representatives of national identity places the story of Ashridge within a broader intellectual debate in Britain about cultural hierarchies.[9]

Third, this book engages with the historiography of the middle class and its 're-making' between the wars. Ashridge was part of a larger response by Conservatives to the arrival of a mass electorate. In this respect, the book seeks to extend works by Ross McKibbin and Jon Lawrence on political language, popular conservatism and political culture more generally.[10] Thus, *Training minds for the war of ideas: Ashridge College, the Conservative party and the cultural politics of Britain, 1929–1954* is a study of the interaction of political, social and intellectual history and it offers a new interpretation of the construction of that 'peculiar, Conservative modernity' Peter Mandler detected in the inter-war years.[11]

The study of Ashridge's cultural project to train Conservative 'intellectuals' raises a series of questions. The history of intellectuals in Britain is in itself a delicate topic.[12] To articulate this history with that of the Conservative party might seem a fraught enterprise, for several reasons. To begin with, the very term 'intellectuals' has been a matter of contestation since it first started to become current in English at the end of the nineteenth century. It was initially perceived as a foreign import, and its associations were with Dreyfusism in France and Bolshevism in Russia, giving it a largely pejorative force. In many respects, the 'intellectual' referred to all things non-English. The historiography has long reflected this vision and accredited the idea of an 'English exceptionalism', whereby 'intellectuals' were altogether absent from English society.[13] Ashridge's attempt to make 'Tory intellectuals', but of a distinctively 'middlebrow' kind, offers to provide a further strand of complexity to the long history of British ambivalence towards this contested category.

The historiography of the Conservative party seems to confirm the importance of anti-intellectualism as part of the Conservative identity, and numerous historians have dissociated the study of Conservatism from the study of political ideas. John Ramsden wrote that '*A History of the Conservative Party* ... does not owe much to the work of philosophers'.[14] Likewise, Andrew Gamble explained that 'It is in vain that armies of researchers set out to discover whether Conservative practice reflects a coherent "philosophy."'[15] Conservative ideas and Conservatism were left to philosophers and political scientists, who were more interested in the presentation of Conservatism as a system of ideas rather than in the historical context in which these ideas had emerged and how they were received. Noel O'Sullivan, Michael Freeden, Robert Eccleshall, W. H. Greenleaf, Roger Scruton and Ted Honderich focused on the formalisation of Conservative ideas, several of them drawing particular inspiration from the work of Michael Oakeshott.[16] Freeden wondered 'Why is there a dearth of capable, sophisticated enquiry into the nature of conservatism, by comparison with the reams of print on liberalism or socialism?'[17] One might raise the same question with regard to intellectual history or the history of ideas. Even though the number of historians interested in the history of Conservative ideas has increased since the 1990s, they remain less numerous than their counterparts for the Labour party. That Stuart Ball's impressive recent monograph on the Conservative party devoted a whole chapter to 'Conservatism. Principles and Temperament' is a tribute to these changes.[18] E. H. H. Green and Philip Williamson considered Conservatism as 'non ideological ideology'. They explained that 'The party's claim to be non-ideological is in itself an ideological statement.' 'The notion of Conservatism as a "non-ideology" should be taken seriously only insofar as it is in itself an aspect of Conservative ideology.'[19] There are more numerous studies on the Thatcher period,[20] insofar as Thatcherism aimed at being an ideology. Margaret Thatcher declared in 1975: 'We must have an ideology. The other side have got an ideology they can test their policies against. We must have one as well.'[21] For some, this claim to an ideology was precisely what distinguished Thatcherism from Conservatism.[22] Freeden reconciled Thatcherism and Conservatism by presenting the latter as essentially a 'swivel-mirror'[23] which reflects everything it sees and adjusts to it. The emphasis placed by Margaret Thatcher on the free economy and the strong state, in Andrew Gamble's words,[24] would be a reaction to the Socialism of the Labour party in the 1970s. Freeden explained that Conservatism was 'an ideology that attains self-awareness when exposed by its ideological opponents, rather than at its own behest, and it reacts to them in looking-glass manner'.[25] The Conservative party reacted to circumstances, so the argument went, rather than acting according to its own principles. Green and Williamson, on the other hand, considered Conservatism to be anchored in certain principles. Green referred to Martin Seliger, who distinguished between the immutable principles of an ideology and the means to express those principles, which can take different forms according to the different circumstances and contexts.[26]

To train Conservative intellectuals, which was the explicit objective of Ashridge, one needed to define what an intellectual was and the role that he or she (nearly always he in this period) was to play in British political life. More specifically, it was a question of knowing whether it was possible for Conservatives to appropriate the term 'intellectual', which had been annexed, so ran the argument, by the Left, or if another term should be found. That was a recurring question for the Conservatives. In 1968, T. Szamuely wrote: 'That there could be an intellectual right ... would have seemed patently absurd – so closely had "intellectual" become identified with "progressive", "liberal" or "Leftist".'[27]

The period that follows the Second World War is probably the only period, apart from the Thatcher years, when the Conservative party was seen as engaging in wide-ranging intellectual reflection. The Conservative Research Department (CRD), under R. A. Butler, became a 'thinking machine',[28] and the Conservative Political Centre (CPC) and the One Nation Group acted as 'think-tanks'. This explains why Kenneth Clarke stated in the 1990s that 'In the late 1950s university students such as myself rarely heard the tired old allegation that we were supporters of a "stupid party". The illustrious names of Butler, Macleod, Maudling and Powell acted as our shield.'[29] By underlining the importance of the Conservatives' intellectual activity after 1945, Clarke, like many others, did not recognise that there had been any Conservative intellectual engagement before then. The 1930s in particular are often considered as a failed decade for the Conservatives, who, despite being in power, or perhaps because they were in power, were seen as not having engaged in a broad debate of ideas, like numerous Socialists at the time. The extreme Right has, for a long time, been an important subject of interest for historians of the 1930s.[30] The historiography of the 1930s seems on the whole to imply that the Conservatives' unique *raison d'être* was their *Appetite for Power*, in the words of John Ramsden. Ramsden examined the organisation of the Conservative party and the efficiency of its electoral machine in *The Age of Balfour and Baldwin*. This was also the main theme of Stuart Ball's work on *Baldwin and the Conservative Party. The Crisis of 1921–1931*, as well as Neal McCrillis in *The British Conservative Party in the Age of Universal Suffrage: Popular Conservatism, 1918–1929*. Tom Stannage and Andrew Thorpe also examined the Conservatives' electoral strategies in 1931 and 1935.[31] The numerous studies on foreign policy and the issue of appeasement contribute to giving a very different image of the Conservative party in the 1930s, and a series of works focus on the official policy of the Conservative party.[32] The party's luminaries have been the object of numerous biographies.

The Bonar Law Memorial College (BLMC) was meant to act as more than a centre for adult education. According to the Trust Deed, it must train people to become 'Lecturers Speakers Writers and Workers', with an ability to think about the content of the teaching, but also the means of conveying this content. This was an attempt to counter the supposedly pervasive influence, domination and even monopoly of the intellectual Left. There was thus a need to train intellectuals who adhered to the principles of Conservatism and who could teach the principles of citizenship through education 'in Economics in Political and Social Science in Political History with special reference to the development of the British Constitution and growth and expansion of the British Empire',[33] from a 'traditional' point of view. Indeed,

For more than a generation the *intelligentzia* of the Left have been strengthening their hold on those who form opinion – among the educated reading public, the universities and the teachers. To-day most of the best-read writers on political and economic subjects and the holders of the key University teaching posts in political science, economics and education, belong to the Left. In the academic, literary and journalistic professions, the expression of Conservative views – regarded as a hall-mark of stupidity and insensibility – has already become a serious handicap to a man's career, the expression of advanced Left views an advantage.[34]

The fear of a cultural, intellectual and artistic domination of the Left increased with the progressive expansion of the suffrage in 1918 and 1928, as the Conservative party feared universal suffrage might benefit its political opponents.[35] Since the 1880s, the forward march of Labour had been one of its main concerns, and at the turn of the century, Labour's growing importance in politics seemed linked to its influence in the intellectual sphere.[36] The rapid expansion of the Labour movement was understood by the Conservatives to be the result of the role played by Socialist, Progressive and Labour intellectuals.[37] These intellectuals were seen as shaping the doctrine that the Labour movement diffused to the new electorate. In 1931, J. C. C. Davidson wrote: 'Anyone who has thought deeply about politics must have dreaded that the country had been given manhood suffrage, which is democracy, before the people had received sufficient political education to use their new power aright.'[38] The fear that universal suffrage might lead to some form of disruption and chaos had been present since the end of the nineteenth century, but it reached its acme between 1917 and 1926, when the Conservative party was hit by what Maurice Cowling named *The Impact of Labour*.[39] In these years, the Conservative party faced a combination of events and political developments, both nationally and internationally, which questioned its values and beliefs. The expansion of the vote had followed closely upon the Bolshevik revolution in 1917, whose shockwaves were felt across Europe, in including Britain, as demonstrated by civil unrest in 'Red Clydeside' in 1919.[40] This heightened fears within the party, which resolved at its annual party conference in 1920 'to combat the Socialists and extremists in the ranks of organised labour'.[41] Thereafter the struggle against Socialism became the party's watchword and rallying cry, and the Labour party became the Conservative party's main target.[42] The creation of the first Labour government in 1924 and, two years later, the General Strike were important stages in this Conservative mobilisation.

The Conservative political tradition was by no means anti-reformist and there had always been a Tory working-class vote.[43] Also, between the 1880s and the 1930s, the Conservative party included an increasingly important element of former Liberals (most importantly the Chamberlains) who promoted radical and social-reformist ideas. However, the existence of a separate Labour party was perceived to imply that not only trade unions but the working class in general would identify themselves solely with the Labour party.[44] And with 78 per cent of the British population belonging, in terms of income, to the working class, Conservatives feared they would remain a permanent minority.[45] Thereafter the most urgent question facing party leaders was how they could attract the new voters to Conservatism.

The party responded to this mounting threat in a number of ways. One was to borrow from the new social sciences in the effort to provide 'scientific' responses to current political issues. An implicit assumption of the Conservative analysis of the success of Labour and Socialist propaganda and action was that the nature of political engagement had changed since *circa* 1880. In the eyes of the Conservatives, the founding in 1884 of the Fabian Society[46] and its subsequent creation of the London School of Economics (LSE) transformed the rules of the political game. Knowledge of history, philosophy and economics, and the emerging disciplines of political science and sociology, were all absorbed into the world of political debate. Politics was no longer seen as simply the art of government or administration in the narrowest sense of those terms, but required a broader and yet more specialised knowledge of and approach to social and political life. These changes reflected similar shifts in the academic world, where universities witnessed the emergence of new disciplines and specialist areas of study.[47]

The expertise displayed by university academics was necessarily of a specialist and formal nature. But expertise was not confined solely to academia, for it was also essential to the claims for social status asserted by the professional middle classes – notably doctors, lawyers and senior civil servants and, at a lower level, managers, accountants, clerks, low-grade civil servants, shopkeepers, etc. All of these groups and occupations could lay claim to a degree of expertise of some kind. It was this claim that enabled them to exercise what Max Weber referred to as 'social closure',[48] that is to say, a process which enabled them to establish a degree of exclusivity with regard to their occupational activities. In many cases, social closure could take the form of examinations, drawn up and marked by members of the profession that the examinee was seeking to join. This rise of 'professional society' was, as Perkin has shown, a general social phenomenon in Britain, which gathered strength and speed in the late nineteenth century. It had two particularly important effects upon the structure of Conservative politics. First of all, the urban and suburban professions, whether high or low, became the basis for the construction of new constituencies of support and 'the transformation of Victorian Conservatism'.[49] Of course, one should not exaggerate this point, since such groups also continued to include many Liberal intellectuals and professionals. Still, and this is the second effect, this social group played an essential part in the professionalisation of Conservative politics. If, in the mid-Victorian era, the Conservatives were to the forefront of professional party organisation, by the late nineteenth century, local Conservative party agents were for the most part salaried professionals who had been hired because of their expertise in electoral law. With pensions as well as salaries, they could be described as professional political apparatchiks. The expansion of the electorate after 1884 and even more so after 1918 ensured that the Conservatives could no longer rely simply upon local notables to meet the challenge of attracting voters. They required a political machine, which in turn demanded expert administration and guidance. Not only were the Conservative party's permanent agents salaried after 1891, but by 1925 they were encouraged to take an examination to demonstrate their knowledge of electoral law; by 1933 passing this examination had become compulsory. This was by no means a seamless process, of course.

In the late nineteenth and early twentieth centuries the Conservatives thus created a professional political machine capable of communicating to a democratic electorate. Methods of communication to the expanding electorate grew apace. Until the Edwardian period, the chief means of political communication was speeches 'on the stump', with politicians addressing mass meetings and large-scale audiences. This was how some politicians, perhaps most notably Randolph Churchill and Joseph Chamberlain, then a Liberal, established their political reputations. Also important, were poster campaigns, mass distribution of political leaflets and the use of both national and local newspapers to get political messages across.[50] The Conservative party was also very quick to apply new technology, in that phonograph recordings of statements and speeches by leading Conservative politicians first made their appearance at party political meetings shortly after the turn of the century – an early example of politicians being on the virtual stump.

The inter-war years saw an explosion of mass political communication, and again it was the Conservatives, largely because they were the most affluent party, who proved most audacious and ambitious in employing it. From 1922 on the party published on average 100 new pamphlets a year, and in the first months of 1927 the party distributed a total of 14,500,000. This literature was deliberately designed for the mass audience, for which many Conservatives clearly had very little respect. Cuthbert Headlam, the Conservative MP for County Durham, described the party's literature as 'designed for the illiterate' and for 'thick skulls filled (more or less) with primitive and sluggish brains'.[51] But whether it respected its audience or not, Conservative Central Office (CCO) continued to pour out material designed for mass consumption. For example, by the late 1920s its magazines, The Young Briton, Man in the Street, The Elector and Home and Politics, had circulations of, respectively, 13,000, 110,000, 190,000, and 200,000. Davidson also expanded the Conservative Press Office, which had first been created in 1911, and established the Lobby Press Service, which each day provided information to more than 230 dailies and weeklies.

In addition to pamphlet literature, the Conservatives also employed the new medium of cinema to get the Conservative message across. In 1925, Davidson commissioned the Thorneycroft company to build the first 'cinema van', and several of them were soon touring the country. In the 1929 general election campaign, ten Conservative cinema vans toured the country broadcasting feature films in tandem with political films, and in the 1935 election campaign an estimated 1,500,000 voters saw these films in village and town halls.[52]

That the Conservatives were able to place themselves at the cutting edge of political communication was not simply due to the continuous migration of many former Liberals – aristocrats, businessmen, intellectuals and political entrepreneurs – from Liberalism to Conservatism over the crucial period from the 1880s onwards. It was also made possible by the transformation of the party's financial base. Whereas before the war its budget amounted to £300,000, by 1922 it had reached more than £1,000,000. The situation improved even more dramatically when Davidson became party chairman in 1926 and set out to tap the party's wealthy business supporters for funds. For example, he secured £12,000 per annum from the Rothschilds and £5,000 per annum from the shipping magnate Sir John Ellerman, and eventually he found generous benefactors in the fields of 'Oil. Newspapers. Prudential. Banks. Railways. Merchant [bankers] – London; – South America'.[53] He managed to raise £1,000,000 in three years, and at single lunch in 1928 in the City of London he collected £130,000 for the party's coffers. In 1927, Stanley Baldwin, the leader of the Conservative party, stated that they should take advantage of 'Our one great advantage: WEALTH'.[54] Baldwin was fortunate in being able to rely on Davidson, who was not only one of the most successful British political fund-raisers of all time, but also an effective party manager.

Davidson recalled that when he became chairman of the party, 'The first job on which I set my mind was to apply the lessons of the Great War to the organization of political warfare.'[55] However, fighting a war required not just money but an effective staff corps, and here Davidson set about reorganising aspects of the CCO to carry out more effectively the party's campaigns. Hence in 1927 he established the party's first centralised communication department, with the former secret service agent Joseph Ball at its head. Davidson deliberately chose Ball because he felt he was an expert 'in the seamy side of life and the handling of crooks',[56] qualities Ball had demonstrated in his use of the fraudulent Zinoviev letter prior to the 1924 general election.[57] In short, Davidson was not only an adroit fund-raiser but was also unafraid, if necessary, to deploy funds to back political 'dirty tricks'.

But even with ample party funds, professional organisation and a readiness to engage in unorthodox measures, Davidson and other senior Conservatives became aware that they must also engage with the other parties in the 'battle of ideas'. It was here that the Conservatives felt themselves to be at a serious disadvantage. This, as noted earlier, was partly due to the lead the other major parties appeared to have gained in organising propaganda activity through intellectual organisations such as the Fabian Society, adult education groups, party summer schools and so forth. It was also perceived to be the result of the hegemony the other parties had secured in intellectual endeavour, including the writing of British history and economic analysis.

That the Labour party, without ever forming a majority government in the inter-war period, should have created such panic within Conservative ranks might seem surprising and exaggerated. After 1931, the Conservative electoral dominance was constant.[58] The perception of the Left as an ever – increasing and unstoppable threat, endangering the very foundations of British society, came with the expansion of universal suffrage to voters who were considered unprepared for this change. The exaggeration of the enemy forces was also the product of political calculation, since the demonisation of the Left enabled the party hierarchy to mobilise the grassroots more easily and to prevent them from apathy after the 1924 and 1931 electoral victories. The memory of the electoral defeats of 1923 and 1929 was used as a reminder that defeats were possible. A year before the general election of 1935, which saw a landslide victory of the Conservatives,[59] Robert Boothby wrote to Stanley Baldwin:

> There is little enthusiasm for the National Government; and I am firmly convinced that we are now moving towards a very considerable electoral debacle. This seems to me to be due 1) to the absence of any political philosophy, or theme, or policy adequate to the needs of the time; and 2) to the lack of constructive measures, and a reactionary tendency on the part of the government which has become apparent lately.... Some new guiding principles will have to be laid down.[60]

Boothby's anxieties with regard to the weaknesses of the Conservative party were also a way for him to put forward his own ideas about

Conservatism.[61] Harold Macmillan, J. W. Hills and other Conservatives expressed similar concerns. They advocated state intervention within the economic sphere and sought to make themselves heard within the party.

The over-emphasis on the dangers attributed to Socialism was not simply due to minorities within the Conservative party. Anti-Socialism was, more generally, part of the Conservative political culture, in particular during the inter-war period.[62] When Christopher Dawson[63] referred to 'Socialist absolutism, whether in its revolutionary or in its Fabian form',[64] he deliberately assimilated 'evolutionary' and 'Fabian' and linked all forms of Socialism – be it the most gradualist – to the destruction of society. The term 'bolshevik' was used as a synonym for 'socialist' and even for 'Labour' to frighten the voters, as shown by Urban Broughton's declaration quoted above. Dawson feared 'the complete subordination of the individual to the State and of the State to the economic machine'.[65] The new electorate might be convinced by Socialist propaganda. This was the explanation given by Neville Chamberlain to the 1929 defeat: 'The politicians & agitators, working on the most ignorant & credulous section of the people, have had an easy task in attributing the troubles & difficulties of the post-war period to the Govt. which they have always represented as a class Govt. with a bias against working people.'[66] This ongoing concern saw the Conservatives produce remarkable attempts to respond to what they saw as a challenge.

In September 1923, the Conservatives set up a political education centre, the Philip Stott College, at Overstone in Northamptonshire. At its opening, Baldwin stated that it would have to struggle against 'Quackish fungoids',[67] who spread 'Cant and ... fallacy', and would need to instruct people to be 'faithful guardians of such civilisation as we have already attained'.[68] The classes at the College were aimed at 'Working men and women of the party who have not access to facilities for post-school education which Socialists obtain at the various Labour colleges'.[69] The fight against Socialism was the explicit object and indeed the primary function of the College. At its opening, the secretary of the Conservative party in East Anglia advised all the Conservative associations in his region to send students to the College in order to receive 'an instructional course in Anti-Socialist organisation'.[70] The experience of the College, albeit not a wholly successful enterprise, convinced Conservatives that they must engage more forcefully in political education, and define their objectives not merely in negative terms – that is, purely anti-Socialism – but rather by offering training in the true principles of conservatism itself. The Philip Stott College closed in 1928, but the following year saw the Conservatives activate institutions of political research and education on a far grander scale.

Twice in 1929 Baldwin stressed the need for the Conservatives to provide political education for the mass electorate. Writing to Lord Irwin that summer, he stated: 'Democracy has arrived at a gallop, and I feel all the time it is a race against time – can we educate them before the crash comes?'[71] To avoid the crash, Baldwin warned,

> The Conservative Party must realise the need of getting hold of the intelligent, ambitious working man, whom Labour is ready to look after so well. It must make an effort to capture the brains in the labouring classes, and teach them early on Conservative lines, through the right type of employer and the right type of M.P. I want their brains. I want to train them, and I don't know how to get them.[72]

Although Baldwin may not have known how to get to the brains of the intelligent working man, he certainly knew how he did not want to get to them, namely via their intellects. Baldwin was proud to describe himself as 'not a clever man',[73] and in an exchange of letters with his friend the historian Arthur Bryant, he wrote that, having read Bryant's latest book, he had been taken aback because 'I never regarded you as an intellectual!', but completed his missive by remarking that 'When you have got over the shock you may realise that that is the very nicest thing I could say of you.'[74] This elided with Baldwin's earlier statement that intelligentsia was a 'very ugly word for a very ugly thing',[75] and was consistent with the long tradition of alleged anti-intellectualism within the Conservative party.

However, one of the major paradoxes of Baldwin and the inter-war Conservative party was that, as this study will show, the Conservative party, under Baldwin's leadership, set out to create one of the most ambitious and original intellectual projects undertaken by a British political party. In the late 1920s, the Conservative party produced numerous memoranda on political research and education, of which the most influential was probably one prepared by John Buchan for Baldwin in 1927. 'Until quite recently', Buchan wrote,

> research was a word little used by Englishmen; perhaps because the mental habits that it presupposed were foreign to the national temperament. England has secured commercial dominion by vigorous, if rough-and-ready, methods, and long after the eyes of her competitors had been opened to the need for patient and scientific investigation her industrial leaders, as interpreters of the attitude of the masses at large, remained staunch empiricists.... The union of scientific research and political action has yet to break. The empirical night still holds sway.... Most of the ills from which we now suffer descend from the negligent regard paid to the Industrial Revolution by statesmen of the earlier part of the century.... There was in their time no tradition of patient, dispassionate, and unbiased investigation.[76]

But although Buchan felt that the 'empirical night' was still largely dominant, he also worried that the only people for whom dawn had broken were on the Left, since the Labour party had established a research bureau which was helping to 'make a solid groundwork for the future advance of Labour'.[77] As a consequence, he considered that the Conservative party must urgently establish its own research department, which would enable it to achieve 'two main ends; the first of which is to inquire as to the means by which a party may remain in power; the second, as to the use to which such power should be devoted'.[78]

In his memorandum to Baldwin, Buchan had emphasised that 'political research would best be carried out by a voluntary organisation within the confines of, or linked to, a political party'.[79] Buchan's position was stated still more strongly by Anthony Ludovici, who asserted: 'At the present day, a political party cannot survive that is not supported by an independent body of students and thinkers from which it can obtain its ideas, its policies and its programmes.'[80] Ludovici's belief that genuine intellectuals had to be independent prompted unending debate on what exactly the relationship was to be between intellectuals and the political party with which they sympathised. When Buchan laid out his ideal of how political research could and should be undertaken, he stressed four essential tenets:

1. To liaise with outside social and cultural bodies;

2. To establish influence, if it is found desirable, within Trade Unions and Co-operative Societies;

3. To attract to the service of the Party young men of brains and character;

4. To utilise the services of economists, historians and other writers of note.[81]

The definition of Ashridge's role was very similar to that of the LSE. Emphasis upon the Empire was never an intrinsic part of the LSE's curriculum or interest, although many of its founders had been imperialists, but the more general stress on economics and history carried strong echoes of the LSE's original interests, and here it is worth noting that the first director of the LSE, W. A. S. Hewins, was to lecture at Ashridge on Empire trade and imperial defence. Indeed, the overlap between the two institutions went well beyond that. In May 1931 the *Ashridge Journal* noted that the college's goal was to inspire its students with 'the same crusading spirit as that of the young men who ... founded the Fabian Movement and gave birth to the Socialist Party', except in the College's case the aim was 'To destroy Socialism, which is now destroying England'.[82] The founders of Ashridge deliberately sought to turn out students who 'would in fact aim at performing the same pioneer service for Conservative Education as that of the early Fabian publications for Socialism'.[83] The Fabian Society was in fact the model for the project of Ashridge. The influence it was deemed to have had over the Labour party and the development of Socialism in Britain made it both feared and admired by Conservatives. With the same careful management, preparation and commitment, the Conservatives felt they could match the Fabians' achievement and, indeed, that it was essential for them to do so.

Viewed in terms of the history of British Conservatism, and indeed the history of twentieth – century politics more generally, Ashridge can appear as a think-tank *avant la lettre*. Its role was that of a political echo-chamber within which Conservative politicians and activists exchanged and discussed ideas with the specific purpose of tailoring strategies for particular contemporary problems. It may have been the case that Ashridge, as Neville Chamberlain had suggested, was sent policy documents and suggestions from the CRD for discussion, but Ashridge was not part of the Conservative party's policy-making apparatus. Rather, its role in this context was to generate through debate and discussion an alternative political and social culture to that which had been generated by the Left and which Conservatives felt was becoming increasingly dominant – 'the credo of the masses' and 'the policy of England'. Ashridge is perhaps best described as a counter-hegemonic project. A good example of this is the rich and wide-ranging discussion of economics at Ashridge. In 1920, one future lecturer at Ashridge, Arthur Steel-Maitland, in a discussion of Marxism, had described economics as particularly prone to the arguments of 'quacks and frauds'.[84] However, by 1930, Eustace Percy conceded that the 'quacks and frauds' had triumphed and that classical economics had been overshadowed by Marxian thought. 'Socialism' rather than Liberal 'free-trade' economics had become the economic doctrine that Conservative theorists most objected to, even if many Conservatives favoured some form of 'protection' of agriculture and key industries. In this sense, a major part of Ashridge's task was to expose the fallacies of the ideas of 'exploded Continental theorists'.[85] This was to be done not by offering monologues on the rectitude of classical economics but through a genuine dialogue on the nature of economic theory. In so doing, the Ashridgeans felt they were presenting the complete opposite of what they saw as 'the Left's' arguments, which according to F. J. C. Hearnshaw were '[t]he grossest perversions of the truth, by an extensive suppression of relevant facts, by a shameless fabrication of lies, and by a passionate animosity towards opponents and critics'.[86]

The story of Ashridge is really the story of a series of paradoxes. The first of these was the exaggerated fear of the influence of Fabian Socialism over British political and intellectual life, at a time when, in electoral terms, the Conservative party was largely dominant. This fear emerged as Fabianism took shape in the Edwardian period and, arguably, lasted until the 1980s. The second apparent contradiction, which stemmed from the first, is that the inter-war Conservative party, whose leaders claimed to be deeply suspicious of intellect, chose to engage in such an ambitious intellectual project. Neither Baldwin himself nor his party (with a few individual exceptions) enjoyed a positive reputation for intellectual debate, although, arguably, Baldwin was far too clever to confess to being 'clever'. Not for nothing did John Maynard Keynes describe a speech of Baldwin's in Manchester in November 1923 as an example of 'the exaltation of a sort of mystical stupidity, with which the Tory, generally sentimentalising himself on these occasions as the "plain, business man", likes to present his nostrums for the cure of economic facts'.[87] Baldwin's subordinates inspired Keynes to even greater heights of condescension, as when in 1929 he complained that the Conservative president of the Board of Trade, Laming Worthington-Evans, had produced an argument against public expenditure to boost employment that was so foolish it could be explained only by the fact that 'He is a Conservative. The reasons are wrapped in the mists of history ... He half understands an ancient theory, the premises of which he has forgotten.'[88] Yet, despite the fact that Keynes seemed to relish patronising Conservative opponents of his ideas, his theories and their apparent application in the United States were discussed at some length at special conferences at Ashridge. Furthermore, Conservatives such as Harold Macmillan, who saw themselves as particularly close and intellectually sympathetic to Keynes, were given the opportunity to expound their ideas at great length to audiences at Ashridge. Nor, as will be seen later, was this the only example of the comprehensive engagement with economic theory at Ashridge in the 1930s.

Keynes's remarks cited above present the clichéd view of the Conservative party as unalterably 'stupid'. But what was displayed at Ashridge was the construction of a different form of intellectual engagement. This engagement consciously eschewed abstract reasoning as an imperfect guide to comprehending the modern world and its problems. For Conservatives, with their long-established empiricist tradition, the fundamental question they faced was how to construct a theoretical model of the intellectual which would not be open to the critique of abstraction.

A third tension was related to the challenge of keeping oneself free from the charge of intellectual abstraction. Alongside the vision of Socialists and Socialism as obsessively over-theoretical, Conservatives also condemned them for being obsessively 'political'. For Conservatives, politics was a very particular part of life, and one that should not intrude into the normal modes of everyday life: it was separate and special. As the Conservative thinker T. E. Utley wrote in 1949, '[t]he great dividing line in British politics has always been between those who regard politics as supremely important and those who conceive it to be the handmaid of religion, art, science and society'.[89] It was this dividing line that the Baldwinian Conservative party sought to preserve and indeed strengthen. In 1928, Neville Chamberlain explained Stanley Baldwin's strength as being due to his ability to '[h]old the mugwumps and the clericals and the conscientious, earnest, theoretical Liberals as no one else in any party can',[90] and Baldwin's instrumental role in creating the National government in 1931 and holding it together through the 1930s confirmed his unique skill at playing the game of 'unpolitical politics', that is to say, mastering and enunciating a rhetoric with a broad-based appeal, which effectively acted as a language of political excommunication for those who did not accept its precepts. Baldwin's national appeal was based upon the presentation of his own party and its partners within the National government as the incarnation of the political mainstream. Ashridge, which was an important institutional embodiment of Baldwinian Conservatism, acted as a reservoir for the language that married Conservatism with the nation. Hence, in the *Ashridge Journal* in 1932, Christopher Dawson, in an essay on 'Conservatism', stated that popular conservatism 'has its roots very deep in the national character and is perhaps the most distinctive feature of English political life'.[91]

A fourth paradox to be considered is that while Ashridge's legacy pervaded the post-war Conservative party, the college as an institution ceased to play a part within the party after 1939, and all links were severed in 1954. As an embodiment of the Baldwinian heritage, there was no place for Ashridge within Churchill's Conservative party. More importantly perhaps, Ashridge's trust deed prevented Churchill from recovering the College and its grounds. It is with some irony, doubtless pleasing to many of Ashridge's contemporary critics, that the Conservative party's greatest intellectual project became one of Britain's first management schools in 1954, with the archive of this extraordinary venture in political education lying forgotten. The title deeds of the management school are still held by the BLMT, which indicates that Bonar Law was not only 'the unknown prime minister'[92] but also the unremembered one, even in the institution where his legacy was memorialised.

Notes

1 Bonar Memorial Trust Deed, 21 Nov. 1929, Ashridge papers, Ashridge College, Berkhamsted (hereafter Ashridge papers).
2 Summary of Reasons for the Ashridge (Bonar Law Memorial) Trust Bill, no date, 1954, Conservative Party Archive (hereafter CPA), CCO 3/4/29.

3 Minutes of the Ashridge Education Committee, 5 Feb. 1930, Ashridge papers.
4 Stuart Ball used the archive for his book, *Portrait of a Party: the Conservative Party in Britain 1918–1945* (Oxford: Oxford University Press, 2013).
5 See C. Berthezène, 'Ashridge College, 1929–54: A Glimpse at the Archive of a Conservative Intellectual Project', *Contemporary British History*, 19(1) (Spring 2005), pp. 80–95.
6 *Ashridge Journal*, Dec. 1935, p. 2.
7 Ball, *Portrait of a Party*.
8 E. H. H. Green, *The Crisis of Conservatism: The Politics, Economics and Ideology of the British Conservative Party, 1880–1914* (London: Routledge, 1995); *Ideologies of Conservatism, Conservative Political Ideas in the Twentieth Century* (Oxford: Oxford University Press, 2002). D. Jarvis, '"Mrs. Maggs and Betty": The Conservative Appeal to Women Voters in the 1920s', *Twentieth Century British History*, 5, 1994, pp. 129–52; 'British Conservatism and Class Politics in the 1920s', *English Historical Review*, 110, 1996, pp. 59–84; 'The Conservative Party and the Politics of Gender, 1900–1939', in M. Francis and I. Zweiniger-Bargielowska, *The Conservatives and British Society, 1880–1990* (Cardiff: University of Wales Press, 1996), pp. 172–93; 'The Shaping of the Conservative Electoral Hegemony, 1918–39', in J. Lawrence and M. Taylor (eds), *Party, State and Society: Electoral Behaviour in Modern Britain since 1820* (Aldershot: Sage, 1996), pp. 131–51. P. Williamson, *Stanley Baldwin: Conservative Leadership and National Values* (Cambridge: Cambridge University Press, 1999). D. Thackeray, *Conservatism for the Democratic Age: Conservative Cultures and the Challenge of Mass Politics in Early Twentieth Century England* (Manchester: Manchester University Press, 2013).
9 See the work and projects of the 'Middlebrow Network', http://www.middlebrow-network.com.
10 R. McKibbin, *Classes and Cultures: England, 1918–1951* (Oxford: Oxford University Press, 1998); *Parties and People, England, 1914–1951* (Oxford: Oxford University Press, 2010). J. Lawrence, *Electing Our Masters: The Hustings in British Politics from Hogarth to Blair* (Oxford: Oxford University Press, 2009); *Speaking for the People: Party, Language and Popular Politics in England, 1867–1914* (Cambridge: Cambridge University Press, 1998, [pbk, 2002]).
11 P. Mandler, *The Fall and Rise of the Stately Home* (Newhaven, CT: Yale University Press, 1997), p. 226.
12 With the important exception of Stefan Collini's work, the history of intellectuals is to be found essentially at the intersection of the history of elites and the history of education.
13 There are numerous examples. P. Anderson, 'Components of the National Culture', *New Left Review*, 50, 1968, in *English Questions*, London: Verso, 1992, pp. 48–104. B. S. Turner, 'Ideology and Utopia in the Formation of an Intelligentsia: Reflections on the English Cultural Conduit', in *Theory, Culture and Society*, 9 (1), 1992, pp. 183–210, as well as 'The Absent English

Intelligentsia?', *Comenius*, 38, 1990, pp. 138–51. G. Stedman Jones, 'The Pathology of English History', *New Left Review*, 46, 1967, pp. 29–44. M. S. Hickox, 'Has there Been a British Intelligentsia?', *British Journal of Sociology*, 37 (2), 1986, pp. 260–8. J. A. Hall, 'The Curious Case of the English Intelligentsia', *British Journal of Sociology*, 30 (3), 1979, pp. 290–306.

14 J. Ramsden, *The Age of Balfour and Baldwin* (London: Longmans, 1978), p. ix.

15 A. Gamble, *The Conservative Nation* (London: Macmillan, 1974), p. 2.

16 N. O'Sullivan, *Conservatism* (London, 1976). R. Eccleshall, *English Conservatism Since the Reformation* (London, 1990). W. H. Greenleaf, *The British Political Tradition*, 4 vols (London: Methuen, 1983–1987), Vol. 2, *The Ideological Heritage*. R. Scruton, *The Meaning of Conservatism* (London: Macmillan, 1980); *How to be a Conservative* (London: Bloomsbury Continuum, 2014). T. Honderich, *Conservatism* (London, 1990).

17 M. Freeden, *Ideologies and Political Theory: A Conceptual Approach* (Oxford: Oxford University Press, 1996), p. 318.

18 Ball, *Portrait of a Party*, pp. 9–81.

19 Green, *The Crisis of Conservatism*, p. 312. Williamson, *Stanley Baldwin*, p. 17.

20 H. Young, *One of Us* (London: Macmillan, 1990). K. Minogue and M. Biddiss, *Thatcherism: Personality and Politics* (London, 1987). R. Skidelsky (ed.), *Thatcherism* (London, 1988). A. Gamble, *The Free Economy and the Strong State* (London: Macmillan, 2nd edn, 1994).

21 M. Thatcher, quoted in S. Blake and A. John, *The World According to Margaret Thatcher* (London: Michael O'Mara Books Ltd., 2003), p. 159.

22 I. Gilmour and M. Garnett, *Whatever Happened to the Tories?* (Basingstoke: Macmillan, 1997).

23 Freeden, *Ideologies*, p. 337.

24 Gamble, *The Free Economy and the Strong State*.

25 Freeden, *Ideologies*, p. 337.

26 M. Seliger, *Ideology and Politics*, 1976, quoted in E. H. H. Green, *Ideologies of Conservatism: Conservative Political Ideas in the Twentieth Century* (Oxford: Oxford University Press, 2002), p. 2.

27 T. Szamuely, 'Intellectuals and Conservatism', *Swinton Journal*, 14 (1), 1968, p. 5.

28 R. A. Butler, *The Art of the Possible* (London: Hamish Hamilton, 1971, 1982).

29 Foreword by K. Clarke to M. Garnett, *Alport: a Study in Loyalty* (Teddington: Acumen, 1999).

30 R. Griffiths, *Fellow Travellers of the Right, British Enthusiasts for Nazi Germany, 1933–39* (Oxford: Oxford University Press, 1983). R. Griffiths, *Patriotism Perverted, Captain Ramsay, The Right Club and British Anti-Semitism, 1939–40* (London: Constable & Co. Ltd., 1998). R. Thurlow, *Fascism in Britain: A History, 1918–1945* (London, 1987). K. Lunn and R. Thurlow (eds), *British Fascism* (London: Croom Helm, 1980). N. J. Crowson, *Facing Fascism: The Conservative Party and the European*

Dictators, 1935–1939 (London: Routledge, 1997). J. Gottlieb, *Feminine Fascism: Women in Britain's Fascist Movement* (I. B. Tauris, 2000).

31 J. Ramsden, *An Appetite for Power. A History of the Conservative Party since 1830* (London: HarperCollins, 1998). S. Ball, *Baldwin and the Conservative Party. The Crisis of 1921–1931* (New Haven, CT: Yale University Press, 1988). N. McCrillis, *The British Conservative Party in the Age of Universal Suffrage: Popular Conservatism, 1918–1929* (Columbus, OH: Ohio State University Press, 1998). T. Stannage, *Baldwin Thwarts the Opposition: the British General Election of 1935* (London: Croom Helm, 1980). A. Thorpe, *The British General Election of 1931* (Oxford: Clarendon Press, 1991).

32 M. Cowling, *The Impact of Hitler, British Politics and British Policy, 1933–1940* (Cambridge: Cambridge University Press, 1975). J. Charmley, *Chamberlain and the Lost Peace* (London: Curtis, 1989). R. A. C. Parker, *Chamberlain and Appeasement: British Policy and the Coming of the Second World War* (Basingstoke: Macmillan, 1993). R. A. C. Parker, *Churchill and Appeasement* (Basingstoke: Macmillan, 2000). G. Stewart, *Burying Caesar: Churchill, Chamberlain and the Battle for the Tory Party* (London: Phoenix, 2000). R. Shepherd, *A Class Divided: Appeasement and the Road to Munich, 1938* (London: Macmillan, 1988).

33 'The Work of Ashridge', (no date) Dec. 1929, Education Committee Correspondence, 1930, Ashridge papers.

34 A. Bryant, Memorandum on the Means of Combatting Left-Wing and Communistic Propaganda in Literature and in the Universities, 22 Apr. 1937, 1st Viscount Davidson Papers, House of Lords Record Office, London (hereafter Davidson papers), DAV/226.

35 See Chapter 1.

36 The 'Labour Representation Committee' (LRC) was founded in 1900. In 1906, twenty-nine members of the LRC were returned to the House of Commons. The LRC then became the Labour Party.

37 See P. Clarke, *Liberals and Social Democrats* (Cambridge: Cambridge University Press, 1978).

38 J. C. C. Davidson, 'The Foundation of Ashridge', *Ashridge Journal*, Dec. 1931, pp. 49–51.

39 M. Cowling, *The Impact of Labour, 1920–1924. The Beginning of Modern British Politics* (Cambridge: University Press, 1971).

40 A trade union demonstration in favour of workers controlling the naval construction sites in Glasgow. The British government sent in the army with tanks to suppress the demonstration.

41 T. J. Whittaker, NUCA conference in Birmingham, 10 June 1920.

42 In the 1918 general election, the Labour party became the main opposition party.

43 M. Pugh, 'The Rise of Labour and the Political Culture of Conservatism, 1890–1945', *History*, 87, 2002, pp. 514–37. M. Pugh, *The Tories and the People, 1880–1935* (Oxford: Basil Blackwell, 1988).

44 On the Conservative party's fears see Green, *The Crisis of Conservatism*.

D. Jarvis, 'The Shaping of the Conservative Electoral Hegemony, 1918–1939', in J. Lawrence and M. Taylor (eds), *Party, State and Society: Electoral Behaviour in Modern Britain since 1820* (Aldershot: Sage, 1996), pp. 131–51. D. Jarvis, 'Stanley Baldwin and the Ideology of the Conservative Response to Socialism', 1918–31 (PhD dissertation, Lancaster University, 1991). R. McKibbin, '"Class and Conventional Wisdom": the Conservative Party and the "Public" in Inter-war Britain', in *The Ideologies of Class: Social Relations in Britain, 1880–1950* (Oxford: Oxford University Press, 1990), pp. 259–93.

45 McKibbin, *Classes and Cultures*, p. 106.

46 Other Socialist and radical Liberal organisations such as the SDF, the Socialist League and the Land Nationalisation League were also prominent in the early 1880s, but it was the Fabian Society that attracted most Conservative attention.

47 It was in the late nineteenth century that the first chair of political science was established at Cambridge. Meanwhile, Alfred Marshall, professor of political economy at Cambridge, with his *Principles of Economics* (1890) played a singularly important role in promoting modern, neo-classical economics, with its emphasis on mathematical calculation and on 'marginal utility' as a basis for income and wealth distribution. These principles were largely propagated in England by radical Liberal economists.

48 For Weber's view of 'social closure', see H. H. Girth and C. W. Mills (eds), *From Max Weber: Essays in Sociology* (London: Routledge, 1998).

49 See J. Cornford, 'The Transformation of Conservatism in the Late Nineteenth Century', *Victorian Studies*, 7, 1963, pp. 35–77 and F. Coetzee, 'Villa Toryism Reconsidered: Conservatism and Suburban Sensibilities in Late-Victorian Croydon', in E. H. H. Green (ed.), *An Age of Transition: British Politics, 1880–1914* (Edinburgh: Edinburgh University Press, 1997), pp. 29–47. M. Roberts, '"Villa Toryism" and popular Conservatism in Leeds, 1885–1902', *Historical Journal*, 49 (2006), pp. 217–46. A. Windscheffel, *Popular Conservatism in Imperial London, 1868–1906* (London: Royal Historical Society, 2007).

50 Some politicians, one notable example being Winston Churchill in the Liberal phase of his career, would circulate his speeches to the press before he had made them, inserting at points brackets indicating 'cheers' or 'laughter', although not all politicians who employed this practice were quite so confident about assuming the audience's response.

51 S. Ball (ed.), *Parliament and Politics in the Age of Baldwin and MacDonald. The Headlam Diaries, 1923–35* (The Historians' Press, 1992) diary entry for 30 Mar. 1925.

52 R. Cockett, 'The Party, Publicity, and the Media', in A. Seldon and S. Ball (eds), *Conservative Century: The Conservative Party Since 1900* (Oxford: Oxford University Press, 1994), pp. 547–77.

53 A. J. Davies, *We, the Nation: The Conservative Party and the Pursuit of Power* (London: Little, Brown & Co., 1995), p. 174.

54 S. Baldwin, 1927, quoted in Davies, *We, the Nation*, p. 164.

55 R. R. James (ed.), *Memoirs of a Conservative: J. C. C. Davidson's Memoirs and Papers 1910–1937* (Weidenfeld & Nicolson, 1969), p. 337.

56 *Ibid.*

57 L. Chester, S. Fay and H. Young, *The Zinoviev Letter* (London: Heinemann, 1967).

58 In October 1931, the Conservatives obtained 55 per cent of national votes and 470 seats in the House of Commons.

59 In November 1935, the Conservatives gained 47.8 per cent of the national votes and 387 seats in the House of Commons.

60 R. Boothby to S. Baldwin, 31 Jan. 1934, 1st Earl Baldwin of Bewdley Papers, Cambridge University Library, Cambridge (hereafter Baldwin papers), SB169.

61 Robert Boothby was in a minority within the Conservative party because he defended radical ideas in terms of economic policy.

62 See Chapter 1.

63 Christopher Dawson was a professor in 'Cultural Evolution' at South Western University. He attempted to construct a Conservative sociology. Dawson's ideas are briefly presented in S. Collini, 'The European Modernist as Anglican Moralist: The Later Social Criticism of T. S. Eliot', in M. S. Micale and R. L. Dietle (eds), *Enlightenment, Passion, Modernity: Historical Essays in European Thought and Culture* (Stanford University Press, 2000), pp. 207–29.

64 C. Dawson, 'Conservatism', *Ashridge Journal*, Sep. 1932, p. 43.

65 *Ibid.*

66 N. Chamberlain to I. Chamberlain, 2 June 1929, Neville Chamberlain MSS, Special Collections, University of Birmingham Library, Birmingham (hereafter Chamberlain papers), NC 18/1/656.

67 S. Baldwin, *On England and other Addresses* (London: Philip Allen & Co, 1926), p. 152.

68 *Ibid.*, p. 151.

69 *The Times*, 29 Mar. 1923, quoted in N. McCrillis, *The British Conservative Party*, p. 166.

70 Eastern Provincial Division, Minutes of Annual General Meeting, 24 Mar. 1923, CPA, ARE 7/1/6, quoted in Green, *Ideologies of Conservatism*, p. 135.

71 S. Baldwin to Lord Irwin, 20 June 1929, quoted in Jarvis, 'Stanley Baldwin', p. 36.

72 S. Baldwin, conference at Ashridge, 14–16 Dec. 1929, Ashridge papers.

73 S. Baldwin at the NUCA Conference, Oct. 1923, quoted in S. Ball, *Baldwin and the Conservative Party*.

74 S. Baldwin to A. Bryant, 19 Jan. 1938, Arthur Bryant Papers, Liddell Hart Centre for Military Archives, King's College, London (hereafter Bryant papers), C62.

75 S. Baldwin, *Our Inheritance. Speeches and Addresses* (London: Hodder & Stoughton, 1928), p. 295, quoted in P. Williamson, *Stanley Baldwin* (Cambridge: Cambridge University Press, 1999), p. 256.

76 J. Buchan, 'Political Research and Adult Education', 1927, Baldwin papers, SB53, fos 79–92.

77 *Ibid.*

78 *Ibid.*

79 J. Buchan, 'Political Research and Adult Education', 1927, Baldwin papers, SB53, fos 79–92.

80 A. M. Ludovici, *A Defense of Conservatism*, 1927, p. 244, quoted in F. J. C. Hearnshaw, *Conservatism in England: An Analytical, Historical and Political Survey* (London: Macmillan, 1933, New York: H. Fertig, 1967), p. 9.

81 J. Buchan, 'Political Research and Adult Education', 1927, Baldwin papers, SB53, fos 79–92.

82 *Ashridge Journal*, May 1931.

83 Memorandum, 13 June 1929, Bryant papers, C13.

84 A. Steel-Maitland, *Foreword to the Socialists' Bible: Karl Marx's Theory Discussed* (1920), quoted in Green, *Ideologies of Conservatism*, p. 76.

85 S. Baldwin, *On England*, p. 154.

86 Memorandum by F. J. C. Hearnshaw, Ashridge Weekend Conference, 14–16 Dec. 1929, Education Committee 1930, Ashridge papers.

87 J. M. Keynes, 'The Liberal Party', *The Nation and Athaneum*, 17 Nov. 1923, in D. Moggridge (ed.), *The Collected Writings of John Maynard Keynes*, Vol XIX: *Activities 1922–1929, The Return to Gold and Industrial Policy, Part I* (Cambridge: Macmillan/ Cambridge University Press, 1981), pp. 142–6, 144.

88 J. M. Keynes, 'A Cure for Unemployment', *Evening Standard*, 19 Apr. 1929, in D. Moggridge (ed.), *The Collected Writings of John Maynard Keynes*, Vol XIX, *Activities 1922–1929, The Return to Gold and Industrial Policy, Part I* (Cambridge: Macmillan/ Cambridge University Press, 1981), p. 811.

89 T. E. Utley, *Essays in Conservatism* (London: Conservative Political Centre, 1949), p. 1.

90 N. Chamberlain to Lord Irwin, 12 Aug. 1928, Halifax Indian papers, C 152/18/114a, quoted in Williamson, *Stanley Baldwin*, p. 355.

91 C. Dawson, 'Conservatism', *Ashridge Journal*, xi, Sep. 1932, p. 41.

92 Asquith first described Bonar Law as the unknown prime minister at his funeral, but it was also the title of the first scholarly biography of Bonar Law. See R. Blake, *The Unknown Prime Minister: The Life and Times of Andrew Bonar Law, 1858–1923* (London: Eyre & Spottiswoode, 1955).

I

The Conservatives' great fear

Between 1918 and 1940, the Conservative party held power for nineteen years, either alone or at the head of coalition governments; it was in opposition merely for three years, in 1924 and between 1929 and 1931, when its opponents were able to form only minority governments. In electoral terms, this was, in fact, the most successful period in the party's history. Yet, despite this success, the party appeared to be on the defensive and could not shake off a sense of vulnerability, which grew as the electorate itself grew. The new electorate was deemed unpredictable and the Socialists had, or so it seemed, devised or co-opted institutions capable of carrying their message to the enlarged electorate. Conservatives felt that they lacked both the institutions and a cogent formulation of their own principles.[1]

Most Conservatives agreed on the importance of promoting the education of the working class and challenging Labour's arguments, which, as they saw it, falsely claimed to protect everyone's interests while in fact defending only sectional interests. They felt that the basic themes of Britain's political culture were being defined by the Left. This was seen to be a consequence of the Left's success in permeating the intellectual world of learning, literature, publishing and journalism, where it had planted the seeds of a political and social credo that questioned and criticised established norms. 'The Socialists are steadily and relentlessly leading a crusade, using every means to advance their aims. Literature, arts, science; all are used to bear witness to the goodness of the Socialist creed,' wrote John Buchan, who was closely involved with the work of the Education Department at Central Office in 1926–27, before becoming Chairman of the Conservative Educational Institute which succeeded it from March 1928.[2] The Conservatives felt that the Labour Party had complemented the academic, 'highbrow' activities of the Fabians with a wide-ranging network of political education institutions, in the form of Ruskin College, the Workers' Educational Association (WEA), the Plebs' League and the National Council of Labour Colleges. These institutions in turn were seen as benefiting from the widespread dissemination of Socialist ideas by the new technologies of film, gramophone and wireless, but also by the British Broadcasting Corporation (BBC) and the media in general.[3] The 'highbrow' cultural domination – through the Bloomsbury Group for example – as well as the 'democratization of culture' both posed significant challenges to the Conservatives. The inter-war period was seen as an era of cultural formation and Joseph Ball, a key figure at CCO,[4] explained: 'I have been told by those in close touch with political movements at the universities today, that our cause is greatly handicapped by the fact that the average undergraduate who is interested in politics has nowhere to turn to-day but to the *New Statesman* or the books of left-wing Socialist intellectuals.'[5] He concluded that the Conservatives had a long way to go to catch up with Labour in terms of adult education and to capture the minds of those who would choose Labour as a default choice. The Conservative party also appeared to have neglected the educated middle classes.[6] For them, Ball suggested the creation of a weekly magazine edited by young journalists, 'capable of exposing effectively the fallacies upon which the public is being regularly fed, not only the periodicals to which I have referred [*New Statesman, Saturday Review*], but also in the books published from time to time by Gollancz'.[7] Buchan, reviewing the history of the Labour party and its successes, emphasised how far behind the Conservative party had fallen in adult education:

> The Labour-Socialists, from the moment they formed themselves into a party, realised to the full the immense importance of education, and saw by what methods they could permeate great numbers of people with their own particular doctrines.... The Adult Educational Movement was in its childhood; here lay a path direct to the hearts and brains of the nation. More, here was something to attract all thinking people, especially the intelligent young who were interested in social and political problems.[8]

Whereas the Labour party, it seemed, methodically spread its ideas, the Conservative and the Liberal parties '[relied] too much on chance and emotional appeals'.[9] Thus, according to Buchan, since the 'left' exercised its influence among all elements of society, the Conservative party must, without delay, throw itself into the 'battle of ideas', for 'battle must be given on their own ground'.[10] 'The Socialist Party, 10 years ago drew up plans and formulated operations that in the intervening space of time have accomplished almost entirely their aims and purposes.... The tide of Socialism is steadily increasing. There is a possibility, which by comparison, inclines one to believe it a probability, that Socialism can be fought and conquered along its own line of action; but only if there are used the means and methods of the time.'[11]

Constructing the enemy

To pursue the 'battle of ideas', it was necessary to identify both the enemy's doctrine and the means for diffusing it. Conservatives considered as 'Socialist' all views of society based upon class analysis, and which called upon the government to correct inequalities of wealth by raising income and inheritance tax and the nationalisation of big business. From 1918, the Conservatives tended to replace the term 'Labour' with the word 'Socialist', with its connotation of a foreign ideology. Stanley Baldwin spoke of Left-wing activists, 'befogging themselves and their fellow-countrymen, by filling their bellies with the east wind of German Socialism and Russian Communism and French Syndicalism'.[12] Any other word might give the impression that they were a moderate organisation, and obscure the revolutionary nature of their proposals. In 1929, at the annual conference of the NUCA, Charles L. Nordon, vice-chairman of the party, proposed: 'The Socialist Party should be called the State Control Party, and that as Conservatives stood for the union of all classes their true title today was Unionists.' He added: 'anti-Socialism was a negative creed', and 'the result of the 1929 election necessitates a new and more intelligent attitude towards the problems and dangers of the political theories and programmes masquerading under the label of "Socialism", and, at the same time, the adoption of more accurate and intelligible political terminology, both internally and externally, and to be expressed in clear and simple language'.[13] The source of many of these alarmist views was the Fabian Society, which Conservatives feared above all.

The Fabian model

The Fabian Society was founded in 1884 and its objective was the 'spread of socialist opinion' 'by the general dissemination of knowledge as to the relation between the individual and the Society in its economic, ethical and political aspects'.[14] The idea was to reform society 'by a slow process of evolution, not by revolution and bloodshed'.[15] Edward Pease, one of the Society's founding members, explained that Socialism was inevitable; the question was knowing how to prepare for it: 'If we prepare the way before it, and receive it gladly, it will come to us peaceably and as a welcome friend. If, on the other hand, we harden our hearts, and close the gates of our minds against the truth, it will come upon us none the less, but as a destroying angel, with fire, and bloodshed and confusion. On us, of the upper and middle classes, rests the burden of this choice.'[16]

The historiography confirms Pease's description of the Fabian Society as a product of the middle classes.[17] In his work on the Fabians, Eric

Hobsbawm notes that they represented the emergence of a 'new *couche sociale*', composed not only of the middle classes in the traditional sense of the word, but also of writers, journalists, senior civil servants, teachers, artists and white-collar workers issuing from the working class.[18] Above all, they were people who were recognised for their skills and expertise, along with their interest in the evolution of society and the role of the state. Their main target was not capitalism but 'administrative nihilism'.[19] They did not want a government of the people by the people but a government of experts for the people. The Fabians were 'bureaucrats, not democrats'. The sociologist L. T. Hobhouse described them as 'socialist officials' who sought to resolve the problems of society from above.[20] When leading Fabians established the London School of Economics and Political Science in 1895, it was in response to the need for a skilled civil service.

The myth of the Fabians as Machiavellian *éminences rouges* was the product of the Conservatives' anxieties. These anxieties stemmed in part from having worked closely with the Fabians. In 1902, some Conservatives such as Lord Milner, J. L. Garvin, Leo Amery, W. A. S. Hewins and Leo Maxse participated in the Fabian-inspired Co-Efficients Club.[21] This rapprochement lasted until 1904 when the Conservatives founded the Compatriots Club, which was even more favourable to the Empire than the Co-Efficients. The Fabians' role in creating the Labour Representation Committee (LRC) in 1900, their drafting of the Labour party's first constitution in 1918, and the presence in Labour's first government in 1924 of nine Fabian ministers, of whom five sat in the cabinet, contributed to the widespread belief that the Fabian Society was the genius behind the Labour party's growing influence. From the Fabian Society's inception, it had defended nationalisation and a social security system, a draft of which William Beveridge, director of the LSE from 1918 to 1940, would propose in 1942. However, the Fabians' role in these reforms and the impact they actually had on the political choices of the Labour party, were no doubt less significant than they seemed.[22] Maurice Reckitt ironically expressed the Conservatives' fear. Referring to G. D. H. Cole, a member of the Fabian Society and Labour party activist, he wrote: 'Mr. G. D. H. Cole / Is a bit of puzzle; / A curious role / That of G. D. H. Cole / With a Bolshevik Soul / In a Fabian muzzle'.[23] For the Conservatives, the Labour party was just like Cole: his Bolshevik, or at least his Radical, sympathies were disguised behind a progressive Fabian rhetoric.

The over-estimation of Fabian ruse and support was matched by an under-estimation of Conservatism as 'intellectually a lost cause',[24] in the terms of Lord Eustace Percy, a Conservative MP and president of the Board of Education between 1924 and 1929. Eustace Percy believed that in order to remain in power, Conservatives must explain to the voters what

Conservatism was and the world-view it proposed, since the Socialists' appeal seemed to rely upon their ability to present a different and better world. Frank Pakenham, a lecturer at the LSE, complained that it was 'difficult to think of any Conservative writer in the last 140 years who has made any serious impression whatever on working-class mentality'.[25] This point was of course quite untrue, Benjamin Disraeli being a prominent counter-example, but Pakenham's remark captures well the sense of being intellectually beleaguered.

From 1918, the grass roots of the party betrayed increasing concern with the influence of 'leftist' views on voters. In 1919, Conservative activists in the constituency of Glasgow organised one of the first civic education courses for its members and open to all voters. That same year, the Primrose League established training courses 'against Bolshevism' in all constituencies. In 1921, the Conservative party's women's organisation proposed lectures on current affairs for London's women voters. Numerous constituencies started to offer civic education classes, and at the annual Conservative party conference in 1923 a motion was passed proposing the creation of a national network of study groups. The 1920s thus witnessed a demand for civic education across the whole of Britain.

As one observer put it, Conservatives must encourage 'a wider outlook and a continuous interest in Toryism as an intellectual and moral thing',[26] with the aim of producing 'well-equipped, well-informed workers for the party, able to *think*, so as intelligently to counter arguments'.[27] Thus came about the idea of creating a school. The initial step involved the recruitment of 'experts' capable of drafting textbooks and expressing Conservative 'principles'. The idea of expertise was at the heart of this undertaking, since many Conservatives wished to distance themselves from the gentleman-amateur label associated with the aristocracy. They believed the party must present itself in a new light, communicating modernity as synonymous with professionalism and expertise, in order to adapt to the new demands of democratic life.

The second step, that of spreading the word, consisted of attracting 'educated people of moderate views, who, though small numerically have considerable influence in forming public opinion and who have hitherto tended to lean towards the left'.[28] This was precisely the goal the Fabians had set themselves at the time they created their Society. In October 1886, Sidney Webb wrote, 'nothing in England is done without the consent of a small intellectual yet practical class in London not 2000 in number. We alone could get at that class.'[29]

The third step, that of education, consisted of creating a school for instruction on current affairs presented and analysed from a Conservative perspective. 'Our aim is to influence in the right direction the kind of young man whom on the other side of politics our political opponents have used so much in the past to capture educated opinion, from the time of the Fabian Society to the present day.'[30] The goal was to attract young people and turn them into committed party activists: 'In all the instruction given attention was paid to the importance of both inspiring and equipping students to continue their studies after leaving Ashridge and to impart their knowledge to others.'[31] Dissemination of knowledge through students was an essential element in the Fabians' strategy. On all these points, the Conservative party attempted to imitate the Fabian Society and directly borrowed its educational project.

The Conservatives' ambition was to create a 'Fabian Society of the Right'. However, in contrast to the Fabians, the Conservatives hoped to reach a wider public than merely the educated middle classes, and aimed in particular at the working class. To achieve this goal, the Conservatives took inspiration from the adult education movement, comprising Ruskin College, which was located in Oxford but financed by the trades unions, the University Extension Movement, which offered free courses given by university lecturers independently of the university, Labour colleges and the WEA.

The Workers' Educational Association

The beginning of the twentieth century saw the creation of some forty educational associations, of which the most important was the WEA.[32] Founded in 1903 by Albert Mansbridge, a co-operative education activist, thanks to subsidies from Oxford University, the Board of Education and its local education authorities,[33] the WEA's goal was 'to federate working-class and educational interests, to stimulate and to satisfy the demand of working men and women for education'.[34] Its objective was 'not to take men out of their class or trade, but to equip them, whatever their occupation in life should be, for the work of citizenship'. The teaching should be 'broad, impartial and scholarly'. The Association was founded '[upon] the belief that an educated democracy is the only permanent basis for the structure of modern society and it [the WEA] is working to secure educational equality of opportunity for all'.[35] The WEA developed rapidly and in 1933 enrolled approximately 50,000 students a year across Britain. For the Conservative party, 'the influence of those Associations under the sheltering care of which the Adult Educational Movement waxes strong, is already great, and in the future is likely to be enormous.... The substance of what they teach will be the political and social "credo" of the masses; actually, the policy of England.'[36]

The Conservatives, though in principle favourable to the WEA, complained that it had fallen under Socialist influence: 'The leading figures in adult education in the last twenty-five years had also happened to be the leading academic Socialists – A. D. Lindsay, the Master of Balliol; G. D. H. Cole; R. H. Tawney, etc.' This Leftward drift was all the more annoying for Conservatives, given that the WEA claimed to be politically neutral. Yet it appeared to be 'passing more and more in the control of the Trade Union Congress'.[37] That the WEA was linked to the trades unions was not in itself objectionable, since trades unions represented the working class for whom the teaching was intended. However, the Conservatives found it unacceptable that the WEA had been infiltrated by the 'left' and affirmed that 'the Socialists are spending a great deal of time in long-range education, and are able to do it most effectively through having captured the Workers' Educational Association which preaches continuously on half-baked Socialist theories to the electorate all over the country'.[38] The Conservatives found it difficult to accept that 'a State-financed body such as W. E. A. had come to be such a powerful political weapon'.[39] A report by the party's central office complained:

> There is now ample proof ... that the Association is becoming more and more linked up with the Socialist movement. There is undoubtedly a close relationship between the WEA and the Trade Unions.... There is evidence of a definite Socialist bias in some of the lectures delivered under its auspices. In some districts there is close co-operation between the WEA and the local Socialists Party Organisation, and there are even indications that the classes are used for the purpose of propagating Socialist ideas and doctrines.[40]

They concluded that the state, on the pretence of educating the working class, was actually subsidising the Socialist movement.

To study how the WEA functioned, the Conservative party seconded several lecturers, including Lord Eustace Percy, whom the Association sent to teach in Staffordshire. He recounted his experience in a memorandum to the CRD in 1930:

> The WEA is, for good or for ill, the most truly democratic body in the world. By this I mean that the tutor is ultimately dependent for his livelihood, or at any rate for his appointment to the classes, on the goodwill of his students.... What struck me very forcibly was that all were Socialists; chiefly as a result of the fact they had all been taught to believe that no intelligent person was anything else.... They were not particularly bitter against Conservatives but to them the typical Conservative was the unthinking person whether he be squire, or flapper, or frequenter of the pub. Capitalism for them had been destroyed by modern, that is to say Marxian and neo-Marxian economics, in much the same way as Christianity in the last century for the clever young atheist has been destroyed by Huxley. I

am speaking now of men among whom I lived and some of whom I count
as personal friends. Considering their opportunities one could not wish for
a more intelligent band of students and yet on this one issue, capitalism v
socialism, their minds were closed.[41]

The analysis of Percy's report went beyond criticising the Socialist seizure
of the WEA. It affirmed that it was the Conservatives' inaction that had
allowed the WEA to fall into Socialist hands. Marjorie Maxse, chief
organisation officer of the Conservative party, hopefully suggested that
there were 'possibilities of "peaceful penetration" of the WEA'.[42]

John Buchan referred in his memorandum of 1927 to other adult
education organisations that had fallen into Labour's hands. Ruskin
College had been established in Oxford in 1899 by Charles Beard, the
American progressive historian, with the help of his compatriot the
philanthropist Walter Vrooman. It employed eleven full-time tutors but
was known for its distance teaching. It was financed one half by the trades
unions and one half by the dons.[43] From the beginning, relations between
Ruskin College and the University of Oxford were strained. Teaching
at the college was provided to bursary-holders from the working world,
whereas Oxford trained elites. Tensions reached boiling point in October
1908 when the Plebs League, which comprised Marxist students, decided
to leave Ruskin College, criticising it for its lack of independence from the
University, and aiming 'to bring about a more satisfactory connection of
Ruskin College with the Labour Movement'.[44]

In September 1909, after its break from the college, the Plebs League
created the Central Labour College at Oxford, which was allegedly closer
to the preoccupations of the working class than Ruskin College, which
was said to have become remote from its working-class roots on account
of its overly academic teaching. Lord Curzon, the chancellor of Oxford
University, wrote in a letter made public, that there was a 'danger that
a Working-men's College, outside the University, and subject neither to
its influences nor its discipline, may develop into a club dominated by
the narrow views of particular political or economic schools'.[45] Ruskin
College was created for a strictly educational, and not a political, purpose:
'An institution framed by charter on non-party lines'.[46]

The Central Labour College (CLC) in Oxford extended across the
country. In 1911, the college moved from Oxford to London, which
brought it closer to two trade unions, the Amalgamated Society of
Railway Servants and the South Wales Miners' Federation, which were
particularly committed to the idea of adult education. The London Labour
College, as it was now called, operated as a boarding school and offered
two sessions per year, mainly for trade unionists: 'The object is to provide

independent working class education to equip members for service in the movement generally, in the work of bringing to an end the system of capitalism and enabling the workers to achieve their social and industrial emancipation'.[47] In 1920, the CLC, the trade unions and the Plebs League joined forces to form the National Council of Labour Colleges (NCLC).[48] In 1927, according to Buchan's report, the NCLC, financed by thirty-five trade unions, had a budget of £35,000 per year and definitely represented 'the "left" wing of the Socialist movement'.[49] Its establishment worried the Conservative party, and at the annual party conference in 1920, David Davis, Conservative counsellor for Newport, solemnly declared that the Labour party had created a college and a network of more than thirty 'schools' for training its activists and open to the general public. These schools disseminated Socialist ideas, and Davis explained that the Conservative party would be well advised to follow suit.[50] By 1927 the NCLC had enrolled a record 31,000 students.[51]

The Philip Stott College

From 1923 to 1928, the experience of the Philip Stott College in Northamptonshire convinced the party that training Conservative officials and activists was 'not enough and that a more ambitious project was needed, combining political education with the formulation of Conservative principles and their dissemination. In 1928 the first plans were drafted for a 'Ruskin College of the right'.

The idea for the new college was to borrow Ruskin's working methods, including the adoption of Ruskin's political autonomy. Sidney Ball, a member of the Ruskin executive committee, recalled that Ruskin College's charter formally eschewed political engagement, and explained that the committee was 'quite willing to put as liberal interpretation as we could on the connexion between the College & the "labour movement" (though there is no reference to this in the charter)'.[52] The Conservatives similarly hoped to interpret the ties between their college and party as loosely as possible, to secure the college's autonomy and a reputable educational framework. Although the WEA and Ruskin College affirmed their political neutrality, the Conservatives saw them nonetheless as belonging to the Socialist movement. They expected their college to occupy the same place in the educational movement, with the same interpretation of political neutrality.

In 1927, Buchan explained, 'In the past, men were apprentices to "Masters" of the trade in which lay their future, masons, weavers, builders; now, men, and women too, apprentice themselves of their own free will to Masters and Professors of the mind. With no view except the cultivation of their own minds they attend evening classes, weekend or Summer Schools, and sometimes even residential Colleges.'[53] The upheaval since 1918 was due to the fact that the 'apprentices' had themselves become the 'masters' because of their new electoral power, and the Conservative party's fate now lay in their hands.

The Conservative party and the new electorate

The Conservative party took active measures in the post-war period to draw in different categories of the expanded electorate, including the young, women and Liberal supporters. The Junior Imperial League (JIL), founded in 1906, was reorganised under Davidson's presidency. In 1928, each branch of the JIL, which until then had enjoyed quasi-autonomy, was integrated into the local Conservative party. In 1930, there were 473 JIL councils in 507 of the Conservative divisions in England and Wales, with Scotland having its own JIL. In 1925, the Young Britons was established for children of 6 to 14 years of age, in order to 'counteract the blasphemous and seditious doctrine of the Communists'.[54] During the inter-war years, the Young Britons had 500,000 members.[55] Conservative leaders supported the JIL and the Young Britons as a means of involving young people in the electoral battle. However, their effectiveness was disputed in several letters to Lord Alec Dunglass, the JIL president in 1937. Critics accused the JIL of organising too many society balls and not enough political meetings. Dunglass replied that it was 'better that [the indifferent] should be danced into Conservatives than drift into Socialist ranks'.[56]

The women's vote

Recent research has shown that the Conservative party's attempts at stratified electioneering began in the 1890s and became more sophisticated in the pre-war years, which were important in advancing women's position within Conservative activism.[57] The Conservative party was responsible for the grant of full voting equality to women in 1928. Between 1918 and 1928, women's votes seemed to favour the Conservatives.[58] Women also occupied a central place in the social activities of the Conservative party between the wars. In 1927, the party had 887,000 women members – one woman in twelve being a member – or 9 per cent of the electorate. 'By the early 1920s, reliance of Conservative Constituency Associations on their female members had become a truism within the party. Almost all agents, M.P.s and candidates acknowledged that women were outdoing men in terms of canvassing, propaganda work and fundraising.'[59] In May 1924, there were 1,500 women's associations within the Conservative party. That same year, Marjorie Maxse, one of the party's most influential women in the 1930s, declared in the *Conservative Agents Journal* that 'the great thing they were out to do was to teach women to be voters and Conservative voters'.[60] In 1928, the Fifth Reform Act aligned women's right to vote with that of men: henceforth women aged 21 and over became eligible. The party's policy on women was seen as a great success: at the 1935 general election the Conservatives won 386 seats, with women constituting more than 50 per cent of the electorate. In comparison, the trade unions and the Labour party seemed to be exclusively male preserves.[61]

The integration of women into the Conservative party was the fruit of a long effort. Contrary to the feminist movement and its egalitarian aspirations, the Conservatives projected the image of a woman who assumed, even embraced, her differences, and whose domestic work was appreciated. Her role within the family was something to be proud of and celebrated in the country. Pamphlets, magazines and brochures were written with the sole purpose of promoting this image. *Home and Politics*, one of the Conservative journals that stressed the role of the housewife, became hugely successful.[62] It presented women as the 'domestic Chancellors of the Exchequer', and the family shopping basket was compared to managing the country's finances: testimony to the party's reverence for the housewife. Above all, it acknowledged her role in society and the community. Particularly for the middle classes in the prosperous suburbs, community life as promoted by the party was a natural extension to domestic life. Whist drives, fêtes, charity sales and balls played a central part in social life and were often as important in terms of meeting people and sharing ideas as were official meetings of the local Conservative party. Belonging to the Conservative party was synonymous with an active social life. As the wife of a sales representative declared, 'unless you're in the swing, like being an active Conservative, suburbia is *hell*'.[63]

The importance of women was fully recognised by the party's hierarchy. Davidson, the party chairman, wrote in his memoirs:

> The dominant feature at this time was the rise in the importance of the women electors. They were organized in branches in every constituency, and had enormous enthusiasm behind them. I appointed Miss Marjorie Maxse with much wider responsibilities as Deputy Chief Agent to make it quite clear to the Party that the women were to play a very important part in the development of Conservatism in the country. We fortunately had at our disposal some excellent women politicians – people like Dame Caroline Bridgeman (who was the first woman to be Chairman of the Annual Conference) and Lady Iveagh, Dame Regina Evans and several others of great ability. And of course the fact that the Conservative Party had led the van in the electoral field as regards women gave us a very definite lead ... [64]

Not everyone in the party shared this open-minded attitude and one of the challenges of Ashridge was to make the party a more congenial home for women. There were many who did not look favourably upon the role taken by women within the party and complained of their intrusion into what had until then been an exclusively male world.[65] Indeed, a fraction of the party strongly criticised the presence of women in political life; some rejected what they saw as the feminisation of the party. 'In politics ... women's influence was accused of promoting the ephemeral, the superficial and the decorative at the expense of more important concerns.'[66]

The role played by women within the party created tensions not only at the local level but also within the parliamentary party. It contributed to the party's anxieties and to what its saw as a new challenge. Nancy Astor, the first female MP, complained that her colleagues never took her seriously and showed little interest in the questions that she raised about the lives of women. In 1927, she declared in parliament: 'We women of the Unionist party have to fight a great battle, there are so many men who say such amazingly stupid things about women in our party.'[67] Conservative leaders had to convince their male colleagues to accept this new situation. During the debates on women's right to vote in 1917, Archibald Salvidge, chairman of the Conservative Association of Liverpool, wrote:

> They will form nearly two-fifths of the parliamentary electorate and the Unionist Party will, of necessity, be compelled to attract them ... Their importance in elections will be paramount and already the Labour Party are bent on a programme which will attract women. There seems no reason why women should not be welcome in the Unionist organisation on equal terms with men.
>
> It is highly probable that Clubs and Branches will have to be formed for women or arrangements made for their inclusion in present clubs or a separate meeting night assigned to them. Much opposition to such proposals may be expected from men ... The bold course of 'equal rights' for males and females seems to be best ... It would perhaps be desirable to make some proviso that the representation of women on divisional councils be limited so as to prevent them securing a predominance of power in the direction of party affairs.[68]

The Conservative party's crushing defeat of Labour in the 1931 general election seemed to confirm the importance of the women's vote for the party. As Davidson wrote: 'the causes of the defeat of the Socialists were in the main the profound contempt, especially of the women electors, for the men who ran away from the crisis'.[69]

The Liberal vote

Between 1918 and 1922, the Labour party gradually replaced the Liberals as the main opposition to the Conservatives.[70] This situation led the Conservative party to formulate an anti-Socialist strategy and to review its relationship with the Liberal party. Between 1916 and 1922, the Conservative party had formed a coalition government with the Lloyd George Liberals to lead the country through the war and prepare for its aftermath. On account of the Labour party's progress, many Conservatives, including Austen Chamberlain and F. E. Smith, considered that an alliance with the Liberals was the best way to fight Socialism. From 1922, however, the Lloyd George Liberals appeared to be too Radical, and the majority of the Conservative party believed they must end the coalition and fight the Labour party on their own.[71] Yet, despite the breakdown of the Conservative–Liberal alliance, the Liberal vote, whether for the Asquith or the Lloyd George wing of the party, remained vital for the Conservative party. It was essential to obtain it or risk losing it to the Labour party. In December 1923, after Stanley Baldwin led the Conservatives to defeat in the general election, Leo Amery reported a conversation when he attempted 'to convince him [Stanley Baldwin] that our main object in the immediate future is the destruction of the Liberal Party and the absorption of as much of the carcass as we can secure'. 'One of the three parties has to disappear and the one that is spiritually dead and has been so for thirty years or more is the natural victim.'[72] Buchan echoed Amery's thoughts in 1927: 'There have been five Elections since 1910, during which time we have witnessed the practical extermination of the Liberals, the erratic course of the Conservative vote, and the steady gradually increasing popularity of the Socialists.'[73]

To attract the Liberal electorate, the Conservative party had to learn the lessons of its 1923 defeat. During the election campaign, Baldwin had attacked the principle of free trade, which was central to Liberal thinking. In proposing import duties on manufactures, he had provoked criticism from the Liberals and, inadvertently, a rapprochement between Lloyd George and Asquith. Following the refusal of the Liberals to form a government or to support a Conservative cabinet, the Labour party formed a minority government. Paradoxically, the Liberal position contributed to the Conservatives' return to power, since the Liberal leaders were accused by their own supporters of contributing to the victory of the Socialists. This was exactly what Amery had hoped for when he wrote, shortly after the election, that the best strategy for the Conservatives was to 'force the Liberals to face the necessity of supporting Labour which is bound to mean their eventual break-up and disappearance as a party'.[74]

During the 1924 general election campaign, 'anti-Socialism' became the Conservatives' watchword, especially by exploiting the emotions aroused when the 'Zinoviev letter'[75] was published, thereby gaining many Liberal votes. After the election victory in 1924, Baldwin, at the risk of offending certain party members, appointed Winston Churchill as chancellor of the exchequer. Appointing a supporter of free trade was a gesture of good will towards the Liberals. It signalled that the principle of free trade would not be abandoned over the next parliament.

Similarly, Baldwin tried to open up the Conservative party to different churches. While painting the Labour party as anti-religious it presented itself as *the* Christian party, uniting Methodists, Baptists and Congregationalists with Anglicans. Baldwin was the first Conservative leader to speak at the annual Methodist conference, where he called for a Christian democracy ruled by tolerance.

To attract the Liberals, the Conservative party felt it needed a programme focused on anti-Socialism, free trade and religious tolerance. But while this policy proved successful in 1924, it did not guarantee the loyalty of Liberal voters. In June 1927, for example, E. L. Spears, the Conservative candidate who had just lost in a by-election, wrote to Davidson that the reason for the defeat was a 'last moment swing of Conservative votes to the Liberals to keep out the Socialists'.[76] Although the Liberals were losing ground, they were still a force to be reckoned with, and the instability of a political system based upon three political parties made the Conservatives' position vulnerable. In June 1929, just before the Preston by-election, Churchill suggested that, in order to beat the Labour party, they should 'ostentatiously encourage Conservative support' for the Liberal candidate.[77] In short, they should maintain a close relationship with the Liberal party in order to unite anti-Socialists. This concern came to a head during the general election in the summer of 1929, when the Liberal party seemed to recover politically and Labour emerged as the largest party. Churchill acknowledged: 'I am deeply impressed with the critical character of the present situation. Eight million Tories, eight million Labour, five million Liberal. Where will those five million go?... We must recognise the conditions of the new franchise; they are inexorable.'[78] Electoral boundaries and the electoral system permitted the Labour party to take power.

The Conservative party sought to attract those Liberals who rejected Lloyd George, who seemed a 'dynamic force' and a 'very terrible thing':[79] an uncontrollable force destroying everything in its way. The party mainly attracted those who were disturbed by the radicalism of the 1929 Liberal programme[80] and the Liberal party's decision to support the Labour party. Neville Chamberlain admired the skill of Baldwin, who knew 'better than anyone in any party how to attract the non-aligned voters and office workers as well as the conscientious and earnest element of the Liberal party'.[81]

The Conservatives not only looked to rally Liberal voters while weakening their party, but also to draw the lessons of their experience in the field of political education. Here the Liberal summer school offered useful insights. The idea of a Liberal summer school was first advanced at a conference in Grasmere in September 1921, and afterwards the school opened its doors every summer, alternately at Oxford or Cambridge. In 1926, the Liberal *Daily News* observed that 'the abler sort of young man turned after Grasmere as naturally to the Summer School Movement as in an earlier generation he turned to Fabianism'.[82] While the first session at Grasmere attracted mainly 'the intellectually expert',[83] the management subsequently sought to widen participation. Ramsay Muir, the Liberal journalist and writer who founded the Liberal summer school, explained that 'ideological innovators were rarely to be found within the upper ranks of a party machine and that a wider net had to be cast in order to reformulate the core and range of Liberal thinking'.[84] Six hundred people took part in the first summer school, held at Oxford in 1922, which was considered a success. In 1926, nine hundred people took part in the summer school. The Liberal press offered grants to working-class students and awarded literary prizes to the best lecturers. The summer school, albeit a Liberal innovation, could not be politically aligned if it wanted to attract as many students as possible. Muir explained that 'many of the best minds engaged in the study of the economic and political scenes were in fact Liberals, though not active politicians, and they planned to provide for them at once a nucleus and a platform'.[85] However, 'despite its non-party profile, the Liberal Summer School Movement attempt[ed] ... to secure the co-operation and ears of the party elite'.[86] The participation of the party's elite in the summer school shaped its educational content just as the debates that took place there were seen as influencing the party's policies. In *Liberalism Divided*,[87] Michael Freeden shows how far William Beveridge's participation at the Liberal summer school advanced his views on family allowances and social security. The Liberal summer school aimed to make up for the fact that 'the Liberal Party, up to the present, has not concerned itself much with Research, believing with the Conservative Party, that the older electioneering methods are sufficient not only to win elections but also to inform the Party, and to mould the public to the right way of thinking'.[88] In January 1927, the Liberal party created the *Liberal Industrial Enquiry*, a journal of economic research that aimed to improve the analysis of unemployment. Working alongside the Liberal summer school, it produced the Liberal party's 'yellow book' on 'Britain's

Industrial Future'. Walter Layton, Hubert Henderson, J. M. Keynes, Ramsay Muir, John Simon, Edward Gilpin and Herbert Samuel participated in the summer school and contributed to the formulation of a radical response to Britain's economic problems. They proposed extensive state intervention and the implementation of a large-scale programme of public works financed by loans. These views formed the basis of the Liberal party's *Yellow Book* and its 1929 manifesto, 'We Can Conquer Unemployment'.

The Liberal summer school left an important legacy in the development of a new approach to economic and social policy, anticipating the Keynesian policies implemented in Britain twenty years later. But in the short run it seemed only to aggravate divisions within the party. Intellectuals like Keynes gave the impression of wanting to cut the party from its past. Leaders of the party, including John Simon and Walter Runciman, were reluctant to accept the principles of the manifesto, 'We Can Conquer Unemployment'. This reluctance was even more marked among activists at the grass roots of the party.[89] After the party's defeat in 1929 they decided to close the summer school. Yet the wealth of intellectual thinking that it generated offered a fine example of the contribution such an institution could make. At any rate, this was the lesson the Conservatives took from its ephemeral existence. If the Conservatives, like the Liberals, were beaten in the 1929 general election, it was, they thought, largely because of the lack of imagination evident in their election programme, which appeared so prudent as to seem worn out, as suggested by its title, 'Safety first'.

The Conservative party and intellectuals

In 1933, F. J. C. Hearnshaw published a collection of lectures he had delivered during the first two years of Ashridge College under the title *Conservatism in England*. While reflecting upon the founding principles of Conservative doctrine, Hearnshaw also discussed the challenges and objectives at the time of Ashridge's foundation. As a starting point, he examined the problems the college aimed to resolve and the void it needed to fill. 'The comparative inarticulateness of Conservatives also explains the comparative scantiness of Conservative literature.'[90] Compared with Socialism, Conservatism had been practically ignored, although he added, 'Socialism is little else than literature.'[91] However, 'Conservatism ... has a small select library of great classics which constitute a magnificent heritage of sound principles and inspiring ideas.'[92] In particular, he singled out the works of Hugh Cecil, Geoffrey Butler, R. M. Banks, Walter Elliot and Arthur Bryant,[93] all of whom 'helped to remove the charge of inarticulateness from the conservative party as a whole'.[94]

Conservatives felt the need to challenge the world-view of their opponents at the most fundamental level. They opposed Marx's claim in *The Eighteenth Brumaire of Louis Bonaparte* that 'men make their own history, but they do not make it as they please'. They also challenged what they perceived to be the Whig or Liberal interpretation of history in which the idea of progress was the driving force behind events. The Whig interpretation of British history, they claimed, had governed history teaching for over a century and universities, and in particular Oxford and Cambridge, were largely dominated by the 'lights of liberalism'.[95] These lights were the progress brought by the 'Glorious Revolution' of 1688, the progressive extension of popular sovereignty, the supremacy of parliament, equality before the law and the extension of universal suffrage. At the social and economic level, the development of industry, the gradual increase of religious tolerance and greater social harmony had turned Liberalism into the new political creed. E. A. Freeman could thus write in 1870 that 'our ancient history is the possession of the liberal'.[96]

F. J. C. Hearnshaw, Keith Feiling, Arthur Bryant and other Conservative historians believed that an overly determined interpretation of history resulted in policies derived from the hegemony of a mode of thought. It was thus necessary to correct this bias, these errors and omissions, conscious and unconscious, of Whig history. As Butterfield wrote: 'Though there have been Tory – as there have been many Catholic – partisan histories, it is still true that there is no corresponding tendency for the subject itself to lean in this direction.'[97] By implication, there already existed, albeit fragmentary, an alternative to the Whig interpretation of history. It would become one of the major tasks of Ashridge to develop this alternative and construct a 'Tory intrepretation of history'.

Although the main target of Conservative historians was the Whig interpretation of British history, they also criticised other forms of history writing. Lytton Strachey's *Eminent Victorians*, published in 1918, and its sequel, *Queen Victoria*, published in 1924, were the expression of 'the Bloomsbury interpretation of history', which ridiculed British institutions and the British establishment.[98] Although the books enjoyed 'amazing success' in terms of sales, they were all the more successful for the fact that they 'inspired countless "debunking" biographies in [their] wake.'[99] Conservatives focused their criticism upon the Bloomsbury group, seeing in it the deliberate destruction of all social, moral, sexual, artistic and literary conventions. Contrary to the Fabians, who, they thought, conformed to traditional morals and were rather conservative in their behaviour, the Bloomsbury group was unrestrained and its intellectual domination of the arts and literature seemed complete. Although it was only a small group of artists, mostly living in London, the social background of its members, the networks to which they belonged and their ties with universities and the press appeared to give them enormous control over ideas and their expression.

In reaction, Conservatives sought to promote the literary heritage of Britain which the Bloomsbury group had dismissed in its quest for 'modernity'. Thus Hearnshaw explained:

> It must be remembered, there is an inexhaustible storehouse of the finest Conservatism in much of the best of the general literature of our country. Where, for instance, can the genius of Conservatism be found more magnificently embodied than the historical plays of Shakespeare? How finely inspired by the Conservative spirit are the poems of Dryden, Pope, Wordsworth and Coleridge! What wealth of Conservative thought in the prose works of Swift, Johnson, Southey, and Scott![100]

That both Coleridge and Wordsworth had pro-revolutionary phases did not seem to be an issue and one of the aims of Ashridge was to revive the taste for studying these English classic texts.

The strategy the Conservatives adopted in reaction to the supposed dominance of the Bloomsbury group comprised several key components. Far from being merely the gatekeepers to the past, they hoped to design an alternative intellectual model to that of the Bloomsbury group, capable of fighting on equal terms. In the literary domain, and the arts in general, they hoped to identify suitable 'Conservative' writers and artists. In the first place, Ashridge should bring together writers and artists whose works conformed with Conservative traditions, to make them aware of their political affinity and the role they should play as intellectuals. In fact, a large number of writers, Conservative or not, published books that were very different from those of the Bloomsbury group, and which, if less critically acclaimed, enjoyed important sales. Agatha Christie, Jan Struther, Ivy Compton-Burnett, John Buchan, James Hilton, Hugh Walpole and many others formed a substantial group of Conservative writers[101] whom critics unfairly rejected in favour of the Bloomsbury group, who enthralled them. To reflect upon literary and artistic canons, and to propose an alternative to what they claimed to be the dominant tastes of the highbrow elite of the Bloomsbury group was one of the first tasks of the Conservative college.

The creation of the Conservative Research Department

In 1927, Buchan, as chairman of the party's educational committee, proposed the creation of a research department as well as a college. The idea of subjecting policies to study and analysis to assess their electoral value was not completely new. The establishment of expert committees in parliament prefigured this development. Already in 1903, Joseph Chamberlain had called for a 'tariff commission' to provide him with the necessary statistics and economic facts required for tariff reform. In December 1904, Andrew Bonar Law wrote to W. J. Ashley, professor of economic history at Birmingham University: 'There is nothing ... which tells more against us than the idea that scientific authority is against us'.[102] Chamberlain and the tariff reformers had looked for the support of economists and experts. Chamberlain explained to W. A. S. Hewins, secretary of the tariff commission: '[you must] supply the economic arguments'.[103] An economic and statistical approach to customs regulations,[104] clarifying the reasons for import duties, was fundamental to convincing the industrial and agricultural worlds of their legitimacy. Similarly, between 1911 and 1914 the Unionist Social Reform Committee (USRC) studied the social reforms to be undertaken, such as the revision of the poor laws, industrial relations, rural housing and agricultural wages. Created by Arthur Steel-Maitland, chairman of the Conservative party,[105] the USRC comprised academic economists such as Hewins, Ashley and L. L. Price, and politicians such as J. W. Hills, who had completed studies at the turn of the century, when the concept of social investigation was starting to take shape. Hewins described the committee as playing two roles: first, to draw up 'a true Conservative theory of the State', and second, to propose social reforms based upon this theory.[106]

In April 1924, Baldwin formed a committee of former ministers to consider new policies. This committee was assisted by 'the policy secretariat', which would become the research department when it was established in 1929.[107] The lengthy miners' strike of 1925, followed by the General Strike of 1926, prompted many Conservatives to question how they should handle social conflict within firms. Tariff reform and the General Strike demonstrated the urgency of creating an organisation for political and economic reflection. Questions of tariffs, unemployment, the defence budget, restructuring industries in decline, health and the role of local authorities were also subjects that needed to be addressed without further delay.

The CRD was created with a different charter to that of the Conservative party. Although financed by the party and employing the same personnel, the subjects studied in the CRD and the policies it devised were determined by the CRD officials themselves. The party's Central Office did not intervene in the process: symbolically, CRD offices were not at party headquarters. Neville Chamberlain described it in 1930 as 'an office of information providing data and briefs for party leaders, and a centre for long-term research whose output is intended not for the general public but for different party groups, for central office and Ashridge'.[108] Ashridge and the CRD were intended to meet similar needs by different means.

Notes

1 On the Conservatives' sense of vulnerability, see D. Jarvis, 'Stanley Baldwin'. Green, *Ideologies of Conservatism*, pp. 135–56. Ball, *Portrait of a Party*, pp. 52–81.

2 J. Buchan memorandum, 'Political Research and Adult Education', 1927, Baldwin papers, SB53, fos 79–92. John Buchan was Director of the Education Department of CCO in 1927. He became Chairman of the Executive Committee of the Conservative Educational Institute, which succeeded it from March 1928. (See *Gleanings and Memoranda*, Mar. 1928, p. 181, CCO, CPA). Buchan was appointed Chairman of the Education Committee at Ashridge on 29 Nov. 1929. I am grateful to Stuart Ball and Jeremy McIlwaine for their help in finding information on the 'Education Department' at CCO.

3 D. L. LeMahieu, *A Culture for Democracy: Mass Communication and the Cultivated Mind in Britain between the Wars* (New York: Oxford University Press, Clarendon Press, 1988).

4 Ball was a secret agent during the First World War and director of the Conservative Research Department from its inception in 1929 until 1939.

5 J. Ball to S. Baldwin, 6 Dec. 1935, Baldwin papers, SB48, fos 251–60.

6 The 'educated middle classes' refers to a heterogeneous class of people, some of whom were university graduates, the majority of whom held professional qualifications, a secondary leaving certificate or were self-educated.

7 J. Ball to S. Baldwin, 6 Dec. 1935, Baldwin papers, SB48, fos 251–60.

8 J. Buchan memorandum, 'Political Research and Adult Education', 1927, Baldwin papers, SB53, fos 79–92.

9 *Ibid.*

10 *Ibid.*

11 *Ibid.*

12 S. Baldwin, 'Political Education', lecture at the Philip Stott College, 27 Sep. 1923, in Baldwin, *On England*, p. 153.

13 Minutes of the annual Conservative party conference, London, 21 and 22 Nov. 1929, CPA, NUA 2/1/45 (117–119).

14 N. MacKenzie and J. MacKenzie, *The First Fabians* (London: Weidenfeld & Nicolson, 1977), p. 84.

15 A. Besant, quoted in *ibid.*, p. 78.

16 Andrew Pease, quoted in *ibid.*, p. 81.

17 A. McBriar, *Fabian Socialism and English Politics, 1884–1918* (Cambridge: Cambridge University Press, 1962). W. Wolfe, *From Radicalism to Socialism: Men and Ideas in the Formation of Fabian Socialist Doctrines, 1881–1889* (New Haven, CT: Yale University Press, 1975). MacKenzie and MacKenzie, *The First Fabians*. P. Pugh, *Educate, Agitate, Organize: 100 Years of Fabian Socialism* (London: Methuen & Co., 1984).

18 E. J. Hobsbawm, 'The Fabians Reconsidered', in Hobsbawm, *Labouring Men, Studies in the History of Labour* (London: Weidenfeld & Nicolson, 1964), pp. 250–71.

19 T. H. Huxley, 'Administrative Nihilism', in *Collective Essays*, Vol. 1. *Methods and Results* (Cambridge: Cambridge University Press, 2011), pp. 251–89.

20 L. T. Hobhouse, *Liberalism* (Oxford: Oxford University Press, 1911).

21 Lord Milner was high commissioner in South Africa during the Boer War. J. L. Garvin was news editor of *The Outlook*, a Conservative monthly, before joining *The Observer*. Leo Maxse was publisher and editor of the Conservative magazine *The National Review*.

22 On the myth of the importance of the Fabians, see Hobsbawm, *The Fabians Reconsidered*; McBriar, *Fabian Socialism and English Politics*. On the origins of the Beveridge Report and the Welfare State see J. Harris, *William Beveridge. A Biography* (Oxford: Clarendon Press, 1997). J. Harris, 'Political Thought and the Welfare State, 1870–1940: An Intellectual Framework for British Social Policy', *Past & Present*, 135, 1992, pp. 116–41.

23 M. Reckitt, quoted in Clarke, *Liberals and Liberal Democrats*, pp. 197–8.

24 Memorandum on the WEA from E. Percy to Director of the CRD, Sep. 1930, CPA, CRD 1/12/1.

25 Memorandum from Pakenham to the Director of the CRD, 1 Dec. 1931, CPA, CRD 1/12/1. Frank Pakenham worked for the CRD from 1930 to 1932 and lectured regularly at Ashridge. He also worked with the WEA as a tutor in the Potteries from 1929 to 1931. He left the Conservatives and joined the Labour party in 1936 and became a Labour peer in 1945.

26 K. Pickthorn, Memorandum, Ashridge conference, 14–15 Dec. 1929, Education Committee, 1930, Ashridge papers.

27 R. Northam, *Conservatism, the Only Way* (London: John Gifford for the Right Book Club, 1939). Underlining in the original.

28 Unsigned and undated memorandum (probably by Hoskins Jan/Feb. 1934), Education Committee 1934, Ashridge papers.

29 Sidney Webb to Edward Pease, 24 Oct. 1886, in MacKenzie and MacKenzie, *The First Fabians*, p. 62.

30 Letter of invitation to speak at Ashridge, 13 Nov. 1936, Bryant papers, C52.

31 'The Work of Ashridge', undated (? Dec. 1929), Education Committee 1930, Ashridge papers.

32 Undated memorandum, 'The Workers' Educational Association', 1933, CPA, CCO 3/1/90.

33 The ministry of education was then known as the Board of Education. As the result of the 1902 Education Act, local education authorities were created to administer and finance local education. With the passage of the Fisher Education Act in 1918, public subsidies were increased.

34 Undated memorandum, 'The Workers' Educational Association', 1933, CPA, CCO 3/1/90.

35 *Ibid.*

36 *Ibid.*

37 Memorandum, 'The Importance of Conservative Education for the Working Man', 30 Nov. 1931, CPA, CRD 1/12/1.

38 J. C. C. Davidson to Sir Alfred Goodson, 10 Mar. 1928, 1st Viscount Davidson Papers, House of Lords Record Office, London (hereafter Davidson papers), DAV/182.

39 Memorandum, 'The Importance of Conservative Education for the Working Man', 30 Nov. 1931, CPA, CRD 1/12/1.

40 Undated memorandum, 'The Workers' Educational Association', 1933, CPA, CCO 3/1/90.

41 Memorandum from Eustace Percy on 'The WEA and the National College of Labour Colleges', 16 Feb. 1930, CPA, CRD 1/12/1.

42 Marjorie Maxse to Joseph Ball, 3 May 1932, CPA, CRD 1/12/1.

43 L. Goldman, *Dons and Workers, Oxford and Adult Education since 1850* (Oxford: Clarendon Press, 1995), p. 167.

44 W. H. Seed (ed.), *The Burning Question of Education: Being an Account of the Ruskin College Dispute, Its Causes and Consequences* (Oxford: Plebs' League, 1909), p. 14, quoted in Goldman, *Dons and Workers*, p. 171.

45 Lord Curzon, *Principles and Methods of University Reform; Being a Letter Addressed to the University of Oxford* (Oxford, 1909), p. 63, quoted in Goldman, *Dons and Workers*, p. 175.

46 S. Ball to J. R. MacDonald, 6 Apr. 1909, quoted in Goldman, *Dons and Workers*, p. 173.

47 W. H. Lee, secretary of the Pudsey and Otley National Unionist Association in Alport, 21 Feb. 1938, CPA, CCO 4/1/85.

48 On the NCLC, see S. MacIntyre, *A Proletarian Science: Marxism in Britain, 1917–1933* (Cambridge: Cambridge University Press, 1980), pp. 78–85.

49 J. Buchan, 'Political Research and Adult Education', 1927, Baldwin papers, SB53, fos 79–92.

50 Green, *Ideologies of Conservatism*, p. 135.

51 Goldman, *Dons and Workers*, p. 178.

52 *Ibid.*, p. 173.

53 J. Buchan, *Political Research and Adult Education*, 1927, Baldwin papers, SB53, fos 79–92.

54 Young Britons' Working Group, 'Background Brief', 15 June 1965, CPA, CCO 506/8/4. S. J. Ball, 'Local Conservatism and the Evolution of the Party Organisation', in A. Seldon and S. Ball (eds), *Conservative Century: the Conservative Party since 1900* (Oxford: Oxford University Press, 1994), p. 275. Socialist Sunday schools existed from the end of the nineteenth century, but they only really developed between the wars.

55 *Ibid.*

56 Lord Dunglass to T. C. Dugdale, 29 Jan. 1943, quoted in J. W. B. Bates, 'The Conservative Party in the Constituencies, 1918–39' (PhD dissertation, University of Oxford, 1994), p. 69.

57 D. Thackeray, 'Rethinking the Edwardian Crisis of Conservatism', *The Historical Journal*, 54, 1 (2011), pp. 191–213.

58 Ball, *Portrait of a Party*, p. 118.

59 D. Jarvis, 'The Conservative Party and the Politics of Gender, 1900–1939', in M. Francis and I. Zweiniger-Bargielowska (eds) *The Conservatives and British Society, 1880–1990* (Cardiff: University of Wales Press, 1996), p. 176.

60 Marjorie Maxse, *Conservative Agents Journal*, May 1924.

61 See McKibbin, *Classes and Cultures*, pp. 127–87; D. Jarvis, 'British Conservatism and Class Politics in the 1920s', *English Historical Review*, 110, 1996, pp. 59–84.

62 In 1929, *Home and Politics* sold 200,000 copies a month.

63 P. Wilmott and M. Young, *Family and Class in a London Suburb* (London: Routledge & Kegan Paul, 1960), p. 108, in McKibbin, *Classes and Cultures*, p. 93.

64 James (ed.), *Memoirs of a Conservative*, p. 266.

65 On the Conservative party and women, see G. E. Maguire, *Conservative Women: A History of Women and the Conservative Party, 1874–1997* (London: Basingstoke, 1998).

66 *Ibid.*, p. 182.

67 N. Astor to Parliament, 9 Feb. 1927, quoted in Jarvis, *The Conservative Party and the Politics of Gender*, p. 173.

68 A. Salvidge, 'The Representation of the People Bill' (1917), Report of the Secretary, Bonar Law papers, 82/4/7, quoted in McCrillis, *The British Conservative Party*, pp. 19–20.

69 J. C. C. Davidson to his uncle William, 5 Nov. 1931, quoted in James (ed.), *Memoirs of a Conservative*, p. 37.

70 On the Conservatives coming to terms with the progress made by the Labour party see Cowling, *The Impact of Labour*.

71 E. H. H. Green, 'Conservatism, Anti-Socialism, and the End of the Lloyd George Coalition', in Green, *Ideologies of Conservatism: Conservative Political Ideas in the Twentieth Century* (Oxford: Oxford University Press, 2002), pp. 114–34.

72 J. Barnes and D. Nicholson (eds), *The Leo Amery Diaries*, Vol. 1: *1896–1929* (London: Hutchinson, 1980), p. 361, diary entry for 8 Dec. 1923.

73 J. Buchan, 'Political Research and Adult Education', 1927, Baldwin papers, SB53, fos 79–92.

74 *Ibid.*

75 The Zinoviev letter, published in the *Daily Mail* in 1924, suggested an alliance between the Komintern and the Labour party. It was in fact a forgery, which the Conservatives used to undermine Labour's credibility. See Chester, Fay and Young, *The Zinoviev Letter*; Davies, *We, the Nation*, pp. 222–26.

76 E. L. Spears to J. J. C. Davidson, 2 June 1927, Baldwin papers, 51, fos 80–82.

77 W. Churchill to O. Stanley, 23 June 1929, Baldwin papers, 51, fo. 84. Reproduced with permission of Curtis Brown, London on behalf of the Estate of Sir Winston Churchill. Copyright © Winston S. Churchill.

78 W. Churchill to S. Baldwin, 29 Nov. 1929, Baldwin papers, 164, fo. 37.

Reproduced with permission of Curtis Brown, London on behalf of the Estate of Sir Winston Churchill. Copyright © Winston S. Churchill.

79 This was the way Baldwin described Lloyd George at the Carlton Club in 1922. Williamson, *Stanley Baldwin*, p. 65.

80 The Liberals' political programme in 1929 was presented in pamphlet form. 'Britain's Industrial Future' and 'We Can Conquer Unemployment' had J. M. Keynes's support. Keynes himself wrote a pamphlet entitled 'Can Lloyd George Do It?'

81 N. Chamberlain to Lord Irwin, 12 Aug. 1928, Halifax Indian papers, C152/18/114a, quoted in Williamson, *Stanley Baldwin*, p. 355.

82 S. Hodgson, 'The Story of the Liberal Summer Schools', *Daily News*, 24 July 1926, quoted in M. Freeden, *Liberalism Divided; a Study in British Political Thought, 1914–1939* (Oxford: Oxford University Press, 1986), p. 83.

83 *Ibid.*, p. 87.

84 R. Muir, 'The Liberal Summer School and the Problems of Industry', *Contemporary Review*, 132 (1927), 282–89, quoted in *ibid.*, p. 82.

85 *Ibid.*, p. 82.

86 *Ibid.*, p. 84.

87 Freeden, *Liberalism Divided*.

88 J. Buchan, 'Political Research and Adult Education', 1927, Baldwin papers, SB53, fos 79–92.

89 See Thorpe, *The British General Election of 1931*.

90 F. J. C. Hearnshaw, *Conservatism in England* (London: Macmillan, 1933), 1967 edition, p. 8.

91 *Ibid.*, p. 9.

92 *Ibid.*, p. 10.

93 See the Select Bibliography.

94 Hearnshaw, *Conservatism in England*.

95 C. Harvie, *The Lights of Liberalism* (London: Allen Lane, 1976).

96 E. A. Freeman, *The Growth of the English Constitution from the Earliest Times*, 3rd edn, 1870, quoted in J. W. Burrow, *A Liberal Descent: Victorian Historians and the English Past* (Cambridge: Cambridge University Press, 1981), p. 3.

97 *Ibid.*, p. 7.

98 L. Strachey, *Eminent Victorians* (London, Chatto & Windus, 1918).

99 P. Clarke, *Hope and Glory, Britain 1900-1990* (Penguin Books, 1996), p. 166.

100 Hearnshaw, *Conservatism in England*, p. 10.

101 Mrs Miniver, one of Jan Struther's characters, featured in a well-known film adaptation during the war. John Buchan was known, amongst other things, for writing *The 39 Steps*, which Hitchcock adapted for the screen. James Hilton was the author of a number of romantic melodramas, most notably *Lost Horizon* and *Random Harvest*, which were also adapted for film. On Conservative writers during the inter-war years, see A. Light, *Forever England: Femininity, Literature and Conservatism between the Wars* (London: Routledge, 1991), and R. M. Bracco, *Merchants of Hope:*

British Middlebrow Writers and the First World War, 1919–1939 (Oxford: Berg Publishers Ltd, 1993).

102 A. B. Law to W. J. Ashley, undated, Dec. 1904, quoted in Green, *Crisis of Conservatism*, p. 177.

103 J. Chamberlain to W. A. S. Hewins, 12 June 1903, in W. A. S. Hewins, *The Apologia of an Imperialist*, 2 vols (London: Constable, 1929), vol. 1, p. 60, quoted in Green, *Crisis of Conservatism*, p. 177.

104 On the Tariff Commission, see A. J. Marrison, *British Business and Protection, 1903–1932* (Oxford: Clarendon Press, 1996) and Green, *Crisis of Conservatism*, pp. 184–93.

105 A. Steel-Maitland was one of the researchers on the Royal Commission on the Poor Laws between 1905 and 1909 and his report 'The Relation of Industrial and Sanitary Conditions to Pauperism' was published as an appendix to the Royal Commission's report on the Poor Laws in 1909.

106 Minutes of the USRC, 28 Feb. 1911, Steel-Maitland papers, cited in Green, *Ideologies of Conservatism*, p. 240.

107 Lancelot Storr, who became Ashridge's college secretary, was also the college political secretary. See Ramsden, *The Making of Conservative Party Policy*, pp. 30–2.

108 N. Chamberlain to I. Chamberlain, 22 Mar. 1930, Chamberlain papers, 18/1/686, in Ramsden, *The Making of Conservative Party Policy*, p. 43.

2

Founding the Bonar Law Memorial College at Ashridge

J. C. C. Davidson, the Conservative member of parliament for Hemel Hempstead since 1920 and parliamentary private secretary to Baldwin in 1921 and 1922, then to Bonar Law in 1922 and 1923, became chairman of the Conservative party in 1926 and continued in that office until 1930. In 1929 he established the CRD and the BLMC at Ashridge in his constituency.

These two institutions were intended to be complementary, although initially there was some confusion over the allocation of their respective work. Lord Eustace Percy, the first director of the CRD, described the differences between Neville Chamberlain's point of view and his own with regard to the CRD's role: 'He [Chamberlain] wanted a group of men who would "devil" for him personally, or would at least work out the application of measures which would be given to them as the Party's policy.... My conception was the more academic one of a group ranging at large over the whole field of unsolved problems, and suggesting conclusions out of which a Party policy might be constructed.'[1] Chamberlain described Percy's approach as 'hopelessly academic'.[2] In the event, Ashridge was more like a university, although this was not to say it could not contribute to party policy. Ten days after the CRD was established, Joseph Ball, representing Lord Percy, went to Ashridge, which had been open since July, to explain the basis of collaboration between the two institutions. He wanted to organise training for CRD members on economic issues, at which time business leaders would be guest speakers. He spoke of creating a 'pool' of information as well as collaboration between the central office, its communications department, created in 1927, the CRD and Ashridge. Ball insisted upon 'the importance of exhaustive research, leading to accurate, trustworthy results'.[3] Two days later, F. J. C. Hearnshaw, professor of history at King's College London, took up the same idea: 'It is very important that Ashridge should become known as a centre where specialised information on political problems can be obtained at short notice, where expert enquiries can be competently conducted, and where authoritative sources of knowledge are collected and classified.'⁴ If there was initially any overlap between Ashridge and the CRD, their objectives were clear: the CRD's role was not to dispense general information, Ashridge's role was not to draft a political programme.

Ashridge, a site of memory

The Ashridge estate is near Berkamsted in Hertfordshire, half an hour north of London. In Arthur Bryant's words, it is 'an epitome of the history of England',⁵ or more precisely the embodiment of rural, traditional England, the beauty and virtues of which Baldwin loved to boast about. The site itself and its history formed an integral part of the Conservatives' plans for Ashridge.

The estate's history began in 1283 with Edmund Plantagenet, second earl of Cornwall. On his return from Germany he founded a monastery at Assherugge, where he deposited a holy reliquary said to contain Christ's blood. He brought monks from the Order of Bonhommes and canons from the order of St Augustine, who were doubtless from the south of France.⁶ The College of Bonhommes was given responsibility for sheltering the holy relic and welcoming pilgrims. In the fourteenth century, Edward, the Black Prince and son of Edward III, became the monastery's protector, and on his death he bequeathed it considerable riches. In September 1534, the monastery had to sign the Act of Supremacy, which declared the king to be head of the Church of England. In November 1539 the second Act of Supremacy led to the dissolution of the monasteries, including the College of Bonhommes. The monastery then became the property of the Crown and royal residence for Henry VIII's children. In 1550, Ashridge passed to Princess Elizabeth. In February 1554, Queen Mary, who sought to distance her sister from the royal court, ordered her to leave the estate. When Elizabeth was crowned in 1558 she took up residence in the palace of Whitehall and at Hampton Court. Ashridge was leased until 1575, when Queen Elizabeth decided to sell the property, which then changed hands several times until 1604, when Thomas Egerton acquired it. Thereafter it remained the Egerton family residence until the 1920s. Ashridge was relatively unscathed by the Civil War in the 1640s, although Egerton's son, the first earl of Bridgewater, was a royalist. When, at the beginning of the nineteenth century, the seventh earl of Bridgewater inherited the estate, he decided to undertake important building works directed by the architect James Wyatt. He built a vast residence whose façade was at the time the largest in England. As the monastery had been partly destroyed over the course of the years, Wyatt demolished all that was left except for the well, the crypt and the tithe barn. Between 1808 and 1813, he constructed a castle in the Gothic revival style, with numerous medieval touches. Down to the last detail, its architecture and decoration celebrated chivalric glory.

The building itself was constructed using the same local white Tottenhoe stone as that used in the monastery.[7] The castle, with its turrets and clock tower, and its woods and gardens designed by the famous landscape gardener Humphry Repton, was considered at the time to be one of the most beautiful residences in England. In the nineteenth century, 'medieval culture' and the symbols of 'Merrie England' generated a huge following, and they can still be seen in the architecture of the time as well as in the art and literature of the Victorian period. This history and architecture explain the appeal of Ashridge for Davidson and the Conservatives. It represented the period in English history associated with values of feudalism, a system based upon a set of reciprocal rights and duties within the community.

In 1849, the countess of Bridgewater died without a direct heir. After numerous quarrels and a protracted lawsuit, a distant relative, Viscount Alford, inherited the estate, becoming the second earl of Brownlow. Aged twelve and already the proprietor of a number of properties in Lincolnshire and Shropshire as well as Ashridge, he was reputed to be the richest man in England. Under Lord Brownlow, the estate grew in size. Records show that eight hundred employees worked there. Ashridge became the place where the cream of Victorian, and later Edwardian, society met; its receptions were popular with the royal family and the most famous politicians of the day. Lord Brownlow died in 1921. His will specified that Ashridge should be sold in order to settle the rights of succession and protect his other properties.

The size of the estate and the importance of its collection of works of art and valuables made the sale long and complex. It took eight years for the sale to be completed. Christie's auctioned off the estate's furniture and works of art in May 1923. On 5 October 1925, *The Times* announced the sale of the castle and its grounds. Fears were aroused that the property would fall into the hands of speculators who would disfigure the park and gardens by building houses. The National Trust[8] received an anonymous donation of £20,000 for the purchase of a part of the grounds, and a press campaign was launched to prevent this historic estate from falling into the hands of property developers. Miss Bridget Talbot, Countess Brownlow's cousin, proposed the establishment of a fund for the purchase of Ashridge and looked to Stanley Baldwin for support. On 20 October 1925, *The Times* published a letter calling on the National Trust to acquire the property. It was signed by Baldwin, J. R. MacDonald, Lord Grey of Fallodon, the National Trust's vice-president, and Lord Asquith. By mid-November, £40,000[9] had been raised, enabling the National Trust to announce it had purchased nearly 2,500 acres. However, in November 1927 the home and grounds were sold to M. E. C. Fairweather, who divided the land into lots which he immediately put up for sale. But in May 1928, Thomas Pace bought the whole property: the castle and 1,500 acres of land. The following month he resold the castle, along with 100 acres of parkland, to J. C. C. Davidson.

Davidson does not figure among the most illustrious members of the Conservative party, yet Charles Petrie wrote of him: 'Few men have wielded so much influence in British public life for so long as John Colin Campbell Davidson.'[10] In 1923, Davidson had played an important role in Baldwin's accession to power. Baldwin was grateful for this and the two men became close friends. This friendship partly explains Davidson's nomination to the post of chairman of the Conservative party in 1926: Baldwin was looking for someone in whom he had complete confidence. Almost inevitably, such a privileged relationship generated a certain amount of animosity towards Davidson within the party, and forced him to retire in 1929, following the Conservative party's defeat in the general election. However, it did not herald the end of Davidson's influence, since Baldwin continued to regard him as his closest advisor. Moreover, according to Petrie,

> No one who had any connection with the Bonar Law College during those years could be in any doubt as to the influence which Davidson exercised through it over the fortunes of the Conservative Party. Ministers might come and go, but he was in control of what may be called the higher education of the party, and although he never appeared in the forefront of the battle it was largely due to him that Baldwin emerged victorious from the struggle against Sir Winston Churchill and Lord Lloyd in the controversy over the Indian reforms in the early thirties.[11]

Charles Petrie perhaps exaggerated Davidson's political importance when he wrote that 'all roads lead to him in the end'.[12] It seems certain, however, that numerous roads led to him and that he controlled all the roads to Ashridge.

When in 1924 Davidson learnt that Ashridge was for sale, he convinced Baldwin and Asquith to sign the letter of 20 October 1925 to *The Times* to launch the fund-raising appeal. In his memoirs he wrote, 'I did not appear very much in the publicity but preferred to work in the background.'[13] Davidson did not want his name to be directly linked with the purchase. At the same time he publicly defended the need to save Ashridge because of its heritage value, and he already had in mind the creation of a college there. The press campaign was intended to prevent speculators getting hold of it and enable the Conservatives to acquire it. In becoming involved with Ashridge, Davidson had several objectives in mind. In his memoirs he wrote:

> When I became Chairman I set out to make good three defects which my predecessors had scarcely thought existed. They were each immense undertakings. The first was the organization of a great system of political education in every constituency focused on and in Ashridge. The second the establishment of a really efficient Research Department to provide the facts free from any bias upon which our leaders can found a practicable policy.... The third is ... the coping stone of the women's movement in our Party ...[14]

Ashridge, near London, in his own constituency, and a heritage site, seemed to Davidson the ideal place to realise his project, and he skilfully manoeuvred to acquire it. Miss Bridget Talbot reproached him for having misled and betrayed her. She wrote, 'My idea was to have Ashridge as an Empire or Commonwealth College Club where people coming from the Dominions could come on arrival and meet members of the Government and others.'[15] She accused Davidson of having betrayed her and stolen her project. Thus 'the hideous and false name of Conservative had settled like a blight on the structure of Ashridge'.[16]

Bridget Talbot knew that Davidson had bought Ashridge for the party's benefit in order to set up a college. However, the press did not mention Davidson's name, but instead that of Urban H. Broughton; she suggested that he had bought it to donate to the Conservative party in honour of his friend, Bonar Law.[17] In fact, Broughton donated £100,000 to Davidson for the purchase of Ashridge. Davidson handled the negotiations with the seller, Thomas Place, and signed the purchase agreement. The property was thus in his name and on the official documents his name alone was mentioned. As a gesture of thanks, Davidson granted Broughton a peerage. Broughton died on 30 January 1929, before he was ennobled. Instead, his son took the title and became Lord Fairhaven. In the summer of 1929, Davidson received a donation of £100,000 from Edward Brotherton in exchange for a peerage. He also benefited from the generosity of Lord Inchcape. In fact, Davidson even called on prominent Liberals for support. Robert Rhodes James writes:

> Not all big contributors were Tories. Indeed, Davidson was able to make use of wealthy Liberals who were disillusioned by Lloyd George. One notable example was Lord Inchcape. As he was still a member of the Liberal Council, he called on Baldwin with a brown parcel containing a very large sum in bearer bonds. Baldwin asked him to see Davidson, and the money was put into the Ashridge fund. As Davidson subsequently recorded, 'that was an example of where a lot of support for the new Toryism came from

– old Liberals; he wouldn't have given one penny to Lloyd George, although he supported the Liberal Party, and Cowdray was the same.'[18]

Davidson used his talent to raise money for the purchase of Ashridge, just as he had done during the Conservative election campaigns. Setting out his plans for Ashridge, he tailored his presentation to the expectations of his audience. A year before Ashridge officially opened, Davidson wrote to Lord Beaverbrook explaining that 'for a long time past there has been a movement steadily growing in the Party that the preaching and propagation of the broad principles of constitutional government should be undertaken on a larger scale'. He added that he had 'given a great deal of thought to the subject', and that it had three distinct aims:

> (1) The instruction in current politics and organisation of the keen spirits in the Party ... (2) The training of Party supporters who are technically qualified to teach in study circles and by similar means in their own locality the working class men and women who are yearning for knowledge which is at present much more easily obtained through the Workers' Educational Association, which is a Socialist body. (3) A research institution to which problems can be submitted and worked out by resident experts in collaboration with outside experts.[19]

While Davidson's third point led to the creation of the CRD, the first two directly anticipated Ashridge. The acquisition of Ashridge would enable the creation of 'an institution which was open all the year round, was accessible to London and could perform the functions outlined above'.[20] Davidson thus highlighted for Beaverbrook the benefits for the party from this initiative. However, when communicating with Broughton, Brotherton and Inchcape, he insisted upon Ashridge serving to perpetuate Bonar Law's memory and Ashridge's contribution to the broader political life of the country.

Ashridge and the party

The legal act passed on 21 November 1929 led to the creation of two distinct but complementary institutions, the BLMT and the BLMC, and defined the purpose of these separate entities. The BLMT was called upon to oversee the whole project and be responsible for honouring the memory of 'a great statesman' (Bonar Law). It should also preserve Ashridge's historical heritage and establish a centre for education. The trust was to be managed by a board of governors with responsibility for transforming 'the buildings ... and a competent part of the land itself into a College or Institution for the study of political and social science and political history with special reference to the development of the British Constitution and the growth and expansion of the British Empire and other subjects as a memorial to the Right Honourable Bonar Law, P.C., M.P'.[21] The trust's financial affairs were entrusted to Lloyds Bank,[22] 'under the direction of the Governing Body' of the BLMT.[23] The property deeds stipulated that the role of the college (BLMC) was to develop lecturers, teachers and writers who should in turn teach the above-mentioned subjects, and to organise lectures and debates for the general public and for students who had paid enrolment fees. They would provide the personnel required to manage the college accommodation. The deeds clearly established the division of responsibilities of the college and the trust.

There is no prescription in the statutes for a 'Conservative college', as there was in the statutes for the Philip Stott College and would be after the Second World War in the statutes of the Swinton Conservative College. Indeed, the plan for the college was not explicitly political, although reference was made to the Empire. Its educational objectives, so far as they were enunciated, could be interpreted in many ways. Davidson's role was equally ambiguous. It was never clear whether he was acting in his role as chairman of the Conservative party or in his own name. The collection of funds for the purchase of Ashridge was not carried out in the name of the party. And the contribution of the party to the financing of the college was limited to a relatively modest loan of £25,540 in 1929, which was repaid two years later. This loan was the only financial link between Ashridge and the Conservative party.

Nonetheless, the party's role was far from negligible, especially within the board of governors. The statutes allowed for the board to comprise up to fourteen members: four founding members with life membership, six life governors who enjoyed the same privileges as the founding members, two representatives of the NUCA and two *ex officio* members, the leader and the chairman of the Conservative party. The council's composition demonstrates the importance of the role of the party in the operation of the trust and in the college, which was subordinate to the trust.

Baldwin and Davidson were among the four founding members. Since at the time the trust was created they were, respectively, leader and chairman of the party, they were also *ex officio* members of the board of governors. Consequently, the places on the council for *ex officio* members were temporarily 'in abeyance'. The following was added to the statutes: 'If any question shall at any time hereafter arise as to who is the Leader or Chairman of the said party … such question shall be decided by the vote of the other Governors.'[24] This rather surprising clause can be explained in the context of the period. In 1929, Baldwin and Davidson had reason to fear a division within the party.[25] The two other founding members were Lord Fairhaven, the son of Urban Broughton, who owed his title to

Baldwin and Davidson, and John William Beaumont-Pease, chairman of Lloyd's Bank, who was also close to Baldwin and Davidson. A few years later he would offer Baldwin a position on the bank's board of directors. Beaumont-Pease became the BLMT nominee. Baldwin and Davidson played keys role in the nominations of other members of the board of governors. Viscount Hailsham and Neville Chamberlain were the only two chosen for lifetime membership, when there could have been six. The ordinary members were also close to Baldwin and Davidson: John Buchan, Lord Astor, Viscountess Bridgeman and Lady Greenwood. Baldwin and Davidson evidently sought to surround themselves with loyal supporters.

In 1931, a memorandum by the research department on political education questioned the links between the college and the party: 'The most important immediate question is: should the scheme be National or Conservative?'[26] 'National', though probably alluding to the National government formed in October 1931 by Ramsay MacDonald, should be understood in a broader sense. The question referred to the nature of the links between Ashridge and the Conservative party. The impartiality of research was the central issue of debates generated by the creation of the CRD and Ashridge: the research and the independence of the researchers. Buchan asked in his memorandum:

> To whom then, or to what, should such co-ordinating research be entrusted? Preferably not to any government department, not because of any lack of intelligence, industry, or devotion, for high qualities are as familiar to Civil Servants as to ordinary men, but because such research must have as its parents a definite philosophy of life.... Political research would best be carried out by a voluntary organisation within the confines of, or linked to, a political party.[27]

The research department produced several memoranda on the proposal for a Conservative college, independent of the party: 'that Ashridge supplies an essential want in the Conservative movement is obvious',[28] a teacher wrote several years after Ashridge was established. Everyone underlined

> the lack of Conservative writings, the inadequate formulation of Conservative ideas, and the absence of a Conservative 'thinking staff' [compared to] the wealth of pamphlets, the precision of policy, and the phalanx of philosophers presented by such socialistic organisations as the Fabian Society. 'At the present day, [A. M. Ludovici observes] a political party cannot survive that is not supported by an independent body of students and thinkers from which it can obtain its ideas, its policies and its programmes.'[29]

Unanimity was evident on the necessary political independence of the college. This independence held promise not only for the college and those who worked there, but also for the party itself. Ashridge could fail 'by unimaginative handling.... In the rigid search after efficiency it is possible to lose the Spirit. Rigidity would prove fatal to the future of Ashridge as it has so often done to many other institutions.'[30] This reference to 'other institutions' was an allusion to the Philip Stott College, which because of the narrowness of its objectives was scarcely a success for its personnel or for the party.

The search for funding

The initial endowment had to finance the realisation of the trust's objectives, which were, as seen above, the upkeep of the property and its transformation into a teaching establishment. From its first year, however, it was clear that the trust's resources could not cover all the expenses, particularly those of the college. During the twenty-five years of its operation, the college accounts were in deficit, which from 1929 to 1939 were approximately £10,000 a year, and exceeded £25,666 a year when it reopened after the war.

In March 1930, at a board of governors' meeting, Davidson insisted upon the need for the college to develop its activities in order to become better known and more influential. These activities, he continued, were essential to recruit more students from different backgrounds, and therefore to increase revenue from tuition fees, for 'people imagined that the College was self-supporting, but this at present was not the case'.[31] In May 1930 the trust's finance commission produced a full report on the college's financial position. Alluding to the trust's position, the commission declared that 'that every endeavour should be made to keep capital sums [i.e. the original endowments] intact; [and that] the interest on same, and any income tax recovered, [was] to be used as revenue'.[32] It added:

> Every endeavour should be made to render the College self-supporting as such, failing which, strenuous efforts should be made to obtain invested capital of the Trust sufficient to produce income to meet any loss on the College, and that in any case an amount of £200,000 should be arrived at as to the invested funds of the Trust, the ideal result being an endowment fund of £200,000 apart from other assets of the Trust which could be utilised to meet losses or to extend the activities of the College.[33]

The recommendations of the finance commission were clear. To make the college financially independent, it must increase the revenue from teaching by enrolling a larger number of students. Failing that, the trust must acquire further capital contributions, to produce enough revenue to cover the college's current and future losses.

This alternative or double objective – to increase tuition fees or capital contributions – was a recurring theme in the 1930s. The question of student recruitment and the level of fees arose in the very first year. On 2 July, the finance commission concluded after one of its meetings: 'The Committee understood that the College would never get a working profit unless there were more than 100 students on an average attending each Course throughout the year. To make Ashridge a really paying concern would involve a tremendous amount of hard work.'[34]

In June, the college's education committee in turn became concerned that the number of students enrolled on the summer courses was insufficient.[35] In July, Lord Stanhope, chairman of the finance committee, asked the principal, Reginald Hoskins, to find £4,000 to develop new activities, to remunerate full-time and part-time area officers and for communications. He added that at the last meeting of the board of governors, Davidson was not able to 'stand and deliver' the promised funds.[36] A month later, Stanhope wrote to Hoskins that: 'I have now had replies both from Mr. Neville Chamberlain and from Davidson. I am sorry to say that the former is not prepared to find the £4,000 required for this [extra-mural] work. Davidson has hopes of being able to raise some money, but he is not at present able to say either how much he will get or when he will get it.'[37]

In October, Stanhope again wrote to Hoskins to inform him of the finance committee's decision to halt the recruitment of local represent-atives responsible for training, as well as any plans for ventures outside the college, because of the trust's financial problems.

Faced with this setback, the finance committee stated: 'every effort must be made to induce benefactors to increase the endowment or to provide a constant stream of regular subscriptions or donations on a large scale'.[38] At the end of June, at a dinner at Lord Astor's, Davidson, who was renowned for his persuasive skills, appealed 'to certain guests, who were known to be interested in educational work, for donations towards the endowment of Ashridge College'.[39] An Astor scholarship fund was created. In 1939, it had collected £10,000, which was considered a success. These funds provided bursaries for students from modest backgrounds. Nevertheless, the college's financial situation remained precarious. Lord Stanhope explained that it was difficult to obtain donations, 'even when the appeal was made on non-Party lines'.[40]

In January 1931, Neville Chamberlain, who had succeeded Davidson as chairman of the Conservative party (the latter having resigned in June 1930), pointed out to the finance committee that the loan provided by the party must on no account be considered a subsidy, and that the trust must reimburse the loan.[41] In a letter of 30 October to his sister, Chamberlain revealed his frame of mind: 'I am working away hard at C.O. reorgani-sation and begin to see light. But the legacies (Ashridge and Ladies

Carlton) are heavy burdens to start under. They have played the d— with our finances.'[42] Chamberlain was determined to obtain repayment of the loan. In March, the finance committee was informed that 'since the last meeting, through the kind offices of Mr. Davidson, a generous gift of £25,000 had been provided by an anonymous donor for the purpose of paying off the loan received from the Conservative and Unionist Central Office'.[43]

Despite the increase in the number of students, the deficit continued to grow each year. When war broke out, the college was rented by the government, which transformed it into a hospital. Educational activity ceased for seven years. From a strictly financial perspective, the college's closure was a source of economy for the trust. The years 1940 to 1946 were the only ones in the history of the college when its revenues exceeded its income. However, financial problems arose again in 1946, when the college was returned to the trust.

In 1953–54, a bill approved by parliament transformed the statutes of the trust and the college, which became a public charity. New statutes were drawn up, which finally cut the ties between the trust and the Conservative party. The college's new status as a charitable foundation exempted it completely from taxes. It also allowed the college to be converted into a school of business and management, which could seek financial support from business. The changes to the statutes in 1954 were an admission of failure, which could have been predicted from the day Ashridge was established. In 1930, Ashridge's board, and in 1935 the trust's auditors, had already noted the fact that the college's activities would require an endowment equal to that which had been required to purchase the college and open it in 1929.

Notes

1 E. Percy, *Some Memories* (London: Eyre & Spottiswoode, 1958), p. 149.

2 *Ibid.*

3 J. Ball, 12 Dec. 1929, Minutes of the Education Committee, 1929–1934, Ashridge papers.

4 Memorandum by F. J. C. Hearnshaw, Ashridge Weekend Conference, 14–16 Dec. 1929, Ashridge papers.

5 A. Bryant, 'The Story of Ashridge', Mar. 1929, Bryant papers, M62.

6 On the history of Ashridge, see D. Coult, *A Prospect of Ashridge* (London: Phillimore & Co, 1980).

7 The stained-glass windows can now be seen in the Victoria and Albert Museum in London.

8 The National Trust for Places of Historic Interest or Natural Beauty was

established in 1895. It is a private foundation for the public benefit, for the conservation of historical sites and monuments.

9 For a rough equivalent in pounds sterling today, multiply the total by three hundred.

10 C. Petrie, *The Powers behind the Prime Ministers* (London: MacGibbon & Kee, 1958), p. 116.

11 *Ibid.*, p. 135.

12 *Ibid.*, p. 136.

13 James (ed.), *Memoirs of a Conservative*, p. 291.

14 J. C. C. Davidson to Sir Charles Hall-Cain, Dec. 1929, in *ibid.*, p. 267.

15 Miss Bridget Talbot, *Ashridge. The History of the College*, p. 2, Ashridge papers.

16 *Ibid.*, p. 7.

17 See, for example, *The Times* article of 2 Apr. 1930.

18 James (ed.), *Memoirs of a Conservative*, pp. 291–2. Lord Inchcape was an industrialist and Lord Cowdray a financier who made his fortune in oil.

19 J. C. C. Davidson to Lord Beaverbrook, 25 May 1928, Baron Beaverbrook Papers, House of Lords Record Office (hereafter Beaverbrook papers), BBK/C111.

20 *Ibid.*

21 *Ibid.*

22 Lloyds Bank acted as a custodian trustee, in other words as a depository of titles (actions, obligations and cash).

23 Bonar Law Memorial Trust Deed, 21 Nov. 1929, Ashridge papers.

24 *Ibid.*

25 Political instability in 1929–30 was such that divisions across the political camps seemed likely. Within the Conservative camp, Neville Chamberlain or the Imperial Free Traders such as Lord Lloyd and Lord Beaverbrook could have broken away.

26 Frank Pakenham, Draft Scheme on Education, Dec. 1931, CPA, CRD 1/12/1.

27 J. Buchan, 'Political Research and Adult Education', 1927, Baldwin papers, SB53, fos 79–92.

28 F. Lee, quoted from a letter from G. Ellis to A. Bryant, 23 Mar. 1934, Bryant papers, C52.

29 Ludovici, *A Defense of Conservatism*, 1927, p. 244, quoted in Hearnshaw, *Conservatism in England*, p. 9.

30 F. Lee, 1934, Bryant papers, C52.

31 Minutes of the Governing Body, 11 Mar. 1930, Ashridge papers.

32 Minutes of the Finance Committee, 14 May 1930, Finance Committee Minute Book, 1930–36, Ashridge papers.

33 *Ibid.*

34 Minutes of the Finance Committee, 2 July 1930, Ashridge papers.

35 Minutes of the Education Committee, 18 June 1930, Education Committee Minutes and Correspondence, 1930, Ashridge papers.

36 Lord Stanhope to R. Hoskins, 3 July 1930, Falmouth Correspondence, Ashridge papers.
37 Lord Stanhope to R. Hoskins, 2 Aug. 1930, Ashridge papers.
38 Minutes of the Finance Committee, 2 July 1930, Finance Committee Minute Book, 1930–36, Ashridge papers.
39 *Ibid.*
40 Minutes of the Finance Committee, 3 July 1930, Finance Committee Minute Book, 1930–36, Ashridge papers.
41 Minutes of the Finance Committee, 14 Jan. 1931, Finance Committee Minute Book, 1930–36, Ashridge papers.
42 N. Chamberlain to I. Chamberlain, 18 Oct. 1930, in R. Self, *The Neville Chamberlain Diary Letters*, Vol. 3, *The Heir Apparent, 1928–1933* (Aldershot: Ashgate Press, 2002), p. 215.
43 Minutes of the Finance Committee, 4 Mar. 1931, Finance Committee Minute Book, 1930–36, Ashridge papers.

3

The ideal of the expert:
Ashridge and the new middle classes

The growing representation of the middle classes in the Conservative party was the result of a slow process which stretched back into the nineteenth century and culminated in the inter-war years. From the end of the 1890s until 1914, one of the challenges the Conservative party faced was finding a balance between the interests of the traditional rural electorate and those of the new electorate made up mostly of the urban middle classes. In the 1890s, for example, the urban middle classes opposed the halving of property taxes paid by landowners while the taxes imposed on urban properties remained unchanged.[1] In rural communities, tenant farmers resented the fact that it was only the landowners themselves who benefited from these changes, since their rent was not changed. In the words of the Liberal party, these measures represented 'doles for parson and squire'. During the Edwardian period, the complex and changing nature of the protectionist policies proposed by the Conservative party reflected the diversity of interests of its electorate, rural and urban.[2] Reconciling the multiple interests of the Conservative electorate on the subject of state intervention proved difficult. It was in fighting Socialism that the different components of this electorate would eventually unite.

At the general election of 1900, 39 per cent of Conservative members of parliament were landowners or professional soldiers;[3] 61 per cent belonged to the liberal professions and the world of commerce and industry. By 1931, the division had become 23 per cent and 77 per cent, respectively.[4] However, these figures applied only to the highest echelons of the party's hierarchy and failed to reflect the importance of middle-class represen-tation at the local level. Numerous sources dating from the inter-war years indicate that membership of the middle classes was determined by income: roughly speaking, anyone earning more than £250 per year belonged to the middle classes.[5] But many who earned less than this considered and described themselves as middle class, notably office workers, commercial representatives, insurance agents or salesmen – those who were called 'black-coated workers'.[6] They differentiated themselves from the working classes by the fact that they did not perform manual work and were paid monthly by cheque rather than weekly in cash. Above this first group of employees were the lower professions such as laboratory technicians, industrial draftsmen, librarians and social workers, who formed the first layer of 'white collar workers'. In England, this category represented around 560,000 people in 1911 and around two million in 1951. The most considerable hike in numbers took place in the 1930s.[7] The higher professions, the category above 'white collar worker', comprising clergymen, solicitors and doctors, were gradually overtaken from the 1930s onwards by engineers, architects, professionals from the fields of science and technology and, above all, businessmen. The increase in these categories is one of the most significant changes in the structure of society in the decade between 1939 and 1949. Ross McKibbin explains: 'This hugely expanded managerial middle-class … [was] self-consciously modern … [and] saw itself, rather than organised labour as the "progressive" class.'[8] At the heart of this new middle class, executives, civil servants, accountants and businessmen were well represented. These changes in the class composition reflected changes in the British economy between the wars. In 1938, 85 per cent of Britain's industrial profits came from corporations, and 50 per cent of factory workers were employed in factories of more than 500 employees. Family businesses were gradually being replaced by shareholder-owned companies, whose size and scale meant that managers, technicians and accountants were needed to run them. These were the people who largely augmented the ranks of the middle classes and altered the class structure. They played a growing role within the Conservative party. Ashridge and the CRD served to strengthen their position within the party and reinforce their influence.

Historians and political commentators often consider the 1949 Maxwell-Fyfe[9] report on the organisation of the Conservative party as the culmination of the process of 'embourgeoisement' of the party. It would be inaccurate to think that the 1930s were a period only of gestation for these ideas; in fact, they were largely applied in the inter-war period.[10] Many constituencies no longer depended upon the wealth and generosity of their local parliamentary candidate, and instead drew upon local sources of finance. The managerial middle class, aware of its growing importance within the party, placed new demands upon it. Dissatisfied with its role in organising the party at a local level, it sought a voice in the development of the 'new Conservatism'.[11] This new Conservatism was associated with meritocratic values and with the end of aristocratic paternalism. The introduction of examinations and diplomas was the most visible sign of the rise of meritocracy within the party. In 1925, examinations were introduced for all party officials, and in 1933 diplomas became obligatory.

Ashridge issued certificates at the completion of its courses. It then became a question of deciding whether these certificates could serve as a shortcut to obtaining posts within the party organisation. R. A. Butler declared in 1937: 'I should like to see more diplomas issued by Ashridge, which would ... enable people to graduate as Conservative lecturers, and would, for example, be one of the credentials demanded of those who serve in the party organisation. It would be a little difficult at first to insist that all agents should have an Ashridge diploma, but restricted posts in the Party organisation might be reserved for those so qualified.'[12] These certificates represented a new political culture based upon competence, which excluded both the 'gentleman' who was considered a political amateur and the working-class man.

Expertise was at the very heart of the Ashridge project. The meritocratic ideal of the managerial middle class was linked to the figure of the expert, the principle that everyone should be recognised for their skills and not their backgrounds, and that their social status should depend principally upon their expertise. In December 1929, a meeting was held at Ashridge to decide on the teaching objectives and the way subjects were taught. 'Selected educationalists from universities, Conservative politicians of standing',[13] were invited to express their views and recommend the preferred type of courses, lecturers and students. Academics and experts in the field of education such as F. J. C. Hearnshaw (King's College, London), Kenneth Pickthorn (Corpus Christi College, Cambridge), Keith Feiling (Christ Church, Oxford), Reginald Northam (Queen's College, Cambridge) and Arthur Shadwell (University of London), and prominent Conservatives such as Stanley Baldwin, John Buchan, Lord Astor, Walter Elliot, Geoffrey Ellis, Lady Bridgeman, Marjorie Maxse and Mary Pickford gathered at Ashridge for three days. During this first meeting, they decided that the teachers should be 'professors and dons who were experts in their particular branch, and distinguished public men'. The expertise of the lecturers was deemed more important than their political affiliation. In fact, 'it was desirable as a matter of principle to invite lecturers to address students on the grounds of their expert knowledge in any particular subject, apart from any question of their politics'.[14] 'The work [shall be] carried out by means of lectures given by well-known authorities. The ideal aimed at is to get each subject presented by the expert best qualified to explain and expound it, and without any attempt at party propaganda. The lectures [shall be] supplemented by class-discussions, tutorials, and debates, in which it is sought to develop the individual character of the students.'[15]

Putting the emphasis on character building linked back to the traditional idea employed by the public schools[16] for the education of the aristocracy.

At the end of the nineteenth century, physical education was recommended for character building, sometimes at the expense of intellectual disciplines.[17] Ashridge proposed an alternative to this approach to character building: emphasis was put on knowledge and scholarly and academic success. It was a way of reconciling the ideal of the eighteenth-century gentleman-scholar, for whom education and erudition were fundamental to his character, with the educational ideal of the middle classes. When Lord Allen of Hurtwood, editor-in-chief of the *Daily Herald*, the Labour party's official newspaper, between 1925 and 1930 and who participated in a number of radio programmes on current affairs, was invited to give a talk at Ashridge, the board of governors, anxious about the unease in the Conservative circles at lectures by individuals who did not belong to the party, defended its decision:

> The lecture in question was an entirely specialist one on a technical aspect of Broadcasting for a special weekend course on Broadcasting which we held last year to arouse interest in a subject where we felt that the 'left' were getting all their own way. The syllabus which was necessarily a specialist one was drawn up in a consultation with Lord Bridgeman, who opened the course, and Sir John Reith, who has recently lectured here to the MPs' conference (this, however, is confidential), and we were advised that Lord Allen was the person who could deal with this subject most adequately.... Lord Allen gave an admirable address which was entirely non-political and which completely satisfied the Conservative audience who heard him.[18]

Lord Allen was a member of the Fabian Society, and had been imprisoned three times for being a conscientious objector during the First World War. His invitation to speak at Ashridge illustrates the college's desire to prioritise expertise.

Defining moments

In November 1929, the board of governors was formed. It comprised Stanley Baldwin as honorary president, Viscount Astor, Viscountess Bridgeman, John Buchan, Neville Chamberlain, J. C. C. Davidson, Lord Fairhaven, Lady Greenwood, Viscount Hailsham and J. W. Beaumont-Pease (who became Lord Wardington in 1936). In June 1930, Sir Hildred Carlile and Mary Pickford, *ex officio* NUCA representatives, became governors for two years, as defined by the statutes. The board of governors was all powerful. It met four times a year at the CRD offices on Old Queen Street in London, a choice of location that highlighted Davidson's importance to proceedings. His private office was there, in the building he had rented in 1929 for the CRD and Ashridge. At the first meeting, General Sir Reginald Hoskins was appointed principal of the college. Hoskins was a professional soldier, in retirement since 1923. He had been principal of the Philip Stott College, the training centre for Conservative party officials, which had closed in 1928. The board created three committees: a finance committee, chaired by Beaumont-Pease and including Davidson and Fairhaven; an education committee, chaired by Buchan and including Astor, Elliot, Ellis, Ormsby-Gore, Pickford, Stanley, Chamberlain and Sir Walter Buchanan Riddell; and a so-called house committee, including Fairhaven, Bridgeman, Davidson and Greenwood, which was responsible for the maintenance of Ashridge and its grounds. What is striking about the names on these committees is the under-representation of the landowning gentry. With the exception of Buchan and Viscountess Bridgeman, who could be considered part of the 'gentry',[19] all the others hailed from the worlds of finance and industry – big business – and the liberal professions. Fairhaven, Astor, Bridgeman, Greenwood and Hailsham were from families that had earned their wealth in industry and at the bar. They shared the meritocratic ideal of the educated middle classes and regarded peerages as recognition of their merits. Stanhope, the only real aristocrat amongst them, was the point of contact between the different committees. He was chosen for his competence, as Baldwin explained: 'He was a large landowner, with special knowledge of forestry, and he had considerable administrative and departmental experience.'[20] This description of Stanhope fits the image of the 'new nobility' that Ashridge sought to create for itself. They did not adopt the traditional lifestyle of the landowning artistocracy, usually associated with hunting, balls and extravagant living. Rather, they wanted to be seen as inspired by the ideal of 'noblesse oblige' and community service. Apart from Stanhope and Neville Chamberlain, who were invited for political reasons, members of the board of governors were all long-time friends. Members of the board and the committees changed over the years, but their social backgrounds did not change. Apart from Stanhope, the only real aristocrats were Lord Falmouth, who replaced Stanhope in March 1933, Lady Falmouth and Oliver Stanley, the son of the seventeenth earl of Derby.[21]

Although most members of the board and the committees belonged to the upper middle class, the same could not be said for the college's teaching body. The principal, Sir Reginald Hoskins, was paid £800 per year, accommodation included, which was a decent salary but not enough to maintain an upper middle-class lifestyle (a doctor earned on average around £1,000 per year). Arthur Bryant, part-time director of the department of education and pure product of the educated middle classes, earned £400 per year, while L. H. Sutton, from 1933 the senior tutor, earned £500 per year. The college had three secretaries, respectively Lancelot Storr, research assistant for the Conservative party between 1926 and 1929,

Dorothy Spencer, another Conservative party official, and T. N. Graham, who worked for the Philip Stott College in Scotland. All came from modest backgrounds, but all excepting Graham had studied at Oxford or Cambridge. Their degrees and their involvement in the Conservative party allowed them to take up positions of responsibility. Hoskins, Graham and Sutton all worked for the Philip Stott College. Storr had worked with Davidson. They formed an ambitious team; for them, Ashridge would be a combination of public school, Oxbridge college and aristocratic residence. It thus represented an ideal mix of good education and traditional values in equal measure, although this did not come without its problems. Graham was accused of being a social climber by a party activist, who criticised him for having 'the mentality of the clever little middle class mind getting into power, and venting its inferiority complex on the people, and class, it believes have stood in its way in the past'.[22] Bryant, Hoskins, Sutton and Graham considered themselves best qualified to run Ashridge.

In December 1929, during the inaugural conference which brought together teachers and politicians to discuss the future of Ashridge, five questions were posed:

- what do the electorate require to be taught at Ashridge?

- what is the best way of teaching such subjects?

- whom should we approach to undertake the teaching?

- what kind of students are most in need of the teaching Ashridge can offer?

- how can such students best be recruited and who should be employed to recruit them?[23]

From 1931 to 1954, with the interruption of the war, sixteen tutors succeeded each other at Ashridge. In most cases, Ashridge was their first full-time position; they stayed on average for eighteen months before obtaining a teaching position at a university or public school, or a post within the Conservative party. Most of them were Oxbridge graduates.[24] In 1931, the starting salary was £200 per year including board and accommodation. In 1950, it was £400, which, adjusted for inflation, was roughly the same. The college was a social and professional gateway. Many went on to teaching posts at provincial university colleges such as Hull and Southampton,[25] and this was only the first step up. Ashridge was also a stepping-stone into politics. Cuthbert Alport, for example, was a Cambridge graduate in history and law who taught at Ashridge between February 1936 and February 1938. Alport came to the attention of R. A. Butler, who put him forward for a position in the Conservative party's education department, where he became director in October 1945.[26]

In 1950, he was elected MP for Colchester. With others, he founded the One Nation Group.[27] In 1951, he served as assistant postmaster-general, and in 1961, as Lord Alport of Colchester, he became high commissioner to the Central African Federation. Thus Ashridge also served as a social ladder.

The teaching staff

Politicians and academics made up most of the teaching staff of Ashridge. Often coming from the landed aristocracy, the social origins of the MPs contrasted with those of the management of the college. Having for the most part studied at a public school and then Oxford or Cambridge, they shared with the board of governors the aim of developing the skills of those who attended.

Politicians were invited to speak on current affairs or the functioning of institutions. 'It was most desirable that Conservative MPs who were interested and expert in these matters should be invited to attend the special courses on Local government, coal, etc...'.[28] Of the 529 speakers at Ashridge between 1929 and 1939, 23 were hereditary peers from the House of Lords (4.5 per cent) and 132 were members of the House of Commons (25 per cent). Detailed information can be found on 106 ministers. All but nine were Conservatives, six belonged to the National Liberal party, two to the National Labour Party and one was independent; forty belonged to the gentry or the landowning aristocracy, twenty belonged to the upper middle classes and forty-six to the liberal professions, mainly barristers. The social background of the parliamentarians who attended Ashridge was not different from that of Conservative members of parliament, with a slight over-representation of the aristocracy or gentry:[29] thirty-two went to Eton, thirty-three to other exclusive public schools such as Harrow, Rugby, Winchester and Westminster and twenty-two to minor public schools or studied abroad; sixty-four studied at Oxford or Cambridge, nine at other universities, mostly in Scotland; seven were women. Most were graduates in the humanities, such as Latin, Greek and history. It was a socially homogeneous milieu, similar to that in parliament and in numerous clubs, particularly the Carlton Club. Forty-eight of them had several publications to their name, on a wide range of subjects. Some had published political essays: 'Toryism and the Twentieth Century' by Walter Elliot, 'The Conservative Outlook' by R. Mitchell-Banks and 'The Creed of a Tory' by Pierce Loftus. Others had written on current affairs: 'Through Tariffs to Prosperity' and 'Britain's Economic and Financial Position' by Herbert Williams, 'Reconstruction' by Harold Macmillan and 'Industrial Leadership' by Samuel Hammersley; historical monographs and biographies: *Sir Edward Carson* by Edward Marjoribanks, *Lessons of the Russo-Japanese War of 1906* by Sir Edward Spears; poetry: *From One Vagabond to Another* by Anthony Crossley, *The Ghosts of Parliament* by Carlyon Bellairs, president of the Poetry Society; and science: the *Textbook of Embryology* by Sir John Kerr. The number of publications by Conservative MPs during the inter-war years is remarkable and evidence of the willingness of the Conservatives to take part in the 'battle of ideas'.[30]

The parliamentarians can be divided into three categories. The first category comprises MPs whose political careers were largely behind them. For them, Ashridge offered the opportunity to share their experience in debates on current affairs. Their presence echoed the past, giving the Ashridge project the seal of approval from respected party members. Earl Winterton, Leo Amery and Sir Henry Page Croft were three examples of Conservatives who had entered parliament before 1914. Amery and Page Croft found ministerial positions and relaunched their political careers in 1940. The political careers of the Earl of Crawford and Balcarres and Sir Robert Horne had ended in 1922 with the downfall of Lloyd George's coalition government. In 1921–22, Horne had been an innovative chancellor of the exchequer, proposing the first budget deliberately in deficit to counter the effects of the recession.[31] If Horne anticipated, in some respects, Keynesian thought on fiscal matters, Sir Arthur Steel-Maitland, minister for labour between 1924 and 1929, explicitly adhered to much of Keynes's economic programme and wrote an enthusiastic book on the New Deal in the United States.[32] He did not hold a position in government after 1931 and was replaced by his deputy. Another example was Sir Samuel Hoare, whose ambition and political career came to a sudden end after the signing of the Hoare-Laval pact on Abyssinia in 1935.

The second category consisted of senior figures in the party who held high-ranking ministerial posts. They went to Ashridge to share their experiences of cabinet and lend their support to the college. Their regular attendance at Ashridge was an endorsement of the work done there. Despite their hectic schedules, Stanley Baldwin, the honorary chairman of Ashridge, Neville Chamberlain, Lord Halifax, Anthony Eden, Philip Cunliffe-Lister, Duff Cooper and Lord Hailsham regularly attended the lectures and debates at Ashridge. Initially, Chamberlain, Davidson's rival, had reservations about the establishment of Ashridge. But in May 1933, when he was chancellor, he wrote: 'I ... discoursed for 50 minutes on Finance, War Debts, Economic Conference & such like, after which questions were called for ... I must say I was very much impressed.'[33] Six Liberal National members of the government were frequent visitors to Ashridge: Sir John Simon, Walter Runciman, Geoffrey Shakespeare, Leslie Hoare-Belisha, Ernest Brown and Edward Burgin. Their presence illustrates the fact that Ashridge aimed to be non-partisan and that expert

knowledge was the criterion for selection. It earned the college criticism
from grass-root party organisers, forcing the management to justify itself.
Thus, for instance:

> Mr. Runciman, who is lecturing here on Trade Agreements at the beginning
> of March, has lectured before; in this case he is coming to explain the
> Trade Agreements concluded by the government, which at the present
> time the Conservative Party is supporting. It would obviously be unfair to
> Conservative students attending this College not to give them some chance
> of hearing the point of view of the leaders of the government to which their
> Party is giving its official support.[34]

Ashridge also invited two National Labour members of parliament,
Malcolm MacDonald and Earl de la Warr. Despite criticism, it welcomed
the different elements of the National government. The persistent tension
between the management at Ashridge and the rank and file of the
Conservative party over their relationship with the National Liberal
Nationals was not resolved until 1947, when an agreement was signed
between Lord Woolton, chairman of the Conservative party, and Lord
Teviot, chairman of the National Liberals. This agreement officially
allowed them to form a common front against Socialism.

The last category was that of members of parliament close to the
academic world and interested in training for politics. This was numerically
the most important category and the closest, at the time the college
opened, to the ideal of 'Conservative Fabians'. Eustace Percy, for example,
was head of the CRD in 1929 and taught at the WEA. He was also, from
1935, president of the British Council. Walter Elliot was rector of the
University of Aberdeen between 1933 and 1936, then of the University of
Glasgow. He had a doctorate in science and medicine from the University
of Glasgow and honorary degrees from seven universities. R. A. Butler,
from a family of academics, was head of the Conservative education
department in the latter part of the 1930s. John Buchan was the first head
of the education department in 1927. He was also the successful author
of many adventure novels and works of history. Sir Malcolm Bullock,
Geoffrey Ellis, Waldorf Astor, Carlyon Bellairs and Anthony Crossley
were other examples of parliamentarians interested in political training.

Of the thirty-six politicians involved with Ashridge who were not
members of parliament, twenty-seven were officials of the Conservative
party: twelve worked for central office and fifteen at local level, illustrating
Ashridge's willingness to represent the whole party and avoid criticism for
being excessively centralist. The social background of the Conservatives
from central office was similar to that of the members of parliament: a
third came from aristocratic families; those from the constituencies were

mainly from the middle classes and liberal professions. Of the fifteen representatives from the constituencies, three had published books, further confirmation of the importance of publications within the Conservative party during the inter-war years.

There were eighty-eight academics (16 per cent), of whom forty were historians, an indication of the importance of history at Ashridge. A Tory account of history was to be at the centre of the new formulation of Conservative principles.[35] Four historians, Alfred Cobban, R. B. Mowat, A. L. Rowse and G. M. Trevelyan (though changing his political allegiance in the 1930s) were originally Liberal or Radical. Six apart, all were trained historians. The great majority worked on British history, with only three focusing on the history of foreign countries. Most were specialists on the nineteenth century, and in particular the Victorian era. Six were medievalists. The college distinguished between specialist and generalist historians, and feared that the amateur or generalist historian would naturally lean towards a Whig interpretation.[36] But in general, it engaged the new generation of historians, whose work was based upon scientific research.

As proof of their interest, they worked alongside economists, who attended Ashridge in relatively large numbers (there were nine altogether). Ashridge was established at a time of profound economic crisis. In January 1930, Ormsby-Gore explained: 'I am sure that all the courses should have a strong economic bias; Economic and social issues rather than political issues are going to be the main issues in this country during the next few years if not longer.'[37] Ashridge claimed to be 'chary about announcing economic laws', above all because 'others with no such scientific caution [have] entered the field. Bankers, businessmen, politicians, and all sorts of people with little training in economics and less in scientific method.' Economic expertise was prioritised, and the contributions of historians were important because, 'with a science like [economics] … it is impossible to isolate a phenomenon for study in the laboratory, or to produce artificially the conditions … to examine'.[38] Economic history enabled one to study economic phenomena over the long term. In this regard, the economists of Ashridge regarded themselves as heirs to the historical economists of the turn of the century. That the highly regarded historical economist, W. A. S. Hewins, lectured at Ashridge seems to confirm this.

After history, the subject later known as town and country planning had an important place at Ashridge: the preservation of rural heritage, town planning and relations between town and country. This was a new and rapidly growing field of study. The 'garden-city movement' at the beginning of the century had been associated with the Liberal Left, and agrarian reforms with Radical Liberals and Lloyd George. In the inter-war years, the Conservatives entered the field and became interested in the issues. Academic specialists in rural economy, agriculture and the environment were invited to Ashridge. Representatives from pressure groups, like Sir Lawrence Chubb, secretary of the Commons, Open Spaces and Footpaths Preservation Society, and John G. Martin, secretary for the National Housing and Town Planning Association, were regular speakers at Ashridge. The college also had close links with the National Trust. The Council for the Preservation of Rural England (CPRE) held meetings at Ashridge, and John Bailey, president of the National Trust, was a frequent guest. These experts on rural Britain were all from urban milieux, and their expertise was based on research they had conducted in the towns and not as part of the rural world.[39]

Other academic visitors were specialists in international relations, the Empire and languages and literature. What is striking in the list of academics at Ashridge was their collective desire to establish 'the link between the enlightened amateur of the nineteenth century and the professional expert of the twentieth',[40] as Lord Holford commented with regard to Sir Patrick Abercrombie, a specialist in town planning who taught at Ashridge.

Ashridge also attracted journalists, writers and men from the theatre world. Sixteen journalists regularly went to Ashridge, including Geoffrey Crowther, Hartley Withers and Donald Tyerman of the *Economist*. C. R. S. Harris, a fellow of All Souls, Oxford and editor of *The 19h Century and After*, the monthly political magazine. Seven writers, known at the time for their successful novels, came to speak on Conservatism and literature. Charles Morgan, for instance, wrote several bestsellers, including *Portrait in the Mirror* (1929) and *The Fountain* (1932), which won the Hawthornden Prize, and a biographical essay, *Epitaph on George Moore* (1935). Baldwin commented in a letter to Davidson on his presence at Ashridge:

> I am particularly delighted to learn that there is a possibility that Charles Morgan may be persuaded to write a volume on The Monarchy. Anything which he writes has an appeal far wider than its sheer literary merit, and I really do hope that he will be persuaded to undertake the work, which might well prove to be a turning point in the intellectual outlook of the country. I would rather see him engaged upon the scheme than anyone else, for it would be a guarantee of its intellectual independence.[41]

To convince Morgan to write a study directed at the general public on the monarchy was an essential goal, considering the constitutional crisis in 1936, but it also pointed to Baldwin's more general concern for 'the intellectual outlook of the country' and the valorisation of a certain type of traditionalist literature. This concern found an echo with Eric Gillett, then an editor at Longmans Green & Company, who wrote in 1937: 'I suggested a literary talk because I believe that in view of the communistic standpoint taken up by the young intellectuals (Spender, Day-Lewis, Auden, etc) it is most important to explain to people with a serious interest in politics, what forces are at work in journalism and literature to-day, subversive and otherwise.'[42] This fear that the cultural world would pass completely into Socialist hands pushed the management at Ashridge to invite as wide a range of speakers as possible. Walter de la Mare, poet and children's author, who received many awards for his writing, provided an example of classical writing that was readable by all. The presence of Val Gielgud, head of television drama at the BBC, Sir Cecil Graves, head of programming at the BBC, and Sir John Reith, director-general of the BBC, attests to Ashridge's wish to appeal to as wide an audience as possible. Reith said that 'the BBC must lead, not follow its listeners, but it must not lead at so great a distance as to shake off pursuit'.[43] Many of these lecturers cultivated a 'middlebrow' identity, something which recommended them to Ashridge.[44]

Many civil servants also received invitations to Ashridge. Of the thirty-eight who were invited, eighteen were specialists in foreign policy and were or had been diplomats. The largest proportion was made up of experts on the Empire and came from the aristocracy or gentry. Another twelve worked in the social services as medical officers, in social housing or urban development. Two were senior officials at the treasury and experts in public finance and the economy. Other invitees worked for voluntary associations such as the Salvation Army. Their presence tends to show how amenable Ashridge was to recruiting informed speakers across different professions who would be able to speak on subjects such as foreign and social policies. As they were not able to publish anything in their name while working for the state, Ashridge was a way of getting their opinions heard. That civil servants were permitted to lecture at the college suggests that Ashridge was successful in portraying itself as 'non-party' in official circles.

Nineteen participants at Ashridge were from the military. Among them were several war heroes from the First World War, including the naval chief, Admiral Jellicoe. He spoke on the subject of 'maritime power and the Empire'. General Sir Frederick Maurice, professor of military studies at the University of London and a specialist on the subject of disarmament, also attended Ashridge as a speaker, as did Captain Basil Liddell Hart and General J. F. C. Fuller, well-known experts on the 'strategy of indirect approach'. Records show that Fuller and Admiral Domville, a naval expert and close friend of Arthur Bryant, the director of studies at Ashridge between 1929 and 1939, were both far-Right supporters. Fuller actually belonged to the British Union of Fascists (BUF).

Ashridge welcomed five members of the clergy, two of whom were highly regarded. W. R. Inge, professor of theology at Oxford and Cambridge between 1880 and 1911 and dean of St Paul's Cathedral from 1911 to 1934, was a prolific writer. He published thirty-nine books, such as *Lay Thoughts of a Dean* in 1926, *A Rustic Moralist* in 1937 and *A Pacifist in Trouble* in 1939. The bishop of Chichester, G. K. A. Bell, worked with the WEA and was a close friend of its founder, Albert Mansbridge. He was named dean of Canterbury in 1924 by the first Labour government, and had a close relationship with the Socialist William Temple, who went on to become archbishop of Canterbury. Bell became bishop of Chichester in 1929. That an extreme High Tory churchman and a pro-Labour bishop – though he was also a close friend of T. S. Eliot – both lectured at Ashridge was remarkable. Bell's international ecumenism, his national campaigns against Hitlerism in the 1930s and his plans to settle refugees in his diocese stood in stark contrast to Inge's dislike for democracy and ambivalence towards Nazism.

Finally, the industrial world was also well represented, with thirty-three leading industrialists and company directors regularly visiting Ashridge: 6 per cent of the total visitors. Guy Locock, for example, was the director of the Federation of British Industries and Sir William Larke was director of the National Federation of Iron and Steel Manufacturers and a representative of industry at the Ottawa imperial conference in 1932. W. L. Hichens, chairman of the shipbuilding firm Cammell Laird and Co, was another regular attendee. Their presence was an integral part of the Ashridge intellectual project. In 1927, Buchan mentioned in his memorandum on research and political education,

> the efforts of a vigorous middle class, which, so soon as it had won power, came to look upon politics as an unreal game that did not warrant the attention of earnest business men. That attitude has persisted up to recently, and besides being responsible for the contempt that 'big business' feels for politics, is also largely responsible for a certain lack of coordination in industrial, commercial and economic matters. Such coordination is to-day ... the main affair of politics, and of politicians.[45]

From 1929, following the Wall Street crash and the onset of the slump, most industrialists favoured state intervention and sought the support of politicians. In Buchan's words, they hoped that 'The rôle of the politician will be to coordinate the efforts of the industrialists, and by considered legislation, to give expression to scientific interpretations of economic laws, and even, it must be owned, of economic expenditure.'[46] To legislate in the area of economics, the advice of experts such as those who attended Ashridge was required. In 1932, Lord Melchett, chairman of Imperial Chemical Industries (ICI), explained at Ashridge the benefits of creating an 'industrial parliament', which would act as an economic and social council. 'A member of Parliament is not elected for his expert knowledge, but is elected in the oddest way and largely haphazard.... People do not ask whether he is an expert on coal or on anything else ... I believe we shall have to go so far as to set up possibly a third House of Parliament.'[47] The idea of a third house of parliament or 'industrial parliament' was widely shared in the 1930s. It was supported by capitalist planners[48] such as Lord Melchett or D. J. Colville, and by the Next Five Years Group,[49] which included Lord Allen of Hurtwood and Harold Macmillan, both of whom were regulars at Ashridge. Macmillan incorporated their proposals in *The Middle Way*. The links between Ashridge and organisations such as the Next Five Years Group are numerous. In his memoirs, Macmillan thanked Sir Geoffrey Ellis, a member of the board of governors at Ashridge, for his support in developing his economic programme.[50]

In 1949, Roy Lewis and Angus Maude, two Conservative writers,[51] published *The English Middle Classes*, in which they reflected on the structural changes of the middle classes during the inter-war years. They reviewed the difficulties of small merchants who suffered from 'the growing competition of chain stores, co-operatives, and departmental stores'.[52] 'The English middle classes are destined to become increasingly "managerial".... Such an evolution, [is] already far advanced.[53] The desire to integrate senior managers into the political world, or rather to get them to participate in formulating economic policies, according to Buchan, required a culture of enterprise able to reconcile big business and politics. The idea of management training, which was the main function of Ashridge after 1954, already existed in embryo in 1929.

Notes

1 A. Offer, *Property and Politics, 1870–1914: Landownership, Law, Ideology and Urban Development in England* (Cambridge: Cambridge University Press, 1981). Green, *The Crisis of Conservatism*, pp. 113–14.

2 *Ibid.*, pp. 184–266.

3 These two categories are often confused.

4 B. Criddle, 'Members of Parliament', in Seldon and Ball (eds), *Conservative Century*, p. 147.

5 See McKibbin, *Classes and Cultures*, p. 45.

6 See D. Lockwood, *The Blackcoated Worker* (Oxford: Oxford University Press, 1958).

7 McKibbin, *Classes and Cultures*, pp. 46–7.

8 *Ibid.*, p. 49.

9 The Maxwell-Fyfe report on the organisation of the Conservative party was symbolically very important. It signified a certain social democratisation, notably reducing how financially dependent senior civil servants were on their local MP.

10 On the minimal effects of the Maxwell-Fyfe report, see J. Ramsden, *The Age of Churchill and Eden, 1940–1957* (Harlow: Longmans, 1995), pp. 127–35.

11 See J. Ramsden, *The Age of Balfour and Baldwin, 1902–40* (London: Longmans, 1978).

12 R. A. Butler, letter memorandum, 23 July 1937, R. A. Butler Papers, Trinity College, Cambridge (hereafter Butler papers), H87, fos 116–119.

13 Minutes of the Education Committee, 18 Nov. 1929, Education Committee, Ashridge papers.

14 Minutes of the Education Committee, 2 Apr. 1930, Education Committee, Ashridge papers.

15 Minutes of the Governing Body, 27 July 1934, Governing Body, Ashridge papers.

16 On the notion of 'character' during the Victorian era, see S. Collini, 'The Idea of Character: Private Habits and Public Virtues', in Collini, *Public Moralists*.

17 A. Mangan and J. Walvin (eds), *Manliness and Morality: Middle Class Masculinity in Britain and America, 1800–1940* (Manchester: Manchester University Press, 1987). See also J. A. Mangan, *Athleticism in the Victorian and Edwardian Public School* (Cambridge: Cambridge University Press, 1981).

18 Minutes of the Governing Body, 24 Apr. 1934, Governing Body Agenda and Minutes 1934, Ashridge papers.

19 John Buchan and Viscountess Bridgeman had backgrounds in business and the liberal professions though they were both landowners. However, in order to belong to the gentry, the land had to be in the family for at least two generations. John Buchan was the son of a Free Church of Scotland minister in a small mining village. He was 'essentially liberal tory', as H. C. G. Matthew put it. H. C. G. Matthew, 'Buchan, John, first Baron Tweedsmuir (1875–1940)', *Oxford Dictionary of National Biography*, Oxford University Press, 2004; online edn, Jan. 2011.

20 S. Baldwin. Minutes of the Governing Body, 11 Mar. 1930, Governing Body Minutes 1930, Ashridge papers.

21 He wrote *Industry and the State* with Harold Macmillan, Robert Boothby and John Loder (London: Macmillan, 1927).

22 Barbara Smythe to Arthur Bryant, 24 June 1938, Bryant papers, C54.

23 Ashridge conference, 14–16 Dec. 1929, Education Committee Minutes 1930, Ashridge papers. Questions 4 and 5 are examined in Chapter 4 below.

24 For the names of the teachers and arrival and departure dates, see the Governing Body Agenda and Minutes and Minutes, and the Education Committee Minutes, Ashridge papers.

25 R. K. Kelsall, tutor at Ashridge in 1933, obtained a post teaching economics at the University of Hull. Donald Balmer, tutor at Ashridge in 1938, became a teacher at Rugby School in 1939. J. A. A. Cross, a Cambridge graduate and tutor at Ashridge between 1950 and 1952, obtained a post at Southampton University.

26 See M. Garnett, *Alport, A Study in Loyalty* (Teddington: Acumen, 1999).

27 The One Nation Group was created in 1950 by a group of Conservative MPs. Most went on to hold ministerial posts: among them Iain MacLeod, Enoch Powell, Robert Carr and Edward Heath. The group aimed to find a truly Conservative approach to social and economic problems.

28 Ashridge conference, 14–16 Dec. 1929, Education Committee, Ashridge papers.

29 In 1935, 35 per cent of the Conservative MPs belonged to the 'gentry': see S. Haxey, *Tory M.P.* (London: Gollancz, 1939), p. 117–75.

30 Some Conservative MPs wrote during the Edwardian period, but the majority of them addressed only the question of customs duties. From 1950, the majority of the work written by the Conservatives came from groups such as the One Nation Group, rather than individuals.

31 See M. E. Short, 'The Politics of Personal Taxation; Budget-Making in Britain, 1917–1931' (PhD dissertation, University of Cambridge, 1984).

32 A. Steel-Maitland, *The New America* (London: Macmillan, 1934).

33 N. Chamberlain to H. Chamberlain, 26 May 1933, in Self (ed.), *The Neville Chamberlain Diary Letters*.

34 Board of Governors report, Feb. 1934, Governing Body Agenda and Minutes 1934, Ashridge papers.

35 See Chapter 6.

36 H. Butterfield, *The Whig Interpretation of History*, p. 6 (London: G. Bell & Sons Ltd, 1931, Penguin, 1973).

37 W. Ormsby-Gore to Acting Secretary, 15 Jan. 1930, Education Committee, Ashridge papers.

38 L. H. Sutton, review of Sir Henry Penson, 'The Economics of Business Life', in *Ashridge Journal,* Mar. 1934, pp. 39–40.

39 On the importance of the idea of preserving the rural heritage, see Chapter 9.

40 Lord Holford, entry on Sir (Leslie) Patrick Abercrombie, *Dictionary of National Biography* (Oxford: Oxford University Press, 1971).

41 S. Baldwin to J. C. C. Davidson, 20 July 1936, Baldwin papers, SB17.

42 E. Gillett to A. Bryant, 15 Jan. 1937, Bryant papers C53. Eric Gillett later became a contributor to the *Children's Newspaper.*

43 J. Reith, quoted in A. Briggs *The History of Broadcasting in the United Kingdom*, vol. II (Oxford: Oxford University Press, 1965), p. 56.

44 On the 'middlebrow', see Chapter 8.

45 J. Buchan, 'Political Research and Adult Education', memorandum, 1927, Baldwin papers, SB53, fos 79–92.

46 *Ibid.*

47 Lord Melchett, 'Internationalism and Big Business', *Ashridge Journal*, Sep. 1932, pp. 18–19.

48 See D. Ritschel, *The Politics of Planning: The Debate on Economic Planning in Britain in the 1930s* (Oxford: Oxford University Press, 1997).

49 The Next Five Years Group was a group of intellectuals and politicians from all parties who were active in the 1930s. They advocated greater state intervention.

50 H. Macmillan, *Winds of Change, 1914–1939* (London: Macmillan, 1966).

51 R. Lewis was a journalist who also worked for the Conservative Research Department. R. A. Maude became a Conservative MP in 1950 and was one of the founding members of the One Nation Group.

52 R. Lewis and A. Maude, *The English Middle Classes* (London: Pelican Books, 1949), p. 151.

53 *Ibid.*, p. 235.

4

Ashridge and the student community

F. J. C. Hearnshaw, speaking at the inaugural conference at Ashridge in December 1929, affirmed: 'The purely educational instruction of our schools and universities is wholly cultural in its end; Ashridge education must be strictly practical in its purpose.'[1] In fact, the college had three objectives: to play the role of a think-tank alongside the CRD;[2] to be a centre for debate and a political training ground for Conservative members of parliament and party representatives; and as a centre for the study of civics for the general public. In 1931, the principal of the college explained: 'Ashridge is not merely providing instruction for convinced Conservative supporters but is impressing its views of political education on members of the general public, hitherto unconnected with any political organisation.'[3] However, it was a question of attracting students who were likely, in the long term, to support the Conservatives. The educational project, the choice of teachers and the ideal type of student all became the subject of debate, which recurred frequently in later years.[4]

The organisation of the teaching

The organisation of the teaching sessions remained little changed between 1930 and 1939. One of the principles of Ashridge was that the students should remain in residence throughout the session in order to develop a common outlook. In 1932, the principal, Reginald Hoskins, said that if students did not stay in college, 'that would change the whole character and atmosphere of the college'.[5] Ashridge was known for its social life and extra-curricular activities. The students had use of the extensive grounds as well as a swimming pool and tennis court. They could play 'hockey, tennis and badminton; and [enjoy] Spring in Ashridge Park'.[6] A billiard-table and a gramophone facilitated the organisation of games and dances. As at Oxford and Cambridge, socialising was an integral part of college life.

The college could accommodate up to a hundred students. Every year it offered on average nineteen weekend sessions, fifteen week-long sessions, one session of two weeks, and a long session of two to three months for the study of citizenship. The weekend sessions focused on a specific topic. Students attended six lectures from Friday evening to Monday morning. For example, the weekend of 3 to 6 March 1932 was devoted to 'The Present Position Abroad: India and the Far East'. Six lectures were devoted to topics such as the crisis in Manchuria and constitutional problems in India. Some weekend sessions were less specialised and tackled subjects such as 'the Legacy of British history', 'the Present Position in Europe', 'India' and 'the Constitution since 1832'. The sessions were divided into levels: elementary, advanced and specialist, the more general sessions being reserved for beginners. The vocabulary used to describe the courses was the subject of debate during the first few months. In July 1930, 'it was agreed ... that the word "elementary" should be avoided as far as possible',[7] as it was too reminiscent of compulsory schooling. At this time more than 50 per cent of children left school between the ages of 12 and 13, in order to begin work.[8] In November 1930, the college banished the word 'advanced' and replaced the adjective 'elementary' with 'introductory course'.[9] These changes indicated the concern of management to avoid appearing either too highbrow or too lowbrow, or to discourage students.

The week-long sessions comprised one or two lectures a day, followed by discussion. The session called 'Week's Introductory Course for Beginners' between 21 and 27 May 1932, for example, comprised the following lectures: 'The Empire's Resources' (one lecture), 'The Modern Citizen' (three lectures), 'The Economic Growth of the Modern State' (three lectures), 'Constitution Building in India' (one lecture), 'The National Education System' (one lecture) and 'The Need for Public Economy' (one lecture).[10]

The two-week sessions consisted of seventeen lectures: one or two a day followed by discussion, with the weekends dedicated to sport and games in the grounds. For example, the session between 28 May and 10 June 1932 included the following lectures: 'Post-War Europe' (three lectures), 'Industrial Revolutions, Past and Present' (three lectures), 'Money and Banking' (two lectures), 'Institutions of the World' (three lectures), 'Problems of Contemporary Political Thought' (two lectures), 'The Future of a Global Currency' (one lecture), 'The Problem of India' (one lecture), 'The Development of Social Relations in England' (one lecture) and 'The Five-Year Plan' (one lecture).

Every year a longer session of several months addressed the subject of citizenship. In 1931, this session lasted three months, from January to April. It was divided into two parts. The courses in the first six weeks were grouped together under the heading 'History' and included economic history, the history of British agriculture and industry, the history of political ideas, constitutional history, the history of local government and public administration, and the history of the Empire, with a series of classes on the Dominions and colonies and another series on India and European history. The courses over the following six weeks were organised under the heading 'Modern' and dealt with economics, with classes on current economic issues, banking, industry, the rationalisation of industry, finance, trade unions and tax; with political ideas with classes on Conservatism, Liberalism and Socialism, on the Fascist state and the Soviet Union; with national and local government, with classes on parliament, local government, welfare services, urban planning, health and public education; with the development of the Empire, with classes on the Dominions and colonies, problems of India; and with international relations, with classes on the League of Nations. The sessions on citizenship conformed precisely to the college statutes, according to which the objective was 'the study of political and social science and political history with special reference to the development of the British constitution and the growth and expansion of the British Empire'.[11] Each session concluded with the awarding of diplomas graded according to performance. In 1931, the length of these sessions was reduced to eight weeks. According to the principal's report,

> experience proved that the period of residence was somewhat too long for such an intensive course of studies, that the lectures were rather too many and that the students showed signs of staleness during the last week or two. Accordingly the second Long Course was confined to eight weeks, and the number of lectures considerably reduced [...] though the intellectual attainment of this Course was perhaps not quite so high as that of the first, the general morale was decidedly higher. In fact, the standard of discipline and of enthusiasm attained by this Course over a period of eight weeks was most remarkable.[12]

Sessions of eight weeks on citizenship became the norm until 1938. Subsequently, they lasted only four weeks, allowing the college to offer several courses of this kind every year.

The creation of bursaries

The number of students attending Ashridge grew year on year, rising from 1,758 in 1930, the first full year of operation, to 3,366 in 1938. The management of the college welcomed this growth. Nonetheless, the question remained as to the ideal student profile: whom the courses would most greatly benefit and who would prove to be the greatest asset for the Conservatives.

The governing body insisted on the presence of 'a nucleus of wage-earning students in each course. Such men are invaluable to the conservative cause, not necessarily as Speakers but as missionaries among their fellow workers.'[13] The enrolment of students of working-class origin posed several problems. The first concerned their prior level of studies and their ability to follow the courses. The difficulty for Ashridge was to reconcile its policy of largely open education with the need to maintain a minimum standard: 'The not very highly educated students sometimes came away from a lecture, when the subject had been approached by the lecturer from every angle, before his final summing-up, with a rather confused mind.'[14] The wish to attract students of modest background stemmed from the desire to counteract Socialist organisations such as the Labour colleges and the WEA. But as Ashridge recruited its students from among professionals, recent graduates, teachers from grammar schools and colleges, and middle-class women, it was difficult to establish a minimum standard. In December 1929, at the inaugural meeting at Ashridge, Hearnshaw declared that the college must absolutely not be a place for professional training or a simple continuation school.[15] The aim was not to play the role of 'social ladder' for the working classes. In the statutes creating bursaries for working-class students, it was stated that recipients should 'return to the ordinary work after finishing the course at the said College [Ashridge]'.[16] Evidently a misunderstanding existed on this matter. The education committee explained in December 1930, for example, that 'Some of the students, especially of the working classes, returned to their constituencies with an exaggerated idea of their knowledge and capabilities and with a desire to receive payment for their political work.'[17] The question of the respective expectations of the management and the students was the subject of numerous discussions, but the management maintained that 'it would be a mistake to lower the intellectual standard of students admitted to the college'.[18] It proposed a dual solution: in the first place, students should complete a preparatory course at home before attending Ashridge; second, Ashridge should operate a selection process.

The education committee stated that 'lectures were often over the heads of students and not of use to them in their day-to-day political work. The Committee agreed that it could only restate its views, that there was need for preliminary educational work in the Areas for students of a certain standard.'[19] In fact, 'It was agreed that this … was partly due to lack of education in the students who were unable to apply the information given to the particular points of policy and the questions of the day.'[20] This explains why the emphasis in the college's first year was on 'extra-mural' teaching in the constituencies by charitable organisations. In October 1930, for financial reasons, the decision was taken to cease all extra-mural work.[21] Davidson explained at a meeting of the education committee that he

> was of opinion that the difficulty was due to the lack of money in the country which had caused some of the educational work to stop, and partly to the fact that Ashridge, which should be the final stage, had come into being before there was a national organisation of education in the constituencies. The problem was how to produce a local organisation of education in the constituencies, to fit students to go to Ashridge.[22]

The following month, the principal reported 'some anxiety' with regard to the number of students signed up for the August and September sessions.[23] The constituencies were requested to prepare students for Ashridge, since 'any necessary educational work of a preliminary character should be carried out in the constituencies'.[24] However, their work also involved selecting candidates: during the college's first three years, around 50 per cent of the students came from Conservative party networks. This percentage fell in the second half of the decade. At the end of July 1931, the college decided to resume its 'extra-mural' activities and work with the constituencies, thanks to money raised by Davidson.[25]

Students attending Ashridge were on average between 21 and 35 years old. The education committee reported in February 1931 that 'some of the middle-aged women felt that they were not made so welcome as the young; this was unfortunate as, while we want to encourage and teach the young, the older people are often of great use in the constituencies'.[26] While there was tension between students of different ages, the number of women present at Ashridge was another source of friction. On average, 60 per cent of the students were women. The majority of the students from working-class backgrounds were men, whereas most of the women came from middle-class backgrounds, which partly explains why the education committee stated in 1933 that 'the majority of students were drawn from classes other than the wage-earning one'.[27] A certain misogyny seemed present among the management. In 1934, Arnold Wilson, a Conservative member of parliament and regular visitor to Ashridge, wrote to the education committee: 'The atmosphere of the place was too agreeable and thus attracted many "old women" of both sexes [sic] among whom working men would never feel at home.'[28] By the same token, Ellis hoped 'there was not too much feminine examination of small details' during the meeting of the education committee on the development of programmes.[29]

Targeting working-class students was a priority for Ashridge. From the first months of operation, a system of bursaries was introduced. A weekend session cost £2 10s, a week-long session £3 10s, a two-week session £7, and the eight-week session £21.[30] In the 1930s, the average weekly wage for a worker was £2 15s, the equivalent to the fee for the shortest course. Furthermore, a factory worker taking time out to attend Ashridge was sacrificing a part of his wages as well as his or her useful time. A memorandum from a representative of the Conservative party in the South-West pointed out that 'Our Conservative working men will not go to Ashridge because as a general rule they only get a fortnight's holiday a year, this they wish to spend with their families.'[31] A system of bursaries was therefore necessary, to cover the cost of enrolment and also the cost of travel and lodging and the loss of wages.

In June 1930, the principal explained: 'The important thing was to attract men and women of the wage-earning class, and to induce individual patrons to finance them by paying their fees and their wages while absent from work.'[32] In October 1930, Lord Astor proposed the creation of a fund to subsidise students from modest backgrounds. Two months later, the fund was created 'with the object of promoting the political education of the poorer classes'. Lord Astor donated £2,000 to this trust, for 'the founding of a scholarship or scholarships at the College at Ashridge Park'.[33] The rules of the trust provided that the bursaries 'shall preferably be awarded to Trade-Unionists especially any who have attended Worker's Education Association classes or shown a practical desire to take an active part in adult or higher education'.[34] Admitting trade unionists among the students demonstrated both a willingness to fight Socialism and the conviction that it was possible to 'reform' students of this background. Those who had already attended the WEA were exempted from the preparatory course, as this demonstrated that they would understand the subjects taught. The restrictive conditions for obtaining a bursary were the result of a decision taken in the summer of 1930 by the education committee: 'It was agreed that the well-educated type of student need not be considered, as he and she could thresh out things for themselves; but that rather special consideration should be given to the less well-educated type, which it was especially desirable to attract to and teach at Ashridge.'[35]

From 1931, two 'Astor scholarships' were awarded every year to students of modest background to attend the eight-week sessions on citizenship. That same year, A. J. Grant, a steel-manufacturer and lecturer at Ashridge, created a fund to cover 'Grant scholarships'. From 1932, a dozen of these bursaries was awarded annually.

In June 1931, a scholarship committee was set up. It received several offers of funding. Following a mass-meeting at the Royal Albert Hall on 15 May 1931, the central women's advisory committee raised money for bursaries for 'working women, covering fees and travelling expenses, and where necessary, making a grant to cover cost of domestic help or loss of wages. 19 such scholarships had been awarded.'[36] CCO and constituency organisations contributed substantially towards the financing of bursaries in the early years. Between three and four hundred bursaries a year were financed by the party.

Although working-class students at Ashridge never became the majority, the system of bursaries enabled a large number to attend. Working-class students made up a half of those who attended the citizenship courses. However, the other courses at Ashridge generally remained inaccessible to working-class students, even though new scholarships were introduced in 1937.

Education or propaganda?

The ties between Ashridge and the Conservative party were often strained, primarily because of misunderstandings over the management of the college. In June 1930 it heard that 'there was in the constituencies a general apathy, and a reluctance to go beyond the existing routine'.[37] However, it was not just the Conservative constituency organisations that were criticised for their lack of dynamism. Members of parliament were also in the firing line. The principal wrote in 1932, 'Enrolments for the new Conservative Members' Course have as yet only totalled 21 in figures. We have now heard that Mr. Baldwin will be addressing the Conference.... As a result we hope for a large increase in enrolments.'[38] Ashridge wanted Conservative constituency organisations actively to recruit, select and prepare students. The college also expected MPs and constituencies to raise funds especially for scholarships. The initial responses from the different regions appeared to be marked by indifference. The education committee complained:

> By far the most valuable potential recruiting source for Ashridge lies in the constituency organisations of the party. How valuable this is is proved by the fact that, if the annual enrolments received from constituencies like Market Harborough and Roxburgh and Selkirk, where the agents are prepared to take great trouble on behalf of the College were paralleled in other constituencies, the College would be packed from one end of the year to the other. But taken as a whole, it cannot be said that the constituency organisations are active in their support of Ashridge ... the total number of students sent in any one year through the ordinary party channels has never exceeded 1,000 and seems, if anything, to be decreasing ... active support from even 50% of the constituency organisations would double our numbers.... It seems a regrettable waste of opportunity that this wider support is not forthcoming.[39]

The attitude of local sections of the party towards the college was due less to indifference than to incomprehension and even suspicion. Some confusion existed over the financing of the college and its objectives. For most local sections, Ashridge was a Conservative college, funded by the party, whose mission was to promote Conservative principles. The principal complained that 'a belief prevails that the college is supported by Party funds which ought to be deflected to more immediately useful purposes'.[40] Even as the Depression hit Britain hard between 1930 and 1932, the idea that Ashridge would train 'Conservative Fabians' with party funds profoundly shocked local sections. The anti-intellectualism of many activists went hand in hand with the complaint that the college was not offering professional training and had no direct usefulness for the party. The principal explained:

> The most important criticisms were the legitimate ones which ever since the College's foundation have come from the constituencies: that the College failed to provide a practical training centre in essential propaganda for Party workers. The answer, of course, is that the College was not endowed for this purpose and would not cater for the needs of the majority of its present students were it to do so. But in many constituencies, the purpose for which Ashridge was founded and the nature of the work it is performing are not understood.[41]

Misunderstanding of the college's objectives persisted, and the local sections of the party regularly complained that Ashridge offered highbrow education that was remote from the real world. In 1932, for example, the education committee reported that 'further general criticisms had been made that the lectures were often over the heads of students and not of use to them in their day to day political work'.[42] A striking similarity existed between the criticism of Ashridge from party activists and the criticism by Ashridge and party leaders of the Left: in both cases, their target was abstract and theoretical intellectualism. The strained discussions between the college and constituency organisations forced the Ashridge management to develop a variable and differentiated training. Without being a catch-all programme, the 'middlebrow' offered the largest training spectrum across the different levels of the party, from the 'Conservative Fabians' at one extreme to the local militants at the other: what they all agreed upon was the necessity for skills and expertise accessible to all.

Ashridge faced the further criticism that it did not provide a sufficiently Conservative education. The local sections and constituency organisations constantly complained 'that there was not enough teaching on definitely party lines'.[43] To win elections, activists were more interested in having propaganda weapons than broad education. In March 1931, following the criticism from local sections to CCO on the content of the courses, Neville Chamberlain, the party chairman, requested the education committee to take note of the criticism. The committee 'resolved that it should be definitely laid down that, at the end of each course, a lecture should be given from the Conservative standpoint, relating that standpoint to the lecture given during the Course and to any special difficulties or misunderstandings that might have arisen from these lectures'.[44] The principal and Chamberlain engaged in a lengthy correspondence on the subject, which confirmed 'the existence of an impression in the Party that it [Ashridge] is too far removed from Conservative sympathies.... [Theses criticisms] whether well-founded, or not, certainly represent an impression that has been produced in the minds of many members of the party.'[45] The decision in March 1931 that the party's official point of view would be made clear at the end of each course failed to end the criticism. At the beginning of 1934, an important exchange of letters between the Ashridge management and central office revealed continuing misunderstanding over Ashridge's role within the Conservative party.[46] The management asked whether it was essential to have the Conservative point of view communicated at the end of each lecture, or whether it was better to limit it to certain classes, and suggested that the 1931 decision should be modified. In February 1934, following discussions with central office, the education committee took note of the 'criticism put forward by Conservative workers that the teaching given was not of practical use to them and the difficulty in which the Central Office would find itself in urging Party workers to attend Ashridge if the minute were rescinded'.[47] The March 1931 decision was not amended but the principal and the education committee were given more leeway to decide which classes should end with a statement of the party's position. The principal explained:

> The proposal to include a special lecture on Conservatism in each Course at Ashridge was first made by Mr. Neville Chamberlain in March, 1931.... We accordingly arranged at the end of each general course a lecture on ... basic Conservative philosophy and principles.... [These] in all probability served a valuable purpose in strengthening the Conservatism of those who were already Conservatives and in some cases of inclining students who had come to Ashridge with open or even radical minds, to the Conservative standpoint.[48]

The division of roles between the Conservative party and Ashridge was problematic. While the party refused financial support for the college's extra-mural activities, the management and the constituency organisations did not envisage the college undertaking these activities. Thus the education committee – at the same meeting when it took the decision on adding a reference to Conservative policy at the end of every lecture – noted:

At a Meeting of the Education Committee on the 25th of March 1931, Mr. Chamberlain stated that the Central Office had been considering whether to start an Educational Scheme for the provinces, and this idea had been approved by the Business Committee of the Party.... If the Central Office Scheme is to be comprehensive and include Study Circles, – and logically it should, the whole question of Ashridge in the Educational Scheme comes under review. Should the College be the centre from which all educational work emanates, or is it desirable for it to pursue its own course for the time being, leaving the Central Office Scheme to prepare students by their own methods for the particular end they have in view?[49]

These tensions convinced the management of the college that it should function autonomously. In 1934, the principal explained: 'Central Office declined all responsibility for Ashridge enrolments four years ago and forced on our shoulders the burden of finding students.'[50] This display of independence was due not only to criticism from within the Conservative party, but also to the desire for independence which had existed from the outset. In 1938, the finance committee of the college decided to return £700 to the party, 'in order to clear off all indebtedness on the part of the Trust to the Party funds',[51] and thus demonstrating its independence from the party.

The management at Ashridge constantly reminded central office that the college was not an organ of partisan propaganda. The debates in 1934 on the teaching of Conservative principles highlighted these tensions. When Dorothy Spencer, a member of central office and secretary of the BLMT until 1935, suggested 'relating each lecture to *present day politics and to the policy* and principles *supported by the Conservative Party*',[52] the principal rejected the idea, arguing that

> would transform the work of Ashridge from that of political education to that of propaganda, and the ultimate object of all lectures would have to be to present the current and necessarily changing Conservative policy of the moment. This would presumably necessitate an alteration in the Trust Deed of Ashridge. It would certainly in my view alienate the body of favourable opinion towards Ashridge which has been gradually built up in the universities and among educated people of moderate views, who, though small numerically have considerable influence in forming public opinion and who have hitherto tended to lean towards the left. It would at once deprive the College of nearly all our distinguished University and most of our industrial and economic expert lecturers, who to my knowledge support the College because they believe that it is endeavouring to teach a sane and traditional view of citizenship without bias or propaganda.[53]

The distinction between education and propaganda was a recurrent issue for Ashridge. The idea that the college could be a conduit for the Conservative party was contrary to the objectives set for Ashridge. Conservatism, as conceived by Ashridge's management, was communicated through diversified teaching that respected the students' freedom of thought. The tension between the party and the management continued to grow during this period. In 1937, Bryant wrote to Ellis:

> We have already tried to co-operate on the most friendly terms with the Central Office and the Constituency Organisations; it is to our mutual benefit that we should do so. But too close a cooperation, amounting to a common control, is impossible, because it is the essential function of a party organisation to insist on unanimity on every issue before Parliament and the Electorate, while it is an essential feature of education, as opposed to propaganda, to offer students many points of view and different angles of the truth before bringing them to the right one.[54]

The wish for autonomy for Ashridge grew during the 1930s. Disagreement with the party was due not only to the way it saw education, but also to a different view of the means to employ for converting students to conservatism. Using Baldwin's method, the Ashridge management adopted a strategy which corresponded with what Ross McKibbin and Ewen Green called 'unpolitical politics'.[55] In parallel to the explicit propaganda carried out by central office and local sections, Baldwin gave speeches on harmony between the classes and in society, the nation and the idea of serving the nation, all of them ostensibly consensual themes.

Ashridge played a propaganda role when it hosted special events for party agents, members of the House of Commons and House of Lords, the JIL and the Young Britons,[56] who represented Conservative youth. The college was also used on some weekends for conferences of regional sections of the Conservative party. Every year, however, fewer than 10 per cent of the courses were for the party itself.

The political role that the Ashridge management agreed to play took the form of a rather traditional Conservatism, expressed in an indirect manner. In December 1929, in a memorandum written at the time of the inaugural conference at Ashridge, Hearnshaw clearly set out the college's objectives:

> The Conservative education of Ashridge should, in my opinion, avoid equally the necessary unpracticality of academic instruction, and the pernicious perverseness of propagandist cramming. Conservative education simply means the impartation of instruction in such portions of universal knowledge as are relevant to Conservative purposes, as such portions of knowledge are seen from the Conservative point of view. The impartation of knowledge from the Conservative point of view does not involve any suppression of fact, any tampering with truth, or any denial that other points of view exist. It merely means the presentation of the picture of the

course of history or the play of economical forces as they are seen by one who is inspired by that reverence for the past, that respect for tradition, that love of England, that devotion to the Empire, that zeal for the ancient British Constitution that marks the Conservative from his opponents.[57]

Ashridge offered a Conservatism that was synonymous with Englishness, the nation and constitutional development. The identification of Conservatism with British society, or rather English society, made possible a teaching programme that was ostensibly non-partisan. For those who subscribed to it, the constitution signified respect for law, order and institutions such as the monarchy, the Church and private property; love of England meant patriotism: 'my country right or wrong'; and the Empire symbolised the expansion of England and a quasi-obsessive devotion to the imperial cause.

Notes

1 F. J. C. Hearnshaw, memorandum from the Ashridge conference 14–16 Dec. 1929, Education Committee Minutes 1930, Ashridge papers.

2 The CRD gave problems or projects to Ashridge so that they could be debated there.

3 Principal's report, 1931, Minutes of the Governing Body 1932, Ashridge papers.

4 Principal's report, 1934, Education Committee Minutes, 27 Nov. 1934, Education Committee Minutes 1934, Ashridge papers.

5 Education Committee Minutes, 19 Oct. 1932, Ashridge papers.

6 'Easter Weekend Course', 1931, Ashridge Journal, 1930.

7 Education Committee Minutes, 10 July 1930, Ashridge papers.

8 McKibbin, Classes and Cultures, p. 207.

9 Education Committee, 12 Nov. 1930, Ashridge papers.

10 'Coming Courses', 1932, Ashridge Journal, 1931

11 Bonar Law Memorial Trust Deed, Nov. 1929, Ashridge papers.

12 Principal's Report on the Session of 1931, Minutes of the Governing Body, 1932, Ashridge papers.

13 Minutes of the Governing Body, 14 July 1931, Ashridge papers.

14 Minutes of the Education Committee, 10 July 1930, Ashridge papers.

15 F. J. C. Hearnshaw, memorandum at the meeting of 14–16 Dec. 1929, Education Committee 1930, Ashridge papers.

16 Trust Deed of the Astor Scholarship, 31 Dec. 1930, Ashridge papers.

17 Minutes of the Education Committee, 9 Dec. 1930, Ashridge papers.

18 Minutes of the Education Committee, 10 July 1930, Ashridge papers.

19 Minutes of the Education Committee, 15 Dec. 1932, Ashridge papers.

20 Minutes of the Education Committee, 9 Dec. 1930, Ashridge papers.

21 Minutes of the Education Committee, 15 Oct. 1930, Ashridge papers.

22 Minutes of the Education Committee, 24 June 1931, Ashridge papers.

23 Minutes of the Education Committee, 22 July 1931, Ashridge papers.

24 Minutes of the Education Committee, 10 July 1930, Ashridge papers.

25 'A Scheme for Educational Work in the Provincial Areas and in the Constituencies', July 1931, Education Committee Minutes 1931, Ashridge papers.

26 The Secretary for the Eastern division of the Conservative Party to Lady Newton, 15 Feb. 1931, Education Committee, Ashridge papers.

27 Report to the Education Committee, 22 Feb. 1933, Education Committee Minutes 1933, Ashridge papers.

28 A. Wilson, joint comments on a memorandum on the subject of a letter sent by the Head of the Education Committee to Conservative MPs, undated, Jan. 1934, Education Committee Minutes, Ashridge papers.

29 G. Ellis to R. Hoskins, 21 Nov. 1933, Education Committee Minutes 1934, Ashridge papers.

30 £1 in 1930 was equivalent to perhaps £100 today.

31 Memorandum from Captain J. W. Lancaster (Central Office Agent for South-Western Area) to the Principal, 23 July 1930, Education Committee, 1930, Ashridge papers.

32 Minutes of the Governing Body, 3 June 1930, Ashridge papers.

33 Trust Deed of the Astor Scholarship, 31 Dec. 1930, Ashridge papers.

34 *Ibid.*

35 Education Committee Minutes, 10 July 1930, Ashridge papers.

36 Education Committee Report, 24 June 1931, Ashridge papers.

37 Minutes of the Education Committee, 18 June 1930, Ashridge papers.

38 Progress Report from the Principal, 19 Oct. 1932, Education Committee Minutes 1932, Ashridge papers.

39 'Advertising: Report for 1933 and Proposals for 1934', Oct. 1933, Education Committee Minutes 1933, Ashridge papers.

40 1933 Principal's report for the Governing Body, 24 Apr. 1934, Governing Body Minutes 1934, Ashridge papers.

41 *Ibid.*

42 Education Committee Minutes, 15 Dec. 1932, Ashridge papers.

43 Education Committee Minutes, 9 Dec. 1930, Ashridge papers.

44 Education Committee Minutes, 25 Mar. 1931, Education Committee Minutes 1933, Ashridge papers.

45 N. Chamberlain to R. Hoskins, 17 Apr. 1931, Education Committee Minutes, 1931, Ashridge papers.

46 See Education Committee Minutes 1934, particularly Jan. and Feb., Ashridge papers.

47 Education Committee Minutes, 8 Feb. 1934, Ashridge papers.

48 Unsigned and undated memorandum, (?R. Hoskins), Jan. 1934, Education Committee Minutes 1934, Ashridge papers.

49 'Study Circle', undated (?May) 1932, Education Committee Minutes, 1932, Ashridge papers.

50 R. Hoskins to G. Ellis, 10 Apr. 1934, Education Committee Minutes, Ashridge papers.

51 Finance and General Purposes Committee Minutes, 19 Oct. 1938, Ashridge papers.

52 Unsigned and undated memorandum (?R. Hoskins, ?Jan. 1934), Education Committee Minutes, 1934, Ashridge papers. Also see D. Spencer to R. Hoskins, 30 Jan. 1934, Education Committee Minutes, 1934, Ashridge papers.

53 Unsigned and undated memorandum (?R. Hoskins, ?Jan. 1934), Education Committee Minutes, 1934, Ashridge papers.

54 A. Bryant to G. Ellis, 20 Oct. 1937, Bryant papers C58.

55 McKibbin, *Classes and Cultures*. Green, *Ideologies of Conservatism*.

56 The JIL was created following the Conservatives' electoral defeat in 1906. In 1928, it was reorganised by Davidson, and two JIL branches were set up in every constituency. It was replaced in 1946 by the Young Conservatives. The Young Britons was created in 1925 for children aged 6 to 16 to '[instill] into the minds of children good citizenship, love of country, love of Empire, and realisation of simple Conservative principles'. In *Handbook on Constituency Organisations*, cited in Seldon and Ball, *Conservative Century*, pp. 273–6.

57 F. J. C. Hearnshaw, Memorandum at the 14–16 Dec. 1929 conference at Ashridge, Education Committee Minutes, 1930, Ashridge papers.

5

Redefining the principles of Conservatism

Ashridge is ... an ideal, but it is a thoroughly practical ideal.[1]

In 1926, the dean of St Paul's Cathedral, the Reverend Inge, wrote that 'the Conservatives have passed through as many changes as a chameleon, and it may be difficult to say for what principles, if any, they stand'.[2] The idea that the Conservative party had no political philosophy was widespread amongst its supporters and opponents alike. One of the objectives of Ashridge was precisely to offer a 'Conservative education ... to make the character and nature of Conservatism more widely known'.[3] Ashridge sought to answer the question posed in 1930 by the historian Keith Feiling in his book *What is Conservatism?*[4]

In 1938, L. H. Sutton, a lecturer at Ashridge, referred to a lecture given by the Conservative author and minister of health in the 1930s, Walter Elliot, as 'the most brilliant and encouraging... [he had] ever heard'.[5] Elliot had reflected upon the nature and meaning of conservatism. In 1927, in a book entitled, *Toryism and the Twentieth Century*, he argued that conservatism was based upon 'an observation of life and not *a priori* reasoning'.[6] Similarly, John Buchan wrote in his preface to Arthur Bryant's *The Spirit of Conservatism* that conservatism was 'above all things a spirit not an abstract doctrine'.[7] Elliot and Buchan were members of the education committee of Ashridge, where Dean Inge was regularly invited to lecture. As Davidson wrote:

> On the whole the Conservative Party is fairly free from the bondage of abstract ideas ... realising that as one of George Meredith's characters says: 'it is useless to base any system upon a human being' ... [and that] devotion to logic in politics produces extremism. 'Extremists alone' said Samuel Butler 'are logical, and they are absurd. Man alone is practical and is always illogical.'[8]

Davidson liked to recall the advice that Stanley Baldwin gave him: 'when you come in to public life use your common sense and avoid logic'.[9] At first glance, it may seem as if the Ashridgeans adhered to the view that conservatism was not an ideology, and that it existed only in reaction to the events that it confronted. That, however, would be an inaccurate conclusion, for Ashridge sought to provide a place for reflection on the principles of conservatism, for dialogue and for debate on the varied meanings of those principles, in order 'to teach, learn and discuss principles [and] shades of conservatism',[10] in the words of a teacher at Ashridge. The analysis of the lectures and vocabulary reveals the nuances between different types of conservatism, and while certain themes were common, their importance varied according to sensibility. The common denominator for all forms of conservatism was the disdain for abstraction. Writers considered by Conservatives to belong to the Conservative tradition, like Richard Hooker, shared this disdain.[11]

This commitment to empiricism and opposition to theory and abstraction did not contradict the existence of fundamental principles. The Conservatives opposed principles that emerge from practice to the 'doctrines' of other parties. In his *Conservatism in England*, F. J. C. Hearnshaw listed twelve principles that formed the foundation of conservatism:

> (1) reverence for the past (2) the organic conception of society (3) communal unity (4) constitutional continuity (5) opposition to revolution (6) cautious or evolutionary reform (7) the religious basis of the state (8) the divine source of legitimate authority (9) the priority of duties to rights (10) the prime importance of individual and communal character (11) loyalty (12) common sense, realism, and practicality.[12]

Conservatism and progress

From 1929 to 1939, numerous lecturers contributed to the reflection initiated by Hearnshaw on conservatism and its principles. The first, second and last of Hearnshaw's principles recurred most frequently, although the first and last ones were linked in so far as respect for the past was based upon the importance given to experience as opposed to abstract reasoning. The concept of an organic society stemmed from the pre-industrial era, as Reginald Northam, who lectured at the Philip Stott College and continued to lecture regularly at Ashridge, explained: 'It was in this old rural England – before the days of the use of considerable capital equipment, of large factories and great aggregations of people in towns – that our national tradition came into being.... In that rural society each was a part of an easily accepted structure. No one was wasted. Everyone counted. The work of each was necessary.'[13] 'Organicism' meant harmony between social classes, based upon the reciprocal rights and duties of everyone in the community.

Claiming the heritage of Edmund Burke, in order to present an exclusively empirical interpretation,[14] Davidson explained in a lecture on 'The History and Principles of the Conservative Party':

> If the Conservative Party was born from the French Revolution, Burke was its midwife.... (1) Burke laid great stress on the importance of religion and on the value of its recognition by the State.... (2) Burke saw in the French Revolution the same sort of threat to private property that the Russian revolution and the doctrines and practice of Communism displayed 130 years later.... He considered private property to be vital to the well being of society. That was then and still remains today the view of the Conservative Party.... (3) Human society is an organism rather than a mechanism. (4) Closely connected with the organic character of society is the need for keeping continuity with the past and making changes as gradually and with as little dislocation as possible.[15]

Burke was regarded as the spiritual father of modern conservatism. Ashridge claimed a lineage that ran from Burke to Baldwin, passing through Peel and Disraeli. Peel's presence in this quartet might seem surprising, given that he was reputed to have divided the Conservative party in 1846, and indeed some said betrayed it by repealing the Corn Laws and thus damaging the interests of the great cereal-growing landowners. After the Reform Act of 1832, Peel

> therefore cast about him to see how he could capture this natural if rather sordid and selfish conservatism of the *petit-bourgeoisie*, and use it for the maintenance and reconstruction of the older and loftier conservatism that was concerned primarily with the conservation of the church, the constitution, the crown, the landed interest, the nation and the empire.[16]

The difficulty lay in the fact that this 'sordid and selfish conservatism' was committed to free trade and freedom of enterprise, to which Peel had subscribed. Hence, his '"surrender" involved not only the temporary decline of Conservatism, but also the passing of the old England and the victory of the individualistic ideals of the middle classes in every department of social life'.[17] Peel allegedly made a similar mistake in 1846 as had been made in 1830–32, the difference being that after 1830–32 the Conservative party spent nine years in opposition, whereas in 1846 it went into opposition for thirty-five of the next thirty-eight years. The negative image of Peel within the Conservative party was linked to these defeats. On his death, one Conservative allegedly exclaimed: 'He lived like a coward and he died like a coward.'[18] The work of the historian George Kitson Clark[19] and that of Hearnshaw began his rehabilitation, which culminated with Norman Gash's biography of Peel at the end of the 1950s.[20] Hearnshaw declared at a conference at Ashridge, 'The great disservice ... which Peel did to the country when he shattered the conservative party in 1846 ... must not blind us to the fact that Peel was a great and good man, a remarkable parliamentarian, an administrator of outstanding ability, and a legislator who placed upon the statute book a number of measures of the utmost beneficence.'[21] Peel's failure stemmed from the fact that he was unable to restore the predominance of the Conservative party after 1832. For Hearnshaw, the question confronting the party in 1832 was: 'would it be feasible in any shape or form to restore it [the influence of the Conservative party]? Such was the problem which first Peel (unsuccessfully) and then Disraeli (successfully) tried to solve.'[22] Peel was considered as a moderniser who had failed because his attention had been too exclusively focused on the interests of the middle classes, thus neglecting other sections of the population. His desire to modernise the Conservative party and society led him to underestimate the importance of the rural world. Hence, 'he had shattered the party that he had laboriously constructed, and in doing so had inflicted an enduring injury upon the politics of the nation that he had hoped to serve'.[23] Ashridge supporters endorsed his commitment to modernisation and regarded his failures as lessons to be learned in the way to proceed with change.

Tory democracy

Disraeli's reputation also passed through different stages. At the beginning of his political career, Disraeli was a Radical. In the 1830s, when he rejoined the Conservatives, he was considered an adventurer. In 1846, he was acclaimed by the protectionists opposed to Peel, who saw him as their representative in the House of Commons. However, while they recognised his talent, their initial suspicion due to his past as a Radical, his Jewish origins and his intelligence never wholly disappeared. Lord Derby remained the real leader of the Conservative party and Disraeli was merely his deputy. It was only in the 1870s, and notably after his election victory of 1874, that the party as a whole recognised and accepted him.[24] During debates on universal suffrage, he invented a new way of speaking of the people and of democracy. He advanced the idea of 'Tory democracy', linked aristocracy to the idea of duties and contributed to the emergence of a new political culture which accepted the phrase 'social class' without making it synonymous with 'class conflict'. Summing up the Disraelian concept of 'Tory democracy', J. E. Gorst, the chief agent of the party between 1867 and 1881, wrote:

> The principle of Tory democracy is that all government exists solely for the good of the governed; that Church and King, Lords and Commons, and all other public institutions are to be maintained so far and so far only, as they

promote the happiness and welfare of the common people; that all who are entrusted with any public function are trustees, not for their own class, but for the Nation at large; and that the mass of the people may be trusted so to use electoral power, which should be freely conceded to them, as to support those who are promoting their interests. It is democratic because the welfare of the people is its supreme end; it is Tory because the institutions of the country are the means by which the end is to be attained.[25]

Disraeli established a distinction between the institutional reforms supported by the Liberals and the social reforms proposed by Conservatives. He accused the Liberals of being too interested in constitutional change and not interested enough in improving the living conditions of the people. Despite the fact that Disraeli had no real programme of social reform and attached little importance to it, he succeeded in creating the myth of a Conservative party engaged in social reform.[26] Thus he contributed to a profound transformation of the party's image. In the 1840s, Richard Oastler and Lord Shaftesbury had been precursors in social reform, but Disraeli was the first to elaborate a theory of social conservatism. He also constructed a discourse on the Empire, borrowing Palmerston's idea of converging national and imperial interests. As with social reform, he distinguished between the policy of Radical Liberals like Cobden and Bright, characterised by indifference and even hostility to the Empire, and the Conservative policy of imperial grandeur.

The construction of the Disraelian myth of 'One Nation', based on a mixture of imperialism and social reform, found its clearest expression after his death. Between 1881 and 1914, his speeches were taken up by his successors, sometimes with different content. The expression 'Tory democracy' became the rallying cry for the new electors. Disraeli's phrases, often very general, were taken up by politicians such as Randolph Churchill in order to address not so much the working class as the urban and industrial elites, the 'cultivated, self-denying, noble-minded men of power and position'[27] who felt best able to talk to the new electorate and to transmit Conservative principles. Subsequently, Joseph Chamberlain, F. E. Smith, Lord Milner and the Unionist committee for social reform took up Disraeli's expressions, especially to address the working class. They all described themselves as 'Disraelians', even if they defended policies that Disraeli had scarcely dreamed of.[28]

Ashridge published the works of Disraeli, and a compilation of his thoughts appeared in the *Ashridge Journal*. One can find, for example, an excerpt from his Crystal Palace speech in 1872: 'The ... great objects of the Tory Party are ... to maintain our institutions, to uphold the Empire, and to elevate the condition of the people.'[29] Davidson repeated Disraeli's statement in his 'Notes on Conservatism' in 1937, under the

heading 'Tory principles', in which he sought to 'examine the faith of
the Conservative party as laid down by Disraeli', and to 'discuss whether
these principles have been departed from, and show that far from any
departure having been made, Conservatives to-day are working solidly
for the fulfilment of the conception of a country's need, expressed so
long ago by Benjamin Disraeli'.[30] Disraeli was presented as a moderniser
and a progressive, a promoter of social reforms financed by the state.
Through him, the Conservative party associated itself with the tradition
of progress. Ashridge contributed to the incorporation of this tradition
and use of this language in the face of the economic, social and political
changes that occurred between 1914 and 1937. Davidson insisted on
the fact that 'the popular conception of Conservatism – namely that
it is static – is not true Conservatism ... [and] that Conservatism, if
it means anything at all means progress'.[31] He went on to discuss the
social reforms introduced by Neville Chamberlain when he was minister
of health in the 1920s, declaring that these measures were the basis of
'what might be termed the New Conservatism'. He added, 'Conservatism
must not be narrow nor rigid. Its broad, basic principles must be given
generous application.'[32] The Chamberlain family – Joseph Chamberlain,
the Radical Liberal who converted to support the Conservatives over
Empire, Ireland and fiscal protection, succeeded by his sons, Austen
Chamberlain, Conservative foreign secretary, and Neville Chamberlain
who became Conservative prime minister – were an essential backcloth to
the story Ashridge was unravelling, as important authors and purveyors
of changing political ideas. In July 1936 and February 1939, Joseph
Chamberlain was the subject of two special courses, one of them on
Joseph Chamberlain as a maker of the Empire. He was also the subject
of an article in the *Ashridge Journal*.[33]

The language of the nation

Stanley Baldwin was seen as the embodiment of these principles of 'New
Conservatism', 'given generous application'. As Davidson later wrote:
'Lord Baldwin in effect ruled Parliament and the country by means of a
union, not expressed in the division lobbies, but often implicit in debate,
between the right wing of the Socialist Party and the left wing of his
own.'[34] If this statement is perhaps excessive, it remains true that Baldwin
was respected by the Labour party and the trade unions.[35] Thanking
Baldwin for his comments on the publication of one of his books, Harold
Laski, the Socialist political philosopher, wrote:

> I rarely escape the conclusion, especially when I read your major speeches,
> that it is tradition rather than fundamentals that has put you among the

forces of the Right. For, if I may venture to say so, there is in you something of the temper of George Savile, Lord Halifax[36] that tinges all principles which claim finality with a recognition that novelty is inescapable.[37]

Baldwin was esteemed beyond the Labour party. Gilbert Murray, professor of classical languages at Oxford and a well-known Liberal pacifist, wrote to Baldwin, 'I think it is rather interesting to see how you, from your Conservatism, and I from my Liberalism come to so much the same conclusion about the present dangers of the world.'[38]

Baldwin's ability to unite people of all sorts was linked to his talent as an orator. He was, to an important degree, the heir to Disraeli as he was recalled at the beginning of the twentieth century, and of the myth of 'Tory democracy'. In the 1880s, Baldwin belonged to the Primrose League, founded in honour of Disraeli.[39] As a student at Harrow, he studied Disraeli's speeches.[40] The use he made of Disraeli was not new,[41] but the context of the inter-war years was profoundly different from that of the 1860s. The opposition between the Conservatives and the Labour party in the inter-war years bore little resemblance to the opposition between the Conservatives and the Liberals. The rules of the game had changed. The Labour party used the language of 'class struggle', hitherto unknown in British politics, and considered by Liberals as well as Conservatives as 'indecent' and contrary to the interests of the country.

In the face of the language of class struggle, Baldwin spoke of the 'nation'. He accused the Labour party of serving only the interests of the trade unions, and in his speeches he developed the old idea that the Conservative party embodied the nation as a whole.[42] He employed the vocabulary of 'industrial peace' and 'social harmony' and affirmed that the interests of employers and employees were linked to those of their firm. In every aspect of political and social life, Baldwin opposed the vocabulary of confrontation with that of social harmony. Seeking to jettison the idea of class struggle while becoming the defender of the non-unionised working class, he earned the favour of the Liberals.[43] Joseph Ball recalled that Baldwin said to him after the 1935 general election that the Conservatives should work to 'destroy the pathetic faith of the rank and file of the Labour Party and of the T.U.C. in the quack doctrines of such men as G. D. H. Cole, Laski, Mitchison, Cripps and others'.[44] Baldwin hoped the Labour party would abandon its projects of nationalisation and adopt a policy close to that of the National government. The situation would then look like that which existed before the birth of the Labour party, when both the Conservative and the Liberal parties defended 'sound evolutionary methods'. Baldwin wished the Labour party would be 'detached from the revolutionary policies which its intellectuals have succeeded in foisting upon it'.[45] His speeches never presented the working class as a threat. In this respect, he adhered to Disraeli's claim that 'in genuine Toryism there is no shrinking from democracy'.[46] Similarly, he was also careful never to present the Labour party as a threat. The danger came from the seduction the Labour party exercised over the working class through Socialist intellectuals and propaganda. Baldwin insisted upon the foreign origins of Socialism, which disqualified it from representing the nation. For him, class conflict was a foreign import. British society consisted of different, but not antagonistic, social classes; Socialism fomented national division, not unity, and as such it was contrary to the interests of the country. He skilfully deployed this argument during the General Strike of 1926, describing it as unacceptable because it was contrary to the constitution and the interests of the country as a whole. He portrayed the trade unions as traitors to the nation and to their own class. Using the vocabulary of inclusion and exclusion, Baldwin considered that the trade unionists had put themselves outside society. However, his hostility was not directed against the workers in whom he tried to instil a sense of belonging to the community.

If Baldwin rallied the majority of the population against the strike, it was because his speeches were addressed simultaneously to different sections of the population. In 1942, Davidson described the inter-war political situation thus: 'As the Liberal Party became shorn of its numbers and influence ... the field was left to the Conservative and Socialist Parties, the one reputed to be the Party of property, and the other property-less.' Davidson praised Baldwin's qualities and greatness, because 'we owe it largely to Lord Baldwin that this juxtaposition was never allowed to develop into a class war'.[47] Baldwin presented conservatism as the foundation of social and political harmony at a time when many feared political conflict and a fragmentation of society. His 'national-anti-socialism' received a favourable echo in the country. For him, the Socialists' mistake and the reason why they believed in class conflict was that they were interested only in the material dimension of life. As Christopher Dawson put it in the *Ashridge Journal*: 'For Socialism, the only social values are the economic ones.'[48] Baldwin went further still: 'Wealth was made to be a servant and not a master ... as a master it meant damnation.'[49]

He also used religious vocabulary to address the country, and tried to give an 'ecumenical' dimension to his speeches, to place himself above political parties. Like Disraeli, he referred to the nation, but his speeches reached beyond the framework of the Anglican church. In Disraeli's time, adherence to one or another church was common to practically all party activists. The non-conformists belonged to the Liberal party, while Conservatives usually belonged to the Anglican church. In the inter-war period, church membership declined as a component of political identity, and Baldwin sought to draw a majority of non-conformists to his cause.

He rejected the idea of a hierarchy between churches and gave broader and more inclusive meaning to the idea of nation and citizenship.

In their search for a suitable lineage, from Pitt to Liverpool, Derby or Salisbury, Conservatives at Ashridge opted for individuals who could be called 'progressives'. As Burke wrote, 'A state without the means of some change is without the means of its conservation',[50] and he proposed a model of evolutionary reforms as an alternative to the brutality of revolution. In Peel, they admired the lucidity which led him to advocate, against his own party, the necessity of transforming itself, even if his impatience led him to miss certain stages. They held the 'ultra-Tories' responsible for delays in adopting certain reforms, in the same way that they criticised Peel for reforms that were too radical and rapid. Disraeli was the model of the accomplished reformer, and Baldwin allegedly embodied the qualities of Peel and Disraeli. Davidson insisted that Baldwin 'has many resemblances with Peel',[51] and he explained that

> If the Conservative Party had not passed through many changes it would have become ossified and atrophied. It has retained its life and vitality because it has been able to meet new conditions and often anticipate new needs. Much of that ability is due to its two great leaders and educators in the nineteenth century, Peel and Disraeli, and neither of them was essentially Conservative. 'I am neither Whig nor Tory' said Disraeli, 'My politics are described by one word, and that word is 'England'. Much the same can be said of a third great leader and educator of the Party, Lord Baldwin. He too was not really a Conservative. In fact the best description of him is one that I believe he applied to himself – a Baldwinian Liberal.[52]

Progressive conservatism

In his speeches, Baldwin made no reference to 'Toryism' or to 'conservatism'. He considered himself above parties. Ashridge, too, claimed to be above parties, and refused to be labelled 'Conservative'. Burke was a Whig. Disraeli had been a Radical. Of Peel, Davidson wrote:

> I'm not sure whether in those days he could rightly be considered a Conservative; at any rate he was what we should call on the left wing of his party, and indeed most great leaders of the Conservative Party have been on the left of it.... I do no think that he bothered himself much about Tory or Conservative principles.... By the repeal of the Corn Laws he antagonized the landowners who formed a large section of his party, just as Lord Baldwin antagonized many of his party by the India Bill.[53]

The Ashridge Conservatives claimed they belonged to the tradition of politicians who favoured change, even against their own party. Baldwin embodied this tradition: a skilful dialectician, mixing the old with the new to formulate a conservatism that met the difficulties of the inter-war period. Writing to R. A. Butler on 13 February 1938, C. J. M. Alport referred to 'forces which exist today and which are bringing about strange changes in the life of our country. Industrialism, urbanisation and the scientific inventions.... Conservatism is conscious of these great changes and is reorientating itself to them.'[54] Reorientation implied an evolution of ideas and the words to express them. The loss of influence of the aristocratic elites and awareness that the 'the squire sleeps with his fathers'[55] did not prevent Baldwin from retaining their essential values and applying them to modern life. 'We have to find a new form for the indestructible force of aristocracy,'[56] Feiling wrote in 1930, 'the word aristocracy meaning, not the rule of money or the peerage, but rule by the best.'[57] As Hugh Sellon explained, 'it is true to say that conservatism is an essentially aristocratic creed, for it values quality above all things.... Since the whole emphasis of the conservative creed is thus laid on quality, we may readily understand how it is due to the Conservative party that the modern state gives so much affection to the mental and physical welfare of its citizens.'[58] The 'mental and physical welfare' of citizens could be attained only through major social reforms.

Repeated use of the word 'aristocracy' echoed Baldwin's use of the vocabulary of the countryside. Baldwinian Conservatives took up traditional aristocratic ideals and adapted them to their cause. Attempting to create new concepts from old ideas, they qualified their conservatism as both traditional and progressive. 'We shall achieve progress by preserving continuity', Reginald Northam wrote in 1939, paraphrasing Burke.[59] The term progressive was itself borrowed from the nineteenth-century Whigs. Its use was meant to show that the Conservatives belonged to the modern world and understood the social upheavals taking place. Northam insisted: 'Those who use the word "reactionary" about Conservatives do so to-day only with their tongues in their cheeks.'[60]

One of the most significant developments of language involved the term 'Unionist'. From 1912, the party was officially 'the Conservative and Unionist party', although the term 'Unionist' had regularly been used since 1886 by Conservatives and Liberals who opposed Home Rule and sought to preserve the union with Ireland. The Irish Treaty in 1921, which established the Irish Free State, ended the union and thereafter the term 'Unionist' referred only to the Ulster Unionists. However, in the 1920s Baldwin gave unionism a new meaning: the will to unite all social classes. In a speech at the Albert Hall in 1924, he defined the term explicitly: 'Unionist in the sense that we stand for the union of those two nations of which Disraeli spoke two generations ago; union among our own people at home which, if secured, nothing else matters in the world.'[61]

Different forms of conservatism

The unifying and progressive conservatism advocated by the Ashridge management led it to accept different schools of thought. Hence Davidson stated that 'it is no small wonder that Conservative principles as such are not readily distinguishable under Lord Baldwin's regime.'[62] However, certain fundamental principles were always present and strongly defended, such as the recognition that human societies were living organisms and not machines, or the need to maintain continuity with the past and to ensure that changes made provoked the least possible disruption to society. Thus, L. H. Sutton declared, 'We must have a real Conservative Government.... This government will have to be in a sense reactionary, but it must be not be only reactionary, it must be progressive as well.'[63] Sutton defended the idea of a government that would include both reactionary elements who were critical of reforms passed by the Liberal and Labour governments since 1906, and progressive elements to counterbalance the reactionaries. These different conceptions of conservatism were present at Ashridge.

Ashridge played the role of an echo chamber for the ideas of the Conservative party, and more generally of the National government, to enable them to face current problems. The problems were of three kinds: the economic crisis, the Empire and the international situation.

The economic crisis: Keynes and the Conservatives

The majority of Conservatives displayed caution in the face of the economic situation. To combat the Depression, they unanimously supported recourse to trade protection. This was introduced around the time of the Ottawa conference in 1932, which led the Samuelite Liberals to resign and enabled the National government to promote a truly Conservative programme. Joseph Chamberlain's dream in 1903, taken up briefly by Baldwin in 1923, had finally been realised. Preferential tariffs for the Empire and, in the autumn of 1932, a protectionist system for British industry were the two elements of what the Conservatives considered an historic success. The principal negotiator of the Ottawa agreements, Neville Chamberlain, wrote to his sister on 30 August 1932: 'It is a great addition to my satisfaction that Ottawa has given you two so much pleasure and there are still so many of the family left to rejoice in the fulfilment of Father's policy.'[64] While the Ottawa agreements were welcome, however, they did not end debates on protectionism. Each industry had to apply for tariff protection and to defend its claim before the Import Duties Advisory Committee, established in 1932. Tariff protection was not accorded to all, and the question remained to whom and by what criteria protection should be given. Debates on trade policy took a lively turn at Ashridge. In 1932, during the Ottawa conference, a special session on commerce within the Empire was introduced. From 1929 to 1939, 54 lectures or discussions on tariffs were held and102 on imperial trade, as well as 12 special sessions on trade within Empire.[65]

Twenty-five lectures and two special sessions dealt with Britain's heavy industries, notably those most affected by the slump, such as cotton, steel and shipbuilding. Fifteen lectures and two special sessions dealt exclusively with coal, which was the most severely affected of all the industries. In 1930, the independent MP Austin Hopkinson gave a lecture on the coal industry in which he criticised the Labour government and the 1929 Act on the fusion of the mining companies. Hopkinson defended a Liberal position: 'No other industry affords so grave a warning against the perils of political interference with the economic life of the people, or exhibits so clear [sic] the falsity of the prevalent idea that a nation can be made prosperous by Acts of Parliaments.'[66] According to him, the cost to the government and tax-payers was too heavy. In contrast, Lord Melchett endorsed the 1929 Act and adopted a more flexible position. He proposed the creation of an industrial parliament, the aim of which was to bring together the representatives of industry, including the trade unions. He supported state intervention in industry, if it was well done. As he wrote: 'Agriculture and coal, two of the biggest industries in England, have been radically interfered with by Parliament. The trouble is that they have not been very well interfered with. I think there is considerable justification for the community doing anything that is to benefit all the people of the country.'[67] Contrary to Hopkinson, he insisted on the necessity of planning the future of each industry, and not letting each company decide on its techniques or policies to adopt.[68] Along with Harold McGowan, president of ICI, which was created by Melchett's father, Guy Locock, president of the Federation of British Industry, William Larke, director of the National Federation of Iron and Steel Manufacturers, and W. L. Hichens, president of Cammell Laird, one of the biggest shipbuilding companies, Melchett represented large industrial corporations.

Harold Macmillan advocated yet another position. Although he favoured the idea of an industrial parliament and was one of the instigators of a reform bill on the self-government of industry,[69] he considered that the state must act as a catalyst in the process of industrial reorganisation. He also defended the idea that certain industrial sectors should be controlled by the state, and hence began a reflection on the 'mixed economy', as it would later be called.[70] In December 1938, the year Macmillan published *The Middle Way*, he was invited to lecture on 'Planning and the Future' during a weekend course at Ashridge on 'Some Modern Economic Problems'. Geoffrey Ellis, a member of Ashridge's governing body and education committee, worked regularly with Macmillan; in 1938 he lectured on 'Money, Finance and Capital in Future Years'.[71] Macmillan wrote in his memoirs of his collaboration with Ellis:

> One of the wisest and most powerful of all my friends in all these activities was Geoffrey Ellis, a deeply respected Member of the party, who had an influence altogether disproportionate to any outward political achievement. He preferred commerce and industry to office, but he was effective in the background.... From him I learnt a great deal, especially on the practical problem of translating general ideas into effective action.[72]

The history of large corporations within the British economy dated back to the turn of the century, but it was not until 1918 that they occupied a central place in the economy.[73] Their growth is a testimony to the radical changes occurring in the world economy as well as in Britain. It is striking to notice that the lecturers who dealt with industrial issues at Ashridge were all associated with large corporations: an indication of Ashridge's willingness to address questions raised by the emergence of the modern economic system. In June 1933, for example, during a course on 'The Constitution and its Reform', W. L. Hitchens spoke on 'The Growth of the Industrial Corporation'. He was followed by Charles Petrie on 'The Corporate State'. In October 1933, Hitchens lectured on 'The Growth of the Big Industrial Corporation'. In August 1934, K. Headlam-Morley spoke on 'The Future Organisation of Industry', followed in December 1934 by W. S. Morrison on 'Modern Industrial Organisation' and by L. H. Sutton on 'Economic Nationalism'.[74] Other lectures addressed seven different industries, including S. S. Hammersley on cotton, Douglas Hamilton on wool, Sir William Larke on iron and steel and Philip Hill on ship transport. All the lecturers were heads of large corporations or experts on their subject.

In 1930, the Labour party responded to the slump by creating an Economic Advisory Council, composed of leading economists and industrialists. Sir John Cadman, chairman of the Anglo-Iranian Oil Corporation,[75] was a member. Ashridge served as the equivalent for the Conservative party.

In 1932, 22 per cent of the British labour force were unemployed.[76] Between 1930 and 1939, forty-seven lectures and four special sessions were devoted to unemployment and to social problems. From October to December 1935, in an eight-week course on citizenship, R. K. Kelsall, a professor of political economy at Ashridge, lectured on 'Economic Theory: the classical economists – modern theories – theory applied to modern problems'.[77] Ashridge was a centre for debate on new theories, in particular those of John Maynard Keynes and Major Douglas, the Canadian economist.

The questions raised by Keynes provoked an important debate within the Conservative party. Party leaders disputed Keynes's political propositions and theories; Baldwin and Chamberlain were chiefly concerned not to raise taxes or revive inflation. Certain Conservatives, however, saw Keynes's proposals as a solution to the economic depression. Ashridge, which fostered the debate, witnessed the beginning of a 'conservative Keynesianism'. From 1934 to 1937, the New Deal in the United States and the American economic situation were the subject of thirteen lectures which examined the issues from different angles. Sir Arthur Steel-Maitland and A. G. Sharp both lectured on the New Deal, which they supported. In 1934, Steel-Maitland wrote *The New America*, in which he stated:

> If great trade depressions can be prevented and capitalism pruned of its excesses, stability in industry may be combined with freedom of individual enterprise.... Capitalism is indeed on trial. So, too, is the freedom of individual initiative. If this is destroyed the chief responsibility for its destruction will lie with those who professed to believe in it, but were too remiss to try and remedy the admitted shortcomings of the existing economic system.[78]

Steel-Maitland was also favourable to the New Deal for Britain, proposed in 1935 by Lloyd George. Lloyd George's New Deal was the subject of two lectures, as were Major Douglas's proposals for reviving the economy through social credit. In November 1934, in a speech in the House of Commons on the economic situation, Steel-Maitland referred to the necessity of reforming the capitalist system 'to provide a cure for poverty in the midst of plenty' and avoid the growth of political extremism.[79] The following summer, during a session on 'Banks and the Nation', a debate was organised on 'Poverty in the Midst of Plenty'.[80]

From 1929 to 1936, the role of the banks was the subject of thirteen lectures and two special sessions. Lord Melchett, Geoffrey Ellis, Arthur Steel-Maitland and Harold Macmillan were the main speakers, and all criticised the role played by the banks. During a weekend course in May 1935, lectures were given on 'Our Money Machine in Relation to Trade and Industry' and the 'Nationalisation of Credit', and debates were organised on themes such as 'Idle Men and Idle Money' and 'Major Douglas and the Credit System'.[81] Describing banks as 'money machines' underlined the divergence between the financial economy and the real economy. Likewise, 'Idle Men and Idle Money' assumed that one of the causes of unemployment was the reluctance of the bankers to lend to productive industry. At Ashridge the City was freely criticised. In the *Ashridge Journal* for 1935, a banker described a lecture he attended on 'The Banks and the Nation': 'at tea ... it was passed from mouth to mouth that there were (in bated breath) a number of bankers present, and there was a sort of furtive scrutiny of one's neighbours which searched for signs of horns or tail!'[82] Criticism of the City and the banks had always been an important component of a certain Conservative sub-culture which was articulated differently, perhaps with more coherence, in the 1930s.

At the beginning of the 1920s, the YMCA (Young Men's Christian Association) was the derogatory name given to a small group of Conservative MPs which included several future lecturers at Ashridge such as Macmillan, Boothby and Oliver Stanley, who advocated radical economic programmes.[83] In the 1930s, it was succeeded by another informal group of Conservative MPs who were equally radical in their economics, and included Macmillan, Ellis, O'Connor, Eustace Percy, Edward Grigg and Anthony Crossley.[84] They conceptualised the idea of 'self-government of industry' and favoured greater state intervention in economic life. In the latter respect, they were close to John Maynard Keynes, who thought the banks and financial institutions were engaged in speculation rather than lending to productive industry.[85]

In his *General Theory*, Keynes called for 'the euthanasia of the rentier'.[86] Keynes's political supporters, however, drew different conclusions from his critique of the financial system. Oswald Mosley,[87] for example, found support for his anti-Semitism by linking finance to the Jewish community. Steel-Maitland, also critical of the banks, proposed an investment commission composed of industrialists and financed by the state, to assist the restructuring of British industry and compensate for the deficiency of British banks. Harold Macmillan went further still. In 1938, he proposed the nationalisation of the Bank of England,[88] which led to his ostracism within the party, where his ideas were likened to Socialism.

Macmillan, Boothby, Steel-Maitland, Ellis and T. J. O'Connor, all lecturers at Ashridge, agreed with Keynes on the need to implement a programme of public works, although unlike Keynes they also emphasised the need to introduce more rationalisation and efficiency in industry. Their preoccupation was at the micro-economic level. Keynes, on the contrary, focused on macro-economics and emphasised the role of the government in increasing effective demand. In 1935, E. J. Garmeson, a banker present at Ashridge, criticised Lord Tavistock's lecture on 'Major Douglas and the Credit System', referring to his 'astounding conclusion' that 'a 10s. note would only purchase one 10s. article, whereas neither currency nor bank money is destroyed when used, but only transferred, and is in fact used over and over and over again'.[89] Douglas's argument

was, in fact, a vulgarisation of the theory of the multiplier at the centre
of Keynes's theory. By and large, Keynes's work was well received by the
younger generation of Conservatives. Garmeson, referring to a lecture
by Macmillan, commented: 'a progressive and sympathetic view of these
matters [economic planning] was not absent from the outlook of the
younger Conservative members of Parliament'.[90]

Thinking about the economy, which became common during the
inter-war period, found a prominent place at Ashridge. Macmillan,
Ellis, Boothby and Steel-Maitland all introduced Keynesian ideas to
the deliberations. The particular feature of Ashridge, as opposed to the
Next Five Years Group, of which Macmillan, Ellis and O'Connor were
part, or to Political and Economic Planning, another cross-party group
interested in Keynesian ideas, was the fact that Ashridge belonged to the
Conservative party. It thus offered progressive Conservatives a space to
express themselves within an institution linked to the party.

The radical wing of the Conservative party and 'pro-Fascist patriotism'

While the more progressive voices within the Conservative party could
be heard at Ashridge, the reactionary wing of the party was equally
represented. Sir Henry Page Croft and Leo Amery, for example, belonged
to the old guard of the Conservative party and to Joseph Chamberlain's
'rebels' at the beginning of the century.[91] Staunch protectionists, they had
supported Chamberlain's Tariff Reform campaign and wrote numerous
books on the subject.[92] In 1917, Page Croft created the 'National party' in
reaction to the Conservative party's participation with the Liberals in the
wartime coalition government. Both represented a non-orthodox form of
conservatism.

The *Ashridge Journal* reproduced some very lively discussions between
progressives and reactionaries. In an article of September 1933 entitled
'A Tory Looks at his World', Sir Charles Petrie, a Right-wing historian,
deplored the materialism of the modern world and its lack of respect for
the monarchy and religion. Norah Case replied in the following number
that Petrie was a reactionary and that

> So many people are engaged to-day in destructive analysis and unfavourable
> comparison of the present age with that of the past.... Sir Charles Petrie
> deplores the flouting of the principles of monarchy by nations which would
> fain be considered progressive. But surely he will admit that the seed of
> dissolution frequently lay in the hypocrisies inherent in certain traditions
> of monarchy?... It is difficult to see how *organised* Christianity is going to
> defend its position unless it is willing to learn a new humility and be more
> objective.[93]

Petrie incarnated the old guard of reactionary conservatism, typically diehard,[94] who advocated not merely continuity with the past but a return to the past. 'I am a Tory, not a Conservative, and when I criticize Conservatism it is because, under the influence of Whiggery and Big Business, it has departed from what I believe to be the basic principles of Toryism.'[95] The debate between 'Tory' and 'Conservative' was the equivalent, for Petrie, of the quarrel between the ancients and the moderns. Although a handful of diehards were invited to Ashridge, the college encouraged the view expressed by Geoffrey Ellis: 'We ought always to stress "Progressive" Conservatism. We really must at Ashridge get away from the idea that we are anchored to diehard trees.'[96] Likewise, Bryant explained: 'It's no use fighting a clever fellow like Gollancz with all the entrenched forces of the "Intelligentzia" of the Universities and Schools behind him with hastily hashed-up books of the English Review, Colonel Blimp kind. Their danger is that they will discredit not only themselves but us too.'[97]

Representatives of an even more extreme Right were also invited to Ashridge: Viscount Lymington, for example, president of the English Mistery, a movement on the margins of the Conservative party which aimed to restore the feudal system in Britain.[98] He was a radical reactionary, opposed to all forms of modernity, who created the English Mistery in 1931 with Rolf Gardiner, Michael Beaumont and Anthony Ludovici, all of whom occasionally appeared at Ashridge. While the English Mistery's fundamentalism can be compared to certain forms of Fascism, it reflected mainly a nostalgia for a foregone and idealised golden age, when society was organised in a strictly hierarchical way and everyone knew their place and role. The Conservatives were by no means alone in eulogising the countryside and looking back to a pre-industrial, pre-urban era, which supposedly had enjoyed superior social values, structures and relationships. There was a surprising degree of cross-party agreement on the existence of a rural golden age in the medieval era.[99] For G. D. H. Cole and the Guild Socialists, the beauty of the medieval period was that it was organically and naturally democratic and in its political aspects egalitarian. For Baldwin and many Conservatives, the medieval period offered an organic, hierarchical and paternalist social and governmental structure. For the English Mistery, the medieval era was to be imitated in part because of its organicism and hierarchicalism, but above all because of its authoritarianism.[100] They saw in the feudal structure a social system that could be drawn upon and imitated. At the start of the 1930s, Viscount Lymington and his friends represented one of the most extreme political tendencies at Ashridge. In a letter to Arthur Bryant in November 1936, Alice Johnston, a teacher at Ashridge, criticised a lecture proposal by

Lord Dawson, the doctor to the royal family who was well-known for his advocacy of eugenics. She wrote:

> The part marked seems to me to be a mixture of Misteries and Nazi-ism.... Also to me it is an absurd idea that our future leaders can be determined by taking their chest measurements at the age of 17.... I think it would be unfortunate if the young intellectuals became imbued with any ideas verging on Mistery at Ashridge.[101]

Aware of the presence of extremist minorities at the college, and facing accusations of being too Right-wing or too Left-wing, Ashridge's management invited representatives of different tendencies in order to play off the one against the other and escape the charge of bias. Responding to an accusation that Ashridge had become a centre for Liberals and Left-wing intellectuals, the governing body stated in 1934: 'To say that only "a mild form of conservatism is tolerated" here is absurd; our lecturing list includes Sir Henry Page Croft ..., Lord Lymington ... and one of the most frequent of our MP lecturers and supporters is Mr. L. S. Amery.'[102] Page Croft and Amery were bracketed with Lymington because in the 1930s they represented the Right of the party as opposed to the young progressives such as Macmillan, Boothby and Butler. Lymington's presence served as a counterweight to the radical wing of the party. In April 1932, the principal of the college corresponded with the secretary of the Eugenics Society concerning a possible lecture at Ashridge on 'The Biological Basis of National Well-Being'. Although the idea was soon abandoned, in December 1936, Professor J. G. Kerr, a Conservative MP and professor of zoology, lectured on 'Biological Aspects of Citizenship'.[103]

Besides representatives of the extreme Right, Ashridge also provided a venue for several 'fellow travellers of the right', such as the military experts General J. F. C. Fuller and Admiral Domville. Domville was president of the Link, the association for Anglo-German friendship. He boasted of being Ribbentrop's friend, and referred to Stalin and Bolshevism as the 'disease' that the 'surgeon' Hitler must cure.[104] Other Ashridge visitors were Arnold Wilson, a former colonial administrator and Conservative MP, and William Teeling, a writer and journalist: both admirers of Nazism who appealed for a moral regeneration of the nation. 'Toryism', Wilson explained, 'is not only a Party spirit but a way of life; not only a political attitude of mind but a regenerative social and moral force.'[105] The fellow travellers of the Right differed from the 'English Mistery', which rejected the modern world, by advocating a corporatist and authoritarian state. In *Why Britain Prospers*, Teeling endorsed the Nazi work camps, where the workers 'gained in health', as well as the Nazi cult of the leader, whose absence in Britain they lamented: 'What are our Conservatives doing in this country to develop our political leaders of tomorrow?'[106]

During the 1930s, a more insidious form of Fascism emerged at Ashridge. Arthur Bryant, director of the education committee of Ashridge, was a notable example. A highly popular historian whose work was appreciated by politicians as different as Winston Churchill and Clement Attlee,[107] Bryant gradually developed a form of sympathy and admiration for Nazi Germany.[108] After Hitler's ascent to power, he published a series of articles, drawn from lectures given at Ashridge, on the theme of leadership in Europe. He examined several political figures including Lenin, Mussolini, Briand, Pilsudski and Hitler. In his conclusion he wrote: 'In awakening her [Germany], Hitler has shown himself to be a great German. Though his ideals are not those which are current in modern Britain, it is a mistake to deny him sincerity.'[109] His Germanophilia led him to an ambiguous admiration for Hitler. A member of the Anglo-German Friendship Society, Bryant went to Germany in July 1939 at the invitation of Walther Hewel, a friend of Hitler. According to one of his biographers, Pamela Street, Neville Chamberlain and Stanley Baldwin asked Bryant to make the trip to Germany in a last attempt to forestall war. On his return to England, he wrote:

> I saw ... a Germany strangely different from the hysterical land of shadows depicted from that other Germany – sad, sullen and divided – which I had seen in the days of the Inflation sixteen years before. For it was a land which, for all the miseries of the minorities tucked out of sight and hearing, seemed at unity with itself and in which the common man felt himself part of a great nation moving, as he supposed, proudly and gladly towards a happier and assured goal.[110]

At the same time, Bryant completed *Unfinished Victory*, a Francophobic book, hostile to the Treaty of Versailles and favourable to Hitler. 'Hitler', he explained,

> like Bismarck ... showed a grasp of the realities of statesmanship. Scorning the safe but ineffectual ways of the academic theorist, he struck boldly out up the perilous paths of urgent action to the summit of his dream. 'The practical wisdom of the statesman', he wrote in *Mein Kampf*, unconsciously following Burke, 'must come to the aid of the abstract conception which is true in itself.'[111]

The association of Burke and Hitler was testimony to the power of attraction that Nazi Germany exercised over Bryant. Bryant compared Hitler to two heroes in history: 'Like King Hal before Agincourt and Joshua at the Jordan, Hitler preferred ... to confine his Movement to people as ruthless and unrelenting as himself.'[112] Published in 1940,

Unfinished Victory caused a scandal. The historian Hugh Trevor-Roper wrote that the book was 'not a plea for political realism but a plea for Nazism itself'.[113] In November 1968, Bryant managed to prevent the Public Record Office from releasing documents relating to his visit to Germany.[114]

Bryant was by no means the only Briton to be fascinated by Germany in the 1930s. Passing admiration for early National Socialism was found cross-party. In a speech to parliament in 1933, Anthony Crossley, a Conservative MP and regular visitor to Ashridge, referred to his recent visit to Germany and expressed his admiration for Hitler's fight against unemployment, suggesting that similar solutions should be applied in Britain.[115] Churchill himself wrote in *Great Contemporaries*, published in 1937, a chapter entitled 'Hitler and His Choice' in which he stated: 'History is replete with examples of men who have risen to power by employing stern, grim and even frightful methods, but who nevertheless ... have been regarded as great figures whose lives have enriched the story of mankind. So may it be with Hitler.'[116] However, after Anthony Eden's resignation on 20 February 1938, Crossley, E. L. Spears, another Conservative MP and regular visitor to Ashridge, and Macmillan, along with eighteen other Conservative MPs, abstained on a Labour party motion censuring the National government's foreign policy. Crossley, Spears, Viscount Wolmer, Leo Amery and Macmillan became members of the 'Group', a small circle of MPs opposed to appeasement.[117]

As late as February 1938, practically the whole country considered Chamberlain's policy of appeasement as an audacious and brave attempt to maintain peace. However, opposition to Chamberlain hardened after the Munich conference in September, and especially after *Kristallnacht* in November. In February 1939, the CRD warned Chamberlain not to call a general election because his popularity was at rock bottom since November 1938.[118] Within a few months, between February 1938 and September 1939, public opinion had rapidly changed. Even Lord Halifax, the foreign secretary and Chamberlain's ally on the policy of appeasement, declared his support for accelerating rearmament.

The *Ashridge Journal*, which Bryant edited, supported the government's foreign policy. In December 1938, with enthusiasm giving way to scepticism, Bryant wrote an article entitled 'Munich: Some Charges and Their Answers'. On the question of the Sudetenland, he wrote: 'The Czechs were probably a good deal less fit to govern Germans than the English twenty years ago were to govern the Irish. The English had been a governing race for centuries: the Czechs in 1919 suddenly found themselves in a saddle to which they were not accustomed.'[119] He continued: 'The Sudeten Germans felt, not so much that they were being enslaved, as en-"Slaved"'.[120] Czechoslovakia, he claimed, was a 'military satellite' of

France, and might have used the Sudetenland to bomb Germany. He concluded: 'It was Mr. Chamberlain's achievement that at the eleventh hour he undid a twenty-year-old injustice and prevented – by firmness, forbearance and persuasion – the German leader from impatiently taking the law into his own hands'.[121] By referring to the Treaty of Versailles as a 'twenty-year-old injustice', Bryant adopted Germany's position and endorsed its territorial claims.[122] In doing so, he departed from the position of the Conservative party. One of the instigators of the Locarno pact, Austen Chamberlain, had declared in parliament in 1933: 'Are you going to discuss with such a Government the Polish Corridor? The Polish Corridor is inhabited by Poles; Do you dare put another Pole under the heel of such a Government?'[123] Bryant's remained an isolated voice. In the aftermath of *Kristallnacht*, he belonged to those whom Richard Griffiths calls the 'pro-fascist patriots'.[124] According to Bryant's friend Francis Yeats-Brown, their admiration for Nazi Germany, Mussolini's Italy and Franco's Spain derived from the desire 'not be involved in a war to make the world safe for Stalin or international Jewry'.[125] Bryant was more cautious than Domville, Fuller, Tavistock, Yeats-Brown and Lymington in so far as he did not join any Fascist organisation. As a result, his 'pro-Nazi patriotism' has long been regarded merely as 'ordinary nationalism'.[126]

In her biography of Bryant, Julia Stapleton explains that 'a prime consideration in the defence of Nazism and other Fascist regimes was to counteract [Bryant]'s perception of the intellectual elite's instinctive reaction against Conservatism, tradition, and nationhood in all their many guises. In his view, this could only serve to benefit the Left.'[127] The link between the defence of Nazism and intellectual insecurity seems confirmed by several of Bryant's writings, and reflecting upon 'the kind of contemptuous attitude (however unjust) which was adopted by young people generally and in the intellectual and academic world towards the word Tory immediately after the war', Bryant wrote in 1937, 'I really think it fair to say that Earl Baldwin has been primarily responsible for changing that'.[128] If Baldwin recognised the need to use a more 'progressive' vocabulary, Ashridge was the place where the language was produced that increased the Conservative party's credibility in academic milieux. Hostility towards abstraction, and the principle of an organic society, remained the two leitmotivs of conservatism. As C. J. M. Alport explained,

> Conservatism pays little heed to the abstract theories of intellectuals,... because it has learnt that these theories usually work out very differently in practice to the ways which their originators expect.... Practical experience

is the basis of Conservatism in action and in theory, because it is the source of all knowledge.[129]

Paradoxically, it was this opposition to abstract theory that attracted the Conservatives to Keynes's work, as Northam observed: 'The object of Mr. Keynes ... is not theoretical but intensely practical.'[130] Ashridge favoured inductive over deductive analysis. Despite his membership of the Bloomsbury group, Conservative interest in Keynes derived from his critique of the classical economists, whose principles were based upon deductive analysis. In this respect, Keynes was close to the British historical economists of the turn of the century, all of whom were Conservatives. In his introduction to the German edition of the *General Theory*, Keynes wrote that, thanks to the German tradition of historical economy, his book would probably be better understood in Germany than in Britain. Ashridge was close to the historical school of economics. One of its members, who frequently visited Ashridge in the early 1930s, was W. A. S. Hewins, the doyen of the school of historical economics and the first director of the LSE. The intellectual origins of protectionism and the imperial preferences adopted in 1932 can be found in the works of the historical economists. At the heart of the historical economists' critique of the classical economists lies a hostility towards individualism and competition. For the historical economists, the economy was regarded as a national economy, just as society was considered as a national organism. Competition should exist between nations and not between individuals.[131] Classes on economics at Ashridge were frequently entitled 'The National Economy' or 'Economic Nationalism'.

Because the concepts of nation and organic society lay at the heart of Burke's and Disraeli's thinking, they were taken as separate subjects of study and lectures. Over the College's ten years of existence before the Second World War, Burke was twice the subject of a special course, and Disraeli four times.[132] However, while Ashridge Conservatives claimed that they belonged to a certain tradition, their aim was first and foremost to consider conservatism in a new light. In 1938, C. J. M. Alport wrote to Butler about *A National Faith*, the book he was currently writing: 'It is not a re-hash of Burke and does not attempt to summon too many dead leaders to testify to us. It is, I hope, an interpretation of Conservatism, which has immediate application to the present day,'[133] and he added: 'It is senility to sit in corners and spin incantations out of Bolinbroke [*sic*] and Disraeli.'[134] Burke's insistence on the organic structure of society needed to be recast and adapted to different historical circumstances. Hence Christopher Dawson wrote: 'There is no doubt that the Conservative conception of the organic nature of society and its ideal of the co-operation of the different classes and economic interests in the nation towards a common cultural end is far more sympathetic to the natural genius than is the socialist absolutism, whether in its revolutionary or in its Fabian form.'[135] Furthermore, he added, 'There was an organised hierarchy of classes each with a specific social function in the life of the whole.'[136] This was the classic Burkean description of society in the eighteenth century, but the industrial revolution had upset that balance, and the resulting individualism reduced society to 'a chaos of competitive units'. In spite of this, Dawson explained, 'though that theory [organicism] was pre-scientific, it rests upon sound sociological foundations and it is capable of being restated in terms of modern conditions. The more complex our civilisation becomes, the more necessary it is to recognize both the autonomous value and the interdependent relations of the different social functions.'[137] Links of mutual and reciprocal interdependence between social groups and individuals were at the heart of the Conservatives' organic vision of society, in contradistinction to the traditional Liberal conception of society as the sum of individuals who compose it and to the Socialist idea that each social class represented particular and conflicting interests.[138]

One of the fundamental principles of conservatism was, as indicated, respect for the past considered as a source of accumulated wisdom, as opposed to ephemeral theories, even the most seductive. History, because it is the knowledge of the past, was an essential part of the Conservative project. Reginald Northam, for example, explained, 'Our Conservative attitude to life arises out of the historic approach. To the Conservative history is not "bunk" for it provides checks against rash action. It is "bunk" only to those who think, in their vanity, that it is possible for a community to start all over afresh.'[139]

When Northam wrote his essay on 'Spiritual Values in Politics', he was already director of the new Conservative College at Swinton,[140] which had been set up in the immediate aftermath of the Second World War as a training centre for Conservative party officials. In many ways, Swinton was a direct institutional successor to Ashridge, but, as a college directly under party control, it did not enjoy Ashridge's autonomy. The reasons for this were largely due to the differing political circumstances in which the two institutions operated. After 1945, the Conservatives were politically, electorally and doctrinally on the defensive, and looked at Swinton to provide them with a core framework of ideas, which would help them confront their predicament. Ashridge had functioned when the party was politically strong but doctrinally uncertain. As a consequence, the range and flexibility of debate on the nature of conservatism that characterised Ashridge's syllabuses, lectures and discussions were very wide. There was, in short, greater political space in the inter-war years for Conservative intra-party debate.

Notes

1 T. N. Graham, 'The Constituencies and Ashridge', *Ashridge Journal*, June 1935, p. 18.
2 Dean Inge, n.d., 1926, quoted in T. N. Graham, 'The Constituencies and Ashridge', *Ashridge Journal*, June 1935, p. 18.
3 D. Boot, 'Some Aspects of Conservative Education', *Ashridge Journal*, Mar. 1936, pp. 34–5.
4 K. Feiling, *What is Conservatism?* (London: Faber & Faber, 1930).
5 L. H. Sutton, 'A Political Diary', *Ashridge Journal*, Mar. 1938, p. 35.
6 W. Elliot, *Toryism and the Twentieth Century* (London: Philip Allen, 1927), p. 4.
7 J. Buchan, Preface to A. Bryant, *The Spirit of Conservatism* (Ashridge: The Bonar Law Memorial College, 1929), p. vii.
8 Davidson, 'The History and Principles of the Conservative Party', Conference, Lancaster Grammar School, 20 Mar. 1942, Davidson papers, DAV/284.
9 *Ibid.*
10 D. Boot, 'Freedom for Political Education', *Ashridge Journal*, Dec. 1934, p. 38.
11 Richard Hooker was the great theologian of Anglicanism. His major work was *The Law of Ecclesiastical Polity* in 1593. Anthony Quinton dates the birth of Conservative thought to Hooker: *The Politics of Imperfection. The Religious and Secular Traditions of Conservative Thought in England from Hooker to Oakeshott* (London: Faber & Faber, 1978).
12 Hearnshaw, *Conservatism*, p. 22.
13 Northam, *Conservatism, the Only Way*, pp. 54–5.
14 Burke's influence was frequently claimed by different schools of thought, which claimed to have adopted his empiricism, his historicism or his reflections on civil society.
15 Davidson, 'The History and Principles of the Conservative Party', Conference, Lancaster Grammar School, 20 Mar. 1942, Davidson papers, DAV/284.
16 *Ibid.*, pp. 197–8.
17 C. Dawson, 'Conservatism', *Ashridge Journal*, Sep. 1932, p. 42.
18 Quoted in D. Read, *Peel and the Victorians* (New York: Basil Blackwell, 1987).
19 G. Kitson Clark, *Peel and the Conservative Party* (London: Bell, 1929). G. Kitson Clark, *Peel* (London: Duckworth, 1936).
20 N. Gash, *Mr. Secretary Peel* (London: Longmans, 1961). See also B. Hilton, 'Peel: a Reappraisal', *Historical Journal*, 22, 1979, pp. 585–614; and P. Mandler, *Aristocratic Government in the Age of Reform: Whigs and Liberals, 1830–1852* (Oxford: Oxford University Press, 1990).
21 Hearnshaw, *Conservatism*, p. 196.

22 *Ibid.*, p. 198.

23 *Ibid.*, p. 206.

24 P. Smith, *Disraelian Conservatism and Social Reform* (London: Routledge and Kegan Paul, 1967). P. Smith, 'Disraeli's Politics', *Transactions of the Royal Historical Society*, 37, 1987, pp. 65–86. P. Smith and D. Richmond (eds), *The Self-Fashioning of Disraeli, 1818–51* (Cambridge: Cambridge University Press, 1997). P. R. Ghosh, 'Disraelian Conservatism: A Financial Approach', *English Historical Review*, 99, 1984, pp. 268–96.

25 J. E. Gorst, 'Summary of Disraeli's Domestic Policy', quoted in D. Boot, 'Let Disraeli Speak Today', *Ashridge Journal*, Dec. 1935, pp. 17–18.

26 See P. R. Ghosh, 'Style and Substance in Disraelian Social Reform', in P. J. Waller (ed.), *Politics and Social Change in Modern Britain: Essays Presented to A. F. Thompson* (Brighton: Harvester, 1987), pp. 59–90.

27 T. Freston to A. J. Balfour, 3 Jan. 1883, in Green, *Crisis of Conservatism*, p. 104.

28 Smith, *Disraelian Conservatism*. R. Blake, *Disraeli* (London: Macmillan, 1969).

29 Quoted in Boot, 'Let Disraeli Speak Today'.

30 Davidson, 'Notes on Conservatism', n.d., 1937, Davidson papers, DAV/233.

31 *Ibid.*

32 *Ibid.*

33 T. N. Graham, 'Joseph Chamberlain', *Ashridge Journal*, Sep. 1936, pp. 15–26.

34 Davidson, 'The History and Principles of the Conservative Party', Conference, Lancaster Grammar School, 20 Mar. 1942, Davidson papers, DAV/284.

35 Williamson, *Stanley Baldwin*, pp. 346–7.

36 George Savile became Lord Halifax in the 1670s. He was known as the Trimmer – the opportunist – for he was allegedly always ready to trim his principles. Those favourable to him said that he was adaptable and that his principles were not rigid. His adversaries accused him of compromise.

37 H. Laski to S. Baldwin, 6 Mar. 1933, Baldwin papers, SB168.

38 G. Murray to S. Baldwin, 9 Apr.1934, Baldwin papers, SB169.

39 The Primrose League was founded in 1883, two years after Disraeli died, to promote 'Tory principles ... maintaining the religious order, the monarchy and the imperial dominion of Great Britain'. The League claimed to have two million members in 1914, but this number is probably exaggerated. Pugh, *The Tories and the People*; A. Cooke, *A Gift from the Churchills: the Primrose League, 1883–2004* (London: Conservative Research Department, 2010).

40 Williamson, *Stanley Baldwin*, p. 131.

41 For a different interpretation of this issue, see *Ibid.*, p. 179.

42 This distinction between the public and sectional interests was to surface again in the early 1950s. See J. Bonham, *The Middle Class Vote* (London: Faber & Faber, 1954), p. 20.

43 McKibbin, '"Class and Conventional Wisdom"'.

44 J. Ball to S. Baldwin, 6 Dec. 1935, Baldwin papers, SB48, fos 252–260.

45 *Ibid.*

46 B. Disraeli, 'A Vindication of the Constitution, 1835', in Boot, 'Let Disraeli Speak Today', p. 18.

47 Davidson, 'The History and Principles of the Conservative Party', Conference, Lancaster Grammar School, 20 Mar. 1942, Davidson papers, DAV/284.

48 C. Dawson, 'Conservatism', *Ashridge Journal*, Sep. 1932, p. 42.

49 S. Baldwin, 'Service', Leeds, 13 Mar. 1925, in Baldwin, *On England*, p. 62.

50 E. Burke, *Reflections on the Revolution in France* (London: J. Dodsley, 1790, Penguin Books, 1978), p. 106.

51 Davidson, 'The History and Principles of the Conservative Party', Conference, Lancaster Grammar School, 20 Mar. 1942, Davidson papers, DAV/284.

52 *Ibid.*

53 *Ibid.*

54 C. J. M. Alport to R. A. Butler, 13 Feb. 1938, Butler papers, H88, fos 92–95.

55 Feiling, *What is Conservatism?*, p. 9, repeated in Northam, *Conservatism, the Only Way*, p. 77.

56 Feiling, *What is Conservatism?*, pp. 29–30.

57 *Ibid.*, p. 21.

58 *Ibid.*

59 Northam, *Conservatism, the Only Way*, p. 270.

60 *Ibid.*, p. 265.

61 S. Baldwin to the Albert Hall, 4 Dec. 1924, in Baldwin, *On England*, p. 73.

62 *Ibid.*

63 L. H. Sutton, 'Conservatism and Ashridge', *Ashridge Journal*, Mar. 1933, p. 24.

64 N. Chamberlain to H. Chamberlain, 30 Aug. 1932, in R. Self (ed.), *The Neville Chamberlain Diary Letters*, Vol. 3, *The Heir Apparent, 1928–1933* (Aldershot: Ashgate Publishing Limited, 2002), p. 345.

65 'Coming Courses', *Ashridge Journal*, 1929–1939.

66 A. Hopkinson, 'Politics and the Coal-Mining Industry', *Ashridge Journal*, May 1930, p. 3.

67 *Ibid.*, p. 18.

68 Lord Melchett, 'Internationalism and Big Business', *Ashridge Journal*, Sep. 1932, pp. 7–22.

69 D. Ritschel, 'A Corporatist Economy in Britain? Capitalist Planning for Industrial Self-Government in the 1930s', *English Historical Review*, 106 (418), 1991, pp. 41–65. Ritschel, *The Politics of Planning*.

70 E. H. H. Green, 'Searching for the Middle Way: The Political Economy of Harold Macmillan', in *Ideologies of Conservatism: Conservative Political Ideas in the Twentieth Century* (Oxford: Oxford University Press, 2002).

71 'Coming Courses, 1938', *Ashridge Journal*, 1938.

72 Macmillan, *Winds of Change*, p. 373.

73 A. D. Chandler, *Scale and Scope: the Dynamics of Industrial Capitalism* (Cambridge, MA: Harvard University Press, 1990), pp. 235–391.

74 'Coming Courses', *Ashridge Journal*, 1933.

75 The Anglo-Iranian Oil Company became British Petroleum in 1954 and was one of the seven largest multinationals in the world.

76 W. R. Garside, *British Unemployment 1919–1939: A Study in Public Policy* (Cambridge: Cambridge University Press, 1990).

77 'Coming Courses', *Ashridge Journal*, 1935.

78 A. Steel-Maitland, *The New America* (London: Macmillan, 1934), quoted in Green, *Ideologies of Conservatism*, p. 113.

79 A. Steel-Maitland to the House of Commons, 26 Nov. 1934, quoted in Green, *Ideologies of Conservatism*, p. 113.

80 'Coming Courses', *Ashridge Journal*, 1935.

81 *Ibid.*

82 E. J. Garmeson, 'As Others See Us: a Visit to the Bonar Law College at Ashridge', *Ashridge Journal*, Sep. 1935, p. 27.

83 The so-called YMCA group existed from 1924 to 1927. It was influenced by Noel Skelton and his book, *Constructive Conservatism* (London: Macmillan, 1924). The name YMCA was given to it by its critics.

84 Macmillan, *Winds of Change*, p. 322.

85 On the Conservatives' hostility towards the City, see E. H. H. Green, 'The Conservative Party and the City in the Twentieth Century: a Troubled Relationship', in P. Williamson and R. Michie (eds), *The British Government and the City of London in the Twentieth Century* (Cambridge: Cambridge University Press, 2004), pp. 153–73. also R. W. D. Boyce, *British Capitalism at the Crossroads* (Cambridge: Cambridge University Press, 1985).

86 J. M. Keynes, *The General Theory of Employment, Interest and Money* (London: Macmillan, 1936, 1973 edition), p. 376.

87 Oswald Mosley did not go to Ashridge. On Mosley's interest in Keynes, see R. Skidelsky, *Oswald Mosley* (London: Macmillan, 1975), pp. 299–315.

88 In *The Middle Way* (London: Macmillan, 1938), where he defended the nationalisation of the Bank of England to halt speculative activity and regulate the British financial system. The Bank was nationalised by the Attlee government in 1946.

89 E. J. Garmeson, 'As Others See Us: a Visit to the Bonar Law College at Ashridge', *Ashridge Journal*, Sep. 1935, p. 29.

90 *Ibid.*, p. 28.

91 L. Witherell, *Rebel on the Right: Henry Page Croft and the Crisis of British Conservatism, 1903–14* (Newark: University of Delaware Press, 1997).

92 H. Page Croft, *The Path of Empire* (Routledge/Thoemmes, 1912, 1988 edn). L. C. M. S. Amery, *Union and Strength, Papers on Imperial Questions* (n.p.: Arnold: 1912).

93 N. Case, 'An Ashridge Student Looks at the World. A Reply to "A Tory Looks at His World"', *Ashridge Journal*, Dec. 1933, pp. 27–9.

94 The diehards emerged within the Conservative party in 1911, in opposition to the Parliamentary Act on the reform of the House of Lords. In 1921, they were opposed to the creation of the Irish Free State. They were the

most vehement critics of the Lloyd George coalition. On the origins of the diehards, see G. D. Phillips, *The Diehards: Aristocratic Politics and Society in Edwardian England* (Cambridge, MA: Harvard University Press, 1979).

 95 Sir Charles Petrie, *Chapters of Life* (London: Eyre & Spottiswoode, 1950), p. 167.

 96 G. Ellis to A. Bryant, 23 Mar. 1934, Bryant papers, C52.

 97 A. Bryant to S. Baldwin, 2 Apr. 1937, Bryant papers, C53.

 98 G. C. Weber, *The Ideology of the British Right, 1918–1939* (Beckenham: Croom Helm, 1986), pp. 60–1.

 99 C. Williams-Ellis, *Britain and the Beast* (London: J. M. Dent & Sons, 1937) is an example of a cross-party collection of essays on urbanism as the Beast.

100 See D. Stone, *Responses to Nazism in Britain, 1933–1939: Before War and Holocaust* (Basingtsoke/New York: Palgrave Macmillan, 2003). 'The English Mistery, the BUF, and the Dilemmas of British Fascism', *Journal of Modern History*, 75 (2), 2003, pp. 336–58.

101 A. Johnston to A. Bryant, 13 Nov. 1936, Bryant papers, C52.

102 Minutes of the Governing Body, 24 Apr. 1934, Governing Body Agenda and Minutes 1934, Ashridge papers.

103 'Coming Courses', *Ashridge Journal*, 1936.

104 Admiral Sir B. Domville to A. Bryant, 10 July 1937, Bryant papers, C46.

105 Sir A. Wilson, *Thoughts and Talks* (RBC, 1934), p. 77, quoted in Green, *Ideologies of Conservatism*, p. 140.

106 W. Teeling, *Why Britain Prospers* (RBC, 1938), pp. 57, 67, quoted in Green, *Ideologies of Conservatism*, p. 148.

107 A. Roberts, 'Patriotism: the Last Refuge of Sir Arthur Bryant', in *Eminent Churchillians* (London: Weidenfeld & Nicolson, 1994), p. 287.

108 For a balanced discussion of Bryant's Tory patriotism/Nazi sympathies, see J. Stapleton, *Sir Arthur Bryant and National History in Twentieth Century Britain* (Lanham, MD: Lexington Books, 2006), chapters 7 and 8.

109 A. Bryant (ed.), *The Man and the Hour. Studies of Six Great Men of Our Time* (London: Philip Allan, 1934), chapter VII, 'Summary of the Editor'.

110 P. Street, *Arthur Bryant. Portrait of a Historian* (London: Collins, 1979), p. 106.

111 A. Bryant, *Unfinished Victory* (London: Macmillan, 1940), p. 233.

112 *Ibid.*, p. 232.

113 Lord Dacre to A. Roberts, 7 Aug. 1993, quoted in Roberts, *Eminent Churchillians*, p. 314.

114 A. Bryant to J. Hewitt, 28 Nov. 1968, Bryant papers, H1, quoted in Green, *Ideologies of Conservatism*, p. 148. The archives were opened in 1989, four years after Bryant's death.

115 A. Crossley to Parliament, 2 Mar. 1933, quoted in N. Thompson, *The Anti-Appeasers: Conservative Opposition to Appeasement in the 1930s* (Oxford: Oxford University Press, 1971), p. 58.

116 W. Churchill, 'Hitler and His Choice', in *Great Contemporaries* (1937), quoted in *ibid.*, p. 59.

117 The Conservative whips called them the 'glamour boys', a pejorative expression that referred to their elegance and concern for their appearance, and implied inefficiency and superficiality. *Ibid.*, pp. 167–8.

118 Stewart, *Burying Caesar*, pp. 339–40.

119 A. Bryant, 'Munich: Some Charges and Their Answers', *Ashridge Journal*, Christmas 1938, p. 26.

120 *Ibid.*

121 *Ibid.*, p. 33.

122 See G. Schmidt, *The Politics and Economics of Appeasement: British Foreign Policy in the 1930s* (Leamington Spa: Berg Press, 1986). Schmidt explains that although many Conservatives and members of government felt that Germany had been mistreated by the Versailles Treaty, which should be revised, they never questioned the post-war frontiers. In this respect, Bryant went much further than his contemporaries.

123 A. Chamberlain to Parliament, 13 Apr. 1933, in Thomspon, *The Anti-Appeasers*, p. 58.

124 R. Griffiths, *Patriotism Perverted: Captain Ramsay, the Right Book Club and British Anti-Semitism, 1939–40* (London: Constable and Co. Ltd., 1998), p. 70.

125 F. Yeats-Brown, *The European Jungle* (London: RBC, 1939).

126 M. Billig, *Banal Nationalism* (London: Sage, 1995). A. Roberts, 'Patriotism: the Last Refuge of Arthur Bryant', in Roberts, *Eminent Churchillians*, and Griffiths, *Patriotism Perverted*, have described Bryant as a Fascist. J. Stapleton offers a more balanced assessment of Bryant's political sympathies in Stapleton, *Sir Arthur Bryant*. See also R. Soffer, *History, Historians and Conservatism in Britain and America: From the Great War to Thatcher and Reagan* (Oxford and New York: Oxford University Press, 2009).

127 Stapleton, *Sir Arthur Bryant*, p. 126.

128 A. Bryant to Mr Greville-Heygate, 19 Oct. 1937, Bryant papers, C53.

129 C. J. M. Alport, 'Conservatism Today', included in C. J. M. Alport to R. A. Butler, 13 Feb. 1938, Butler papers, H88, fos 91–107.

130 Northam, *Conservatism, the Only Way*, p. 104.

131 For the importance for economic nationalist thinking in Britain before the 1930s, see Green, *Crisis of Conservatism*, pp. 159–83 and G. M. Koot, *English Historical Economics, 1870–1926: The Rise of Economic History and Neo-Mercantilism* (Cambridge: Cambridge University Press, 1987).

132 Burke and Disraeli were also studied in courses on Conservatism and on the history of ideas.

133 C. J. M. Alport to R. A. Butler, 13 Feb. 1938, Butler papers, H88, fos 91–107.

134 C. J. M. Alport, 'Conservatism Today', included in *Ibid.*, fos 97–107.

135 C. Dawson, 'Conservatism', *Ashridge Journal*, Sep. 1932, pp. 42–3.

136 *Ibid.*, p. 45.

137 *Ibid.*, p. 45.

138 The idea of 'organicism' was not confined to the Conservatives, but was also shared by New Liberals and Social Democrats, for whom an organic society

was an ideal to achieve. However, for the latter groups, the construction of an organic society required a certain degree of redistribution of wealth and goods. P. Clarke, 'The Social Democratic Theory of the Class Struggle', in J. M. Winter (ed.), *The Working Class in Modern British History: Essays in Honour of Henry Pelling* (Cambridge: Cambridge University Press, 1983).

139 R. Northam, 'Spiritual Values in Politics' (CPC, June 1949), CPA, C.P.C. No. 53.

140 Swinton College opened in March 1948 at Masham in North Yorkshire.

6

The Tory interpretation of history

> Though reason may be a good guide in politics, it is
> inadequate for the writing of history, and the very qualities
> which make Tories detestable as politicians should make
> them good historians.[1]

History constituted the core of teaching at Ashridge. Almost half the
university academics at the college were historians, and the majority of
classes and lectures were on history. After the First World War, recognition
of the influence of the Whig interpretation of English – meaning British –
history, which Conservatives regarded as virtually Socialist, led them to
believe they must rewrite their history. As Butterfield lamented, 'There
is not anything worth the name of "the tory interpretation of English
history".'[2]

The Whig interpretation of history

In 1950, the historian A. J. P. Taylor wrote,

> The Whig interpretation of history is easy to define; all our political thinking
> rests on it. It is the story of English liberty, founded by Magna Carta,
> consolidated by the Glorious Revolution, expanded by the great Reform
> Bill, and reaching its highest achievement with the Labour Government. In
> the words of Ramsay MacDonald, 'Up and up and up and on and on and
> on'. It is the doctrine of history as Progress: men always getting wiser and
> more tolerant; houses more comfortable, food more plentiful; new laws
> always better than old laws; new ideas always better than old ideas; new
> wives, I suppose, always better than old wives (this last much practised by
> the Whig aristocracy).[3]

Albeit supercilious, Taylor's observation summarised a widely shared
opinion, according to which the British political system rested upon
the Whig interpretation of history, that is to say, the idea of progress.[4]
Conservatives did not share this view. Without denying Britain's progress

and the positive evolution of its political system – Conservatives regarding themselves as 'progressives' – they questioned the manner by which the progress was realised and the factors that permitted it. 'Progress' did not exist on its own, and the measures that led a country to evolve were not themselves 'progressive'. Far from being, in Hegel's words, 'the march of God on earth' or the 'cunning of reason', history was the outcome of contingency and chance. Although Conservatives could detect God's presence in certain events, they discerned no overall design. As John Buchan, citing Burke, explained, 'we are therefore obliged to deliver up that operation [historical causation] to mere chance; or more piously (perhaps more rationally), to the occasional interposition and the irresistible hand of the Great Disposer'.[5] Conservatives were as critical of the notion of progress as they were hostile to abstraction in all its forms. In practice, they feared that universal suffrage would lead to the intensification of social demands. In her article against the methodology of certain Tory historians, Jenifer Hart emphasised the danger of thinking that social progress could be the result of chance and 'the historical process', rather than 'fierce battles' led by men and women. She argued that referring to 'impersonal historical forces' was a way of belittling 'the role of men and ideas' and the 'considerable effort and determination on the part of men (even if only of obscure men) who realised that it was worth while making a conscious effort to control events'.[6] For many Conservatives, the Whig interpretation of history seemed to anticipate the Socialist project. Both had in common the search for rationality through abstract theory. Thus Butterfield wrote, 'Men make gods now, not out of wood and stone, which though a waste of time is a comparatively harmless proceeding, but out of their abstract nouns, which are the most treacherous and explosive things in the world.'[7] Progress was one of the abstract words used by Whigs and recast by Socialists, for whom it was synonymous with Socialism. The political situation of the 1920s seemed to confirm this, since the 'new Whigs' from the radical wing of the Liberal party supported the Labour party and appeared to be responsible for the Labour party's victories in 1923 and 1929. There was an obvious parallel between them and the new Whigs of the 1790s, whom Burke criticised for their support for the French Revolution. This comparison reinforced the Conservative criticism of the naïveté of the Whigs, who were allegedly selling the British past to the Socialists. The 'old Whigs' of the 1790s, like Burke, acknowledged the mistakes of the Radical wing of their party, and the 'old Whigs' of the late nineteenth century did the same when they concurred with the Conservatives on the Irish question and became their political allies after 1886. Likewise, the advent of universal suffrage found most Whigs aligned with the Conservatives. After 1884, the

Whig interpretation of history seemed to raise the same problem both to Conservatives and Whigs. It was as if the Whigs lost control of the Whig interpretation of history, which took on a new and frightening dimension by becoming gradually assimilated to Socialist ideas. Just when a number of Liberals joined the ranks of the Conservatives, the latter amplified the dangers of Socialism and exaggerated the dangers of the Whig interpretation of history. J. H. Blaksley, congratulating Bryant on his book, *The Spirit of Conservatism*, wrote: 'I have thoroughly appreciated and enjoyed it, all the more so because I have thought for years that propaganda of the Tory outlook in a popular form was a national need. We shall never know the extent of the harm done by the Whig Radical monopoly of political thought and historical interpretation throughout the 19th century.'[8] The existence of a 'Radical monopoly' of political thought in the nineteenth century was of course quite untrue and testifies to the Conservatives' sense of being intellectually under attack. Blaksley taught at Ashridge and embarked, with others, upon the writing of a Tory interpretation of history of Britain.

An important contribution to this project was made by Keith Feiling in his two volumes on *A History of the Tory Party, 1640–1724* and *The Second Tory Party, 1714–1832*. The period Feiling examined was not a happy one for the Tory party, precursor of the Conservative party which arose after 1832. The Tory party, whose support for Church and Crown had been its *raison d'être*, faced in the seventeenth century the English revolution of 1640, the execution of Charles I, Cromwell's republican interregnum, the difficult Restoration, the 1688 Revolution and finally the Act of Settlement of 1701,[9] which excluded the Stuarts and other Catholics from succession to the throne and ensured the Protestant ascendancy of the Hanoverians, confirmed by the accession to the throne of George I in 1714. Feiling described the history of the Tory party as a series of errors committed by its leaders and certain royal figures such as Charles I and James II. He wrote:

> If obedience, then, were due to rulers, it must be due as Harcourt admitted at Sacheverell's trial and as Swift in public and private, to the whole community as represented in its legislature, and the divine rule was seen to be reflected in no static despotic order, but in the fluid and expanding claims of humanity ... the business of the new Tory thought of Swift, Bolingbroke and Pope was to build this broader conception of Nature, so far as might be, into the older Tory theory.... [Their works] measure the strides made by Tory speculation since the Oxford pundits of 1683 had condemned their party to immobility, and show, taken with their ... works as a whole, that in Tory theory – in spite of some inconsistencies, insincerities, and tawdry emotions – there still hovered a living germ, one day to be revived.... Yet,

from the first, the Whig contract ideas took with Swift and Bolingbroke a more concrete and historical form, and the right of resistance to oppression, conceded by them to be implicit in man's nature, was never by them grounded on the Lockeian system of abstract and equal rights. But the full working out of the historical and rational theory of conservatism was to take the greater part of a century, and in 1714 still lay for the majority far distant and undiscerned.[10]

For Feiling, the Tory party had adhered too long to the idea of a monarchy based upon divine right, which prevented it from developing a different approach to relations between the sovereign and the people that would establish a certain balance between authority and liberty. He did not have the same reading as some Whigs of the 1688 Revolution, which ended divine-right monarchy. For them, the Revolution introduced Locke's principles on a contract between the sovereign and the people. Feiling, on the contrary, saw in it a defence of the tradition wherein the King had authority over parliament. He described William III, who came to the throne in 1688, as 'more than happy to work with the Tories if the Tories would loyally accept him as their King, he was convinced that they were the natural supporters of the throne'.[11] The elections in 1690, which were favourable to the Tories, confirmed their support for the new king: 'this election, and the return of a Tory majority pledged to support King William … may be said to end the year of the Revolution. Monarchy *de facto* had triumphed indeed.'[12] The fact that both the 1689 and 1690 parliaments had declared that James II had abdicated and had not, in Lockean terms, 'broken his contract' and been put to flight, showed, for Feiling, that 1688 was a revolution 'not made but prevented'. He was one of the first historians to hold this position against the Whig interpretation of a revolution after which the king was 'elected' and not 'sacred'.

For Feiling, the period from 1690 to 1714 was a difficult period for the Tory party. The leadership of the party, particularly under Henry St John, later Viscount Bolingbroke, was shown to be maladroit at the time of the death of Queen Anne and the succession of George I. The party was regarded as the defender of the Jacobite cause. The Hanoverians considered the Tories traitors, and the eighteenth century was politically dominated by the Whigs. Feiling saw in the late eighteenth century, notably after 1783, when William Pitt the Younger became prime minister, a renaissance of Tory ideas and values. This revival was confirmed after 1789, when Pitt organised the struggle against the French Revolution both in Britain and in Europe. Feiling admired Pitt, not only for his hostility to the Revolution, but also because in the 1790s he introduced legislation aimed at ameliorating the fate of the poor and used taxes, paid by the rich, to finance the wars against France. For Feiling, it was thanks to

Pitt and Lord Liverpool, one of his successors, that the Tory domination was ensured until the end of the 1820s. But, like Hearnshaw, Feiling reproached Wellington and Peel for their poor leadership of the campaign against electoral reform from 1830 to 1832, as a consequence of which the Tory party suffered a catastrophic defeat in 1832. Feiling cited the Birmingham Radical Joseph Parkes, who remarked in 1832 that 'we have buried the Tories'. Feiling asked, 'What place was there for Tory principle in this charnel-house?' and replied:

> Much: if they [the Tories] realised that since the Revolution they had exhausted themselves in defence of eighteenth-century Whig monopolies, wherein a landed aristocracy should have all political power, and this power should be buttressed by an exclusive Church. If they cut away this incrustation, if they examined their original native forces in the light of the new world round them, they might yet find things to do and survivals of imperishable value. There was a Church, with a spiritual integrity and a spiritual sanction for a historic society. There was a Crown, tarnished ... but still with a role to play. And there was a people ... neglected, faction-ridden, almost revolutionary. But it was capable ... of living its new life and finding new happiness within ancient bounds and old affections.[13]

Feiling regarded the Tory interpretation of the events of 1688 as closer to reality and more just than the Whig interpretation as informed by Locke. Feiling's interpretation was essentially inspired by Burke and the idea of a balanced constitution. The Tories made a distinction between King James II and his attempt to impose radical changes in the structure of monarchical power, and the monarchy as institution. For them, 1688 had nothing to do with revolutionary principles, but rather with the preservation of a constitutional balance, in evolution since the time of Elizabeth. It was James II who was, in fact, revolutionary in his attempt to change the rules of the game in order to become an absolute monarch. His Catholicism and his absolutism made him an English counterpart to Louis XIV. The men of 1688 treated him as a foreigner who wanted to introduce a foreign religion and political principles. The Tories supported the 1688 Revolution and made it possible. Feiling emphasised the Tories' influence in the process that led to the Act of Settlement of 1701. He refused a purely abstract reading of the Revolution considered as the starting point of a contractual relation between the monarch and his subjects. The Whig interpretation, he claimed, presented the Tories, at worst as obstacles to the Revolution, at best as passive agents.

The Tory interpretation of history found echoes after 1918. The challenges confronting the Conservative party were, to some extent, similar to those of 1714 and 1832. In order not to repeat the mistakes made then, the Conservatives tried to understand the reasons for their failures and sought inspiration from Disraeli, who embodied the possibility of a Tory democracy. Contrary to the commonplace view that the Conservatives favoured an authoritarian regime and opposed freedom, Feiling drew upon a more Liberal tradition of Conservatism. For example, he offered a positive description of William Wyndham and the rural Tories' attitudes between 1719 and 1742 and their opposition to the 'robinocracy' of Sir Robert Walpole.[14]

A nation for all?

Rewriting the history of Britain, the Conservatives could demonstrate that they were the originators of important social reforms and that neither the Liberals nor the Labour Party could claim a monopoly of social reform.[15] In his *Sketches in Nineteenth Century Biography*, Feiling perceived in Robert Southey 'that never-yet wholly severed link between one sort of Tory and one sort of Socialist'.[16] For Southey advocated:

> prison reform, law reform, licensing, the game laws, adulteration, limitation of entail, heavier income-tax, restoration of parish government, a federal Empire – for twenty years Southey preached these things, to a generation of Tories worn by war and hag-ridden by economics.... *Laissez-faire* was to him principally the sin against society.[17]

Southey and the other poets of the Lake District were considered precursors of the Young England Movement and the Factory Reformers.[18] In *The English Inheritance*, George Kitson Clark, a professor of history at Cambridge and an occasional lecturer at Ashridge, wrote,

> Southey's theory, and Shaftesbury's for that matter, was really an extension of the old conception of the order of society. Christian society had a paternal duty towards the poor which could not be evaded whatever the economists said. This was essentially a Tory conception,... reflected in the generous romanticism of the Young England group in the 1840s, as also in the pages of Disraeli's best novels.[19]

The reference to the Young England movement and to Disraeli was part of the claim to a Conservative heritage of social reforms. Disraeli claimed he was one of the first working-class MPs elected to parliament in 1879. Alexander Macdonald declared to the House of Commons: 'The Conservative party have done more for the working class in five years than the liberals have in fifty.'[20] Macdonald referred to the Artisans' Dwelling Act of 1875 and to the public health and hygiene reforms of 1876, which Disraeli described as measures to 'elevate the condition of the people'.[21]

Disraeli's measures to alleviate the condition of the people showed his will to bridge the gap between what he called in his political novel, *Sybil*, the 'two nations', the rich and the poor.[22] The Ashridge historians, writing on the contemporary period, similarly sought to present the Conservative party with a human face and as the party of a united nation. Although the nation meant the United Kingdom as a whole, the term was, *de facto*, more often used as a synonym for England. Hence Kitson Clark explained: 'The English ... were English before they were British. What has been inherited from their English past has been and still is of the greatest importance.'[23] He accepted the complexities of this identity:

> there is not one English heritage, there are many ... There are local traditions, North and South, West Country and East Anglia, urban traditions, rural traditions, and the peculiar traditions of London.... Running across these are economic divisions, and social divisions.... Party politics ... have helped to create different types of Englishmen with contrasted ways of thought ... probably the most persistent and penetrating permanent division in English history has been between Church of England man and Protestant Dissenter.... Yet all are Englishmen, the very tension set up by their conflict is an important part of the national heritage.[24]

Despite regional particularism, Englishness was a unifying theme and a rallying cry. The force of this theme was also recognised by Feiling, who wrote in 1930 that the Conservative party was founded on 'specific historical, or unhistorical, claims ... and only in history can be found its philosophical defence. Its own version has sometimes been fanciful, but invariably insular; and if, proceeding farther, we called it an English party, in distinction to Britain at large, historically we should not be much amiss.'[25]

The history of the United Kingdom would in fact be the history of England. Likewise Bryant entitled his book on the history of Britain, *English Saga, 1840–1940*, and dedicated it to 'Lord Queenborough, Englishman'. For Feiling as for Bryant, Englishness and conservatism were synonyms. In this respect, they echoed Disraeli, who declared, 'My politics are described by one word, and that word is England.'[26]

Disraeli had a very precise idea of England in mind. Bryant wrote of him that, 'Like Burke he [Disraeli] preferred the instinctive wisdom and prejudice of the older England. An intellectual himself, he fell back on instinct and precedent: on the accumulated wisdom of generations tested by experience.'[27] The Tory interpretation of history emphasised the English *instinct* formed by English institutions and traditions. This instinct derived from the fact that love of liberty was learnt, not taught. It was acquired naturally by the respect for law and English institutions and by the practice of ancestral traditions. Those traditions, dating back to the Middle Ages, were represented in exemplary fashion in the sixteenth century by the Tudor dynasty. Bryant explained that 'in the two and a half centuries after the Conquest ... England was governed by four very great kings. Afterwards one has to wait for nearly two centuries till the Tudors for any real political leadership.' Although the fourteenth and fifteenth centuries seemed to him politically superficial, he wrote: 'what impresses me about those two centuries is the wonderful creative genius which the English appeared to possess ... most of all, in that wonderful English architecture, the perpendicular'. The Middle Ages witnessed the apogee of a certain form of society, the feudal society, whose cultural creativity was unsurpassed. The only failure was the system of government, which is why 'the Tudor Age seems so splendid to us ... though alot of its new men were vulgarians compared with their predecessors.... Tudor sovereigns, with their splendid political sense, canalized the energies of the race into profitable channels and, above all, into those oceanic channels.'[28] In many respects, Conservative historians sought to construct the equivalent of the Whig version of the seventeenth century, with 'the Ancient Constitution and the Feudal Law'[29] as the origin of English liberties. While the Whigs spoke of 'Tudor despotism', the Conservatives saw in the Tudor dynasty an example of ordered freedom. Claiming the notion of the ancient consti-tution and feudal law for themselves, the Conservatives added the idea of a hierarchical society, and of the importance of customary law in the judicial and institutional system. Bryant added: 'At the back of Disraeli's mind lay always certain ancient English ideals – the one Tudor the other medieval – of a united nation and of a continuing community.'[30] The Ashridge historians thus established a genealogy of Tory history.

Precise national characteristics were associated with this heritage. Bryant explained: 'It was because it had so strong a sense of its own strength, sanity and inherent decency that the England of character and tradition felt it had so little to learn of foreigners.'[31] The vocabulary of decency, character and tradition was a very Baldwinian one and formed part of the semantic field the Conservative party sought to make its own, in response to the idea that the Socialists had a more developed social conscience. Decency signified respect for practices, and mutual respect was a key term of 1930s Conservatism. Recasting the Socialist arguments, Bryant sought to show that Socialism had not invented anything in social matters and that the traditional values of Conservatism had nothing to learn from foreign theories. For Conservatives of Ashridge, the first critics of *laissez-faire* and the first ones who proposed social reforms were not Socialists. Bryant wrote that 'during the middle and later [eighteen] forties the novels of Dickens, Disraeli and Charles Kingsley, the pamphlets of Carlyle and the poems of Elisabeth Barrett Browning educated the reading classes in the Condition of the People question and stimulated their desire for social reform'.[32] Likewise, he described John

Ruskin as 'a great teacher ... who had impressed on younger consciences the ideal of social responsibility'.[33] For Bryant, the difference between the Conservative reformers of the 1840s to 1850s and the Socialists was that the former sought harmony between the social classes, while the latter were adepts of the social struggle.

Baldwin belonged to the tradition of Conservative reformers. The reforms of the health system in the 1920s, and the 1925 Act on widows' and orphans' pensions, were promulgated by his government. Hence, Bryant wrote:

> Despite the obvious disabilities of the existing system, the British electorate, though largely composed of working men, even continued to send Conservative majorities to Parliament. But they probably would not have done so but for Baldwin. This kindly liberal-minded and characteristically English politician so obviously shared the ordinary Englishman's humane ideal that when he told them that he was working to bring about a better England they believed him. They had no idea how he was going to bring it about, nor, it now seems, had he. The only thing that was certain ... was that it was going to take a very long time. For Baldwin, like his Socialist vis-à-vis, Sydney Webb, believed in the inevitability of gradualness.[34]

Beyond the irony of this last remark, the essential differences between the gradualist rhetoric of Baldwin and that of Webb were, first, the involvement of workers in the changes, and second, the role of the state. The Baldwinian Conservatives of Ashridge sought a happy balance between individualism and what Butterfield called 'the deification of the state'.[35] They saw in the happy balance the very expression of Englishness, and it is why Baldwin was the incarnation. Butterfield insisted upon the fact that love of country was not equated in Britain with a deification of the state, just as British individualism was not based on an abstract idea but 'is rooted in tradition and sentiment. The individualism on the one hand, the love of country on the other hand, are less likely to be dangerous when growing in this kind of earth – less likely to devour one another.... Men may sometimes be better than their doctrines precisely as the prejudices, the sentiments, the traditions prevail.'[36]

The Tory interpretation of history was the writing of Englishness and the national characteristics that distinguished England from other countries. Butterfield continued: 'Just as the French from 1789 trumpeted men's abstract rights and broke with history and tradition,... we in the same cause of liberty ran out to greet the past, taking our stand on the historic rights of Englishmen.'[37] For the Conservatives, this Englishness found its most eloquent expression in the expansion of the Empire and the idea of a 'Greater Britain'.

The expansion of England

The history of the Empire was the privileged domain for the writing of Tory history. Butterfield remarked in 1945 that 'the real alternative to whig history in recent times – the real tory alternative to the organisation of English history on the basis of the growth of liberty – was the story of British expansion overseas'.[38] The history of the Empire was the history of a partnership between the colonies and Britain, and not that of domination of the one by the other. C. J. M. Alport, for example, in 1937 wrote *Kingdoms in Partnership*, in which he defended the idea of a Commonwealth with autonomous dominions. Charles Carrington, one of the Ashridge historians, became editor of *The Cambridge History of the British Empire*. The idea of a Commonwealth was to integrate into the Empire colonies that had a strong national identity, in order to demonstrate the Empire's capacity to create harmony at the international level. The history of the British Empire thus became the story of the construction of a liberal Empire with a human face, different from the colonial empires of other powers. Bryant wrote: 'The proud imperialism of England was founded on a very real love of liberty and on a certain innate if vigorous humanity which the Englishman, and the English gentleman in particular, possessed as his distinguishing traits.... The outward march of the Union Jack brought enduring benefits that easily compensated for any temporary suffering and injustice.'[39]

This vision of Empire challenged the criticism made at the beginning of the century by people close to the Labour party. The political economist, J. A. Hobson, for example, published in 1902 a highly critical tract, *Imperialism: A Study*, which appeared in a third edition in 1938 without changes to the original text.[40] He simply added a long introduction to explain the reasons why his opposition to the Empire remained valid.[41] Conservative historians opposed Hobson, who regarded the Empire as anti-democratic and a financial liability. One of the courses at Ashridge in February 1935, for example, was centred on the criticisms of the Empire by authors such as Hobson. It was entitled 'Dictatorship and Democracy' and included classes on 'Germany under Hitler, Italy under Mussolini, Fascism, Socialism and the path to Dictatorship, British Democracy, and *The Democratic Ideal of the British Commonwealth of Nations*'.[42] The Empire was presented as the very embodiment of democracy. From 1930 to 1939, Ashridge proposed twenty-seven courses on the Empire as well as 159 lectures. It was the theme that came up most regularly, which reflected both the aims set at the foundation of the College, that is to say, the study of the British constitution 'with special reference to the Empire'[43] and the conclusions of Hearnshaw's book on the future tasks of conservatism, one of which was to preserve the Empire. As Hearnshaw explained,

> One of the main elements of hope and confidence for the future is the existence of the vast commonwealth of nations known as the British Empire.... Communists loathe it as the main obstacle to the triumph of their propaganda; Bolsheviks ceaselessly plot against it as the chief barrier to their advance towards world dominion; socialists of the milder type speak of it with dislike or contempt as something unfavourable to their little schemes; even liberals tend to be lukewarm.... But to conservatives the Empire's continued existence, its growing solidarity, its closer federation, its progressive development, its increasing prosperity, are matters of vital importance. The Empire stands in the world as a monument of freedom, of justice, of peace, of health, and of general well-being.[44]

Hearnshaw's statement was an eloquent, slightly bombastic riposte to the critics of Empire.

For the Conservatives, the case of India illustrated the mistake made by people like Hobson. Trade with India, in particular British textile exports, had been an important source of income and employment since the nineteenth century; several articles on Lancashire and India in the *Ashridge Journal* focused on this topic.[45] It was therefore not a financial liability: quite the contrary. On the other hand, the fact that Britain had outlawed Suttee,[46] ended the cult of Thugee[47] and introduced the rule of law in place of the authoritarianism of the princes, was proof of the democratic ideal of the Empire, which had abolished India's most barbaric customs while preserving its culture.

In 1929, Lord Irwin, the viceroy of India, supported the objective of granting India Dominion status. This announcement prompted strong reactions within the Conservative party. In October 1932, Ashridge organised a lecture entitled 'The history of the British Empire, India and the Dominions since the war', which was the first of a series of courses and lectures on the status of India. Between 1932 and 1935, they followed the rhythm of government bills: in September 1933 a lecture on constitutional reform in India, in October a debate on the government's White Paper, in August 1934 a discussion on the report of the Royal Commission on India, and in October an extra class on Indian constitutional reform. In 1935 a special weekend course on the Indian question was organised. These courses created controversy, and in 1933 the college was accused of inviting lecturers who were too favourable to the reforms proposed by the government.[48] Tensions within the Conservative party over Indian self-rule, between 1929 and 1935, showed Baldwin as a great reformer. Lord Irwin wrote to Davidson in 1930:

The day is past when you can make nations live in vacuums. The day is also past in my humble opinion when Winston [Churchill]'s possessive instinct can be applied to Empires and the like. That conception of imperialism is finished, and those who try to revive it are as those who would fly a balloon that won't hold gas ... The thing just won't work.[49]

The Ashridge lecturers were, as a whole, favourable to the 1935 India Act. In March 1931, Baldwin declared in the House of Commons that the party sought to achieve 'the granting of self-governing institutions with a view to the progressive realisation of responsible Government in India as an integral part of the Empire'.[50] It was thus not a question of independence, but of a modernised conception of imperial relations. One of the numerous articles on India in the *Ashridge Journal* explained that India had a long tradition of administrative institutions, on which it could rely for government, and that 'no Conservative will deny that the genius of a nation is enshrined in its institutions'.[51] The existence of a strong national identity did not seem incompatible with India's presence within the Empire.

The attitude of Ashridge historians towards India stood in stark contrast to that of the hard-core imperialists such as Page Croft, Lord Lloyd or Churchill. But it was not only on the subject of Empire that the Ashridge historians sought to distinguish themselves from their traditionalist colleagues. Their aim was to write a Tory, but not a reactionary, history which would redefine the Conservatives' position in relation to the Whig interpretation of history.

The Tories, the Whigs and Englishness

In his critical study of the Whig interpretation of history in 1931, Butterfield considered that one of its main errors was that 'it is part and parcel of the Whig interpretation of history that it studies the past with reference to the present ... with direct and perpetual reference to the present'.[52] The Ashridge historians' fear of the Whigs' use of history 'with reference to the present' diminished between 1930 and 1940, while their own historical outlook evolved during the decade and changed radically during the war. In 1945, in *The Englishman and His History*, Butterfield modified his objection to the Whig interpretation of history, affirming that 'the Whigs ... lay hold on an eternal sameness in the English system', and that 'their greatest service is not to the historiography but to the English tradition'.[53] The Conservative opposition to the Whig interpretation of the past was actually more ambiguous than it seemed. For example, practically all Conservative historians admired T. B. Macaulay, the Whig historian of the early nineteenth century and Liberal MP. As Hearnshaw explained:

'It was Macaulay who first roused my enthusiasm for history, and I have never ceased to admire him, and to enjoy reading him, in spite of the criticism to which he has been subjected.'[54] In 1932, Bryant wrote an extremely favourable biography of Macaulay, and in 1935 his grandson, G. M. Trevelyan, wrote to Baldwin:

> What a good Conservative Macaulay would have made if he had lived a few years longer, till the time when the Second Reform Bill came up! The thought comforts me now that I am a Conservative myself, though today conservatism is no longer trying to ward off Democracy, but to sustain Democracy against the consequences which Macaulay prophesied would follow from its adoption – ie communistic or militaristic despotism. Whiggism and Conservatism are not opposed as fundamental principles. Indeed I remember Arthur Balfour saying to me that he agreed with every one of Macaulay's political principles, which would have somewhat astonished his supporters.[55]

That Trevelyan, the Whig historian par excellence, should refer to his grandfather in those terms and admit to his change of political allegiance was remarkable and showed the extent to which, in the 1930s, the Whig tradition converged with that of the Conservatives.

This rapprochement of the Whig and the Tory interpretations followed the rapprochement between the Liberals and the Conservatives. In 1929 the Liberals and the Conservatives had been in opposite camps, which enabled the Labour party to take office, but in 1931 many Liberals supported the National government, which was dominated by the Conservative party. Most of the National-Liberals stuck to the government, even when tariff protection was introduced in 1932. Baldwin's landslide victory in 1935 showed the distance covered by each side, and confirmed that the traditional antagonisms between the majority of Liberals and the Conservatives had virtually disappeared. This evolution was mirrored by the number of National-Liberals invited to Ashridge and can be seen in Trevelyan's declaration to Bryant in 1935: 'It is my hope and belief that your Toryism, without ceasing to be Toryism, is broadening into Englishry, as I hope my Whiggery has to some extent so broadened in the course of years.'[56] Trevelyan was not the only Liberal intellectual to enlarge the ranks of the Conservative party. For example, Ernest Barker, professor of politics at Cambridge, wrote to Bryant in 1938: 'I am bothered to-day by the abstract intellectualism of them with whom I used to associate, and by the conventional lip-service to phrases in my old party – the Liberal party.'[57] The conservatism embodied by Baldwin was easily assimilable by Liberals; and doubtless, the decline of Liberalism diminished the feeling of belonging to the Liberal party. The Second World War marked a further stage in the convergence between Conservatives and Liberals.

It may be said that the aim of the Conservatives was less to replace the Whig interpretation of history than to diminish what they considered to be its excess. In 1945, Butterfield wrote that 'the development of historical study in this country since the time of Coke has been the gradual toning down of this initial Whig interpretation, the curbing of the extravagances associated with its first exuberant period'.[58] The Conservatives' contribution to the history of Britain was one of the crucial elements in the moderation of Whig 'extravagances', which in turn altered the interpretation of the role of the Conservative party in Britain. With regard to the Conservatives' contribution to the historiography of their country, Butterfield wrote: 'The "Tories", when (for example) they return *Magna Carta* to a feudal context, help the cause of historical study by insisting on the differences between the past and the present.'[59] He contrasted this approach to that of the Whigs: 'It is the virtue of the whigs that they not only bent the history, so to speak, but they made it more bendable for all the future; they made it possible to preserve continuity while taking the XIXth century to democracy.'[60] Hence it was the dialectics between the two approaches that made the British constitution possible. For Butterfield, as for Feiling, the British constitution was 'the result of the continual interplay and perpetual collision of [Whig and Tory principles]'.[61] It was this balance that the Ashridge historians sought to attain in their historical writing, at a time when Socialist advances seemed to endanger the very foundation of this dialectic.

Whigs and Tories shared a common definition of Englishness, made of a love of liberty, which was allegedly particular to the English.[62] One of the longest entries in the index of Bryant's *English Saga* was 'Liberty, English passion for'. In 1945, Butterfield suggested that the history of Empire was the Tory alternative to the Whig interpretation of history, since they were both characterised by 'advances in the direction of liberty',[63] while taking different routes. He thus concluded:

> Attempts were made to give currency to this organisation of the story of England, but the whiggism that is in all Englishmen declined to take the imperialistic version to its heart. Now, however, even this structure of the history of England is a tory alternative no more; and only in recent times have we come to see how this epic of British expansion has been swallowed into the original system of the whigs. Perhaps only in the shock of 1940 did we realize to what a degree the British Empire had become an organisation for the purpose of liberty. What power is in this English tradition which swallows up monarchy, toryism, imperialism, yet leaves each of them still existing, each part of a wider synthesis.[64]

Butterfield, like many others after 1940, accepted that the Whig interpretation constituted the very framework of British history, that it was an element of cohesion for the nation, which remained united thanks to its love of liberty in a war against all forms of oppression. But he added that numerous contributions over time had made it less a Whig history than a truly British history. In the face of a common enemy, differences of interpretation faded, giving way to a common conception of the nation. The common enemy was not only foreign dictatorships, but also, he claimed, the more insidious enemy, Socialism in Britain. Butterfield explained that, even if revolution was historically an important force of change, the Whigs sought to avoid it, in contrast with the Radical Socialists. Butterfield praised the English genius of progressive change and gradual evolution which, like other Ashridge historians, he saw as the synthesis of both Whig and Tory interpretations of history.

> The system that we have inherited from the whigs replaces the doctrinaire quest for the highest good.... It implies ... a reluctance to bring things to a decision until something like the general sense of the nation makes itself clear. All these things, so often mute, so often inglorious, weigh heavily on men who have responsibility; but they are mere feathers to the impatient armchair politician. They are aspects of that self-limitation which is necessary for those who seek to co-operate with history.[65]

Writing in 1945, shortly before the general election, it seems likely that Butterfield was seeking to convince Liberals of the Whig tradition to join the Conservatives in the defence of English liberties.

When, in 1930, the Ashridge historians began their research, their aim was to devise an alternative to the Whig interpretation of history. The Socialist threat seemed to be the natural consequence of Whig radicalism. During that decade, their vision of history evolved and their appreciation of the Whig interpretation increased. The acknowledgement of their proximity was the result of the political evolution in Britain and the rise of political extremism on the Continent. The perils created a sense of common inheritance. Just as the Whigs and the Tories had created a common front against Napoleon, so a rapprochement occurred in the face of Nazism. In each case the Continental threat bore a doctrinaire and uncompromising attitude. As Butterfield put it, in 1790, 'at the very moment when the Whigs appeared to be passing over to doctrinarism, they adopted, so to speak, a new resolution in favour of the alliance with history'.[66] The Whigs saw Jacobinism and the Nazi regime as horrific expressions of the consequences of theory and abstraction. Bryant wrote: 'What the menace of Nazi ideology and aggression is to-day, that of French Jacobinism seemed to our stubborn forefathers.'[67] Butterfield went further: 'The French Revolution brought tragedy for the generation upon which it fell – tragedy for France and for Europe not unlike that which resulted from the Nazi Revolution of 1933.'[68] This vision of Britain as the depositary of an anti-doctrinaire heritage shaped the writing of its history and the conception of the British community. It produced a model of democratic evolution, in which the rights of citizens were anchored in history.

Notes

1 A. J. P. Taylor, 'Tory History', in *Essays in English History* (London: Hamish Hamilton, 1976), pp. 18–19.

2 H. Butterfield, *The Englishman and His History* (Cambridge: Cambridge University Press, 1944), p. 2.

3 Taylor, 'Tory History', pp. 17–18.

4 See J. Hart, 'Nineteenth-Century Social Reform: A Tory Interpretation of History', *Past & Present*, 31, July 1965, pp. 39–61.

5 J. Buchan, 'The Causal and the Casual in History', in *Men and Deeds* (n.p.: John Murray, 1935), p. 20.

6 Hart, 'Nineteenth-Century Social Reform, pp. 60–1.

7 Butterfield, *The Englishman and His History*, pp. 128–9.

8 J. H. Blaksley to A. Bryant, 10 June 1929, Bryant papers, C17.

9 The Act of Settlement of 1701 altered the law of succession to the British throne to ensure only Protestant descendants succeeded the kings of England and Scotland. As a result, Sophie of Hanover inherited the Stuart throne, since she was the closest Protestant relation.

10 K. Feiling, *A History of the Tory Party, 1640–1714* (Oxford: Oxford University Press, 1924), pp. 492–3. For an analysis of how Tories sought to 'out-Whig' the Whigs in the early eighteenth century, see Q. R. D. Skinner, 'The Principles and Practice of Opposition: The Case of Bolingbroke versus Walpole', in N. McKendrick (ed.), *Historical Perspectives: Studies in English Thought and Society* (London: Europa, 1974), pp. 93–128.

11 Feiling, *A History of the Tory Party*, p. 256.

12 *Ibid.*, p. 272. This was an English interpretation, for in Scotland the parliament implicitly accepted a contractual interpretation of James's overthrow.

13 K. Feiling, *The Second Tory Party, 1714–1832* (London: Macmillan, 1938), p. 396.

14 *Ibid.*, pp. 29–41.

15 See Soffer, *History, Historians*.

16 Robert Southey, with Wordsworth, Shelley and Coleridge, was one of the Lake poets, who lived in the Lake District between 1790 and 1830.

17 K. Feiling, *Sketches in Nineteenth Century Biography* (London: Longmans, Green & Co, 1930, New York: Books for Libraries Press, 1970), p. 78.

18 R. Faber, *Young England* (Faber & Faber, 1987).

19 G. Kitson Clark, *The English Inheritance* (London: SCM Press Ltd, 1950), p. 155.

20 Hearnshaw, *Conservatism in England*, p. 217.

21 B. Disraeli, 1874 Manchester Speech. Of course, it was Disraeli's home secretary, Cross, who was the real instigator of these reforms.

22 B. Disraeli, *Sybil: or The Two Nations* (London: Longmans, Green, 1871 edn).

23 Kitson Clark, *The English Inheritance*, p. 13.

24 *Ibid.*, p. 16.

25 Feiling, *Sketches in Nineteenth Century Biography*, p. 174.

26 B. Disraeli, *Gallomania*, 1832, in W. F. Moneypenny and J. E. Buckle, *The Life of Benjamin Disraeli, Earl of Beaconsfield*, Vol. I (London: John Murray, 1929 edn), p. 214.

27 A. Bryant, *English Saga, 1840–1940* (London: The Reprint Society, 1942), pp. 99–100.

28 A. Bryant to G. Barraclough, 24 Dec. 1953, Bryant papers, E1.

29 J. G. A. Pocock, *The Ancient Constitution and the Feudal Law: A Study of English Historical Thought in the Seventeenth Century* (Bath: Cedric Chivers, 1974).

30 Bryant, *English Saga*, pp. 98–9.

31 *Ibid.*, p. 31.

32 *Ibid.*, p. 78.

33 *Ibid.*, p. 210. Ruskin in fact came to be seen by Edwardian Conservatives as a key Tory social reformer. See for example George Wyndham's positive views on Ruskin in various letters in J. W. Mackail and G. Wyndham, *Life and Letters of George Wyndham*, 2 vols (London: Hutchinson & Co, 1925).

34 *Ibid.*, p. 330.

35 Butterfield, *The Englishman and His History*, p. 128.

36 *Ibid.*, pp. 132–3.

37 *Ibid.*, p. 104.

38 *Ibid.*, p. 81.

39 Bryant, *English Saga*, p. 30.

40 J. A. Hobson, *Imperialism: A Study* (New York: J. Pott & Company, 1902. The 1938 edition was published in London by Allen & Unwin Ltd.) In 1902, Hobson was a leading New Liberal, but by the 1930s he had joined the Independent Labour Party.

41 P. J. Cain, *Hobson and Imperialism: Radicalism, New Liberalism and Finance, 1887–1938* (Oxford: Oxford University Press, 2002), pp. 220–4.

42 'Coming Courses for 1935', *Ashridge Journal*. My italics.

43 Bonar Law Memorial Trust Deed, 21 Nov. 1929, Ashridge papers.

44 Hearnshaw, *Conservatism in England*, pp. 304–5.

45 For example, B. Ellinger, 'Lancashire and India', *Ashridge Journal*, Sep. 1934.

46 Suttee was the custom whereby, at the death of a man, his wives were all burned with him.

47 The cult of Thugee required its followers to strangle men as a sacrifice to the goddess Kali.

48 R. Hoskins, Report on the courses in 1933, n.d. (Mar. 1933), Education Committee Minutes 1934, Ashridge papers.

49 Irwin to J. C. C. Davidson, quoted in J. Charmley, *Lord Lloyd and the Decline of the British Empire* (London: Weidenfeld & Nicolson, 1987), p. 172.

50 *Ibid.*, p. 178.

51 J. E. Webster, 'An Indian Government for India', *Ashridge Journal*, June 1932, p. 27.

52 Butterfield, *The Whig Interpretation of History*, p. 11.

53 Butterfield, *The Englishman and His History*, pp. 78–9.

54 F. J. C. Hearnshaw to A. Bryant, 4 Nov. 1932, Bryant papers, E2.

55 G. M. Trevelyan to S. Baldwin, 31 Mar. 1935, Baldwin papers, SB170.

56 G. M. Trevelyan to A. Bryant, 1 Aug. 1935, Bryant papers, E2.

57 E. Barker to A. Bryant, 7 Oct. 1938, Bryant papers, E1.

58 Butterfield, *The Englishman and His History*, pp. 72–3.

59 *Ibid.*, p. 78.

60 *Ibid.*, p. 79.

61 Butterfield, *The Whig Interpretation of History*, p. 41.

62 P. Langford, *Englishness Identified* (Oxford: Oxford University Press, 2000).

63 Butterfield, *The Englishman and His History*, p. 81.

64 *Ibid.*, pp. 81–2.

65 *Ibid.*, p. 98.

66 *Ibid.*, p. 81.

67 Bryant, *English Saga*, p. 57.

68 Butterfield, *The Englishman and His History*, p. 110.

7

Educating for citizenship

In *What Is Conservatism?* Keith Feiling explained that the principles of Conservatism must not rest upon 'abstract propositions and theoretical rights', rather 'on history [and] the interpretation of the past'.[1] The importance of history as a discipline led one of the founding members of the Association for Education in Citizenship to place history at the heart of the teaching of citizenship: 'The contribution made by the study of history to an understanding of contemporary conditions and to an appreciation of our national heritage can be pre-eminent if it is recognised that the type of historian required is he who looks upon the study of the past largely as a means of interpreting the present.'[2] The notion of citizenship encompassed the relationship between the individual and the community, the individual's rights and duties and the search for social harmony. Every year Ashridge organised a course on citizenship, which was dedicated to the teaching of civics. It was aimed at young people from modest backgrounds. Ashridge wished to be seen as 'a residential College of Citizenship – the first to be founded in England. It exists for the man and woman in the street.'[3]

Since the 1920s, citizenship had become a subject of study in both the academic and the political worlds. From 1916 onwards, the war, rationing, censorship and new regulations led to an expansion of the concept of solidarity. How would society honour its debts to those who had shed their blood for it? Trade unionists and former soldiers of all political leanings, but also women, particularly those who had worked in arms factories during the war, demanded a new definition of their rights as citizens. Lloyd George's promise made in 1918 to create 'Homes fit for Heroes' must be honoured.

Education and citizenship

Education and citizenship were partly linked. In the inter-war years, when the school leaving-age was fixed at 14, the majority of voters had received only a primary education. Educating the electorate became a preoccupation for successive governments. In 1926, the Hadow Report recommended making secondary school education compulsory up to the age of 15, and that education in citizenship should become part of the secondary school curriculum. The report was very well received. The London County Council's education commission proposed an education for 'public life', which would be compulsory and provided by governmental organisations run by volunteers and politicians.[4] In 1934, Sir Ernest Simon, a Liberal industrialist from Manchester, established the Association for Education in Citizenship. In the foreword to *Training for Citizenship*, 6,000 copies of which were printed by the Association, Herwald Ramsbotham, the Conservative MP for Lancaster and parliamentary secretary to the Board of Education, affirmed that 'fitness for citizenship is one of the objectives which the schools of this country should keep before them'.[5] Education, Simon explained, whether general or professional, commonly 'ignore[s] a man's third great function in life: his membership of the community'.[6] Dictatorships sought their citizens' 'docile obedience',[7] whereas democracies wanted active citizens. They should 'have a deep concern for the good life of [their] fellows,… have a sense of social responsibility and the will to sink [their] own immediate interests, and the interests of [their] class, in the common good'.[8]

It was a matter of working out how citizenship should be taught. Ramsbotham wrote to Simon in 1934, 'if citizenship is, as I suppose it is, a combination of intellectual, moral and social qualities, it is a big job to have to "teach" it, particularly by the direct method as a school subject'.[9] In her article 'Methods of Training for Citizenship', Eva Hubback described the teaching of history and geography as a means of understanding the present. She explained that the study of history, particularly contemporary history, was fundamental to understanding political, economic and social problems. Celebrating events in history and the anniversaries of great men provided good public role models. Team-work was also important in understanding how to live within a community. Voluntary organisations such as the Women's Institute, the Rotary Club, the Women's Citizen Association, political parties and the BBC should contribute to the teaching of citizenship.[10] In May 1936, a newspaper called *The Citizen* was launched. The first edition contained editorials from Norman Angell, Ernest Barker, G. P. Gooch, Cyril Norwood and Lord Passfield (Sidney Webb), academics and writers who favoured the teaching of citizenship and became members of the executive board for the Association for Education in Citizenship. Writing in *The Citizen*, Ernest Simon complained, 'we still believe in common sense and muddling through…. We have no tradition of respect for intellectual solutions in public affairs. We must create one or perish.'[11] Simon's comments were similar to those of the Conservatives at Ashridge, in that he rejected demagoguery and feared dictatorships.

Ashridge participated in a wider movement for the promotion of civic training, and it established many links with associations pursuing the same objective. Bryant was a member of the executive committee of the Association for Education in Citizenship, although he was the sole Conservative to sit on the committee. Similarly, Ernest Barker, who wrote for *The Citizen*, was regularly invited to Ashridge. The management there was keen to prevent Socialists from appropriating and monopolising the term 'citizen'. While preparing for a conference at Ashridge in partnership with the Association for Education in Citizenship, Bryant wrote to Simon:

> With Attlee speaking combined with the predominant Left Wing names on our Council, we must be careful or we may find ourselves defeating our own object which is to secure for our Association the support of all political parties, particularly that of the Conservative Party which has, perhaps, hitherto interested itself less in such matters, and which for some time past has been deeply suspicious of Left Wing views in the world of education.[12]

For Conservatives it was a matter of defining the idea of citizenship in their own way. The College aimed to produce 'good citizens of sound constitutional views',[13] or better, to promote 'a sane and traditional view of citizenship without bias or propaganda'.[14] The words 'traditional', 'sane' and 'sound' were synonymous with 'conservative'. When the principal, Reginald Hoskins, brought up the question of teaching the principles of conservatism at Ashridge, he suggested that direct and explicit references to Conservatism were not necessary. As he explained to a party official, the teachers at Ashridge offered 'sound economic and constitutional views'. He added: 'In the past ... several young men of radical tendencies were awarded scholarships.... The result of the course was that they were converted to Conservatism.'[15] The terminology used at Ashridge differentiated the Conservatives' view of citizenship from that of the Left.

An important difference concerned the rights and duties of citizens. Speaking on the rights of citizens, Stanley Baldwin wrote, 'the assertion of people's rights has never yet provided that people with bread. The performance of their duties, and that alone, can lead to the successful issue of those experiments in government which we have carried further than any other people in this world.'[16] On the duties of the citizen, he invoked 'the spirit of the British regiment',[17] and appealed to the idea of service as it was understood in the army. In his book *Service of Our Lives* he wrote: 'Let us dedicate ourselves ... to the service of our fellows, a service in widening circles, service to the home, service to our neighbourhood, to our county, our province, to our country, to the Empire, and to the world. No mere service of our lips, service of our lives.'[18] Baldwin saw himself as 'a man of service to the nation'. He proved himself a model citizen when, as parliamentary secretary to Bonar Law during the First World War, he refused all pay and in 1919 donated £120,000 to help pay off the war debts.[19] The term 'service', like 'nation', was contrary to the rhetoric of class warfare and was supposedly politically neutral, yet it could be used in extremely politicised contexts. For example, Baldwin praised a public schoolboy for volunteering to break the General Strike in 1926, 'thanking him for his national service'.[20] In Baldwin's speeches, phrases such as 'service to the nation' were linked to the defence of the nation's constitution and consequently British society as a whole. As he saw it, Socialism was the greatest threat to the constitution and to society, as demonstrated by the 1926 strike. Ashridge was established to combat this threat. In 1954, CCO recalled that Urban Broughton had been one of Ashridge's most important donors 'because he was deeply concerned at the danger of what in those days was known as Bolshevism'.[21] The struggle against Bolshevism and all forms of Socialism was a way of defending the constitution and society. Baldwin seldom spoke of Conservatism, but instead of the shared ideas of service, fraternity and the nation. Thus, in 1938 Sir John Simon, leader of the Liberal Nationals, praised his speech 'The Torch I Would Hand On'.[22]

Writing in May 1930, the Conservative MP, Michael Seymour, complained that too many local MPs were creating jobs by employing their supporters, using tax-payer's money and the council budget. In his view, 'municipal life is badly in need of men and women filled with the desire for social service rather than with personal ambition'.[23] Seymour's criticism was aimed at Labour, but also employers who neglected their civic duties: 'The manufacturer or the employer in an industrial area must not keep his sense of social service for his suburban home.... He must concentrate his energies on the place from which he derives his income.' He did not forget the youth: 'Young men and women must not let the natural claims of leisure and pleasure prevent them from serving their country in an environment in which they will find plenty of interest.'[24] He believed it was a matter of overcoming the sense of apathy that stemmed from an increased sense of self-centredness in society, by instilling a sense of duty. As with altruism,[25] service was useful to both society and the individual. The development of the individual within society depended upon it. Altruism went hand in hand with philanthropy, with the richest giving charity to the poorest. The idea of service emphasised duty and equality of sacrifice.[26] In this respect, it was a Conservative concept. The frequent reference to the army (soldiers are of course 'service men') illustrated the importance they attached to the concept. In some ways the soldier was the model citizen, as his duty was to serve king and country.

Although the army was seen as a role model by the Conservatives, they did not worship it in the way dictatorships did. The difference between democracies and totalitarian regimes became the backdrop to a conference on 'The Challenge of Democracy', held at Ashridge in July 1937. It was organised by the Association for Education in Citizenship together with Ashridge, and was 'the first inter-party conference on the problems of democracy to be held in this country since the rise of the modern totalitarian state',[27] according to Sir Ernest Simon. Representatives from the three main political parties were invited. Lord Halifax, Sir William Beveridge and Clement Attlee all addressed the conference. The relationship between Ashridge and the Association for Education in Citizenship appeared to be in good shape, but Bryant's correspondence suggested otherwise. In the months leading up to the conference, T. N. Graham, secretary of the Ashridge Trust, twice wrote to Bryant about the threat posed by the Association. 'I may arrive at 10.20 in order that our forces may be suitably disposed before the enemy attacks', and 'before the Philistines descend upon us'.[28] Bryant, for his part, sought Baldwin's participation in the conference. He wrote to Davidson:

> If the P.M. would agree to address the Conference and make its location at Ashridge the condition of his doing so – which my Socialist colleagues on the Executive are prepared to agree to – there is no doubt that it would enormously strengthen Ashridge's position in the intellectual and academic world. So far as criticism from the stupider elements of our own side is concerned, we should be able to protect ourselves a) by the P.M'.s presence, b) by the strength of the right wing element represented in the lecturing list, which I will take very good care of, and c) by the fact that the course was arranged not by Ashridge authorities, but by the National Council for Education in Citizenship to which in the ordinary, legitimate course of our letting, we have let the College.[29]

Beyond the unease expressed by Graham and Bryant were profound differences of interpretation. In his lecture on 'The Purpose of Democracy',[30] Lord Halifax refuted 'the Benthamite definition of the purpose of government as being "the greatest happiness of the greatest number"'. Instead, he offered his own view of government as an 'instrument to secure conditions favourable to the fullest possible development of personality.... In a sense the British character has always been, and I trust will always remain, strongly individualist.' Attlee and Simon, less in favour of individualism, developed a more communitarian vision. Attlee claimed that a true democracy required economic equality: on this point he differed from both Halifax and Simon. For Simon, economic equality was unnecessary, although economic security and the guarantee of a minimum salary for all were basic conditions for democracy.[31]

Conservatives rejected the universal character of the rights of man, thus distinguishing themselves from Liberal and Labour spokesmen. And because they were unequal, their social rights could scarcely be the same. Keith Feiling wrote of Samuel Taylor Coleridge,[32] of whom he was a fervent admirer: 'He found the roots of this evil system [Jacobinism] in the deduction of all men's social rights from Reason.... Bare reason was, in his eyes,... the science of cosmopolitanism without country, of philanthropy without neighbourliness or consanguinity, in short, of all the impostures of that philosophy of the French Revolution which would sacrifice each to the shadowy idol of all.'[33]

Citizenship and voluntary action

Conservatives rejected the abstract idea of universalism in favour of embedding citizenship within the nation's history. For them, citizenship could not be the product merely of a certain form of government and made sense only as an expression of a particular political system. Far from being a revolutionary ideal, citizenship was something acquired or earned. It was not decreed, but constituted the culmination of a historical process. It contributed to integration and social cohesion. As Hugh Sellon wrote: 'The State, to the Conservative, is not an artificial creation which may be changed and reshaped according to the capricious desires of the moment, but an organic growth, formed with infinite pain and difficulty during many centuries.'[34] The state can only develop organically through the establishment by citizens of voluntary associations. The absence of such associations was one of the weaknesses of totalitarian states, whether communist or Fascist. In Sellon's words, 'There is a weakness latent in Fascist Italy, just as there is in Nazi Germany, and that is the danger of what has been called "Statolatry" – the glorification of the regimented State, to the virtual suppression of all individuals and sectional interests.'[35] By comparison, Britain was a democracy blessed with a vast network of voluntary associations.

Ernest Barker, the originally Liberal professor of politics, who was a regular at Ashridge, wrote that society was 'the whole sum of voluntary bodies and associations contained in the nation ... with all their various purposes and with all their institutions'.[36] They were essential, since they played an important 'educational' role in civic training. Baldwin, referring to friendly societies, created in the nineteenth century to provide insurance to the unemployed and the sick,[37] declared:

It is not wasting words to try to realise what the great friendly society movement stands for.... [It] has been a great instrument during a period of rapid change in instructing our people in some of the greatest of the principles which should guide their lives.... The whole spirit of the movement is service for others.... By teaching our own people the spirit of service which the friendly societies inculcate, we are playing our part in making our democracy fitter and nobler.[38]

The friendly societies depended upon neither philanthropic bodies nor the state. They embodied the ideal of citizenship of Liberals in the nineteenth century and Conservatives in the twentieth. For Liberals, it was a matter of individual freedom; for Baldwin the emphasis was on the communal role of the associations. This ideal explained the Conservatives' attitude towards trade unions. They were in favour of them so long as they operated as economic actors and did not become embroiled in the world of politics. For Conservatives, working conditions were not the responsibility of government but of the trade unions, which must remain apolitical. In his homage to the friendly societies, Baldwin highlighted the importance of separating politics from unions and voluntary associations: 'I am glad that in the friendly society movement we know no politics ... I am thankful that this movement has never been captured by any of the political machines.'[39] In this respect, the model citizen was not interested only in politics but also had many non-political interests, and their contribution to society could be achieved in many other ways. As Bryant wrote in 1945: 'If democracy is not to founder, on the shifting quicksands of apathy, ignorance, suspicion, exploitation, impotence, anarchy and Party despotism, a meeting-place must be found where citizens of all classes and opinions ... can study and debate the problems they have to decide. To say that we cannot afford it is beside the point; if we are to remain a democracy and gather the fruits of victory we cannot afford to do without it.'[40]

Participating in associations not only contributed to civic education, but also served as a springboard for citizens to take a greater part in local life. It was a matter of creating 'some form of public service and so helping to create an active instead of a passive democracy',[41] in which citizens engaged in 'various forms of public service, both statutory and voluntary'.[42] This argument, made in the 1930s, was still a topic for discussion after 1945, with the arrival of the welfare state and the accession of a Labour government.

In 1945, when Labour took office, the Conservative party drew upon the work undertaken at Ashridge in the inter-war years. In 1946, at the annual Conservative party conference, Anthony Eden set out the Conservatives' counter-proposals to Labour reforms. At the heart of this project was the idea of 'a property-owning democracy'.[43] This idea had already been incorporated into Conservative thinking since the nineteenth century. Following the third Reform Act in 1884, many Conservatives, including the party leader, Lord Salisbury, spoke of the need to build 'ramparts of property'[44] against the Socialist menace. From the start of the 1890s until 1914 the Conservatives focused on the development of agricultural small-holdings. Thomas Wrightson, a Conservative MP for Stockton, had envisaged the enlargement of working-class access to property. Throughout the nineteenth century, the relationship between property and citizenship remained at the heart of debates on the extension of the franchise. The suffrage was a badge of citizenship. Being a householder was seen as demonstrating one's ability to be civic minded and socially responsible. Those in receipt of Poor Law relief were denied the right to vote. Being able to support oneself and one's family financially was the first duty of the citizen. Those who could not contribute to the well-being of the community or became a burden upon it demonstrated a lack of responsibility, which was punishable by the withdrawal of citizenship.

The extension of the franchise following the end of the Great War, first in 1918 to all adult males and to adult women over 30 years of age who met certain property ownership qualifications, and later in 1928 to all adult women, led to a new definition of citizenship, which now conferred the right to vote. Yet the relationship between citizenship and property did not disappear. Defining citizenship remained a matter of dispute between Labour and Conservative parties. The decision of the Lloyd George coalition government in 1921 to grant uncovenanted payments, that is to say, unemployment benefit to those who had not paid in to the system, a policy extended by the Labour government in 1924, prompted strong objections from Conservatives; the Conservative government of 1924–29 reduced the number of beneficiaries of this aid. In 1929, in the face of growing unemployment, the Labour government restored this assistance, although it was obliged to reduce it by 10 per cent in 1931. The reduction provoked discontent among the majority of the cabinet and a crisis that led to the resignation of the Labour government and its replacement by a National government in October 1931. When the National government in 1932 introduced means testing for beneficiaries, the Labour opposition, led by George Lansbury, protested vigorously. Outside London, Wal Hannington's National Unemployed Workers' Movement organised numerous demonstrations against the means test and the requirement of the unemployed to prove that they were actively seeking work. Women whose husbands were in work were excluded from the system. The National government introduced steadily more restrictive conditions on assistance to the unemployed. The justification for the restrictions was that the government had a

> Duty to defend and fortify the national character by abolishing the lingering abuses of the dole, by stopping the demoralisation caused by indiscriminate charity, by stirring up the contentedly lazy to useful and elevating self-help, by ending those appeals to anti-social cupidity which have been the main cause of 'the corruption of the citizenship of the working man'.[45]

For Hearnshaw, the deterioration of the 'sense of citizenship among workers' was the result of the Socialist programme wrapped in 'the seductive title of "social reform"'.[46] Hearnshaw and the Conservatives recognised in the October 1931 general election results the resistance to this programme from the majority of the electorate, particularly from voters who 'have long possessed the franchise'.[47] The Conservatives were evidently still nervous about the socio-economic consequences of extending the vote. Those who had obtained the vote before 1918 and owned property had, it seemed, demonstrated their sense of civic responsibility and social maturity. However, since the right to vote could not be reversed, enabling as many as possible to become property owners was the most effective means of developing their sense of responsibility.

In November 1932, during a weekend course at Ashridge, the Conservative member of parliament T. J. O'Connor lectured on 'The Ideals of Toryism: A Property-Owning Democracy'.[48] The Conservative party returned to this subject after the Second World War, although it found that 'it takes an immense amount of reiteration to get a thing of this sort across to the public'.[49] Here, as in other areas, Ashridge was the precursor.[50]

The citizenship training provided by Ashridge reflected the Conservatives' idea that the English were free made, not free born.[51] Citizenship was learned, acquired or merited; it was not a natural and universal right. As set out in the *Ashridge Journal* in 1932,

> Citizens should equip themselves with knowledge of its [the nation's] problems and of current events ... to meet the needs of the present, students will devote their studies to three departments: History – chiefly post-war history, that they may have some understanding of how the present position in the world arose; economics ... and Current Affairs, to give the young citizen a knowledge of the problems confronting the nation at the moment. A nation is, after all, merely the sum total of its citizens. A healthy, contented and prosperous nation can only be built up of healthy, contented and prosperous citizens. This Eight Weeks' Course, brief though it is, aims at showing the way to this conception of citizenship.[52]

Citizenship touched on the relationship between the individual and the state. The political context of the 1930s prompted reflection on democracy and the totalitarian regimes. The conflict between them or, as Hugh Sellon wrote, the 'conflict between the "totalitarian" state and the state of free citizens',[53] did not prevent Conservatives such as Sellon from admiring certain characteristics of totalitarian states. Thus he wrote,

> it [the Italian corporate State] encourages the free producers of national wealth, both employers and wage-earners, to combine among themselves, to settle their own disputes, to make their own regulations regarding contracts .... In short, the producer of wealth in Italy is taught to regard himself, not as an isolated individual,... but as a member of a great confraternity of fellow-workers, whose interests are his own, both because the prosperity of the industry as a whole is his also, and also because on the harmonious working of the industry depends the national wealth in which he, as a citizen, shares. This is a return to a finer and more liberal form of the old trade guild of the middle-ages and to the spirit of medieval Christianity brought into contact with and applied to the needs of the modern state.[54]

The connection between the corporatist state and the feudal system explains the admiration of some Conservatives for authoritarian systems. In corporatism, it was not so much the authority they appreciated as the socio-economic structure that opposed free trade and created a network of social links. The sense of community and mutual relations amongst citizens, as well as the role of the state as catalyst for these relationships, led Christopher Dawson to say he wished for

> a return to the organic conception of society, and the resurrection of the traditional principle of political authority. Conservatism stands above all for the preservation of inherited tradition of our civilisation and the defence of the higher cultural values in a society against the new mass movement that threatens Europe with a return to barbarism.[55]

Britain could benefit from a corporatist state without necessarily becoming Fascist. The mass movements and the fear they aroused were the subject of Ortega y Gasset's *The Revolt of Masses*, published in 1930.[56] Tradition, an organic concept of society and the protection of national heritage pointed to the benefits of the feudal system and rural communities. Conservatives stressed the relevance of feudal values in contemporary society.[57] They were attracted by the idea of citizenship based upon the reciprocity of relationships between the individual and the constitution. Citizenship embodied, as they saw it, the fundamental values of conservatism: it was an individual quality and not a universal right or an abstract concept. It was acquired through education based upon history and the sense of continuity which gave each nation its distinct character. Citizenship flourished in an organic society, that is to say, a society that was more than just an aggregate of its individual members and was a genuine community. Civic equality was seen as a more socially integrative goal than social equality, which was thought to be based on class differentiation, which in turn carried the possibility of class division and conflict. Furthermore, social equality necessarily emphasised the material realm, and was therefore deemed to undervalue all other aspects of daily and community life. Construed in this way, citizenship became a counter-poise to the language of class conflict.

When Arthur Bryant called for a place where citizens could get together, he insisted on the importance of it being a place open to everyone, to encourage debates, 'not merely on the highest level but on that of the ordinary man'.[58] In order to become a citizen and not just a voter, a trade unionist or a campaigner, the man in the street, it was claimed, must receive an education. This was the responsibility handed to Ashridge, and it was there that thought was given to the possibility of creating a middlebrow discourse, or more generally speaking, a middlebrow culture.

Notes

1 Feiling, *What Is Conservatism?* p. 8.
2 E. M. Hubback, 'Methods of Training for Citizenship', in Sir E. Simon and E. M. Hubback, *Training For Citizenship* (Oxford: Oxford University Press, 1935), pp. 17–44, at p. 23.
3 A. Bryant, *The Story of Ashridge, the Bonar Law Conservative College, Mar. 29*, Bryant papers M62.
4 See R. Barker, *Education and Politics, 1900–1951* (Oxford: Oxford University Press, 1972).
5 H. Ramsbotham, foreword to Simon and Hubback, *Training for Citizenship.*
6 *Ibid.*, p. 8.
7 *Ibid.*, p. 10.
8 *Ibid.*, p. 14.
9 H. Ramsbotham to E. Simon, 3 Dec., 1934, Bryant papers, C28.
10 Hubback, 'Methods of Training for Citizenship'.
11 E. Simon, 'Public Opinion and Education', *The Citizen*, May 1936, p. 5.
12 A. Bryant to E. Simon, 3 June 1937, Bryant papers, C92.
13 R. Hoskins, Report on the 1933 session, undated, Mar. 1934, Education Committee Minutes 1934, Ashridge papers.
14 R. Hoskins, undated memorandum, Jan. 1934, Education Committee Minutes 1934, Ashridge papers.
15 R. Hoskins to Mr. Lee, 10 Apr. 1934, Education Committee Minutes 1934, Ashridge papers.
16 S. Baldwin, 'Democracy and the Spirit of Service', speech delivered in London on 4 Dec. 1924, in *ibid.*, p. 71.
17 Baldwin, *On England*, p. 66.

18 S. Baldwin, *Service of Our Lives: Last Speeches as Prime Minister* (London: Hodder & Stoughton, 1937), p. 144.

19 Williamson, *Baldwin*, p. 139. £120,000 is equivalent to at least £3 million today and represented a fifth of his personal wealth. (Given that one could purchase a substantial house near Hyde Park for £1,000 in the 1920s, which would have a market value of several million pounds today, 'at least' is an understatement.)

20 Hughes, *A London Family Between the Wars*, pp. 101–3, quoted in McKibbin, *Classes and Cultures*, p. 59.

21 Summary of Reasons for Ashridge, Bonar Law Memorial Trust Bill, n.d. 1954, CPA, CCO 3/4/29.

22 Sir E. Simon 'The Faith of a Democrat', in Sir E. Simon *et al.*, *Constructive Democracy* (London: George Allen and Unwin Ltd., 1938), pp. 25–6.

23 M. R. Seymour, 'Local Government in a London Industrial Area', *Ashridge Journal*, May 1930, p. 39.

24 *Ibid.*, p. 43.

25 The idea of altruism first appeared half way through the nineteenth century and became an important subject in Victorian and Edwardian society. See Collini, *Public Moralists*, pp. 60–90.

26 In 1931, 'Equality of Sacrifice' became the government's watchword when it came to introducing severe cuts to the national budget, particularly to unemployment benefits.

27 E. Simon, preface to Simon *et al.*, *Constructive Democracy*, p. 16.

28 T. N. Graham to A. Bryant, 28 Jan. 1937 and 29 Jan. 1937, Bryant papers, C53.

29 A. Bryant to Lord Davidson, 27 Nov. 1936, Bryant papers, C53.

30 Lord Halifax, 'The Purpose of Democracy', in Simon *et al*, *Constructive Democracy*.

31 C. Attlee, quoted in Simon, 'The Faith of a Democrat', pp. 16–23.

32 Coleridge was a key figure in British Conservative thinking. In *On the Constitution of Church and State* (Hurst, Chance & Co, 1830), he developed a theory of the organic nature of society which was contrary to Jeremy Bentham's and James Mill's utilitarian ideas.

33 Feiling, *Sketches in Nineteenth Century Biography*, pp. 93–4.

34 H. Sellon, 'The River of Conservatism', *Ashridge Journal*, Aug. 1931, p. 25.

35 H. Sellon, 'The Corporate State', *Ashridge Journal*, Sep. 1933, p. 24.

36 E. Barker, quoted in Green, *Ideologies of Conservatism*, p. 262.

37 The individual paid monthly contributions in order to benefit from unemployment and sickness insurance. The friendly societies insured, for example, burial in a cemetery rather than in a communal grave. See E. Hopkins, *Working-Class Self-Help* (London: UCL Press, 1995).

38 Baldwin, *On England*, pp. 263–4.

39 *Ibid.*

40 A. Bryant, in Street, *Arthur Bryant*, p. 127–8.

41 Education Council Minutes, 5 Oct. 1948, Minutes of the Education Council 1947–1949, Ashridge papers.

42 Education Council: Sub-Committee on the Ashridge Circles and Publications, 5 Oct. 1948, Ashridge papers.

43 A. Eden at the annual Conservative party conference (NUCA), Blackpool, 3 Oct. 1946, quoted in A. Eden, *Freedom and Order, Selected Speeches, 1939–1946* (London: Faber & Faber, 1947), pp. 394–5.

44 De Laveleye, *The Land System of Belgium and Holland*, in J. W. Probin (ed.), *Systems of Land Tenure in Various Countries* (Cobden Club, 1871), quoted in A. Offer, *Property and Politics, 1870–1914: Landownership, Law, Ideology and Urban Development in England* (Cambridge: Cambridge University Press, 1981), pp. 148–58.

45 Ramsay MacDonald, *News Chronicle*, 15 Sep. 1932, quoted in Hearnshaw, *Conservatism in England*, p. 290.

46 Hearnshaw, *Conservatism in England*, p. 291.

47 *Ibid.*, p. 292.

48 T. J. O'Connor, 'The Ideals of Toryism: A Property-Owning Democracy', 18–21 Nov. 1932, Governing Body Minutes, 1932, Ashridge papers. The expression 'property-owning democracy' can be attributed to Noel Skelton in 1924. J. Barnes, 'Ideology and Factions', in A. Seldon and S. Ball (eds), *Conservative Century: The Conservative Party since 1900* (Oxford: Oxford University Press, 1994), p. 326.

49 The Leader's Advisory Committee, 21 Oct. 1946, quoted in J. Ramsden, *The Age of Churchill and Eden*, p. 141.

50 The declarations made by Eden and others in 1946 were again taken up and developed with the abolition of Schedule A Tax on one's main residence in 1963, the council house sales to sitting tenants in 1971 and the Housing Act in 1980 and 1982.

51 One is not 'born' free but rather one 'becomes' free.

52 *Coming Courses*, Oct–Nov. 1932, *Ashridge Journal*, Feb. 1931.

53 H. Sellon, 'The Corporate State', *Ashridge Journal*, Sept. 1933, p. 24.

54 *Ibid.*, p. 19.

55 C. Dawson, 'Conservatism', *Ashridge Journal*, xi, Sep. 1932.

56 J. Ortega y Gasset, *The Revolt of the Masses* (London: Allen & Unwin, 1932).

57 On implementing feudal values in urban society, see Chapter 9.

58 A. Bryant in Street, *Arthur Bryant*, p. 127–8.

8

Fighting the 'battle of the brows'

One of the most consistent claims of the British Conservative party has been its anti-intellectualism. Indeed, the notion that Conservatives were uninterested in ideas and anti-intellectual has been a constant theme in the historiography of British Conservatism and a crucial component of Conservatism itself.[1] The familiar stereotype of the pragmatic, abstraction-avoiding, unintellectual Conservative (an ongoing stereotype since the French Revolution), as well as the equally enduring cliché of the verbose and pretentious Continental philosopher) was reinforced by the Conservatives' claim that they recognised and understood a more general British cultural valorisation of 'common sense' over reason, which led them to present themselves as representatives of 'national' values. The Conservative self-description was thus interwoven into a broader, enduring national stereotype that British culture – or more specifically English culture – was peculiarly hostile to intellectuals. In *Absent Minds. Intellectuals in Britain*, Stefan Collini shows how anti-intellectualism came to be such an important component of the construction of national identity in Britain, and how it was internalised by intellectuals themselves.[2] The debate around intellectuals in Britain is remarkably synthesised by the inter-war Conservative party's simultaneous apparent abhorrence and obsession with intellectuals, with understanding what an intellectual is or should be and what a Right-wing intellectual might be, as opposed to a Left-wing intellectual. In the same way that Collini notes a large presence in Britain of intellectuals who deny being intellectuals – what he calls the 'absence thesis' or the 'tradition of denial' – Conservatives seemed to have internalised that, as Conservatives, they were necessarily anti- or un-intellectual. Julia Stapleton labels them the 'non-intellectual intellectuals'.[3] Against the political extremes that were perceived to have flourished on the Continent, British, or rather English, exceptionalism was seen as deriving from its hostility to abstract-minded intellectuals.

By and large, Conservatives' suspicion has been directed at a specific category of intellectuals, namely 'highbrow' intellectuals who dwell upon abstract theory '*à la française*'. Because the French Enlightenment allegedly gave rise to the Revolution and the Terror, Conservatives have dismissed theorists and the intellectuals of the Left as dangerous, pretentious and dogmatic. Thus, for instance, Hearnshaw accused the French revolutionaries of attempting to introduce 'changes too rapid and too complete, changes made without respect for tradition ... [which] tried, with deplorable results, to start everything afresh on mechanical lines according to the abstract formulae of Rousseau's *Social Contract*'.[4] By the same token Feiling proudly cited a letter of 1791 from a British officer who described a demonstration in London in which participants cried out, 'No philosophers! Church and King!'[5] In this respect the Conservatives' anti-Socialism was derived directly from Burke's *Reflections on the Revolution in France*[6] and his counter-revolutionary contemporaries. In 1923 Baldwin expressed his contempt for 'exploded continental theorists',[7] reflecting Conservative hostility towards an intellectual model imported from abroad.

Against abstraction

Conservatives lay claim to a national intellectual model strongly inspired by Burke, which gave rise to a conception of the 'intellectual' that differed markedly from the French model. In *The Politics of Imperfection*, Anthony Quinton affirms that 'the doctrines of traditionalism, organicism and political scepticism [are] the defining characteristics of a genuinely conservative point of view', and adds that 'these three doctrines are the most prominent and persistent features of Burke's political thought'.[8] They also form the foundation of Quinton's theory of the imperfection of human reason and explain humankind's chronic inability to grasp the complexity of the world around it. Because they too accept the fallibility of reason, Conservatives favour an empirical approach to political and social issues. Burke thus explained: 'The science of constructing a commonwealth, or renovating it, or reforming it, is, like every other experimental science, not to be taught *a priori*.'[9]

Thus the 'Conservative intellectual' was less an oxymoron than an ideal firmly rooted in tradition and established practice. The tensions between various usages and meanings of the term 'intellectual' in the inter-war period became prominent in what Collini called 'the battle of the brows', which culminated in the late 1920s and early 1930s, around the time of the creation of Ashridge College.[10] The terms 'highbrow' and 'lowbrow', which first appeared in the United States before the First World War, were imported into Britain during the war. Originally they described different types of consumers, highbrows being better-off and more selective consumers, lowbrows representing the mass consumers.[11]

The term 'middlebrow' appeared for the first time in Britain in an article in *Punch*, the satirical magazine, which described middlebrows as 'people who are hoping that some day they will get used to the stuff they ought to like'.[12] While Virginia Woolf spoke scornfully of the sort of people who were 'betwixt and between',[13] George Orwell defended the middlebrow, pointing out that 'art is not the same thing as cerebration'.[14] Hostility to all forms of intellectualism is key to understanding the term middlebrow. One of the objectives of the Book Guild, an inter-war book club, was to 'avoid indulging in the deplorable affectation of recommending as a work of "genius" the sort of thing which is dubbed clever simply because it is mainly unintelligible and written in an obscure manner, or boosting some foreign work simply because it is foreign, and the author's name difficult to pronounce'.[15] The 'development of a specifically middlebrow literature'[16] at the end of the 1920s was linked to a glorification of English culture as practical, common sense and middle of the road, with a certain confusion between the social and cultural classifications. Middlebrow writers were not confined to one political party and were to be found on the Right as well as the Left. A. J. Cronin and J. B. Priestley, for example, were middlebrow writers who belonged to the Labour party.[17] Cronin, Priestley and Orwell represented a form of Left-wing anti-intellectualism for whom 'theory is middle-class, experience working-class'.[18] Orwell thus wrote, 'The English are not intellectual. They have a horror of abstract thought, they feel no need for any philosophy or systematic "world-view".'[19]

Although the term middlebrow was not associated with a particular political party, it was soon appropriated by the Conservative party, for which it became a useful defensive strategy against the perceived intellectual dominance of the Left in general. The looseness of the term was precisely what made it attractive. The middlebrow was important 'for those who felt under threat, marking a new boundary of cultural discrimination, which divided the general educated audience from the high intelligentsia'.[20] 'The language of "brows"'[21] offered the educated public a defence against the high intelligentsia and the European sophistications, which were commonly associated with Socialism and appeared to threaten the essential values of British society.

The middlebrow existed only in opposition to the highbrow. The reason for this hostility was eloquently expressed by Leonard Woolf, *bête noire* of the middlebrow. In his satirical study, *Hunting the Highbrow*, published in 1927, Woolf humorously explained why highbrows like himself and other members of the Bloomsbury group were considered dangerous.

> The highbrow intellectual … is an animal in whom this faculty for enjoying the use of his intellect is abnormally developed. Sometimes he is content to

confine the exercise of his intellect to safe subjects.... But there have always been a certain number of highbrows who insist upon applying the intellect to all subjects and all departments of life – and then the trouble begins. If you begin to think about religion, or the relation of the sexes, or the party system, or education, or patriotism, you are lost, but, what is much more serious, they are lost too. They are the superstructures of illusions and prejudices, and as soon as reason is applied to their foundations they come down with a crash.[22]

A 'crash' was precisely what the Conservatives wished to avoid. They, on the contrary, demanded an approach based upon 'illusions and prejudices' derived from a particular historical context. Burke had insisted upon the importance of 'the wisdom of ancient prejudice' as a factor of peace and order in society, claiming that prejudice and traditions formed the very foundation of society and its proper functioning.[23] Proceeding from society's traditions and myths and integrating them into common thought enabled one to understand and shape society. Highbrow intellectuals threatened to sap the very foundations of society by challenging the prejudice on which it was built. In Woolf's words, 'Nothing is so dangerous as thought applied to the structure of society, for once people begin to think, you let in the highbrow, and anything may happen.'[24] Middlebrow intellectuals could only agree with this warning. They set out to write the 'island story'[25] of Britain, with its distinct traditions and institutions, which over a long period and lived experience gave rise to the nation's prejudice and stereotypes. They claimed that it echoed Burke's ideas on the state which required the power to effect change in order to conserve the essence of its identity. The opposite was also true: the state had to know how to save its essence in order to transform itself. In contrast, the highbrow thinker was thought to select certain aspects of the past in order to build an idealised vision of the future. Thus, while the middlebrow was perceived as basing his analysis upon existing structures, the highbrow was seen as proposing only utopian projects.

According to Woolf, 'One's judgement of the intellectual highbrow must depend ... very much upon one's estimate of how far and how widely it is possible that mankind may be induced to apply reason to the arrangement of their communal affairs.'[26] Woolf was 'convinced that if men would allow intellect and reason rather than passion and prejudice to have a say in their communal affairs, a good deal of the sordid ugliness and misery would disappear from society'.[27] Michael Oakeshott described this as the 'jump to glory style of politics':[28] the naïve and dangerous idea that reason is a sufficient tool for understanding and resolving complex social issues.

The golden mean

The post-war work of Michael Oakeshott provided tools for understanding the notion of the middlebrow as it emerged during the inter-war years and the way it was used by Conservatives. Oakeshott distinguished between practical and technical knowledge, a distinction central to the middlebrow critique of Socialism.[29] Technical knowledge was akin to a user's manual, whereas practical knowledge was something acquired through experience, allowing one to formulate judgements. Technical knowledge could be formally taught and learned by rote; practical knowledge was something acquired over time, through a combination of questioning and reflection. Oakeshott contrasted what he called 'rationalist' objectives based upon technical knowledge with Conservative objectives based upon experience, using a maritime metaphor. Rationalists would plot a precise course to attain a certain destination, assuming they had sufficient navigational instruments to do so, whereas Conservatives would seek, more modestly, simply to stay afloat. But to remain afloat did not mean remaining immobile. On the contrary, according to Oakeshott, a ship seeking to stay afloat was akin to a state that permitted civil society and associative life to thrive. The social links would be stronger and more complete than in political life. To focus exclusively upon the ship's capabilities was to focus too narrowly upon pure politics. This is what the Labour party sought to do in organising society according to a formal and uniquely political model, as if one could govern by means of a ready-made model.

Oakeshott's work can thus be used to present one approach to conceptualising the middlebrow. Some space existed between abstract and practical thinking, between the highbrow and the lowbrow, which allowed for the fact that, as Oakeshott put it, 'men are not wholly unintellectual, there is always some modicum of theory behind their actions even if it unexpressed and almost entirely unrealized'.[30] It was precisely this 'modicum of theory' that was important and made the difference between middlebrow thinking and the over-elaborate theories of Socialists and highbrows.

Constitutional history, as written by Conservatives, reflected the notion of 'a modicum of theory' in men, as opposed to an abstract system imposed from outside history. In *Hunting the Highbrow*, Woolf regretted that '[n]ot only the educational system, but the Press, our party system in politics, the theory of the British Constitution, our legal system, the doctrines of religion and patriotism are all ingeniously calculated to make the use of the intellect suspect and unpopular'.[31] Woolf was challenging the stereotypical image of Conservatives. But while some Conservatives did indeed contribute to this stereotype, the 'Fabians' of Ashridge claimed they were not suspicious of reason itself, but rather of those people who imagined they could rely exclusively upon the application of reason. The historians at Ashridge responded to the stereotype in their histories of the Conservative party. Thus Feiling wrote,

> The Whig contract ideas took with Swift and Bolingbroke a more concrete and historical form, and the right of resistance to oppression, conceded by them to be implicit in man's nature, was never by them grounded on the Lockeian system of abstract and equal rights. But the full working out of the historical and rational theory of conservatism was to take the greater part of a century.[32]

Conservatives at Ashridge embraced Swift and Bolingbroke because they did not think in abstract terms, but rather in concrete, historical terms. History was perceived as illustrating man's desire to become free, and observation of human nature similarly confirmed an historical preference for freedom. It was this freedom that Kitson Clark called 'the modicum of theory'. Middlebrow Conservatives located the 'modicum of theory' within history because certain unchanging features of human behaviour emerged only over the course of history, in events and historical processes; and time was essential to discern these unchanging features in human and social relationships. This they saw as echoing Burke's 'wisdom of the ages', and the importance of viewing the continuity of human affairs over the long term. Kitson Clark considered that the fundamental difference between France and Britain derived from the former's respect for abstract theory and the latter's respect for history. Of Britain he wrote:

> As there was no moment at which a new coherent set of ideas was substituted for the old as in France by the Revolution, so there was no moment at which, in modern times at least, a scientific code was received from the hands of a single law-maker. Therefore Englishmen have been apt to look for guidance neither to abstract principle nor to government officials, but backwards to long experience of living in a community which was a complex of individual rights and personal obligations, which they had to vindicate for themselves or to perform for themselves, and a community in which they have had much varied experience of self-government.[33]

If Kitson Clark seemed to promote the most common clichés regarding France and Britain, these clichés served in fact as the starting-point rather than the culmination of his reflections. As Feiling wrote,

> Man, even economic man, is a noble animal ... There are things auguster than a majority of our contemporaries, more comprehending than the largest individual brain, a treasury of merit ordered in the past, and a reality in prosaic fact which theory may condemn but is powerless to destroy.

> Toryism is thus dogmatic, and claims its dogma as *ex cathedra*: infallible,
> not as voicing one party or one age, but as the deposit of a long life, attested
> revelation, a living society.[34]

Playing with the image of a Conservative party hostile to all types of
theory, Feiling set out the party 'dogma', namely the opposite of dogma,
that is to say, flexibility and adaptability to change, since this 'dogma' was
specifically understood as based upon practical reality.

A different approach to constructing the middlebrow was that of the
golden mean, rather than the 'modicum of theory', between high theory
and folk wisdom or common knowledge. The golden mean was not a new
idea of course. It initially stemmed from Horace's *'aurea mediocritas'*,[35]
the precious mean, which referred to moderation against excess and was
taken over and reinterpreted by many poets and philosophers throughout
the centuries. Wisdom was to be found in humility and simplicity, in
'mediocritas', that is to say in the lucid recognition of mankind's limits.
In the sixteenth century, Montaigne defined *mediocritas* as the humanist
ideal *par excellence*, a spiritual exercise against one's propensity to
exaltation.[36] The Conservatives' conception of the middlebrow was drawn
from a general understanding that not only was the 'middle' not pejorative,
it could be in fact constructed in a positive and noble way.

The construction of the 'middle' as a goal to reach was not exclusively
linked to the literary, artistic or academic world, it was equally present
in the economic and social sphere. One of its most remarkable manifestations was Harold Macmillan, as he set out in his research on the 'middle
way'.[37] Macmillan's *via media* or middle way allowed him to achieve his
main objective, which was to address the economic disequilibria that
resulted in mass unemployment among those with whom he had fought
in the First World War and whom he admired. Between laissez-faire
and state Socialism, the middle way constituted a sort of economic and
political balance. He believed blind faith in outdated principles was the
cause of the 1929 economic crisis.

In *English Saga*, Bryant saw in the nineteenth century evidence that 'the
English being bad theorists, though masters of practice and adaptation,
overlooked the fatal error in the logic of laissez-faire'.[38] The search
for a balance between excessive theorising and plain common sense
would have ensured that Britain avoided this mistake. This reliance on
'practical knowledge'[39] was the basis of Keynes's criticism of Macmillan's
book *The Next Step* in 1932, which Keynes admired but criticised for
being 'not nearly bold enough ... [and in] the sort of middle position'.[40]
Macmillan and Keynes were close and shared the same scepticism for old
economic theories. However, according to Macmillan, Keynes's awareness

of his own intellectual superiority rendered him ill-equipped to convince politicians and public opinion of the validity of his thesis.[41] The balance Macmillan sought between his intellectual research and his involvement in politics conformed with the perspective of a *juste milieu*.

The middlebrow, consensus and centrism

Literature was the pre-eminent domain of the middlebrow. 'A good story well told',[42] was the watchword for a whole generation of writers. For John Buchan, Charles Morgan, Walter de la Mare, St John Ervine or A. P. Herbert, the aim was to attract a wider readership than members of the Bloomsbury group and the literary salons of west London. Trevelyan wrote in his preface to Buchan's biography: 'Despising literary coteries, though always at hand to help individual men of letters, avoiding the squabbles and narrowness to which "intellectuals" of all periods are too prone, he claimed no 'privilege of genius' to fail in duty to others.'[43] Modesty and a sense of duty formed an integral part of the middlebrow ethic. Similarly, Trevelyan emphasised the large audience Buchan reached with his novels and history books: 'In our age, when so much popular interest is taken in history but when so many histories are written only for specialists, men are required who are at once good popular writers and real historical scholars. There are not a few, but among them John Buchan was pre-eminent.'[44] Buchan's adventure stories were similar in genre to those of Edgar Wallace and Dornford Yates.[45] The novels of Morgan and de la Mare could be compared to those of Hugh Walpole, Somerset Maugham and E. F. Benson,[46] and the comic works of A. P. Herbert were comparable to those of P. G. Wodehouse (though not nearly as funny).[47] They were all successful authors whose works sold in the tens and even hundreds of thousands.[48] Their novels and plays were broadcast on the radio, particularly those of Wallace and Wodehouse, and some were made into films; for instance, Alfred Hitchcock adapted Buchan's *The 39 Steps* for the cinema. Their plots usually developed within the comfortable surroundings of the gentry or the middle classes and dwelt upon characters confronted with changes brought on by the war and its aftermath and who sought to understand the world they lived in. If Ashridge writers considered themselves middlebrow, some such as Hugh Walpole resented the label. Writing to his friend Virginia Woolf, Walpole described his writing as 'old-fashioned', and expressed envy of her modernism.[49] Similarly, Maugham described himself as 'in the very first rank of the second-raters'.[50] But while they were critical of themselves, they were appreciated at Ashridge precisely for their middlebrow qualities.

The middlebrow public was generally an educated public from the provinces and suburbs, and overwhelmingly from the middle classes. Although educated, its defining feature was membership of a social milieu distinct from the London elite. In his book on national character, Bryant distinguished seven traditional types of Englishmen drawn from different social milieux and reflecting the view of England as essentially a middle-class country.[51] Alison Light emphasises the link between Englishness and the middle classes during the inter-war years.[52] For Baldwin, 'our nation' allegedly meant all its citizens, what McKibbin refers to as the 'public' as opposed to sectional groups who defended their particular interests. Baldwin established a fundamental political distinction between the 'public' who had the 'nation's interests at heart, and particular interests, which were equated with trade unions.[53] The most obvious example of this distinction was militant trade-union action, which in its most extreme form, as in the General Strike of 1926, was described as 'unconstitutional', and even in its more limited forms as antisocial and against the public interest. The action of strikers, especially those engaged in the events of 1926, was looked upon as an abrogation of both their rights and duties as citizens, an antithesis of civil responsibility and middle-class values as defined by Baldwin. During the General Strike of 1926, volunteers offered to work in place of the strikers, standing in for bus and lorry drivers.[54] Baldwin regarded them as defenders of the nation and its institutions. Being against class conflict and accusing the trade unions of creating class tensions was of course the best way to be a class warrior. The middlebrow was a loose enough concept to be used as a cloak to comprise an ensemble of moral values similar to those Baldwin evoked when he spoke of 'service', 'duty' and 'honesty'. The filmmaker Alfred Hitchcock evoked 'this central and vital element of the British people – the middle-classes.... They embody the spirit of Britain.'[55] Hitchcock depicted a middle class that conserved national values and safeguarded the middlebrow, and Baldwin could not have agreed more.

When, in 1937, Ashridge created a book club to compete with the Left Book Club, begun the year before, it named it the National Book Association (NBA),[56] not the Conservative Book Club. The list of NBA members indicates that the majority came from the middle classes. In February 1939, Mrs E. D. Coats, a member of the NBA, wrote to Bryant, its director, saying she used the NBA books to open 'a small library for local tradesmen, and working men and women'.[57] Mrs Coats used the language of the middle class to describe her future clientele. She could have belonged to the British Housewives' League, set up after the war to oppose rationing and which crystallised the discontent of the middle classes with the high cost of living.[58] This league, although it comprised in the majority housewives from England, and more specifically from the south-east of England, called itself British out of concern to employ the language of the nation and to be seen as representative of the nation as a whole. By the same token, in 1956 the Middle Class Alliance was established and held its first meeting on St George's day – England's national day – to emphasise the fact that the middle classes were the heart of England.

When Geoffrey Ellis wrote in 1937 that 'Ashridge seeks to attract ... people of a middle type of mind',[59] he was implicitly referring to the middlebrow as opposed to the highbrow. Ellis was not trying to find a middle ground between Socialism and Conservatism, but rather to convince people of the merits of Conservatism. In this regard, the *juste milieu* was not a compromise between two ways of thinking, but the position the Conservative party allegedly embodied. Butterfield wrote,

> Napoleon was not defeated by men who excelled in intellect and surpassed him in originality.... For there is a Providence in the historical process which sometimes (and indeed perhaps often in the long run) is on the side of the mediocrities. And who amongst us would exchange the long line of amiable or prudent statesmen in English history, for all those masterful and awe-inspiring geniuses who have imposed themselves on France and Germany in modern times?[60]

The 'mediocrities' here is a reference to the wisdom of the *mediocritas*. Playing upon national stereotypes, Conservatives proposed what could seem a consensual vision of Britain, located within the long history of the country. They were not alone in their valorisation of a middlebrow culture as an essential part of national identity and many within the Labour camp would have agreed with them. In August 1943, for example, James Chuter Ede, Labour under-secretary at the ministry of education, recorded a conversation with Labour party colleagues: '[W. H.] Green said he didn't expect to win a General Election with Attlee. We wanted someone more brilliant. Walkden said the country distrusted brilliant men. Mosley, Cripps, R. MacDonald, J. H. Thomas had all been unreliable.'[61] Chuter Ede's unease about the difference of opinion between the Labour party and its intellectuals was expressed by Bryant, who wrote: 'Even many of the Trade Union and Cooperative-Society leaders – often stalwarts of the local Tory working men's club – regarded the new Socialism with disfavour. It was too highbrow and foreign for their shrewd liking: too far removed from the familiar tastes and prejudices of the simple men they represented.'[62] The middlebrow represented a form of national consensus on certain values, which the Conservatives used to present themselves as the representatives of the nation. This was confirmed by the work of Arthur Marwick on middle opinion in the 1930s, and the idea that for

Britain the inter-war period, far from being one of extremes, was in fact the era of the *'juste milieu'*.[63] Marwick claimed the Next Five Years Group was the expression of agreement between men and women of different political persuasions, which anticipated the national consensus during the war and after 1945.

Yet there was by no means a consensus. Instead it was a case of promoting a Conservative position. The 'language of the brows' as it was deployed by the Conservatives served their interests. Thus, for example, Baldwin, speaking in 1925 in the House of Commons on relations with the trade unions, declared: 'Give peace in our time, O Lord.'[64] Baldwin's language could not have been more consensual, yet in 1926 he suppressed the General Strike without making the least concession to the miners. In 1927, his Conservative government adopted the Trades Disputes Act, which barred trade unions from devoting any part of their dues to a political party; a measure evidently intended against the Labour party. Despite his soothing speeches, Baldwin applied a hard-line Conservative policy. One can only agree with Philip Williamson that 'Baldwin drew the TUC leaders into a strike they had not really sought'.[65] Similarly, while Macmillan evoked the middle way and the need to find a *juste milieu* between laisser-faire and state Socialism, he nonetheless remained opposed to nationalisation and a state-managed economy. For him and other Conservatives of the Next Five Years Group, the state could be a 'midwife' but never a 'mother'. If the Next Five Years Group and Neville Chamberlain could agree that *'laissez-faire* [wa]s dead',[66] they were equally agreed in their opposition to large-scale state intervention, as favoured by the Socialists.[67] The idea that the Next Five Years Group represented the beginning of a consensus between the Conservative and Labour parties is scarcely borne out by the evidence. Even the most progressive Conservatives scarcely agreed with the Labour party on economic matters. The eulogy of the 'middle' and the *via media* should by no means be mistaken for a soft compromise. Similarly in social policy, Conservatives sought to retain a large place for philanthropic organisations and voluntary work. In 1947, Quintin Hogg, a member of the Tory Reform group, reacted to the creation of the welfare state: 'Where are the Friendly Societies since the Labour Party came to power? Where are the voluntary hospitals, or the municipal hospitals?'[68] Enoch Powell suggested that one of the major differences between Conservatives and Socialists was their conception of society and the community. For Socialists, he claimed, society and the state were abstract entities, which could be merged into one another, whereas for Conservatives society was comprised of a network of links that developed spontaneously in the course of daily life.[69]

The identity of the middlebrow was by no means to be equated with the search for a compromise. Historians at Ashridge read the works of Burke and Disraeli through the prism of the 1930s and proposed a specifically English notion of the relationship between intellectuals and society. Whereas highbrow thinkers assumed that intellectuals could mould society, middlebrow thinkers believed that intellectuals were moulded by the society in which they lived, and that it was only reasonable to recognise this. In *Culture and Society*, published in 1958, Raymond Williams observed, 'the reforming bourgeois modification of ... society is this idea of service'.[70] Williams added, 'the phraseology of "making a man a useful citizen", "equipping him to serve the community", has become common form'.[71] Ashridge contributed to this discursive change and gave substance to a middle class construction of society as inclusive and consensual, in which 'service' was one of the watchwords. Williams also added, 'the servant, if he is to be a good servant can never really question the order of things'.[72] One of the goals of Ashridge was to instil in members of the working class who attended its courses this sense of duty and service. In 1933, an Ashridge student of working-class origins wrote, '[the college] stimulated me and accentuated my sense of responsibility and gave me some understanding of the problems confronting the world'.[73]

In this respect, Ashridge was not just a political project. It also had a more ambitious purpose of redefining social and cultural norms: it questioned the inclusiveness and exclusiveness of citizenship, and the shared values of service and duty which implied an element of hierarchy in society. The Conservative party in the inter-war period actively constructed constituencies of support by articulating plausible representations of 'identity', and in particular intellectual identity through language. The 'language of the brows' enabled the Conservatives to address a very wide audience and present themselves as defending an English culture of practical knowledge against their imagined enemy.

Notes

1 Green, *Ideologies of Conservatism*, pp. 2–17.
2 S. Collini, *Absent Minds. Intellectuals in Britain* (Oxford: Oxford University Press, 2006).
3 Stapleton, *Political Intellectuals and Public Identities*, p. 114.
4 Hearnshaw, *Conservatism in England*, pp. 168–9.
5 Colonel Delancy to the General, 21 July, 1791, quoted in Feiling, *The Second Tory Party, 1714–1832*, p. 188.
6 Burke, *Reflections on the Revolution in France*.
7 Baldwin, *On England*, p. 154.
8 Quinton, *The Politics of Imperfection*, p. 56.

9 Burke, *Reflections on the Revolution in France*, cited in Quinton, *ibid.*, p. 57.

10 Collini, *Absent Minds*, p. 117.

11 R. Graves and A. Hodge, *The Long Weekend* (London: Hutchinson, 1940), quoted in L. Napper, 'British Cinema and the Middlebrow', in J. Ashby and A. Higson (eds), *British Cinema, Past and Present* (London: Routledge, 2000), pp. 111–12. Also see L. W. Levine, *Highbrow/Lowbrow. The Emergence of Cultural Hierarchy in America* (Cambridge, MA: Harvard University Press, 1988). McKibbin, *Classes and Cultures*. R. M. Bracco, *Merchants of Hope: British Middlebrow Writers and the First World War, 1919–1939* (Providence, RI: Berg Publishers Ltd, 1993).

12 'Charivaria', *Punch*, 23 Dec. 1925, p. 673; *Oxford English Dictionary*.

13 V. Woolf, 'Middlebrow', in *The Death of the Moth* (London: Hogarth Press, 1942), p. 115, quoted in Bracco, *Merchants of Hope*, p. 11.

14 G. Orwell, *Tribune*, 2 Nov. 1945, in *The Collected Essays, Journalism and Letters of George Orwell*, Vol. 4: *In Front of Your Nose, 1945–1950* (Harmondsworth: Penguin, 1970), pp. 37–41.

15 E. Mannin, *The Bookworm's Turn*, quoted in Q. D. Leavis, *Fiction and the Reading Public* (London: Chatto & Windus, 1932), pp. 11–12.

16 Collini, *Absent Minds*, p. 112.

17 A. J. Cronin, *The Stars Look Down* (London: Gollancz, 1935); *The Citadel* (London: Gollancz, 1937). J. B. Priestley, *The Good Companions* (London: Heinemann Ltd, 1929). J. B. Priestley, *English Journey* (London: Heinemann Ltd, 1934). Cronin and Priestley were among the most widely read novelists of the inter-war years. Their books were also adapted for film.

18 T. Eagleton, 'Reach-Me-Down Romantic', *London Review of Books*, 19 June 2003, p. 7.

19 G. Orwell, *The Lion and the Unicorn* (1940), in Orwell, *The Collected Essays, Journalism and Letters of George Orwell*, Vol. 2, p. 140.

20 J. Baxendale and C. Pawling, *Narrating the Thirties* (London: Macmillan, 1996), p. 49, quoted in Napper, 'British Cinema and the Middlebrow', p. 113.

21 Collini, *Absent Minds*, p. 111.

22 L. Woolf, *Hunting the Highbrow* (London: Hogarth Press, 1927), pp. 43–4.

23 '[Prejudice] previously engages the mind in [points the mind toward] a steady course of wisdom and virtue, and does not leave the man hesitating in the moment of decision, skeptical, puzzled, and unresolved. Prejudice renders a man's virtue his habit, and not a series of unconnected acts. Through just prejudice his duty becomes a part of his nature'. Burke, *Reflections on the Revolution in France*, p. 186.

24 Woolf, *Hunting the Highbrow*, pp. 46–7.

25 R. Samuel, *Theatres of Memory*: Vol. II, *Island Stories: Unravelling Britain*, (London: Verso, 1998).

26 Woolf, *Hunting the Highbrow*, pp. 48–9.

27 *Ibid.*, p. 50

28 M. Oakeshott, 'On Being Conservative', in *Rationalism in Politics and*

Other Essays (London: Methuen & Co., 1962, Indianapolis, IN: Liberty Press, 1991), pp. 426–7.

29 Oakeshott, *Rationalism in Politics and Other Essays.*

30 *Ibid.*, p. 15.

31 Woolf, *Hunting the Highbrow*, p. 42.

32 Feiling, *A History of the Tory Party*, p. 493.

33 Kitson Clark, *The English Inheritance*, pp. 28–9.

34 Feiling, *Sketches in Nineteenth Century Biography*, pp. 176–7.

35 Horace, *Odes*, 2.10. 1–8.

36 Montaigne, *Essais*, III, 3.

37 Macmillan, *The Middle Way.*

38 Bryant, *English Saga, 1840–1940*, p. 56.

39 As Oakeshott defines it in *Rationalism in Politics and Other Essays.*

40 H. Macmillan, *The Next Step* (London: E. T. Heron, 1932). J. M. Keynes to H. Macmillan, 6 June 1932, J. M. Keynes papers, Microfilm Reel 61, quoted in Green, *Ideologies of Conservatism*, pp. 157–91.

41 See Green, *Ideologies of Conservatism*, p. 163.

42 J. Agate, 'The Film Till Now, 1930', in *Around Cinemas* (Homes and Van Thal, 1946), p. 80, cited in Napper, 'Cinema and the Middlebrow', p. 113.

43 S. Tweedsmuir, *John Buchan by his Wife and Friends*, with a preface by G. M. Trevelyan (London: Hodder & Stoughton, 1947), p. 17.

44 *Ibid.*

45 D. Yates, *Blind Corner*, 1927; *Deadlier than the Male*, 1932. E. Wallace, *The Crimson Circle*, 1922; *The Green Archer*, 1923. Wallace wrote the *King Kong* screenplay in 1932.

46 H. Walpole, *Rogue Herries* (London: Macmillan, 1931); *The Fortress* (London: Macmillan, 1932). S. Maugham, *Cakes and Ale, or the Skeleton in the Cupboard* (London: Heinemann, 1930); *For Services Rendered*, in the *Collected Plays*, vol. 3, London: Heinemann, 1931). E. F. Benson, *Mapp and Lucia* (London: Hodder & Stoughton, 1931).

47 P. G. Wodehouse, *The Inimitable Jeeves* (London: Herbert Jenkins, 1923).

48 See J. McAleer, *Popular Reading and Publishing in Britain, 1914–1959* (Oxford: Oxford University Press, 1992).

49 M. Drabble (ed.), *The Oxford Companion to English Literature* (Oxford: Oxford University Press, 1996), p. 1051.

50 W. S. Maugham, *The Summing Up* (1938), quoted in Drabble (ed.), *The Oxford Companion to English Literature*, p. 641.

51 A. Bryant, *The National Character* (London: Longmans, Green & Co., 1934).

52 Light, *Forever England*, pp. 61–112; pp. 208–21.

53 McKibbin, '"Class and Conventional Wisdom"'.

54 G. A. Phillips, *The General Strike: The Politics of Industrial Conflict* (London: Weidenfeld & Nicolson, 1976).

55 A. Hitchcock, 'The Real Spirit of England', in *World Film News*, Feb. 1937, p. 15, quoted in Napper, 'Cinema and the Middlebrow', p. 115.

56 See Chapter 6 for more on the National Book Association.

57 E. D. Coats to A. Bryant, 8 Feb. 1939, Bryant papers, C46.

58 See I. Zweiniger-Bargielowska, 'Rationing, Austerity and the Conservative Electoral Recovery after 1945', *Historical Journal*, 37, 1993, pp. 173–97. I. Zweiniger-Bargielowska, *Austerity in Britain: Rationing, Controls, and Consumption, 1939–1955* (Oxford: Oxford University Press, 2000).

59 G. Ellis to R. A. Butler, 27 Oct. 1937, Butler papers, RAB H.87 33.

60 Butterfield, *The Englishman and His History*, p. 99.

61 J. Chuter Ede, diary entry, 3 Aug. 1943, in K. Jefferys (ed.), *Labour and the Wartime Coalition: From the Diary and Letters of James Chuter Ede, 1941–1945* (London: The Historians' Press, 1987), p. 145. W. H. Green and D. Walken were Labour MPs. Clement Attlee became prime minister for the Labour party in 1945. Oswald Mosley had left the party in 1931 to form the New Party, which became the British Union of Fascists. Stafford Cripps was expelled from the party in 1938 for favouring the popular front, which implied a compromise with the Communists. MacDonald and Thomas were also expelled from the Labour party in 1931 for forming a national government with the Conservatives and the Liberals.

62 Bryant, *English Saga*, pp. 229–30.

63 A. Marwick, 'Middle Opinion in the Thirties: Planning, Progress and Political "Agreement"', *English Historical Review*, 79 (311), 1964, pp. 285–98. See also H. McCarthy, 'Parties, Voluntary Associations and Democratic Politics in Interwar Britain', *Historical Journal*, 50 (4), Dec. 2007, pp. 891–912.

64 S. Baldwin, 'Peace in Industry', 6 Mar. 1925, in S. Baldwin, *On England*, p. 52.

65 Williamson, *Stanley Baldwin*, p. 347.

66 For a summary of the Next Five Years Group's position, see S. G. *Note*, 18 June 1934, CPA, CRD 1/65/2. For more on Neville Chamberlain's position specifically, see the minutes from the CRD conference, 2 Mar. 1934, CPA, CRD, 1/64/2, quoted in Green, *Ideologies of Conservatism*, p. 243.

67 For further analysis on the different opinions regarding the role of the State, see Ritschel, *The Politics of Planning*.

68 Q. Hogg, *The Case for Conservatism* (West Drayton: Penguin Books, 1947), p. 67.

69 J. E. Powell, 'The Social Services: Theory and Practice', in *The Listener*, 17 Apr. 1952, quoted in Green, *Ideologies of Conservatism*, p. 274.

70 R. Williams, *Culture and Society* (London: Chatto & Windus, 1958), p. 312.

71 *Ibid.*, p. 315.

72 *Ibid.*, p. 316.

73 Letter from A. Cummins in a joint letter with E. McEwen to H. Gordon, 17 Jan., 1933, Education Committee Minutes 1933, Ashridge papers.

9

Rural elegies

In 1937, Clough Williams-Ellis, a prominent architect and a regular lecturer at Ashridge, edited a collective work entitled *Britain and the Beast*.[1] Williams-Ellis had been commissioned by Davidson in 1928 to 'Clough-up' Ashridge and to turn it from a palace to a college.[2] Although to many, it might have seemed that 'Clough was the official architect to the Conservative Party',[3] in so far as he altered and enlarged the Ladies' Carlton Club, as well as many Tory grandees' mansions, Williams-Ellis refused to stand as a Conservative party candidate when CCO offered him the opportunity to run in an election.[4] Seven Ashridge lecturers contributed to the volume. *Britain and the Beast* examined the damage to the English countryside due to negligence, industrialisation and urbanisation. The Conservative party was not alone in taking an interest in the subject, which was taken up by politicians of all stripes. *Britain and the Beast* received a very favourable reception from the Left as well as the Right. George Lansbury, Stafford Cripps and J. B. Priestley, all members of the Labour party, sang its praises. Cripps wrote: 'We must somehow rest our beauty of the country from the grip of the Beast of industrialism, with all its foul habits of spoliation. We must build again the community life of our villages.'[5] Lloyd George, leader of the Radical Liberals before the First World War and hostile to the persistence of the feudal system in the countryside, wrote that 'a task of supreme importance for our times is the awakening of the nation to the treasures of our neglected countryside'.[6] Many Conservatives signalled their agreement, notably the Marquess of Zetland, Lord Crawford and the Earl of Derby.

In his introduction, Williams-Ellis praised the work of the National Trust for Places of Historic Interest or Natural Beauty (founded in 1895) and of the CPRE. Williams-Ellis, and those he called his 'knights errant'[7] of town and regional planning, had founded the CPRE in 1926, under the chairmanship of Lord Crawford. The Council embraced different views and politics: Lord Crawford was a Conservative, Patrick Abercrombie, one of the 'knights errant', whose 1926 pamphlet, *The Preservation of*

Rural England, inspired the CPRE's foundation and who became its first honorary secretary, was a Liberal. Clough Williams-Ellis, for all his Conservative friendships and connections, briefly joined the Independent Labour party. All three were frequent lecturers at Ashridge. Williams-Ellis wrote that 'The National Trust is very generally saluted ... [and] nearly every contributor also commends the valiant labours of the Council for the Preservation of Rural England'.[8] The National Trust and the CPRE were private charitable foundations set up to preserve the national heritage. The National Trust owned 2,500 acres of Ashridge park and the CPRE organised meetings at Ashridge. The multiple links between Ashridge, the CPRE and the National Trust illustrated the importance the college gave to the protection of rural heritage. 'The preservation movement,' wrote Howard Newby, 'proved to be a strange amalgam of patrician landowners, for whom the preservation of the countryside was closely linked to their conception of "stewardship", and socially concerned Fabians (Hampstead dwellers, but keen hikers on the Downs) who believed in the pursuit of social justice through national planning'.[9] Lord Crawford explained that the objective of the CPRE was to create new villages and new towns that 'shall conform to modern requirements without injuring the ancient beauty of the land'.[10] One of the goals of Ashridge was to adapt a form of aristocratic ideal to the modern world.

In praise of rural life

The idea that the true English character was located in the land and was situated in a pre-industrial past was as frequent in Labour or Socialist discourse as it was in Conservative rhetoric. But it was seized upon by Stanley Baldwin in a particularly skilful way. In his 1924 speech on 'England', he lyrically evoked the English countryside, and equated landscape and national identity, thereby valorising the peaceful essence of England as opposed to war and class conflict.[11] That Baldwin should want to present himself as a countryman, at one with nature and the countryside, sensitive to the simplicity of country living and nostalgic for a rural past, was in many ways ironic for Baldwin who was an iron master and steel manufacturer. Furthermore, Britain, and above all England, had already, by 1911, become the most urban country in the world and it became even more urban in the inter-war years. It was under his government that a large-scale programme of road construction was undertaken and electric pylons were erected which disfigured the countryside. Williams-Ellis could not resist mocking Baldwin and his 'yards and yards of sob-stuff about the beauties of the countryside'.[12] What Baldwin was valorising was not only the organic character of rural England, but also the stately-home idyll and its associations with aristocratic landed elites. This romantic ideal of the country house was shared by numerous contemporaries. Lord Crawford, chairman of the CPRE, also owned major coal-mines in Lancashire and, like many aristocrats, he divided his time between town and country, making him, as F. M. L. Thompson put it, 'amphibious'.[13] The same applied to numerous businessmen who owned country homes and whose numbers grew in the inter-war years.[14] The movement for the defence of the countryside was essentially an urban movement.

If the upper middle classes were buying up stately homes and castles from cash-strapped aristocrats, the middle and lower middle classes generated large-scale tourism, especially engaging in visiting historic houses recently opened to the public. A feature of the inter-war years was the rise of middle-class tourism. Trains and cars enabled them to discover the countryside and national heritage. Meanwhile the working class engaged in new forms of leisure activity. Rambling and touring by bicycle became widely popular: in 1930, ten million bicycles were in use.[15] In 1937, a million cars used the roads. The Youth Hostels Association was created in 1929. In 1939, the four hundred youth hostels in the country offered half a million overnight places for a shilling, breakfast included.[16] Thousands of reproductions were sold of *The Hay Wain* by Constable, the most popular artist in the inter-war years.[17] From Baldwin to the factory workers in Sheffield, city-dwelling England was dreaming of the countryside. Nostalgia for the rural community grew alongside the idea of transforming the countryside into a place for holidays and leisure activities. A large number of books glorifying England's countryside were published. H. V. Morton's *In Search of England*, published in 1927, was reprinted twenty-three times in the next ten years.[18] . For Peter Mandler, this work 'combin[ed] the functions of travel guide and philosophizer on Englishness'.[19] Respect for decency and the values of rural life were perceived as essential elements of Englishness, although or because both were perceived to be threatened with extinction. The Conservative party sought to be their protector and fulfilled its mission of popular education and as defender of the national heritage and its values by encouraging all citizens to discover this national heritage for themselves. During the war, posters calling on Britons to enlist showed a countryside with little villages and church spires and carried the message: 'Your Britain: fight for it.' Ninety-two per cent of the population by now lived in urban areas.[20] The countryside was equated with preserving civic virtue and patriotism.

The choice of Ashridge as the site and the mission it was given make sense in this particular context. Ashridge was a historic home, and for both Baldwin and Bryant the country house was part of the education in citizenship which they sought to provide.[21] Mandler defines a country house as one that embodies 'a physical legacy of the past belonging, however abstractly, to the citizenry of the present by virtue of its contribution to national history'.[22] From 1918 onwards, the gradual changes in the social role of the landed aristocracy led to the redefinition of the country house. The economic depression that struck the agricultural world in the 1870s, the radical political critiques and democratic advances savagely affected the landed aristocracy. The magazine *Country Life* first appeared in 1897,[23] just as the decline of the landed aristocracy gathered pace, as a celebration of a way of life and values that were on the verge of extinction. In 1911, the reform of the House of Lords ended its main constitutional privileges. This reform of the Lords was the consequence of their veto of the People's Budget presented by Lloyd George in 1909, which included a major increase in property taxes. Between 1914 and 1918, death duties rose by 50 per cent, which severely affected the landed aristocracy. In 1925, Baldwin raised them again. As a consequence of fiscal pressure, the aristocracy sold a large part of its land. In the 1920s, many estates changed hands, on a scale not seen since the Norman Conquest.[24] In the inter-war years, the aristocracy thus experienced a serious crisis, which took several forms. The decline in their standard of living led some to emigrate to the colonies, including Kenya. Others sold their land and invested their money in securities, thus becoming *rentiers*; in most cases, they belonged to the most 'glamorous' parts of London society.[25] Still others became *déclassé* aristocrats.[26] Finally, a growing number sought to protect their stately homes and land by opening them to visitors. Not only did this generate revenues, but it also allowed them to present themselves as guardians of the nation's heritage. Some of the aristocracy thus saw their political role metamorphose into that of 'cultural stewardship'.[27] From the 1920s, the Marquess of Salisbury, who was still active in politics, opened Hatfield House to the public.[28] Similarly, the fact that Lord Crawford was head of the CPRE illustrated the aristocracy's progressive conversion to the 'heritage industry', albeit still in its infancy at this time.[29]

The aristocracy was not alone in its nostalgia for a vanished past. Former Radicals like G. M. Trevelyan and H. J. Massingham,[30] although hostile towards the rural aristocracy at the beginning of the twentieth century, recognised in the inter-war years the gentry's contribution to the protection of the countryside, thanks to improved agricultural techniques as well as their shared community ethos. In 1937, Massingham, editor-in-chief of the weekly Liberal magazine, *The Nation*, argued that 'what has to be rediscovered and restored ... is the living spirit of the old village community',[31] stating that he was turning towards 'a conservatism of a much older tradition'.[32] Similarly, Trevelyan had been critical of the gentry, but analysed the problem differently during the inter-war years. He saw speculators and estate agents as the greatest dangers to the English countryside. Massingham, in his contribution to Williams-Ellis's book, went even further by claiming,

> The ruin of the peasantry in the eighteenth century ... was followed by the ruin of the land in the twentieth. Defenceless, its weedy fields with their skinny hedges and choked ditches, its desecrated woods and dales, polluted rivers and deserted hills, lie open to a horde of speculators whose rape far exceeds in violence the worst excesses of the old barbarian invaders.[33]

From its start, Ashridge was intended to safeguard a historical residence and its land from property speculators.[34] Saving Ashridge had indeed launched Trevelyan's career within the National Trust, and from there to his friendship with Baldwin. While Davidson raised the funds to acquire Ashridge and part of its land, Trevelyan saw to it that the National Trust acquired the rest. In June 1926, *The Times* commented on the work of the National Trust: 'its conservation ... rests with students not of the past but of the present, with the *practical* men who would endeavour to keep a thoughtless evolution on tolerably well-thought-out lines'.[35] The students who went to Ashridge acquired, it was claimed, through their stay in historic surroundings, a sense of their responsibility towards the country's heritage.

The statutes of Ashridge themselves assigned to the trust the task 'to preserve a great and beautiful historical Building from destruction'.[36] However, unlike the National Trust and the CPRE, the Ashridge trust was not just responsible for protecting the country's heritage. Its teachers were also to be 'inculcators of atmosphere'.[37] The Conservatives of Ashridge felt that they lived 'in a period of transition ... [and it was] wise to consider whether it is not possible for something of the old tradition to survive'.[38] Old traditions and the atmosphere of the college formed part of the educational project of Ashridge. During its first five years, Bryant contributed regularly to the *Ashridge Journal*, writing of the college as if it were a national hero that would serve as a role model to its students. He explained in 1930:

> For the history of Ashridge is almost as old as that of England. Turn back the leaves of the centuries. The present page reveals the great staircase crowded with ever new successions of eager students, deep in chairs and talk before the fire. A page before and we are in 1830 and Ashridge of the squires.... Always at Ashridge the feet of great men come and go – Richard, King of the Romans, Edward I, the Black Prince, Geoffrey Chaucer, Cardinal Beaufort, Henry VIII, Mary Tudor, Elizabeth, Chancellor Ellesmere, Duke of Bridgewater, Benjamin Disraeli, and now to-day the silent Worcestershire

ironmaster, on whom the mantle of the English country tradition has fallen. So in our Ashridge biography past and present mingle.[39]

The college prided itself on bringing students together in the congenial atmosphere it generated. Ashridge, as a place of memory, was expected to arouse in them a sense of continuity and offer them the opportunity to be, if not a future hero, then at least a servant of the nation and its heritage. Graham explained: 'From its historic setting there radiate those influences which will go far towards the moulding of that intelligent democracy upon which all our future must rest.'[40] It is difficult to measure the influence of the spirit of Ashridge upon its students, but the record left by a number of them indicates that they felt its 'magic'. Arthur Cummins, a student of modest origins in Scotland, wrote that Ashridge was 'a sentinel, guarding the heritage of Britain'.[41] Similarly another student wrote,

> After [the Principal's opening] address, each one of us had made up his or her mind to be a worthy unit of a team, working together in an environment of exquisite charm, rich tradition, and deep-seated culture.... Each and all expressed the corporate life, inspired by the words spoken by the Principal on the first evening, quickened by a short ten minutes in the College Chapel where the ashes of the founder lie and where all gathered each morning to listen to words of wisdom; strengthened by daily contact in discussion and debate; deepened by the tradition of Ashridge.[42]

As mentioned previously, a large proportion of Ashridge students were of middle-class origin. For them, Ashridge initially seemed like a holiday camp. The sporting activities it offered – tennis, croquet, golf and swimming – were very popular. Peter Mandler explains that during the inter-war years, the middle classes in Britain had, as it were, 'annexed' the land and stately homes of the aristocracy, turning them into places for leisure: 'the interwar middle classes ... took symbolic ownership of the whole of the country by travelling and exploring it'.[43] Ashridge contributed to this movement, which saw the middle classes appropriating a part of the nation's heritage, but its objective was more ambitious. Mandler explains that 'the suburb's most conspicuous non-residential building was a cinema, not a church'.[44] Ashridge offered films, but the chapel remained at the heart of the college.

In his article, 'Our Inheritance from the Past', Massingham wrote:

> The constitution of the village community effected an extraordinarily stable balance between socialism and ownership,... [allowing] free human contacts between man and man, the lack of financial incentive in the daily round, the bonds of traditional observance, the absence of social division and enmity, and the deep attachment of one and all to the land of their birth, their work, and their village.... Modern socialism, being a machine

similar in structure if differing in policy and principle from the existing
machine of national government, cannot even conceive the nature of a
society repeated, with a wide range of variations in detail, thousands of
time over.... The village community did accomplish the to us incredible feat
of reconciling independence with interdependence, and tradition with the
free play of the individual within the body of the village.[45]

Creating a community through common activity and customs and the
absence of social conflict was at the heart of Ashridge's project. This
idealised vision of village life was in stark contrast to the anarchical
development of the suburbs. The ideal of the traditional village was born
of urban geography, which seemed to accentuate the differences between
the social classes by separating and ghettoising them. There were some
who favoured this discrimination. The construction in 1934 of Cutteslowe
Walls, a district of Oxford, to separate a working-class community
from a lower middle-class one is a particularly striking illustration.[46]
Others, particularly social planners, wished for what they called 'viable
communities' which were better integrated and demanded civic and social
engagement. Still others saw the village and the social integration of the
working class as the best defence against the scourge of overly rapid urban
development.

For speakers at Ashridge rural life was not only a matter of nostalgia
or a utopian dream. They also addressed the difficulties of agriculture.
Between 1929 and 1939 fifteen sessions and sixty-three lectures dealt with
problems facing British agriculture. Among other things they considered
'economic and social aspects of the mechanisation of farming', 'animal
husbandry', 'the pros and cons of marketing boards' and 'the changing
face of British agriculture'. These lectures were delivered by well-known
figures such as J. A. Scott Watson, professor of rural economy at Oxford,
A. G. Street, an agricultural expert and author of *Farmer's Glory* and Sir
E. John Russell, director of the Rothamsted experimental farm.[47] In 1934,
the college organised a session at Ashridge in collaboration with the CPRE
called 'The Village', in which Bryant examined the history of 'The Village
as It Was', A. E. Richardson, professor of architecture at the University of
London, spoke on 'the rural habitat', and Patrick Abercrombie, professor
of architecture at the University of Liverpool, discussed 'rural disfig-
urement and its remedy', as well as 'recreation and social life in the village',
'small holdings and allotments for village settlements' and 'the powers and
duties of the parish council'. Abercrombie sought to convince his audience
of the importance of zoning regulations to protect the countryside from
property developers and urban sprawl. He was behind the 1932 Act on
urban and rural planning, as well as the Ribbon Prevention Act. Edward
Hilton Young, another lecturer at Ashridge, defended the project in

parliament. That same year Frederic Lee, a member of the Ashridge education committee, wrote:

> Now that the question of town-planning is in the air it seems that there is an excellent opportunity of making a start in what is, after all, not a new direction but a revival of the conditions that have been part of the normal life of the country for hundreds of years. These new plans could be made with a view to giving housing facilities to all classes within the planned area.[48]

Lee's ideas on social integration anticipated the creation of 'viable communities', as advocated in the Uthwatt report of 1942, and Abercrombie's new towns were built according to the principles of old village communities.[49] Massingham wrote in his hymn to the village: 'We do not normally associate vitality with an extreme conservatism, but here [in the village community] the one was the condition of the other.'[50]

The heritage of the manorial system

Given that Britain's urbanisation had proceeded apace with its industrialisation, Baldwin and others of all political persuasions who extolled the virtues of rural, country life were necessarily harking back to a lost golden age before 'England's green and pleasant land' had been invaded by 'dark, satanic mills'.[51] The question for all critics of Britain's industrialisation and urbanisation was when the rural golden age had existed. Here, again, there was a surprising degree of cross-party agreement, namely that it had been the medieval era.

In 1937, Sir Stafford Cripps wrote: 'We cannot go back, we do not want to go back to the conditions of feudalism.'[52] Everything, however, suggests that 'medievalism' was a cross-party phenomenon. Socialists saw in elements of the medieval period structures and lessons that could be valuable. For G. D. H. Cole, for example, as for A. J. Penty, the author of *The Restoration of the Gild System* (1906), the medieval guilds were intrinsically democratic. The guild system was seen as a forerunner of Syndicalism, that is to say, an order in which those who controlled the labour process itself were the key authority. For Cole and others, the control by the workforce itself of its daily activities and its securing of its own welfare was the only true industrial democracy possible. The top-down reincarnation of the medieval structure, which had a particular attraction for Conservatives, was precisely what Left-wing medievalists wished to avoid.

During the second meeting of the governing council at Ashridge, the idea of creating a coat of arms for the college was raised. Lord Fairhaven, who was in charge of the project, should present different alternatives to the Court of Heralds.[53] This move stemmed from the desire to present Ashridge as a place of historical importance. In April 1931, the coat of arms was ready. The design comprised a shield, held by two rampant lions, upon which was engraved a royal sceptre decorated with a Tudor rose. The emblems were chosen because of their links to the Black Prince, who had contributed to the prosperity of the Ashridge monastery, and Queen Elizabeth, who had spent part of her childhood there. The most important element was the college motto: 'This Sceptred Isle', taken from the beginning of Jean de Gand's monologue in Shakespeare's *Richard II*, devoted to the glory of England.[54] Jean de Gand was the Black Prince's brother.

This desire to be associated with medieval tradition can be seen in Bryant's *Ashridge Journal* biographies. They were usually on individuals from the Middle Ages, while subjects from the modern era were nearly always princes and military leaders, such as the Duke of Marlborough and the Duke of Wellington. Medieval-themed performances took place, including pageants and *tableaux vivants*, designed to bring the past to life. Jousting tournaments and battles were also organised. As Julia Stapleton has shown, Arthur Bryant excelled at restoring pageantry to the English scene.[55] Although the pageants at Ashridge were not as large and elaborately staged as the medieval reconstructions held at Eglinton in 1839, they echoed and continued the tradition known in the nineteenth century as the 'the return to Camelot':[56] the return to the Arthurian legends – Camelot being King Arthur's castle – and the knights of the Round Table. This interest in the Middle Ages dwelt chiefly on its chivalry and code of honour.

The nineteenth and early twentieth centuries rediscovered the Middle Ages and, with them, the knightly code of honour 'sans peur et sans reproche'. In July 1912, a great tournament of mounted riders took place in the Empress Hall at Earl's Court to celebrate the tercentenary of 'England's Shakespeare'.[57] This was just one event in a vast celebration of the Tudors and Merrie England, which drew upon the work of poets and writers including Alfred Tennyson, Thomas Malory, Sir Walter Scott and Robert Louis Stevenson.[58] They all advanced the glorious vision of England victorious over France and Spain, commemorating Agincourt and Crécy as well as the defeat of the 'invincible' Armada. The chivalric code of honour lent these victories a special aura, suggesting they were secured without triumphalism but with modesty, in the fulfilment of duty. The alleged conduct of the knights, in victory as much as in adversity, was to inspire the conduct of the English gentleman. 'Fair play' was seen as the centre-piece of these games and tournaments.

The comportment of the English on board the *Titanic* in 1912, so far as it was reported, lived up to this stereotype:

> The inevitable order went out; 'women and children first'. Gentlemen escorted ladies to their boats as though to their carriages, and helped them courteously in.... Mrs William T. Graham, having been helped into her boat by Howard Case,... 'one of the chivalrous young heroes of the Titanic', watched him lean against the rail, light a cigarette and wave good-bye as her boat was rowed away. 'Walter, you must come with me', begged Mrs Walter D. Douglas. 'No', replied Mr. Douglas, turning away, 'I must be a gentleman.'[59]

That same year, Captain Scott's tragic expedition to the Antarctic was an opportunity to praise a gentleman who had died a hero. An article in *The Times* affirmed that Captain Scott had been 'firm in his friendship and chivalrous in his conduct'. One of the patrons of the expedition commented on the 'deeds of devotion unequalled in all the deeds of knight-errantry'.[60]

In *English Saga*, Bryant criticised a society based upon money, produced by the enclosure movement of the eighteenth century, which marked the end of the agricultural small holding, the start of a rural exodus and the growth of towns:

> The England of the rationalists and the money-makers had no time to consider the England of the 'yeomen and the ale house on the heath'. It thus lost the key to its own past and future. Its divided posterity has been seeking it ever since. The social conditions of that older England – Christian, rural, half-democratic and half-authoritarian – were the outcome of centuries of evolution. They combined diversity with great cohesion and strength.[61]

Cohesion in diversity was set up against the Socialist idea of class struggle. Materialism was the product of the industrial and urban development, which reduced human relations in the cities solely to monetary exchange.

In 1925, Baldwin declared, 'People often say that this is a materialistic age. There is much truth in that.'[62] Against Socialist materialism, Baldwin set the spiritual life sustained by Christianity. Far from being an abstract doctrine, Christianity was seen as the fruit of a history incarnated in a single man. He contrasted Christianity with Socialist dogma, which, for him, was close to fundamentalism and obscurantism. He explained that 'all churches have their rule of life, you cannot say that there is any definite code laid down for all political parties.... The party that can claim more than any of the others to have a religious code to-day is the Labour Party, because they still have the Marxian *Capital*.'[63] To Baldwin, the distinction between Marxism and Christianity was that of a rigid and dogmatic approach, and an approach bound up with history, which alone enabled a critical approach towards the world. Baldwin, like the majority of Conservative thinkers, placed Christianity at the heart of his political thought.[64] Unlike his predecessors, Baldwin, in a spirit of ecumenism, sought to open up his party to different Christian groups and not only members of the Anglican church. Like Chamberlain and several of the other Conservative leaders, he came from a 'non-conformist' family. Descended from a long line of Methodists, his parents converted to the Church of England. He considered himself the product of the two traditions.[65] The Conservatives' religious ideal was one that conformed with existing society. It was less a matter of abstract faith than the organisation of community life and the principles that governed it. The notion of 'service', so dear to Baldwin, was echoed in the liturgy, the word 'service' being also used to mean the Church's programme of prayer. In 1925, Baldwin declared at the conference of non-conformist churches: 'the bodies of Christian people, united by a common ideal, have to act not only as individuals but as corporate bodies and communities ... criticising and judging, that we may be told where we fall short of the highest ideals in trying to apply political and social remedies in this country'.[66]

Bryant, writing in 1966,[67] explained English history through Protestantism, although his admiration for England before the Reformation is evident in his other works, especially *English Saga*. There he wrote, for example:

> Their [the English] tradition derived from the Catholic past of Europe. Its purpose was to make Christian men – gentle, generous, humble, valiant and chivalrous. Its ideals were justice, mercy and charity.... A squire or merchant who treated his neighbours with a sense of responsibility could still prosper. As a result of strong and unbroken Christian usage, it became native to the English to live and work in a society in which moral responsibility existed. And when England broke with the Catholic past – partly out of a critical sense of its human imperfections – she still cherished the old ideal of a nation dedicated to the task of breeding just and gentle men.[68]

Bryant's reference to the responsible and prosperous 'merchant' is a critique of a different form of materialism than that of the Socialists: that of the classical economic theory of the early nineteenth century, which was based on individualism and competition. Pushed to the extreme, it led to selfishness and the law of the jungle. For Bryant, as for Baldwin, the Church was the central institution in the medieval and Tudor periods, although the economic and social developments of the eighteenth and nineteenth centuries had reduced its importance. Ashridge, originally a Benedictine monastery, prided itself on understanding the continuity of England before and after the Reformation. The chapel at Ashridge was central to college life. A student, recalling his stay there, wrote, '"'time and tone" ... [were set] by the General's [Hoskins] apt words at prayers in the chapel. Daily these prayers were a delight. Here one found inspiration and guidance. The reading from Holy Writ was so appropriate and read so pleasantly and naturally that one felt obliged to live life at its highest and in its greatest realities.'[69]

Christian metaphors inspired numerous publications at Ashridge. Eric Patterson, Hoskins' successor as principal in 1938, wrote in the *Ashridge Journal*: 'Ashridge must be prepared *to serve* the many needs of the nation so far as its capacity will allow, for in the world of citizenship there are many mansions, and therefore Ashridge can never be narrow in its scope or limited in its endeavour.'[70] Ellis later took up this argument more explicitly, declaring that 'the simple creed [of Ashridge] ... [was to] hold in Trust, untarnished, all our forbears fought for and won, and pass that on, in our turn, to our children'.[71] Ashridge's mission should not be 'conceived within the narrow limits of passing party controversies, but as Seekers after Truth. In a world that has become over-material in its concepts of Life, there is surely urgent need for this teaching.'[72]

The manorial system was based on a dual authority – the secular authority of the squire, and the spiritual authority of the parson. Both were obliged to respect the rights of each member of the community. Relations between the squire, the parson and the community did not involve the exploitation of one by the other, as in the industrial and urban system. Feudal ties were not, as one is often led to believe, a unilateral system of deference from the community towards squire and parson, but rather a system based upon mutual obligations. When agricultural prices declined, squires were expected to adjust the rent paid by the peasants. By the same token, a few centuries later, farm labourers who worked on large estates often benefited from 'tied cottages', which provided lodging as part of their pay. In the event of a bad harvest or if there was not enough work, landowners did not discard their labourers. These rules were part of what was known as the 'the custom of the country': a code of conduct based upon mutual respect and responsibilities.[73] Ellis explained it thus:

> Our aim is simple and direct. To regain Faith through Understanding. To commune as much as to lecture. To read, to think, and to take counsel one with the other. More to examine frankly and faithfully than merely to memorise. To round off one's own corners, and to learn how others live. Freely to give vent to opinion, and get to appreciate the virtues of tolerance. That is the spirit in which we try to teach; to justify what we conceive to be our Mission.[74]

The manorial system shared with Christianity the notion of communion. They were two sides of the same coin; in both cases, the aim was to provide every individual with the means to live together. Massingham thus wrote: 'The manor was a superstructure upon an original foundation.'[75] This foundation was none other than the village. The manorial system was the institutional form taken by the social structure of the village. It represented the ideal that Ashridge sought to incarnate. In 1932, Frederic Lee, member of the college educational committee, described the manorial structure of the village:

> In the village we have a mixture of houses and the different classes growing up round the church, squire, lesser farmers and tradesmen. In such a community we know each other, enjoy a close-up of each other's lives with all the problems, faults and joys that come to all kinds of people. There is no outsider among the decent inhabitants of a normal village community and there is therefore a better understanding among all classes of people who dwell there together. In the village one class may call upon another either in business or for a friendly chat, without comment, or creating an atmosphere of restraint or self-consciousness. Intercourse between classes is natural and easy because it is sanctioned by custom and assisted by the geographical formation of the average village.[76]

Ashridge was 'not an institution, but a house party, and of the most unusual and catholic kind',[77] for 'its beauty and atmosphere is definitely part of what Ashridge gives to the students'.[78]

The Conservatives of Ashridge had a vision precisely the opposite to that of Karl Marx when he spoke of the 'idiocy of rural life'.[79] For them the customs of rural life were the manifestations of ancestral wisdom, which was more reliable than anything that could be found in the town. This ensemble of values inherited from Christianity and the Middle Ages explained the balance achieved in village communities. Solidarity and mutual respect were the keystones of a society that emphasised experience. Ernest Barker wrote to Bryant in 1938, 'I admit more and more the practical wisdom of the good ordinary Englishman, facing the facts and "feeling" the right way through them – as a good countryman feels his way through a new countryside.'[80] If the way of thinking of country people seemed wiser than that of townspeople, the comparison with their way of life was equally preferable to that of the townspeople. A. G. Street, the agricultural expert and lecturer at Ashridge, wrote: 'Our slow old-fashioned country-folk have farmed this island from time immemorial.... Without [their] steadying influence in the background, we should be a nation of chattering town robots.'[81] For Street, the fascination of city dwellers for new technologies was proof of their narrow-mindedness and lack of imagination. It was not that country people neglected or lacked interest in technological advances but they regarded them 'as [their] servant not [their] master,... thereby proving [their] intellectual superiority over the townsmen'.[82] The Ashridge estate, its historical heritage and the ideals of its founders made the college and its spirit a pedagogic tool in itself. Ashridge's manorial spirit was seen as an instrument to seduce, but also shape, its students. Thus Ellis wrote in 1938: '[We] hope that those who come to us will understand; and in understanding perhaps may borrow from this House some small measure of its Spirit, until in ever-widening circles the Message of Ashridge has been spread throughout the land.'[83]

Notes

1 Williams-Ellis, *Britain and the Beast*.
2 Jonah Jones, *Clough Williams-Ellis. The Architect of Portmeirion. A Memoir by Jonah Jones* (Bridgend: Poetry Wales Press Ltd, 1996, 1998), p. 76.
3 *Ibid.*, p. 80.
4 Clough Williams-Ellis was married to Amabel Strachey, whose political inclinations were moving Leftwards. She was an editor of the *Left Review* from 1934 to 1936. He explained, 'it was at her instigation that I ... joined the I.L.P'. C. Williams-Ellis, *Architect Errant. The Autobiography of Clough Williams-Ellis* (London: Constable, 1971), pp. 149–50.
5 Message from Sir Stafford Cripps, foreword to Williams-Ellis, *Britain and the Beast*, p. vi.
6 Lloyd George message in *ibid.*, p. v.
7 Williams-Ellis, *Britain and the Beast*, p. 138.
8 *Ibid.*, pp. xvi–xvii.
9 Howard Newby, *Country Life: a Social History of Rural England* (London: Weidenfeld & Nicolson, 1987) quoted in S. Spiers, *2026. A Vision for the Countryside* (London: CPRE.), www.cpre.org.uk/resources/cpre/about-cpre/item/2025-2026-a-vision-for-the-countryside.
10 CPRE pronouncements, quoted in Spiers, *2026. A Vision for the Countryside*.
11 S. Baldwin, 'England', 6 May 1924, in *On England*, pp. 6–7. L. Black, 'Tories and Hunters: Swinton College and the Landscape of Modern Conservatism', *History Workshop Journal*, 77 (1) 2014, pp. 187–214, at p. 3.
12 P. Mandler, *The Fall and Rise of the Stately Home* (New Haven, CT: Yale University Press, 1997), p. 241.
13 F. M. L. Thompson, *Gentrification and the Enterprise Culture, 1780–1980* (Oxford: Oxford University Press, 2001).
14 Mandler, *The Fall and Rise of the Stately Home*, pp. 226–30. See also M. J. Wiener, *English Culture and the Decline of the Industrial Spirit, 1850–1980* (Cambridge: Cambridge University Press, 1981), *passim*.
15 *Ibid.*, p. 232.
16 *Ibid.*, p. 237.
17 A. Potts, 'Constable Country between the Wars', in R. Samuel (ed.),

Patriotism: The Making and Unmaking of British National Identity, Vol. 3, *National Fictions* (London: Routledge, 1989), pp. 160–86.

18 H. V. Morton, *In Search of England* (London: Methuen, 1927).

19 *Ibid.*, p. 234.

20 J. Stevenson, *English Society, 1914–1945* (Harmondsworth: Penguin Books, 3rd edn, 1990).

21 Stapleton, *Sir Arthur Bryant*, pp. 71–84.

22 Mandler, *The Fall and Rise of the Stately Home*, p. 7.

23 *Ibid.*, pp. 148–9.

24 D. Cannadine, *The Decline and Fall of the British Aristocracy* (New Haven, CT: Yale University Press, 1990).

25 McKibbin, *Cultures and Classes*, pp. 27–34.

26 Déclassé was the French term used in English.

27 D. Cannadine, *G. M. Trevelyan; A Life in History* (London: Harper Collins, 1992), p. 159.

28 Mandler, *The Fall and Rise of the Stately Home*, p. 249.

29 R. Hewison, *The Heritage Industry: Britain in a Climate of Decline* (London: Methuen & Co., 1987).

30 Both were supporters of Lloyd George's land reform campaign between 1912 and 1914.

31 H. J. Massingham, 'Our Inheritance from the Past', in C. Williams-Ellis, *Britain and the Beast* (London: J. M. Dent & Sons Ltd, 1937), p. 31.

32 H. J. Massingham, *Remembrance: An Autobiography* (1941), quoted in Mandler, *The Fall and Rise of the Stately Home*, p. 237.

33 Massingham, 'Our Inheritance from the Past', p. 30.

34 See Chapter 2

35 *The Times*, 21 June 1926, in Cannadine, *G. M. Trevelyan*, p. 154 (my italics).

36 Bonar Law Memorial Trust Deed, 21 Nov. 1929, Ashridge papers.

37 J. Buchan memorandum, 'Political Research and Adult Education', 1972, Baldwin papers, SB53, fos 79–92.

38 W. A. Eden, 'The Landowner's Contribution', in Williams-Ellis, *Britain and the Beast*, p. 49.

39 A. Bryant, 'Ashridge Biographies II', *Ashridge Journal*, May 1930, pp. 13–14.

40 T. N. Graham, 'The Constituencies and Ashridge', *Ashridge Journal*, June 1935, p. 22.

41 A. Cummins, quoted in E. McEwen to H. Gordon, 17 Jan. 1933, Education Committee 1933, Ashridge papers.

42 J. A. L., 'Students' Reminiscences', *Ashridge Journal*, May 1930, pp. 8–12.

43 Mandler, *The Fall and Rise of the Stately Home*, p. 231.

44 *Ibid.*, p. 230.

45 Massingham, 'Our Inheritance from the Past', p.18.

46 McKibbin, *Classes and Cultures*, p. 100.

47 A. G. Street, *Farmer's Glory* (London: Faber & Faber, 1932). See 'Coming Courses', *Ashridge Journal*, *passim*.

48 *Ashridge Journal*, 1934, p. 24.

49 See J. Stevenson, 'Planners' Moon? The Second World War and the Planning Movement', in H. L. Smith (ed.), *War and Social Change: British Society in the Second World War* (Manchester: Manchester University Press, 1986).

50 Massingham, 'Our Inheritance from the Past', in Williams-Ellis, *Britain and the Beast*, p. 29.

51 William Blake, 'Jerusalem'.

52 Cripps, foreword to C. Williams-Ellis, *Britain and the Beast*.

53 The Court of Heralds is comprised of specialists in heraldry, shields and suits of armour. Governing Body Minutes, 11 Mar. 1930, Ashridge papers.

54 W. Shakespeare, *Richard II*, act II, scene 1.

55 Stapleton, *Sir Arthur Bryant*, pp. 49–65.

56 M. Girouard, *The Return to Camelot: Chivalry and the English Gentleman* (New Haven, CT: Yale University Press, 1981).

57 *Ibid.*, p. 6.

58 See P. Mandler 'In the Olden Time: Romantic history and English national identity, 1820–1850', in L. W. B. Brockliss and D. Eastwood (eds), *A Union of Multiple Identities: The British Isles, c. 1750–c. 1850* (Manchester: Manchester University Press, 1997), pp. 78–92.

59 *Ibid.*, p. 4.

60 *Ibid.*

61 *Ibid.*, p. vii.

62 S. Baldwin, 'Christian Ideals', 12 Mar. 1925, in Baldwin, *On England*, p. 209.

63 *Ibid.*, p. 205.

64 On Baldwin and religion, see Williamson, *Stanley Baldwin*, and P. Williamson, 'The Doctrinal Politics of Stanley Baldwin', in M. Bentley, *Public and Private Doctrine; Essays in British History Presented to Maurice Cowling* (Cambridge: Cambridge University Press, 1993), pp. 181–208.

65 Williamson, 'The Doctrinal Politics of Stanley Baldwin', p. 205.

66 Baldwin, 'Christian Ideals', pp. 207–8.

67 A. Bryant, *Protestant Island* (London: Collins, 1967).

68 Bryant, *English Saga*, p. viii.

69 J. A. L. 'Students' Reminiscences', *Ashridge Journal*, May 1930, p. 8.

70 E. J. Patterson, 'The Principal's Message', *Ashridge Journal*, summer 1938. My italics.

71 G. Ellis, 'Founder's Day Address in Ashridge Chapel', 19 Nov. 1938, *Ashridge Journal*, Christmas 1938, p. 5.

72 *Ibid.*

73 See F. M. L. Thompson, *English Landed Society in the Nineteenth Century* (London: Routledge, 1963). On the politics of deference, also see D. Eastwood, *Governing Rural England. Tradition and Transformation in Local Government, 1780–1840* (Oxford: Oxford University Press, 1994).

74 Ellis, 'Founder's Day Address in Ashridge Chapel, 19 Nov. 1938', p. 6.

75 Massingham, 'Our Inheritance from the Past', in Williams-Ellis, *Britain and the Beast*, p. 24.

76 F. Lee, 'National Unity and National Housing', *Ashridge Journal*, Sep. 1932, pp. 23–4.

77 A. Bryant, 'The Story of Ashridge', Bryant papers, M62.

78 Lord Davidson to Sir Patrick Hennessy, 24 Nov. 1954, Ashridge Appeals 1954, Ashridge papers.

79 K. Marx and F. Engels, *The Manifesto of the Communist Party*, 1848, *Selected Works*, vol. I (Moscow: Progress Publishers, 1958), p. 38.

80 E. Barker to A. Bryant, 7 Oct. 1938, Bryant papers, E1.

81 A. G. Street, 'The Countryman's View', in C. Williams-Ellis, *Britain and the Beast* (London: J. M. Dent & Sons, 1937), pp. 130–1.

82 *Ibid.*, pp. 131–2.

83 Ellis, 'Founder's Day Address in Ashridge Chapel, 19 Nov. 1938', p. 6.

10

Ashridge and the media

In 1925, Stanley Baldwin explained: 'My party have no political bible. Possibly you might find our ideals best expressed in one of Disraeli's novels, but I have no power to make people read them, and I have no power to compel them to belief.'[1] The creation of the NBA in 1937 was an attempt to advance, if not a bible, at least the Conservative catechisms setting out the credo of Ashridge.

The battle of the books

In May 1936, Victor Gollancz founded the Left Book Club, a political and literary venture which offered members a discount on the purchase of recommended books. The creation of this new book club politicised what had hitherto been a purely commercial phenomenon. Since the mid-1920s, book clubs, originally an American innovation, had taken a substantial share of the book trade. Two of the clubs, the Book Society and the Book Guild, were created on the model of the American Book of the Month Club. They helped establish, as the literary critic Q. D. Leavis disparagingly put it, 'a middlebrow standard of values', and their books were 'the staple reading of the middlebrow; they will be observed on the shelves of dons, the superior sort of schoolmaster … and in the average well-to-do home'.[2] These book clubs became engaged in a merciless fight to dominate a booming market. From the end of the 1920s, paperbacks also appeared, offering the public light reading for the price of six pence.[3] The most famous were those published by Mills and Boon.[4] In the autumn of 1935, Penguin Specials first appeared, with their iconic orange or green covers, marking the appearance of good-quality books, cheap enough to reach a wide public. In October 1937, *The Times* wrote: 'The cheap book … seems well on the way to being regarded as a staple commodity of home life…. The brightly coloured sixpenn'orths … can be readily sold all the year round to a public with purses, tastes, and habits of the most diverse kinds.'[5] With the creation of the Left Book Club, a new stage in the development of literary societies was reached, clearly politically oriented. Six months after it was established, the Left Book Club had 30,000 members. In March 1938, membership reached 58,000. By the end of 1937, it had created 730 discussion groups, with 12,000 people taking part every fortnight.[6] The 'veritable battle of the books'[7] had now begun; it was no longer just a matter of commercial competition, but also a war of ideas.

The Right Book Club and the National Book Association

The creation of the Left Book Club aroused great concern among all levels of the Conservative party. Before its creation, the Conservatives had already put considerable efforts into identifying the 'camouflaged Red reviewer'.[8] Now that an openly Socialist book club existed, the threat acquired a new dimension. Of Gollancz, Bryant wrote:

> [He can] publish serious political books simultaneously at two prices, one for the well-to-do high-brow – hitherto the only purchaser for this kind of book – and the other for the new popular public of the Left-Wing Book Club.... He has made propagandist publishing a paying proposition. He is using it to subvert the existing system of society.... No right-wing reading public exists comparable to that on the other side.... Writers and reading public have alike to be created.[9]

The real danger posed by the Left Book Club, Conservatives feared, was the infiltration of Socialist ideas among middlebrow readers. Until then, the highbrow had been synonymous with the Left. The Socialists' audience was already clearly defined, Bryant claimed, leaving Conservatives the large middlebrow public, which was precisely the audience that Gollancz now targeted.

In the months that followed the creation of the Left Book Club, Conservatives launched two rival literary ventures. At the end of 1936 William Foyle created the Right Book Club (RBC). Foyle was a senior partner in the most famous publishing house and bookshop of the day, W. & G. Foyle, of Charing Cross Road in London. The 'moving spirit'[10] behind this project was Christina Foyle, Foyle's daughter, who was known for her strongly Right-wing political views. In the spring of 1937, Arthur Bryant, in partnership with Ashridge, the Conservative party and the publishing house Walter Hutchinson, founded the NBA.[11] Bryant, T. N. Graham, Geoffrey Ellis and J. C. C. Davidson, with Baldwin's blessing, had established the NBA in absolute secrecy. The unexpected launch of the RBC led them hastily to bring forward the creation of the NBA. Bryant wrote:

> I had to make up my mind whether to disown the whole affair and leave the field to the Right Book Club under the direction of people who hadn't

the least idea of what we were trying to do, or to risk humiliating failure by accepting responsibility for an open attempt to hold the field with the odds all against us.... Something in me rebelled against letting our arrogant enemies carry the day, merely because fools on our own side made our path more difficult.[12]

If Bryant is to be believed, Baldwin originated the idea of the NBA. In 1937, Bryant wrote to him, 'The National Book Association ... arose out of a suggestion of yours at the Ashridge Governing Body a year ago that steps should be taken to get books written to counter balance the propaganda of the Left "intelligentsia" in the literary and academic world.'[13] Hastily created while Bryant was absent on account of illness, the NBA was a book-of-the-month club rather than a book club as initially proposed. A book-of the-month-club had the advantage of generating a regular monthly income. The disadvantage was that it imposed a rigid demand for recommended books, and frequently led the directors to propose books that had already been published. Unlike the RBC, the NBA aimed to publish its own works.

Bryant complained in June 1937 that,

> The N.B.A. in its present form as a Book of the Month Club was announced in my absence, without my knowledge, and contrary to my judgment, to meet the emergency caused by the launching of the Right Book Club.... The essential difference between such [a] scheme and our own was that theirs was based on the mistaken belief that the books that would do the work we wanted were already written and had only to be chosen; whereas we knew they had actually to be written.... I was then confronted with a promise to supply subscribers with a book every month, though in my opinion many months must elapse before books of the requisite standard could be produced. The books I already had on the stocks were short books of about thirty thousand words: a Book of the Month Club required books of at least 60,000 words that could be offered to the general public at three times the prices charged to members. This meant that they had to be doubled in size and rewritten to meet an entirely new situation.[14]

The NBA never recovered from its precipitous launch. The NBA's directors had thought of it as a complementary activity to Ashridge College, an extension of its cultural policy. However, it provoked acute tensions between the College and the party. Bryant wrote to Davidson in June 1936, 'The less the Central Office is made officially (or even unofficially) aware of what we are trying to do, the safer both for them and us: I should love to have their support, but this is a game we've got to play on our own if it's to have any chance of success.'[15] That same month, Ellis wrote to Bryant,

From what I know of the C.O. I have a certainty in my mind that they will produce just the potted 'one side of the question' which can be used as quick-firing fodder by the lazy minds of our political supporters. They and we appeal to two totally different types of mind.... We are trying honestly to educate not only our own people (most of whom are so static and sub-consciously frightened that they will never vote anything but 'agin Socialism') but the large & indeterminate (& increasing) mass which honestly does demand reason (rather than dogmas) for how they are to order their lives or cast their votes.[16]

Tensions between the NBA and the Conservative party were frequent and similar to those between Ashridge and the party. The same questions continued to arise: education or propaganda, highbrow versus lowbrow, the authority of the party or the autonomy to handle projects independently. The NBA's position was all the more complex, due to the existence of a rival literary society within the Conservative camp. The confusion created by the co-existence of two literary societies and the party's failure to decide which it wished to support aggravated conflicts. The confusion was such that Reginald Hoskins, the former principal at Ashridge, unaware of the rivalry between the two societies, lent his name to the RBC. Bryant was furious and requested Davidson to pressure him to abandon it.[17] Similarly, Miss E. D. Coates, an RBC supporter, wrote to T. N. Graham, director of the NBA, pointing out that she had been 'a subscriber to the *Right Book Club* for some months now', but having learnt of the existence of the NBA, she wondered which of the two societies belonged to the Conservative party. She expressed regret that founders of the NBA were also members of the RBC and that the existence of two book clubs revealed 'the utter lack of cohesion within the Party'.[18] Coates's point of view was shared by others. Bryant complained to Baldwin that

other groups of Conservatives in ignorance both of the real position and the difficulties ahead, if we are to make any lasting effect on the country, are talking of forming other book clubs: Douglas Jerrold and the extreme right, and Ned Grigg with Salisbury and Derby behind him, who also seem to expect your backing, while a number of old-fashioned Liberals, frightened by the foolish use of the word *Right* book club, are talking of forming a Centre Book Club.[19]

At one of the meetings for the executive committee of the NBA in September 1937, 'Mr. Hacking informed the Committee that it was becoming increasingly difficult for Central Office to advance the claims of the National Book Association, as opposed to the RBC. The RBC were determined to get in direct touch with the Constituency Associations.'[20] The RBC and the NBA competed to obtain the support of CCO and the constituency associations. In May 1937, Bryant appealed to Baldwin in favour of the NBA: 'Only you can save the situation by giving us the right to use your name ... as our Chairman or President ... [and] restore unity and confidence to our own people who are horribly confused by the appearance of one leading Conservative name after another on the literature of our rivals, and enable us to continue our carefully prepared plans to meet the very real danger of domination by extremist intellectuals.'[21]

In June 1937, Baldwin gave his approval and became chairman of the NBA, which 'serve[d] the double purpose of keeping the Conservative interest behind us and of aligning the intelligent centre and Liberal opinion we're out to capture. No other name could achieve this double role.'[22] The NBA's line of defence was similar to that of Ashridge: it was a national society, as its name suggested, with no affiliation to any political parties. The NBA, contrary to the RBC, sought to attract a wide range of readers. Bryant explained: 'The Right Book Club, though it possesses a large circulation, has no effect whatever outside Conservative circles; its books are ipso-facto labelled propaganda and Right.'[23] If for these reasons the NBA was opposed to the RBC, it defended itself against the pressure from the Conservative party, which sought to turn it into an openly Conservative organisation. While attempting to reach Conservative readers, the NBA wished to remain independent from the party. In October 1937, Davidson wrote to the Duchess of Atholl: 'You are mistaken in thinking that it [the NBA] is in any way financed by Central Office or Ashridge. From the financial point of view, it is an entirely independent publishing venture.'[24] A few days later, he asked Douglas Hacking, the Conservative party chairman, and members of the NBA executive committee, to confirm the NBA's autonomy. Hacking declared: 'Central Office has not any control over the Association.'[25] Equally, the NBA did not accept the idea that the RBC served as a tool for propaganda for the party. Like Ashridge, the NBA considered itself to be aligned with the party, but not attached to it, or rather the NBA saw itself as serving as the Conservative party's literary society, and all the more effectively by obscuring its links. Like Ashridge, it considered itself to be a better defender of conservatism than the Conservative party itself with its bureaucratic approach to communication problems. As Bryant wrote, 'literature unlike propaganda cannot be rigidly partisan ... Certain of our books will not be representative of the strictly party point of view; in some cases, they may even run counter to it.'[26]

Like Ashridge, the NBA thought of itself as apolitical. In September 1937, the meeting of the NBA executive committee affirmed: 'The NBA is neither a "Left" or "Right" Book Club.'[27] Baldwin's name and presence as head of the NBA guaranteed the neutrality of the project. Although leader of the Conservative party, Baldwin regarded himself as representative of the nation and of an Englishness 'over and above the parties'. This image of Baldwin was shared by many of his opponents, including a former Labour MP who wrote to him in 1939 to congratulate him on his speech 'Peace in Our Time'.[28] He was convinced that hatred between the classes was avoidable and that cordial relations between the different social classes were possible.[29] Baldwin remained true to his reputation, for in agreeing to chair the NBA, he 'had laid down as a condition that the Association must be supported by Members of all Parties behind the National Government, and by representatives of industry, education, etc., throughout the country, so that its appeal could be made upon the widest possible grounds'.[30]

'[T]he widest possible grounds' that Baldwin referred to was 'middle opinion', which, he imagined, principally comprised the middle classes. In March 1938, Frederick Heath, editor of the NBA at Hutchinson, wrote to Bryant about advertising the NBA in the press. He observed that there had been only 20 responses to the advertisement placed in *The Times*, whereas there had been 130 replies to the advertisement in the *Daily Telegraph*. Heath attributed the difference to the fact that readers of *The Times* were not interested in literary societies. '*Daily Telegraph* public is the lower middle class and slightly upwards where it is obvious we shall find most of our supporters'.[31] Similarly, Raymond Savage, administrator of the NBA, wrote that NBA books 'must ... appeal ... to the better educated, more especially the business man and the great "black-coat" public which is either too busy or too lazy to study serious books on serious subjects'.[32] However, middle opinion stretched beyond the petty bourgeoisie. NBA books 'must be published at a price within the compass of the pocket of the "man in the street"'.[33] The first book published by the NBA was *Coal-Miner, An Autobiography* by G. A. W. Tomlinson, a Nottinghamshire miner and student at Ashridge.[34] Its publication in March 1937 was a success, and it was nominated for the Femina prize. The book was aimed at the working class, to offer an example of a non-Socialist miner, and at the middle classes in order to demonstrate that the 'archetypal proletarian' was not necessarily Socialist. However, the NBA was interested not only in Nottinghamshire miners. In February 1938, it published a study called *The Good Patch* on the 'little Moscows' in the Rhondda valley in south Wales.[35] The NBA published several books on the working class to show the diversity of a class the Socialists described as homogeneous. In April 1938 the NBA published *Cast of All Fooling* by John Scanlon. Bryant described it thus: 'John Scanlon's book on Labour politics since the War up to the present time – a scathing denunciation of the upper and middle-class Left Wing Intellectuals, written from the point of view of a working man who really wants something done to better the working-man's wages and standard of living.'[36] The NBA sought to go even further, since in the spring of 1938, 'Mr Scanlon also suggested that it might be possible to obtain a book from Sir Walter Citrine and I asked Lord Baldwin, before he left England, if he would kindly reinforce Mr Scanlon's suggestion with a word to Sir Walter himself.'[37]

The NBA sought not only to present the point of view of workers and trade unionists but also that of employers. In July 1938, the NBA published *Manufacturer*,[38] the autobiography of Frederick Lee, a member of the education committee of Ashridge: 'a small manufacturer's point of view and political and social philosophy'.[39] If *Manufacturer* was an extended study of a small industrial firm, *The Nation Keeps House*[40] by L. H. Sutton, another teacher at Ashridge, offered a more general perspective on the British economy. He intended it as a defence and an illustration of the general domestic virtues associated with the middle classes. Other books published by the NBA focused on Englishness, Greater Britain, the Empire as well as the international situation.

The NBA's aim was 'to combat the growing tendency in political, academic and educational literature to represent Left wing propaganda as if it were an expression of middle opinion, and to ignore altogether the facts and opinions that defend the traditionalist point of view'.[41] It was a matter of conquering and holding this middle ground, which corresponded to the struggle in which the Conservatives believed they were engaged. As Bryant explained, 'Lord Baldwin is convinced that if we are to succeed in doing what we want to achieve, we have got be wary of frightening away the moderate intelligentsia and the centre, who still are very chary of anything that savours of Conservatism and have got be weaned from their "pink" bias gradually.'[42] The NBA targeted 'the man and woman in the street', offering them 'Commonsense Books on & of Fact', describing 'experience NOT fantastic theory'.[43] NBA advertising leaflets announced 'Authoritative books of national importance written in a popular manner by famous authors and eminent experts for every level-headed man and woman.' They described the NBA as an organisation 'Founded for People of Common Sense' who sought 'Balanced and common-sense conclusions arrived at after careful thought ... [with] answers to all extreme and crazy projects, arguments and ideas'.[44] Bryant wrote in a draft brochure for the NBA: 'You being British require no appeals to your emotions, and no fiery denunciations to help you to form judgments on issues affecting your interests. You need only one thing – the unvarnished truth. You, as a man or woman of common sense and sane outlook, can only look upon extreme revolutionary literature, of which there is so much, as dangerous to you, the country, and the Empire.'[45]

The demise of the National Book Association

Although the appeal to common sense was constant, it did not stop the NBA from publishing a work by Admiral Domville, who was known for his Nazi sympathies, and also publishing Hitler's *Mein Kampf* in February 1939.[46] From the NBA's viewpoint, publishing works of the extreme Right avoided the marginalisation of its authors, who would otherwise become still more dangerous. Some individuals within the party advocated a far more Right-wing conservatism. For example, Douglas Jerrold, editor in chief of *The English Review*, a reactionary, Fascistic monthly, wrote to Bryant in 1937, 'Right wing political movements are handicapped by the fact that something like half the Conservative Party are very moderate in their views and that they are the half who control the machine.... If the [Book] Club is simply to be the mouth piece of the great soft centre it will not only be no good, but it will precipitate the drift away from the party of all the people who have got to be kept in the party if we are to avoid Fascism or Communism.'[47] In November 1938, the NBA published the memoirs of Victor Serge, *Destiny of a Revolution*.[48] This account of a Bolshevik who had fled Stalin's purges was insufficient to give credibility to the NBA's declarations of political neutrality and impartiality.

On 28 July 1939, Baldwin's resignation from the NBA's executive committee presaged the end of the club, for his presence alone maintained the pretence of its political neutrality.[49] Already before his resignation the reorganisation of the NBA was the subject of numerous debates. Raymond Savage, one of its administrators, affirmed, 'Book Clubs have been overdone and most of them will find their Nemesis before long.' In consequence, Savage explained, if the NBA were to publish a new series of books on current affairs, 'in no circumstances should the word "National" be used and further that the word "Democracy" has become so familiar that it might breed suspicion, and obvious propaganda is what everyone desires to avoid'.[50] The fact that the words 'national' and 'democracy' could even be considered propaganda shows how drastically opinion had turned against the founding principles of the NBA in the span of two years. This change in vocabulary signified a profound change in the manner of approaching politics. The word 'national' was now associated with the extreme Right, particularly in Germany and Spain. Baldwin's resignation as prime minister in May 1937 marked the end of a certain language of Conservatism. Criticism of Chamberlain's 'appeasement' policy had also begun to affect Baldwin's reputation.[51]

Against a worsening international background, growing tensions between the NBA and the Conservative party were accompanied by a crisis between the NBA and the publishers Hutchinson, since the former's political objectives clashed with the latter's commercial imperatives. The NBA had been possible only thanks to financial assistance from Walter Hutchinson and the support of his publishing house. In July 1936, Bryant wrote: 'The firm is putting about £10,000 into launching it, about half of which will be spent in the first year, a good deal in advertisement.'[52] The importance of this financial support placed Hutchinson in a position of influence over the NBA's strategy. For him, the priority was to sell as many books as possible, whereas Ashridge sought to support authors and create a reading public. In April 1937, Graham wrote to Davidson:

> I gather that you have been made aware of the difficulty which Walter Hutchinson is creating. His trouble is that he expected the scheme on its initial advertisement to receive 40,000 subscribers and to forge ahead of the Gollancz effort. He threatens to call in just those people who would throttle the whole business at its birth. W. H. is out of touch with the realities. He lives a cloistered existence ... I think, therefore, if he can be assured that his effort to combat Communism is very deeply appreciated but he will best serve the Cause of the National Book Association by standing outside the ring and allow those of us who have lived a life of combat to do the fighting.[53]

According to Graham, Hutchinson did not understand the NBA's ambitions and did not understand the kind of readers it was looking for: 'a class whose apathy towards the things that matter is a bye-word'.[54] In order to attract this type of reader without putting them off, Bryant wrote in February 1938, 'We must proceed very cautiously and refrain scrupulously both from propaganda and the showier kind of advertising. We are building for the distant future and trying to make an educated democracy, not for the immediate present.'[55] He concluded his memorandum by suggesting that if Hutchinson did not agree with this policy, the NBA should seek another publishing house. Similarly, Frederick Heath, a colleague of Hutchinson's, explained that 'the scheme must by its very nature be a long term one, since we had to find our authors and create our public as against the existing authors and avid public available to and accountable for the enormous success of the Left Book Club, the slow growth in membership did not necessarily mean failure'.[56] As we have seen, Heath shared the same objectives as Bryant. As the result of his disagreements with Hutchinson, Heath resigned at the end of 1937. He wanted to see the NBA's editorial department, which he managed, leave the Hutchinson premises and move elsewhere. Heath thought the NBA needed 'a definite agreement with Hutchinson that he is merely the publisher and printer and has nothing to do with the editorial work'; this would '[curb] Hutchinson as he will always have to be curbed'. It was a matter of preventing 'arrangements for the NBA ... on his own authority'.[57]

Relations between Hutchinson and the NBA scarcely improved in 1938, during which the NBA recorded a net loss of £4,360. In May 1938, the number of NBA members dropped from 4,000 to 3,500.[58] In January 1939, Graham wrote to Bryant saying that for Hutchinson the 1938 deficit was in fact £5,000. If the contract between the NBA and Hutchinson had to be severed, Hutchinson considered that the books published by the NBA would legally belong to him.[59] In May 1939, Hutchinson claimed the NBA had 5,000 members and that he was in the process of taking sole control of the organisation.[60] This was undoubtedly optimistic on his part. Already in January that year, Ellis had expressed doubts as to the accuracy of the statistics provided by Hutchinson.[61] Ashridge leaders were worried by the manner in which he managed the publishing and commercial sides of the operation. In January 1939, Ellis felt that 'The way WH [Walter Hutchinson] has dealt with *Mein Kampf* would alone justify a first-class war.'[62] Bryant shared Ellis's opinion on this matter and was outraged that Hutchinson had published *Mein Kampf* twice in the space of one month: an unabridged complete edition for the general public and an abridged edition for members of the NBA. Byrant spoke of a 'racket'.[63] Criticism of Hutchinson only stopped with the closing of the NBA in July 1939.

Because of the tempestuous nature of this relationship, Bryant, Ellis, Graham and CCO made contact with other publishing houses. In November 1938, at a meeting of the party devoted to political education, Eric Gillett, a lecturer at Ashridge, told R. A. Butler, head of the Conservative party's department of education, Patrick Gower, head of the department of communications, and Eric Rowe, Cuthbert Alport and Kathleen Curlett, all officers of the party, that the contract between Hutchinson and the NBA was due to expire at the end of that same year. He wondered if this would not be a good moment for the party to regain control of the organisation: 'He favoured this procedure rather than the formation of a new Book Club and his plan would be to carry out the present programme of the National Book Association and then by degrees revitalize it and make it a power.'[64] The rumours circulating within the NBA were different, however. In February 1939, Graham wrote to Bryant, 'I understand that young Alport at C.O. has sent a circular letter asking for information as to what people would like to read not necessarily political. Is a 'Bookclub' under contemplation at C.O.?'[65] Graham's suspicions were perhaps based on Alport's double 'desertion' in publishing *Kingdoms in Partnership* in 1937 with both the RBC and the NBA, which had not gone unnoticed, and in quitting his teaching post at Ashridge in 1938 for a position at CCO.[66] The Conservative Party considered taking control of the NBA in November 1938; it also considered the possibility of a partnership with

Penguin in order to be rid of Hutchinson. Kathleen Curlett explained to Butler,

> I have a feeling that Mr. Allen Lane, having explored the reading public on the Left, is now prepared to do the same on the Right. I think that the proposed slip inside the Penguin books to the effect that his policy is non-sectarian and non-political is only of value if he is prepared to publish a greater proportion of books with a non-socialist bias.[67]

Meanwhile, those in charge of the NBA also sought a solution. In the spring of 1938, before the tensions with Hutchinson reached their peak, Graham proposed that Ashridge should take control of the NBA:

> The idea originally in our minds [was] that the NBA and Ashridge would be linked up. In fact if I remember aright some of us discussed the preparation and issue of books in connection with Ashridge.... [We] might then take over the NBA and absorb it. An ASHRIDGE BOOK ASSOCIATION or CLUB could be formed which would take over such members of the NBA as cared to join it – many of the members of the NBA at present are Ashridge students – and be built up upon the basis of the 20,000 Ashridge students scattered throughout the country.... A BOOK ASSOCIATION or CLUB and ASHRIDGE linked together might well become a strong force in the country.[68]

It went without saying that the Conservative party too wished to make the NBA a 'strong force'. Another proposed solution was to merge the NBA with the RBC into a single organisation. Bryant favoured this idea: 'From our own point of view amalgamation, provided it is on our own political terms, is to be welcome. It would avoid wasteful competition.... The name of Right Book Club, which is likely to antagonise academic and university opinion, should be dropped or merged.'[69] A few months later, Bryant wrote to the chairman of the Conservative party that while he considered the RBC

> a continual threat to all that we are trying to achieve ... I could not be party to any amalgamation which did not leave completely intact the political and educational purposes for which we have been working from the beginning.... Nothing else would do anything so contrary to my own interests and profession as to sponsor a half-a-crown Book of the Month Club. The Right Book Club is at present merely an organisation which exploits Conservative alarm at Gollancz's propaganda to under-sell over the heads of the trade books that are already being published in the ordinary course.... Unless we can obtain complete political and educational control of it, we shall gain none of our ends by amalgamation and merely incur odium in the very quarter which we want to win over to the Conservative cause.[70]

As a result of these doubts and uncertainties, the proposed amalgamation of the RBC and the NBA was abandoned, and with it the hope that the NBA would gain the 10,000 members of the RBC.[71] Thereupon Heath proposed that 'co-operation should be sought with the Penguin Book Company, not only to issue some of our own books in their sixpenny series but to find a means of forming with the Penguin Company an issue of sixpenny series'.[72] He compiled a list of publishing houses to contact: 'Heinemann, Constable, Collins, Methuen, Murray, Longman would ... be quite willing to work the scheme, but they would, I think, require either some financial assistance or a guarantee against loss. [But] any of these publishers would understand the scheme and work sensibly and amicably.'[73] Bryant took up this idea again in November 1938. He noted that Penguin had a 'vast ... public appeal' and that if the NBA were associated with Penguin 'we should be touching a far vaster public than we can hope to do, either through the present National Book Association, through a similar Ashridge Book Association, or through an amalgamation of the National Book Association and the Right Book Club.'[74] In spite of Heath's and Bryant's hopes and those of central office that Allen Lane would demonstrate that it 'was anxious not to be too partial'[75] and counterbalance its Socialist publications with more publications from the Right, no agreement between the NBA and Penguin was reached. Bryant lamented: 'There *is* no right wing reading public of a size comparable to that which the writers and academic bigwigs of the Left have been building up for the past thirty years.... That has to be created, and it will take time, and so has a school of right wing political writers.'[76]

During the summer of 1939, it became evident that the NBA could not meet its creditors. On 28 July 1939, the NBA's executive committee 'resolved that in view of the fact that ... interest in and support for Book Clubs generally has now declined this Committee be and hereby is dissolved'.[77] Some of those responsible for the NBA believed still in the possibility of reviving it. Shortly after the outbreak of war, Raymond Savage wrote to Bryant:

> It will be most unwise for us to sit down and do nothing. After all, our friend Gollancz is carrying on with his Left Book Club, and I understand that the Right Book Club is also carrying on. Surely, just at this juncture, it is very important indeed that an organisation should actually exist which could meet events and situations as they arise. I feel that in spite of everything we ought to get Lord Davidson and Sir Geoffrey Ellis and yourself together to discuss the future.[78]

Savage was wrong. The RBC ceased operating at the start of the war and was never brought back to life. As for the Left Book Club, it closed in 1945.

One of the reasons invoked to explain the NBA's lack of success was revealed in a memorandum by Graham in May 1938, in which he complained, 'we have no real NBA organisation in the country'.[79] One of the solutions envisaged by the NBA was making use of the 'Ashridge circles', which had existed around the country since 1930.

Extra-mural Ashridge

In November 1929, John Buchan, chairman of the education committee at Ashridge, proposed that

> all the educational activities of the Party would centre at Ashridge, which would be the 'power house' and 'generating station' of these activities, functioning under the Educational Committee meeting in London, but in close and constant touch with the College authorities, a 'field organisation' would be established in the different constituencies to arrange for the holding of classes to meet the educational requirements of each district. It was most important to develop without delay an educational network throughout the country in order to meet – as far as possible – similar activities on the part of the Labour Party, which had already been in the field for some time past.[80]

This proposal was reiterated in July 1930 by Neville Chamberlain, then president of the Conservative party, who sent a circular to his party members in his capacity 'as a Governor of Ashridge',[81] encouraging local branches of the party to send students to Ashridge. He explained, 'In practically every constituency, there is a number of men and women who could afford to go to Ashridge and who would do so if they knew more about it, and realised its educational and social attractions and the benefits of a course there.'[82] Chamberlain proposed the creation of 'Ashridge committees' in each constituency, and 'Ashridge clubs' to spread information about the college and its publications. This led to what would become known as the 'Ashridge circles'. These circles constituted the main element of the 'extra-mural' activities of the college. They served two purposes: to represent Ashridge and diffuse its teaching in the constituencies, and to select and recruit Ashridge students.[83] On 5 February 1930, it was decided that Buchan should send, on behalf of central office, a letter to local representatives of the party, explaining the need to create a 'small Ashridge committee' at the local level.[84] Although, after October 1930, the College's financial difficulties led it to shelve its other extra-mural activities, the idea of Ashridge circles was not abandoned. In July 1931, extra-mural activities were taken up once again in co-operation with local sections of the party. A network of teachers was set up across the country, closely linked to Ashridge and the party, the former as educational advisors, the

latter as recruitment agents.[85] A scheme published in July 1931 established
the different roles held by Ashridge and by the Conservative party.
Ashridge circles were placed under the college's authority, while each
locality had a party representative whose mission it was to 'encourage
the development of educational classes in the constituencies' and 'find out
suitable students for Ashridge from among Party workers and others, and
to link up the Area classes with that of Ashridge'.[86] Ashridge advised the
local education committees on teaching and the contents of the teaching
programme.

> It is advisable that Ashridge should draw up a scheme of Courses of lectures,
> varied in type and length with recommended books for the guidance of the
> Area Education Secretaries.... During the summer months when there
> would probably be very little work in the Areas and constituencies it might
> be possible for the Area Educational Secretaries to act as additional tutors
> at Ashridge, which would be a great help during the months when there are
> more students at Ashridge, many of whom require extra coaching.[87]

The decision in July 1931 indicates that 'although the Area Educational
Secretaries should work directly under the control of their respective
Areas, their work should be co-ordinated and the general scheme of
education laid down should be on the same lines as far as possible, since
the work is to be regarded not only as an end in itself but as a preparation
for Ashridge'.[88]

Gradually, Ashridge circles were established around the country. The
Ashridge Journal of May 1931 reported that 'an Ashridge Lancashire
Circle has been formed', and that 'two members of the Harborough
district who have attended courses at Ashridge formed an Ashridge club
last November'.[89] In February 1934 the first reunion of representatives
of Ashridge circles took place at the college.[90] From 1934, the *Ashridge
Journal* regularly published detailed reports on the activities of each circle.
The 1937 report, for example, clearly illustrated the activities and the
expansion of the circles. It reported that new circles had been established
in Fulham East and West as well as in other districts of London such as
West Islington and Finchley, to facilitate the work of Ashridge in London.
By the same token, after the meeting of the Ashridge circle in Yorkshire, a
new meeting was held in Hull to create a local circle there. In January and
February 1937, an Ashridge circle covering the West Midlands area was
created in Birmingham, and another in Manchester.

The activities of each circle were described in detail. The Ashridge
circle in the west of Wales, for example, reported that

> the numbers of Ashridge students in this area are not large, but in Miss
> Phyllis Betts there is one student who is determined to carry into effect the

teaching she received at the College.... The West Wales Circle has been established and has arranged a series of lectures in conjunction with the Swansea Conservative and Unionist Association.... We commend the idea of Ashridge Circles as the basis for such courses of lectures. The appeal is wider than that which is confined to the members of the Circle, and it brings Ashridge to more general notice.[91]

If, as Bryant wrote, 'from England to Ashridge is no very long leap of thought',[92] the Ashridge circles aimed to make the college not merely English but British. Several circles were created in Scotland and Northern Ireland. The one in Ayrshire was among the most active; the Roxburgh and Selkirk circle was one of the earliest. The map of the country was practically filled with Ashridge circles. In numerous localities, the work undertaken by the Ashridge circles matched the goals that were set out in the document of July 1931. In the west of Wales, for example, it was noted that the circle there acted 'as the educational agency of the [constituency] association'.[93] Generally speaking, the circles benefited from 'the practical sympathy and encouragement of many of the Party agents'.[94] In light of the reports on their activities, T. N. Graham wrote that 'considerable progress has been made in connection with the maintenance of existing Ashridge Circles and the formation of new agencies.... More and more it is being realised that Ashridge is playing a very definite part in counteracting the many subversive elements which are at work to-day to undermine the stability of our country, and that there is abundant opportunity for service for all Ashridge students.'[95]

The success of the circles was such that the Conservative party hoped to place them under its direct control. Butler, chair of the party's education committee, acknowledged this to Bryant. However, Bryant rejected the proposal, replying to Butler, 'this might be of some assistance to the Education Committee but it would effectively destroy the Ashridge Fellowship. The whole purpose of the Fellowship is to draw into our net those whom the Party Organisation cannot send to us.'[96] In 1939, some fifty Ashridge circles were functioning.[97] Ashridge's ambition to be present in every region had been realised.

Twenty Ashridge circles continued to operate during the war.[98] From 1945, the other circles reopened their doors. However, the management changes at Ashridge and the change of direction in teaching by the college made the Ashridge circles a 'vexed question'.[99] Some felt 'the Circles could still most usefully perform their dual function of recruiting new students for the College and encouraging their members to take their full share in public service, especially if their members as individuals joined other organisations.... It was probable that gradually the old Circles would be superseded by a new type.'[100] This new type of circle was not clearly defined, however, and the importance of Ashridge circles started to decline from 1946.

If, during the inter-war years, the circles, clubs and other literary societies were the principal instruments for spreading new ideas, the Conservative party was an audacious innovator in the use of new technology such as radio and cinema.

Using new forms of communication

Cinema

During the inter-war years, the Conservative party was the only political organisation to make use of the cinema as an instrument of propaganda. In 1925, at Davidson's request, the first travelling cinema was built by Thorneycrofts. Writing to Winston Churchill in 1928, Davidson proudly explained this innovation:

> For rural districts the phonofilm cinema van is by common consent the most powerful agency at the disposal of the Party, and is one which neither the Liberal nor the Socialist Party possesses.... Right through the summer the vans which the Party possesses will be travelling through the rural districts and carrying on propaganda amongst those who ordinarily it is difficult to get at even through the press.[101]

During the elections in 1929, ten Conservative party vans which were equipped to project films toured the country, offering political films along with films of pure entertainment in public places. The party also had thirteen mobile projectors to show films indoors, in town and village halls. During the electoral campaign of 1935, an estimated 1.5 million people saw Conservative party propaganda films.[102] The content of these films was as original as the method used to disseminate it. Sir Patrick Gower, who became director of the department of communication in 1929 when Ball became head of the research department, created a sub-section for film called 'The Conservative and Unionist Film Association'. It produced documentaries, historical films and animated works. Gower asked William Ward, one of the three best-known illustrators of the period, to produce animated films for the party. Alexander Korda, one of the best-known directors of the 1930s, was involved in several film projects.[103] In 1946, a memorandum from the Conservative constituency of Horncastle described the film showings:

> the show usually opens with a documentary, travel or sport film, and this is followed with a special 'build-up' film to put the audience in the right mood to listen to a serious political argument.... Whenever possible we conclude

every programme with a good feature film which may run for an hour or more.

It is the feature film which draws the large audience which must, however, listen to the speech and/or see the propaganda films before enjoying their treat ...

In conclusion we believe that this is the best possible way of preaching Conservatism in a Rural Area ... We find that not only do our opponents come to these meetings but the floating voters are also attracted as well as the young people. Moreover, our meetings are attended by far greater numbers than we could expect from any other method.[104]

In 1928, Oscar Deutsch created the Odeon cinema chain, with the aim of showing films to the general public throughout the country. The Conservative party took this idea on board and made popular entertainment a means to garner the loyalty of new voters.

In the 1930s, the film industry in Britain was characterised by its determination to protect British films against domination by Hollywood and to develop documentary filmmaking, which was considered as Britain's greatest contribution to the 'seventh art'. Since the 1920s, the House of Commons had frequently debated the role of cinema in society and the influence of cinema upon public attitudes.[105] Conservative members of parliament actively participated in these debates. Documentary filmmaking was generally associated with the Left, and in particular with the work of John Grierson, the most prominent figure in the Documentary Film Movement.[106] But while most speeches on cinema in the House of Commons were delivered by Conservatives,[107] parliament was not the only place where the subject was discussed. Three historians closely associated with Ashridge participated actively in the debates which agitated the film world, and in particular the Documentary Film Movement. From 1934 to 1939, Charles Petrie presided over the history and arts committee at the British Film Institute, of which Arthur Bryant was also a member. From 1936 to 1938, Frederick Hearnshaw presided over the cinematic branch (founded in 1934) of the Historical Association.[108] These organisations shared the same objectives: defending conservatism and educating public opinion through the diffusion of Conservative principles. Intellectual rigour and the choice of 'serious' subjects were deemed essential. Historical films seemed to be the best means of attaining this objective, since they could touch a wide public and pass on civic values.

The film industry was divided between those who sought to entertain and those who wished to *educate*.[109] The Conservative attitude on this matter was similar to that of the Documentary Film Movement. In October 1936, Grierson wrote an article on the 'the role of cinema in teaching citizenship', where he observed that the government used film as a means to communicate with voters. The Empire Marketing Board, for example, created some short films mid-way between documentary and advertisement, to promote products from across the Empire. These films were shown before the main film. Grierson regretted that they did not address the theme of the 'dignity of labour'[110] by showing, for example, the work of indigenous people as he had done the fishermen in the north-east of England in his film *Drifters*. He added that it was time the cinema emerged 'out of the field of publicity and into the field of civic education … at last joining cinema to the service of social purposes'.[111] Petrie, Bryant and Hearnshaw would have concurred with this view. Their difference would have been in the choice of subjects.

Grierson considered that the worker represented the best in British society. His pride, work and dignity in the face of adversity, especially poverty, made him the true hero in Grierson's documentaries. For the Conservatives, the embodiment of national character was often found in the figure of the policeman. The policeman was, in many ways, the antithesis of the worker as depicted by Grierson. Workers regarded him as the defender of the interests of the ruling class. In 1937, Bryant edited, along with the filmmaker Charles Laughton, a script for a film on the daily life of a London policeman. Laughton was to be the director. Bryant wrote:

> What Charles Laughton and I are anxious to do is to make a film with a typical London policeman as its central figure. We want to show him against the background of the London year – controlling the traffic, managing the rush hour, presiding at public ceremonies, frustrating crime, preserving order – always steady and calm amid chaos, both in his public work and his private life. Our motive is to give our own people and the outside world a film descriptive, not of the surface life of cocktail parties, divorce triangles and all that, but of genuine, native English character. And we feel that a typical London policeman is the best subject to illuminate it.[112]

The contrast between the 'genuine, native English character' and 'the surface life' of London society echoed the arguments on the subject of rural values versus those of city dwellers. The London policeman represented rural values to the city. He was the guarantor of the sound moral values of 'old cottage folk of England'.[113] In his *English Saga*, Bryant explained that 'though London was the greatest city in the world, its people still had their roots in the country'.[114] It was just this past and this heritage that the policeman incarnated. The protagonist of the film was called 'Robert of London' or 'Bobby'.[115] Bryant described him as follows,

> His character: plain man, solid as a rock. He never fails in his duty and takes a thousand crises and troubles with cheerful calm as part of the day's

work. But he looks for no promotion and never gets any because being no
scholar, he can't pass examinations. When it comes to tackling awkward
situations with stolid common sense, he is brave as a lion, yet his knees go
all of a tremble at the mention of an examination.[116]

Wisdom born of experience as opposed to wisdom acquired through
books was the key to the manner of work of the policeman, since he
was daily confronted with various situations and people from all walks
of life and professions. No theory applied to the trade of the policeman,
since his work was never the same. Bryant underlined that 'You cannot
possibly teach a policeman by theory.'[117] If 'Robert of London' was fearful
of examinations and their theoretical aspect, it was not because he did not
possess the necessary knowledge, but because he would have to deal with
the administrative and bureaucratic demands, which were far removed
from the practical reality of his work.

Radio

Since its formal establishment under royal charter in 1927, the BBC had
aroused suspicion among Conservatives,[118] a suspicion still evident today.
In 1990, Norman Tebbit, chairman of the Conservative party between 1985
and 1987, observed of the BBC: 'the word "Conservative" is now used by
the BBC as a portmanteau word of abuse for anyone whose political views
differ from the insufferable, smug, sanctimonious, naive, guilt-ridden, wet,
pink orthodoxy of the sunset home of that third-rate decade, the 1960s'.[119]
These acerbic comments are consistent with unrelieved criticism of the
BBC ever since the 1930s. Bryant constantly complained that the BBC
radio programmes were too Left wing.

> I have made contact with Ogilvie [the Deputy Director of the BBC],... I
> made it quite clear that I wanted to discuss with him the Left tendency of
> the BBC.
>   I have been thinking a great deal about it, and I have come to the
> conclusion that it is not advanced politics that is in trouble; it is the fact that
> the Left Wing intelligentsia has got in, and that the Gollancz crowd – whom
> the ordinary honest-to-God working man and trade unionist loathes worse
> than he loathes us – is responsible for the propaganda which we all can put
> our finger on in the talks, etc. If this continues it is the BBC which is going
> to suffer, and it is a point I shall not fail to make when I have a serious talk
> with Ogilvie. The working classes do not like satire on marriage, religion,
> and the acceptance of low moral standards as inevitable in the modern
> age.[120]

Bryant's moralising complaints echoed the critiques of Conservatives about
the behaviour of members of the Bloomsbury group. The loose morals

attributed to them were alleged to be a sign of the deterioration of public morals. His reference to the working class and trade unions suggested that the BBC was too highbrow. The Conservatives therefore decided to launch a campaign to make the BBC a more middlebrow medium. In September 1933, for example, a series of programmes on England was scheduled. Stanley Baldwin delivered the first talk, while Bryant prepared a programme on the 'national character'. He relied upon the historian A. L. Smith, taking up his proposed theme of 'the spirit of cooperation, the spirit of fair-play and give-and-take, the habit of working to a given purpose, which tempered the hard and grim individuality of the national character'.[121] In Bryant's view, 'the hard and grim individuality' was associated with 'laisser-faire' economics of the industrial revolution, and was not the best expression of the national character. National character was meant to show 'her [England's] ability to restate in a new form the ancient laws of her own moral purpose and unity'.[122] To get this message onto the airwaves was a way of 'infiltrating' the BBC and combating the subversive influence of Left-wing programmes. Several BBC programmes prompted criticism from Baldwin and Davidson. Davidson commented on the programme 'Some New Novels', broadcast in London on 26 June 1939 and directed by J. Brophy: 'I understand that without exception every one of the books reviewed was Leftist (if I may use that horrid word).'[123] Baldwin similarly complained of a new programme on 'some new sixpennies'. Investigating this programme, Davidson discovered that the commissioner of the programme was none other than Eric Gillet, 'who often lectures at Ashridge and is also connected with Central Office educational activities, so it would perhaps not be wise to complain about him'.[124] This kind of incident demonstrated the anxiety of the Conservatives, who saw Socialist conspiracies and highbrow activity everywhere. In 1936, Bryant wrote to Davidson, 'The Left always advances behind a creeping barrage of mugwumps! – woolly-minded Liberal professors, devotees of the League of Nations and Bishops with a weakness for the limelight, with the result that it takes a very close observer to see what is really happening.'[125] The substantial correspondence that Bryant received from Conservative activists, complaining of the domination of the Left in the realm of culture, demonstrated just how widespread was the fear of conspiracies.[126]

However, winning back some of the cultural scene from the grip of the Left was not considered a lost cause, but one that required hard work and a careful strategy. In 1936, Bryant welcomed the progress made by Conservatives within the BBC:

> That it's possible to do something is proved by the BBC. Three years ago,
> so far as its 'highbrow' side was concerned, it was almost an advertising

medium for the extreme left, and when I first talked for them I was regarded as a reactionary of the worst die! Now they're essentially moderate and, I think, very fair, without tipping the balance in the least towards the right. But I hope when the new Governors are appointed they won't alter things again: the price of a free intelligentsia is unceasing vigilance![127]

'Unceasing vigilance' was precisely the attitude of the Conservative party and its activists. In 1934, Patrick Gower, who was director of the Conservative party's communications department, wrote: 'I am getting more and more disturbed about the subtle propaganda which is being put out by the BBC ... and I am making arrangements for somebody to listen in every night and take down in shorthand anything that savours of tendentious socialist propaganda.'[128] From 1945, this attitude of defiance and suspicion became systematic both within central office and at the local level. In 1946, the Conservative party created a broadcasting department, directed by the young member of parliament John Profumo, whose aim was to train Conservatives to use radio and television as well as to monitor the impartiality of BBC programming and pressure the organisation in the case of programmes judged too Left-wing.[129] At the local level, a national viewers' and listeners' association was set up at the end of the 1960s by Mary Whitehouse.[130] It brought together different Conservative activist groups to fight against the alleged amorality of television and radio programmes. The monitoring of the media by Ashridge prefigured the more systematic surveillance mechanism put in place after the war.

Notes

1 S. Baldwin, 'Christian Ideals', 12 Mar. 1925, in Baldwin, *On England*, p. 205.
2 Q. D. Leavis, *Fiction and the Reading Public* (1939), pp. 22–4, 37, quoted in McKibbin, *Classes and Cultures*, pp. 478–9.
3 These books were called 'sixpennies' as they were priced at 6 old pence, which today is roughly equivalent to 75p.
4 McAleer, *Popular Reading and Publishing in Britain*.
5 'The Battle of the Books', *The Times*, Oct. 1937, Davidson papers, DAV/232.
6 B. Pimlott, *Labour and the Left in the 1930s* (Cambridge: Cambridge University Press, 1977), p. 156.
7 'The Battle of the Books', *The Times*, Oct. 1937, Davidson papers, DAV/232.
8 Lord Elton's Report, undated, July 1938, Davidson papers, DAV/232.
9 A. Bryant, 'Memorandum on the Means of Combatting Left-Wing and Communistic Propaganda in Literature and in the Universities', 22 Apr. 1937, Davidson papers, DAV/226.
10 A. Bryant to R. Northam, 3 Aug. 1938, Bryant papers, C46.
11 A. Bryant to S. Baldwin, 5 May 1937, Davidson papers, DAV/226.

12 *Ibid.*

13 A. Bryant to S. Baldwin, 5 May 1937, Davidson papers, DAV/226. No mention of this was found in the minutes of the governing body.

14 A. Bryant to D. Hacking, 1 June 1937, Bryant papers, C41.

15 A. Bryant to J. C. C. Davidson, 13 June 1936, Davidson papers, DAV/226.

16 G. Ellis to A. Bryant, 10 June 1936, Bryant papers, C44.

17 A. Bryant, Notes on Mr. Graham's Confidential Memorandum of the 20th of May 1938, undated (May 1938), Bryant papers, C49. See J. C. C. Davidson to R. Hoskins, 24 Mar. 1937, Davidson papers, DAV/230.

18 Miss E. D. Coates to the Manager, National Book Association, 30 Jan., 1939, Bryant papers, C47.

19 A. Bryant to S. Baldwin, 5 May 1937, Davidson papers, DAV/226, emphasis by the author.

20 Minutes of the National Book Association Meeting, 30 Sep. 1937, Davidson papers, DAV/232.

21 A. Bryant to S. Baldwin, 5 May 1937, Davidson papers, DAV/226.

22 A. Bryant to W. Hutchinson, 24 June 1937, Bryant papers, C47.

23 A. Bryant, 'Notes on Mr. Graham's Confidential Memorandum of 20th Nov., 1938', undated Nov. 1938, Bryant papers, C47.

24 Lord Davidson to the Duchess of Atholl, 4 Oct. 1937, Davidson papers, DAV/232.

25 D. Hacking, 21 Oct. 1937, Davidson papers, DAV/232.

26 A. Bryant to G. Ellis, 20 Oct. 1937, Bryant papers, C58.

27 Minutes of the National Book Association, 30 Sep. 1937, Davidson papers, DAV/232.

28 S. Baldwin, 'Give Peace in Our Time O Lord', in *On England*, pp. 23–40.

29 ? to S. Baldwin, 18 Sep. 1939, Bryant papers, C62.

30 Minutes of the National Book Association, 30 Sep., 1937, Davidson papers, DAV/232.

31 F. Heath to A. Bryant, 4 Mar. 1938, Bryant papers, C47.

32 R. Savage, 'Report on the National Book Association to Lord Davidson', 17 July 1939, Davidson papers, DAV/262.

33 *Ibid.*

34 The Nottinghamshire miners refused to take part in the 1926 General Strike. In Nottinghamshire, a separate trade union to the Federation of British Miners was set up, called the Spencerites. See R. J. Waller, *The Dukeries Transformed: The Social and Political Development of a Twentieth-Century Coalfield* (Oxford: Clarendon, 1983).

35 H. W. J. Edwards, *The Good National* (National Book Association, 1938). The little Moscows were mining villages in the Rhondda Valley, so called because of their Left-leaning politics.

36 National Book Association, 'Memorandum on Editorial Policy for 1938', 9 Mar. 1938, Bryant papers, C47.

37 *Ibid.* Walter Citrine was the TUC secretary-general.

38 Frederick Lee, *Manufacturer* (London: Hutchinson & Co, 1938).

39 National Book Association, 'Memorandum on Editorial Policy for 1938', 9 Mar. 1938, Bryant papers, C47.

40 Lawrence H. Sutton, *The Nation Keeps House: An Introductory Study of Money and Trade* (London: Hutchinson & Co., 1938).

41 National Book Association, Notes on Mr. Graham's Confidential Memorandum of 20th May 1938, Davidson papers, DAV/232.

42 A. Bryant to W. Hutchinson, 24 June 1937, Byrant papers, C49 and Davidson papers, DAV/232.

43 Rough draft for a NBA brochure, Davidson papers, DAV/232.

44 Rough draft for a NBA brochure, Davidson papers, DAV/230.

45 *Ibid.*

46 A. Bryant to G. Fry, 14 Feb. 1939, Bryant papers, C62.

47 D. Jerrold to A. Bryant, 23 Apr. 1937, Bryant papers, C46.

48 Victor Serge, *Destiny of a Revolution* (London: Hutchinson, 1937).

49 Minutes of the NBA Meeting, 28 July 1939, Davidson papers, DAV/262.

50 Report on the National Book Association for Lord Davidson, 17 July 1939, Davidson papers, DAV/262.

51 A. Clarke, in *The Tories; Conservatives and the Nation State, 1922–1997* (London: Weidenfeld & Nicolson, 1998), p. 120, explained that 'Neville Chamberlain's accession to power was seamless and smooth. Of all the change-overs in the party's twentieth-century history it was the least contentious.' Chamberlain's policies were considered a continuation of those of Baldwin.

52 A. Bryant to J. C. C. Davidson, 3 July 1936, Davidson papers, DAV/226.

53 T. N. Graham to J. C. C. Davidson, 7 Apr. 1937, Bryant papers, C41.

54 *Ibid.*

55 A. Bryant to T. N. Graham, 'Memorandum to be sent to Hutchinson and circulated to G. Ellis and J. C. C. Davidson', Feb. 1938, Bryant papers, C47.

56 F. Heath, 10 Jan. 1938, Davidson papers, DAV/232.

57 *Ibid.*

58 T. N. Graham, Memorandum, 20 May 1938, Bryant papers, C47.

59 T. N. Graham to A. Bryant, 27 Jan. 1939, Bryant papers, C47.

60 W. Hutchinson to G. Ellis, 15 May 1939, Bryant papers, C44.

61 G. Ellis to A. Bryant, 27 Jan. 1939, Bryant papers, C44.

62 *Ibid.*

63 A. Bryant to T. N. Graham, 26 Jan. 1939, Bryant papers, C47.

64 Meeting on Publicity and Political Education, 11 Nov. 1938, Butler papers, H89, fos 23–25.

65 T. N. Graham to A. Bryant, 1 Feb. 1939, Bryant papers, C47.

66 C. J. M. Alport, *Kingdoms in Partnership; A Study of Political Change in the British Commonwealth* (London: Lovat Dickson for NBA), 1937.

67 K. Curlett to R. A. Butler, 21 Nov. 1938, Butler papers, H90, fo. 50.

68 T. N. Graham, NBA, 'Memorandum on Present Position with Suggestions for Reconstruction', 20 May 1938, Bryant papers, C47 and Davidson papers, DAV/232.

69 A. Bryant, 'Memorandum on suggested proposals for the amalgamation of the Right Book Club with the National Book Association', 29 Apr. 1937, Bryant papers, C49 and Davidson DAV/226.

70 A. Bryant to D. Hacking, 1 Oct. 1937, Davidson papers, DAV/232.

71 A. Bryant, 'Notes on Mr. Graham's Confidential Memorandum of 20th May 1938', Bryant papers, C49.

72 F. Heath, 10 Jan. 1938, Davidson papers, DAV/232.

73 *Ibid.*

74 A. Bryant, 'Mr. Graham's Confidential Memorandum of 20th Nov. 1938', Bryant papers, C47.

75 *Ibid.*

76 A. Bryant to F. Heath, 22 Apr. 1937, Bryant papers, C49.

77 Minutes of the NBA Committee, 28 July 1939, Davidson papers, DAV/262.

78 R. Savage to A. Bryant, 27 Sep. 1939, Bryant papers, C51.

79 T. N. Graham, 'National Book Association, Memorandum re Present Position with Suggestions as to Reconstruction', Davidson papers, DAV/232.

80 Minutes of the Education Meeting, 18 Nov. 1929, Minutes of the Education Committee, 1929–1934, Ashridge papers.

81 N. Chamberlain, Circular Letter on Ashridge to all Conservative MPs, candidates and Party officials, 15 July 1930, Education Committee Appendixes, 1930, Ashridge papers.

82 *Ibid.*

83 See for example J. C. C. Davidson, Governing Body Minutes, 11 Mar. 1930, Ashridge papers.

84 Minutes of the Education Committee, 5 Feb. 1930, Minutes of the Education Committee, 1929–1934, Ashridge papers. In 1937, the Conservative Party divided England and Wales into twelve divisions. Scotland was split into six. See A. Ball, 'The National and Regional Party Structure', in A. Seldon and S. Ball (eds), *Conservative Century: The Conservative Party since 1900* (Oxford: Oxford University Press, 1994), pp. 205–7.

85 'A Scheme for Educational Work in the Provincial Areas and the Constituencies', July 1931, Education Committee Minutes 1931, Ashridge papers.

86 *Ibid.*

87 *Ibid.*

88 *Ibid.*

89 *Ashridge Journal*, May 1931.

90 *Ashridge Journal*, Feb. 1934.

91 'Ashridge Circles During the Past Quarter', *Ashridge Journal*, Mar. 1937, pp. 56–7.

92 'Editorial', *Ashridge Journal*, Dec. 1931, p. 4.

93 T. N. Graham, 'Ashridge Circles During the Past Quarter', *Ashridge Journal*, Mar. 1937, pp. 56–7.

94 *Ibid.*, p. 51.

95 *Ibid.*

96 A. Bryant to G. Ellis, 20 Oct. 1937, Bryant papers, C44.

97 *Ashridge Journal*, Sep. 1945.

98 *Ibid.*

99 Minutes of the Governing Body, 17 Nov. 1948, Governing Body Minutes 1947–1949, Ashridge papers.

100 *Ibid.*

101 J. C. C. Davidson to W. Churchill, 5 Apr. 1928, Davidson papers, DAV/182.

102 Cockett, 'The Party, Publicity, and the Media'.

103 Alexander Korda is best known for having directed *The Private Life of Henry VIII* (1933) and *The Four Feathers* (1939).

104 Memorandum from the constituency of Horncastle, 'The Use of the Cinematograph in County Constituencies', 1946, CPA, CCO/4/4/252, quoted in Cockett, 'The Party, Publicity, and the Media'.

105 A. Higson, *Waving the Flag: Constructing a National Cinema in Britain* (Oxford: Oxford University Press, 1995). M. Dickinson and S. Street, *Cinema and State: the Film Industry and the British Government, 1927–1984* (London: British Film Institute, 1985). M. Landy, *British Genres: Cinema and Society, 1930–1960* (Princeton, NJ: Princeton University Press, 1991).

106 I. Aitken, *Film and Reform: John Grierson and the Documentary Film Movement* (London: Routledge, 1990). A. Higson, 'Britain's "Outstanding Contribution" to the Film: the Documentary-Realist Tradition', in C. Barr (ed.), *All Our Yesterdays: 90 Years of British Cinema* (London: British Film Institute, 1986), pp. 72–97.

107 See S. Street, 'British Film and the National Interest, 1927–1939', in R. Murphy (ed.), *The British Cinema Book* (London: British Film Institute, 1998).

108 S. Harper, *Picturing the Past* (London: British Film Institute, 1994).

109 See J. Chapman, *The British at War; Cinema, State and Propaganda, 1939–1945* (London: I. B. Tauris, 1998).

110 J. Grierson, 'The New Cinema in Teaching Citizenship', *The Citizen*, Oct. 1936, p. 7.

111 *Ibid.*, pp. 6–7.

112 A. Bryant to G. Fry, 22 Jan., 1937, Bryant papers, C62.

113 Bryant, *English Saga*, p. 13.

114 *Ibid.*, p. 13.

115 The name was inspired by Robert Peel, who established the metropolitan police in 1828.

116 A. Bryant, from the script 'The Daily Life of a London Policeman', Bryant papers, ADD/4.

117 *Ibid.*

118 The British Broadcasting Company Ltd was established as a commercial company in 1921. It was dissolved January 1927 and its assets were transferred to the BBC (British Broadcasting Corporation).

119 N. Tebbit, Feb. 1990, quoted in P. Clarke, *A Question of Leadership: Gladstone to Thatcher* (London: Hamish Hamilton, 1991), p. 315.

120 A. Bryant to J. C. C. Davidson, 3 Nov. 1938, Bryant papers, C41.

121 A. L. Smith quoted by A. Bryant, 25 Sep. 1933, Bryant papers, C62.

122 Bryant, *English Saga*, p. 337.

123 J. C. C. Davidson to G. Fry, 30 June 1939, Davidson papers, DAV/262.

124 *Ibid*.

125 A. Bryant to J. C. C. Davidson, 5 Oct. 1936, Davidson papers, DAV/226.

126 See Bryant papers, C44.

127 A. Bryant to J. C. C. Davidson, 1 July 1936, Bryant papers, C41.

128 P. Gower to Miss Gower, undated, Nov. 1934, CPA, CCO 4/1/23.

129 This was the department that organised a campaign to end the BBC's monopoly. It introduced radio stations and commercial TV channels in 1954. Ramsden, *The Age of Churchill and Eden*, pp. 252–4.

130 M. Whitehouse, *Cleaning Up T.V.: From Protest to Participation* (London: Blandford Press, 1967).

I I

Ashridge after the war:
the Baldwinians versus the Churchillians

Ashridge College, in its original form, ceased to exist at the onset of the Second World War. The college was then turned into a hospital. After the war, the fate of Ashridge was extremely uncertain. Already, in a letter to Baldwin of 7 August 1940, Geoffrey Ellis wrote, 'We are all agreed we must have a clean cut because we (none of us) know what will be the position at Ashridge after the war. It looks as though the Ministry of Health will want to keep it.'[1] The question of whether or not there would be 'another Ashridge', and above all the form it would take, provoked debate. 'If again we have "an" Ashridge', Ellis wrote, what would be its objective, its *raison d'être*?[2] The war caused a deep upheaval in the country. 'Never again', the title of Peter Hennessy's book on the period,[3] became a rallying cry; the war, and with it the pre-war period, were cast aside; from 1940, and above all from 1942, reconstruction was the focus of debates. The most ambitious projects were the work of two Liberals, William Beveridge and John Maynard Keynes. The Beveridge report on the social services was published on 2 December 1942.[4] The Conservative party, and particularly former students of Ashridge, actively participated in the debates that preceded its publication. R. A. Butler, a member of the college since its creation – he sat on both the education committee and the governing council of the BLMC between 1936 and 1939 – was the architect of the law that bore his name on the reform of the education system.[5] After the Conservatives' electoral defeat in 1945, Lord Woolton, who had played an active role in the ministry of reconstruction,[6] became chairman of the Conservative party and thus an ex-officio member of the board of governors.

The question of reopening the college was debated with renewed vigour. Was the initial plan to create 'Conservative Fabians' still relevant in a world that was being reconstructed? The catastrophic financial position of the college, largely due to inflation, made it all the more urgent to address the question. In November 1946, when Stanley Baldwin stepped down from his post as chairman of the governing board of Ashridge, he explained that he no longer had a role to play, 'now that Ashridge was starting a new chapter'.[7]

From Baldwin to Churchill

After fourteen years in power, the Conservative party's electoral defeat in 1945 was traumatic. It was all the more humiliating, since Conservatives believed they had led the country to victory. Paradoxically, Churchill's leadership was not questioned.[8] In fact, he seemed to emerge even stronger from the defeat. Since his accession to the leadership in 1940 and during the war, relations between Churchill and the party were tempestuous. In May 1940, J. C. C. Davidson wrote to Baldwin:

> Winston is putting in the jackals and ousting even those who have done well of what I may call the respectable rump of the Tory Party. The 'Glamour Boys' have all got jobs. I think it is clear, however, that Neville will remain leader of the Party, and with Kingsley and Halifax to give some sort of respectability to the firm we ought to be able to keep the Party together and compact on the back benches. What is important is that while the Party must support the Government in the prosecution of the war it will have to play its part, and amongst other things it will have to look carefully for and, if found, secure the next leader of the Party from amongst its own ranks. Geoffrey Lloyd will no doubt be dropped, as will all of those faithful to the Baldwin-cum-Chamberlain tradition. The crooks are on top, as they were in the last war.[9]

In May 1940, the majority of the Conservative party had reacted negatively to Churchill's arrival in Downing Street. Although forced to accept an appointment enthusiastically welcomed by the public,[10] many did not hide their unease at seeing at the head of the country a man whom they considered to be an opportunist and an adventurer. For many of them, Neville Chamberlain, who remained leader of the party until his death in October 1940, provided the standard by which to judge leadership. The animosity between Churchill and the party hierarchy, albeit never erupting into the open, was real enough.[11] For the party, the 'glamour boys' such as Anthony Eden and Duff Cooper, to mention only the best known, lacked respectability. Brendan Bracken, Churchill's right-hand man, and Robert Boothby were considered social climbers and Churchill had the reputation of being an opportunist, having quit the Conservative party in 1904 and then the Liberal party in 1924. Baldwin supporters did not appreciate his imperialist stand with regard to the India Act in 1935, then his support for Edward VIII at the time of his abdication in December 1936. His taste for alcohol contributed to making him 'a study in failure', to borrow the title of Robert Rhodes James's book on Churchill.[12] Harold Crookshank described him as a 'garrulous and bibulous old man'.[13]

From the summer of 1940 until summer 1942, while the war continued, the party's internal power struggles continued unabated. In 1940, Kenneth Pickthorn described Churchill as 'a word-spinner, a second-rate rhetorician' and 'a disastrous war leader, albeit a vigorous personality'.[14] In the summer of 1942, as the internal quarrels reached their peak and the military situation was particularly worrying, Leo Amery wrote in his diary shortly after the cabinet reshuffle: 'The Conservative Party will not like... a War Cabinet containing not a single real Conservative, for they certainly don't class either Winston or Anthony as such.'[15] In March 1942, the departing Conservative party chairman and the incoming chairman agreed on the fact that 'Winston is a difficult leader and [that he] is not a Conservative at all.'[16] Finally, in 1944, Woolton, a member of Churchill's war cabinet since 1940, asked R. A. Butler 'whether the P.M. was really a Conservative', to which Butler replied: 'The PM's fundamental idea of politics was a mixture of old Liberal doctrines of cheap food and free trade, combined with the Tory Democracy of his father.'[17]

The party's suspicion of Churchill began to diminish after 1942, when Chamberlain's former supporters rallied to his support. Without becoming unconditional supporters, many admired Churchill's leadership of the country in the war and stuck by him. The deepest differences arose over reconstruction: the Tory Reform Group, the most progressive element, differed with central office over the Beveridge report. A considerable number of Conservatives hesitated to support any specific project. The Conservative member of parliament and minister of health, Henry Willink, wished to establish a national health service without actually supporting the Beveridge report: 'Our fight was *against* Hitler and his works, not "for" social reforms, however desirable.'[18] In a period of uncertainty likely to end in a political shake-up, former supporters of Baldwin and Chamberlain found themselves caught up in a network of conflicting personal and political loyalties.

In July 1941, a Post-War Problems Central Committee (or PWPCC) was created. Robert Topping, the General Director of the Conservative Central Office, invited Butler to chair the PWPCC, with Maxwell-Fyfe as his deputy. All three had been close to Chamberlain. Despite keeping them at arm's length from decision making on the conduct of the war, Churchill entrusted them with evaluating economic and social questions. Butler sought to surround himself with experts and suggested George Kitson Clark, Douglas Jerrold, G. M. Young, Keith Feiling, Arthur Bryant, G. N. Clark, Kenneth Pickthorn, Arnold Toynbee and Christopher Dawson.[19] All of them had been involved with Ashridge. Butler was an example of divided loyalty. He sought to join the new hierarchy within Churchill's party, even though he was still regarded as Chamberlain's lieutenant. Chips Channon described his house as 'the Belgravian citadel of Chamberlainite Conservatism'.[20] Butler was aware of his reputation. Robert Armstrong, one of his collaborators when he was chancellor of the exchequer between 1951 and 1955, recalled a conversation with Butler on the subject of Munich: 'He waggled his cane at me and said "since that time I have never carried an umbrella", because an umbrella was the symbol of Mr. Chamberlain. I learnt from this that even fifteen years later he [Butler] was very conscious of the fact that he was associated with Chamberlain and I think that he was very conscious of the fact that Sir Winston Churchill hadn't forgotten that.'[21]

The double death of Stanley Baldwin

The electoral defeat in 1945 led to a reconfiguration within the Conservative party. Despite his prominence, Churchill was still widely regarded with suspicion,[22] and many Conservatives held him responsible for the defeat. On 16 July 1945, the day of the general election, Harold Crookshank described Churchill in his diary as a 'beastly man', and spoke of 'Winston's gang'.[23] Former participants at Ashridge were particularly severe. T. N. Graham, who maintained the Ashridge circles during the war and who had led the movement to reopen Ashridge, wrote: 'I make no comment about the Election further than to express the hope that the lessons are plain for Conservatives to learn. I am not sorry that electoral disaster has overtaken the crowd who were in control, though I think Churchill deserved a better fate.'[24] Bryant similarly commented on the defeat: 'the Conservatives ... are under the dominance not only of vested interests but of something a great deal worse – vested ideas!'[25] Those loyal to Baldwin and Chamberlain blamed Churchill for neglecting the party's political activity during the war. For them, Labour's victory was explained by Churchill's lack of involvement in the election campaign and his lack of consideration for the campaigners. In a letter to Davidson, Bryant wrote:

> I'm confident from what I've seen that the younger generation of Tories who take a liberal and sensible view of political education is increasingly going to out weigh the still rather vocal minority of those who can't distinguish between propaganda and education and suppose that if a Conservative listens to a Socialist argument he is in danger of becoming a Socialist.... The change I believe, is partly due to Ashridge's pre-war work, and yours and S.B'.s vision twenty years ago. If Winston had shown the same realisation of that change as S.B. he wouldn't have lost the 1945 Election.[26]

The analysis of the electoral defeat by Crookshank, Graham and Bryant was, however, the work of a minority within the party and the country. The Conservatives' defeat was generally attributed to three factors. In the first place, the campaign had been poorly organised, as Churchill himself complained.[27] Second, public opinion was said to have shifted Leftwards as the result of active propaganda by the Labour party during the war and in particular its promises of social reforms. Third, and perhaps most important, the defeat was attributed to the Conservative party's pre-war domestic and foreign policies.

The party had not known how to take advantage of the victory in the war. It was publicly associated with the economic crisis and the policy of appeasement and Munich. Henceforth, it was more the party of 'guilty men'[28] than the party of the victors. As a party official wrote in October 1947, 'The major obstacle standing between us and a huge-scale swing of opinion in our favour among wage earners is the memory of unemployment in the thirties plus the stream of Socialist lies about the subject. Even our own supporters have come to half believe that we have a bad record.'[29] This was a widely shared analysis. The party's defeat in 1945 was thus the defeat of the Baldwin and Chamberlain Conservative party, not that of Churchill. In August 1961, explaining the role of the CRD in the Conservatives' victory in the 1951 general election, Michael Fraser, the head of the CRD, wrote: 'At the 1945 General Election the Party was identified with the desire to return to unlimited free enterprise, unemployment, slump and so on. The nation was in no mood for this and we were crushingly defeated.'[30] He explained the party's electoral success in 1951 in similar terms: the Conservatives, thanks to the CRD and the CPC had succeeded in shaking off the contested heritage of the 1930s, particularly Baldwin's heritage. The electoral defeat of 1945 was thus attributed to the legacy of Baldwin–Chamberlain, henceforth associated with one another, and the victory in 1951 to the party's rejection of this legacy.

Stanley Baldwin died on 14 December 1947, and along with him a whole era ended. This was the moment for the judgement and condemnation of those responsible for what was considered a shameful past. Baldwin, Chamberlain and the 1930s were cast into oblivion. The judgment of 'Cato' on the *Guilty Men*[31] was widely shared. The Conservative party did not seek to defend its record, and Churchill seemed to eradicate all trace of this period. In 1948, in the index to his book *The Gathering Storm*,[32] Churchill referred to Baldwin in these terms: 'Admits to putting party before country'.

Churchill's appreciation became the official position of the party. It prevailed until the 1980s, when historians re-examined the 1930s.[33] Robert

Skidelsky's *Politicians and the Slump* (1967) and Michael Stewart's *Keynes and After* (1972), in particular, drew a picture of Baldwin once again as an 'indolent' and 'limited' politician.[34] Until the work of Philip Williamson[35] on Baldwin and his role during the inter-war years, Churchill's interpretation prevailed.

The rewriting of the Baldwin years

The rewriting of the Baldwin years has been mainly devoted to economic policy, the fight against unemployment and the lack of preparation for the war. Writing on the Chamberlain years has been almost exclusively devoted to foreign policy. Claiming the Baldwin years for itself, Ashridge sided with Churchill's adversaries. In the autumn of 1945, when the question of reopening the college was raised, the debate between Baldwin and Churchill supporters took a new turn. For Churchill, Ashridge was 'an asset for the party', which he intended to make use of. He therefore swept aside a very clear refusal from the governing body of Ashridge. Lord Davidson – Baldwin's former right-hand man but no longer exercising any official function – seized the occasion to get revenge for being sidelined by the party. His grudge against Churchill dated back to 1929 and the brutal press campaign inspired by Lord Beaverbrook, who blamed him for the electoral defeat of that year. He had been forced to stand down from his position as chairman of the Conservative party. Beaverbrook became a close advisor to Churchill during the war, further fuelling Davidson's animosity towards him. In January 1946, one of Davidson's successors as party chairman, Ralph Assheton accused Beaverbrook of playing the Left's game by promoting books like *Guilty Men* 'for too high a political price'.[36] Davidson was not the only critic of Beaverbook and Churchill, but he was one of the very few to criticise them openly. Drawing upon the ambiguities of the statutes of the BLMC Trust, he established that Ashridge did not belong to the Conservative party. Thereupon, a struggle began between the governing body of Ashridge and the Conservative party. On 4 November 1946, during a particularly heated meeting[37] involving Woolton, the chairman since June, R. A. Butler, chairman of the CRD, James Stuart, the party's chief whip[38] and Davidson, Churchill accused the latter of bad faith and said that Bonar Law must be turning in his grave, since obviously Ashridge was a Conservative institution. Ashridge, he said, should be the 'power house' of the party, to train future party cadres and to teach them the 'doctrine of conservatism'. Davidson responded by emphasising the importance of Ashridge's independence and insisting upon the non-partisan nature of its programme. Churchill angrily replied: 'All this idea about Non Party teaching was sheer bunk, it was just

Left-Wing!'[39] The struggle became so embittered that Churchill demanded a Counsel's Opinion as to the autonomy of the education committee. Davidson stood firm, and on 3 January 1947 Ashridge reopened its doors with a team largely imbued with Baldwin's ideas.

Presenting General Bernard Paget, the new principal of Ashridge, with a volume of Baldwin's speeches, Davidson wrote: '[They] may give you a background to the kind on [sic] Conservatism for which Baldwin stood and for which I stand today.'[40] Although the Conservative party was undergoing great changes and starting to emerge in its new form, Ashridge remained the preserve of Baldwin's legacy and the refuge for those who had been excluded from the new party. The divisions among Conservatives were numerous: on the one hand, there were those who thoroughly rejected the Baldwin/Chamberlain legacy, on the other, those who remained loyal to it like Davidson or Bryant, and between them those such as R. A. Butler who tried, more or less skilfully, to adapt to the new situation. The reopening of the college gave Bryant the opportunity to forget his trips to Germany in 1939, the deals of yesteryear and his book, *Unfinished Victory* (1940). His sympathy for the far Right in the 1930s having marginalised him, Ashridge enabled him to bounce back and regain a place at the heart of the education system.

T. N. Graham wrote to Byrant that Baldwin 'was [his] ideal politically'.[41] Bryant wrote back: 'I was disgusted by Harold Macmillan's remarks about him in the House yesterday – a week after his death – and found it difficult not to endorse Aneurin Bevan's acid remark that the Conservative Party, in spitting on its former leader, hadn't the common instincts of gentlemen.'[42] Reactions of the press, the climate of general denigration and the lack of respect for the party's governing body with regard to their former leader profoundly shocked them:

> I still think that old man, unpopular as he is, did more for England than any living statesman, when we were so bitterly divided by class and party feeling after the last war he gave us back our unity, and so saved us from the terrible division that broke France in 1940. It is what, I feel, Ashridge is doing today, when we need unity even more – by restraint, by regard to truth, by common inspiration.[43]

Ashridge's legacy

The party did not abandon the idea of a 'Conservative university'. After the electoral defeat which saw the country 'sacrificed to Socialist shibboleths, and its people crucified on the cross of dogma',[44] it was urgently necessary to rebuild the party. As it was legally impossible to claw back control of Ashridge, the Conservative party created three organisations (the CRD, which already existed but was to be expanded, the CPC and Swinton College) which, between them, played the same role as Ashridge had done from 1929.

The leadership of the Conservative party, whatever some say, was preoccupied after the end of the war and the electoral defeat of 1945 with the political training of its activists.[45] In July 1945, Marjorie Maxse, deputy chair of the Conservative party, wrote: 'One of our most urgent and important tasks is to plan a system of political education for the Party.'[46]

An Advisory Committee on Policy and Political Education (ACPPE), under the direction of R. A. Butler, was created to make proposals on how to reorganise what had earlier been carried out at Ashridge. In a memorandum of November 1945, the party set out a new programme. 'Political education is high on the priority list of party work. The target is to take up the "slack" of six years of war in the next six months.'[47] The first stage consisted of re-establishing the political education department, under the direction of C. J. M. Alport, a former tutor at Ashridge. In 1938, Alport had published A National Faith under the pseudonym 'A Modern Conservative'. Subsequent steps from June 1946 were, first, the institution of education committees across the country. At the same time plans were made for a CPC in London to act as the focal point for the 'education movement'. Finally, the first proposals appeared for a training college for party officials. Ashridge was swiftly replaced by three different institutions: the CRD, under Butler's impetus, aimed to become a 'thinking machine'.[48] The CPC was headed by Alport. Finally, in March 1948, Swinton College was opened.[49] The CRD and the CPC were supposed to collaborate and establish a dialogue similar to that which had been foreseen between Ashridge and the CRD from 1927 to 1929.

In November 1945, Churchill entrusted Butler with the direction of the CRD, which, seriously weakened by the war, consisted only of two members and two secretaries. After the war, the CRD became the main centre for the formulation of Conservative policy, and remained so until the 1970s, when it was supplanted by the Centre for Policy Studies.[50] The CRD's role thus grew considerably after the electoral defeat.

Under the CRD's authority, the CPC was created in December 1945.[51] The aim of the CPC was to establish 'a continuing partnership between the party leaders and its rank and file in the formation of party policy on political issues', and more generally a dialogue between the leader and the rest of the country. The CPC launched what it called a 'two-way movement of ideas' or the 'contact programme',[52] to promote the circulation of ideas from the top of the organisation downwards and vice versa. A pamphlet entitled 'What do you think?' was drafted by prominent party members with the help of the CRD. This was essentially a questionnaire accompanied by a reading list, which was distributed in the constituencies, which in turn organised meetings where these questions were debated. The responses were then sent back to the CPC headquarters, where they were compiled. The results appeared in a brochure entitled 'What We Think'. The first questionnaires focused on the 1947 industrial charter, the trade unions and local government. Subsequent questionnaires focused on the collieries and economic recovery. Economic policy was an important issue for the Conservatives, who sought to distinguish themselves both from their predecessors and the Labour party. It was a matter of describing and explaining to voters the principles of the new Conservatism. This 'two-way movement of ideas' was an essential tool in generating large-scale debate. It was the 'power house' of the 'education movement'.[53]

Finally, the Conservatives created a third instrument to enable them to win the 'battle of ideas': a new Conservative college. In September 1945, Miss Maxse wrote to Butler: 'We shall have to tackle the question of a residential college in succession to Ashridge.'[54] In July 1946, Davidson wrote that 'Butler was very keen that the Ashridge name and, incidentally, its furniture should be handed to the Party, and that a new education centre should be started.'[55] On 25 March 1948, the Swinton Conservative College opened its doors in Masham, North Yorkshire. It took in only between 65 and 70 students at a time. The objectives at Swinton were more limited than those of Ashridge: it was to be a staff college for party officials and a training centre for party workers.[56] Each constituency was expected to send an average of six students per year and these students, upon returning to their constituency, were expected to 'form a cell from which the influence of an understanding faith could radiate'.[57] In July 1949, a first report indicated that 'The facilities at Swinton during the last few months have, to an increasing extent, been devoted to the training of paid and voluntary workers for the party, and it is rapidly becoming a Conservative Staff College.'[58] However, very quickly Swinton confronted the same financial challenges as Ashridge.

Party control

Contrary to Ashridge, the post-war organisations were integrated into the party: none of them enjoyed the same autonomy as Ashridge. After 1945, the party preferred a centralised system of political training under tight control by party headquarters. Following the electoral defeat, there was no longer any question of 'unpolitical politics' or policies 'above parties', like those of Baldwin. The party insisted upon direct control of training without intermediaries. Accordingly, it tightly controlled the CRD as well as the CPC and Swinton College.

Upon the establishment of Swinton College, 'Mr. Butler stated it had been agreed with Lord Woolton that there would only be three trustees of Swinton: the Chairman of the party, the leader of the party and one other, thus giving the party a majority.'[59] The Conservative party financed Swinton College, constituted the majority on the governing body and oversaw all decisions taken by the college principal. Every six months the principal, Reginald Northam, had to report to the ACPPE. 'The Committee would thus be able to exercise a degree of surveillance and to make suggestions for future courses.'[60] At Swinton, the educational programmes were based upon party policies.

The same can be said for the CRD and the CPC, even if for the latter this was controversial. In November 1945, Maxse drafted a note in which she revealed that 'Col Alport urged very strongly that the Education Dpt should be housed outside the CO. He feels – and I agree – that it would be very difficult to get young people to come in to the Party machine headquarters.'[61] Like Ashridge before the war, the CPC wished to be autonomous '[with]in the party, but not run by the party'.[62] This would be a source of constant tension between the party chairman, Lord Woolton, and Butler. Woolton complained that the CPC 'was independent of Central Office except when the bills came in'.[63] In July 1949, following the Maxwell-Fyfe report on the reorganisation of the party,[64] political education was placed under the direct authority of the party chairman. Butler lost control of the CPC, having already lost control of the CRD in November 1948. He remained chair of the advisory committee on policy, which oversaw political decisions. On this occasion, it was recalled that '[t]he CPC has no constitution and is not a separate entity', and that '[t]he organisation of political education is a CO responsibility, for which the Director of the CPC is answerable to the Vice-Chairman of the Party and the General Director'.[65]

The persistence of Baldwin's legacy

These new structures, albeit integrated into the Conservative party, shared numerous similarities with Ashridge. They seemed to have been inspired more by Baldwin than by Churchill or even Butler. In July 1945, Maxse wrote:

It was only during the war that I realised the far-reaching psychological effect of Ashridge upon people who had been drawn there in order to escape propaganda. I came across these ex-students in every walk of life,

and outside this country, and the hall mark of Ashridge was on them....
Through the efforts of Ashridge and the Central Office, a considerable
amount of useful work was done.[66]

This is one of the rare occasions when Ashridge is mentioned in the party
archives. After the war and its quarrel with Ashridge, the party, as if
obeying some kind of tacit agreement, never mentioned Ashridge again.

R. A. Butler, who was the true founder of the CPC, warned against 'the
present inadequacy of facilities available for the diffusion of Conservative
ideas and the acute danger arising from the present hold which Leftist
intellectualism has on the mind of Britain'. He explained that the CPC's
role was 'Not merely to develop political education methods and to
influence public opinion indirectly by reasoned instruction within the
party, but to create a kind of *Conservative Fabian Society* which would
act as a mouthpiece for our best modern thought and attract that section
of the postwar generation who required an intellectual basis for their
political faith.'[67] This was, to the letter, the objective at Ashridge in 1929.
The education committees of the Conservative party frequently mention
'the need for coordinating specialists namely, economists, historians,
doctors, etc.'[68] and for gathering experts together to create the first 'think-
tanks'. Rab Butler was considered to be the originator of these ideas. There
was even mention of 'Rabians' as one spoke of 'Fabians'.[69] A memorandum
on the CPC explained: 'There is a certain type of person whose interest in
the Party has been created, and will probably only be retained, by the fact
that the party provides, through the CPC what can best be described as *an
intellectual approach to politics.*'[70] The idea of an intellectual approach to
politics was inherited from Ashridge. Once again, one is struck by the fact
that not only was Ashridge not mentioned, but the origin of these ideas
was never acknowledged. The Conservative party under Churchill made
the Ashridge legacy its own without acknowledging it politically. By the
same token, if the CPC had the task of

> stimulating and guiding the Political Education movement of the party. Its
> aims are essentially educational and are to be distinguished from those of
> propaganda in that they include an objective examination and presentation
> of facts together with systematic discussion before firm conclusions are
> reached.... It stands to reason that the persons willing to lecture or tutor for
> the CPC ... will be at least sympathetic with the Conservative approach to
> politics. For those of more independent position we cannot stress too much
> that it is educational instruction as such that we are providing.[71]

Here, too, the similarities with Ashridge are striking. There is no doubt
that continuity within the party between the pre- and post-war period,
though largely invisible, prevailed over the discontinuities.[72] The training

at Swinton was based on that of Ashridge.[73] Apprenticeships in the 'responsibilities of citizenship', which were one of the party's priorities under Churchill, derived directly from Ashridge. The 'new Conservatism' of the post-war period closely resembled Baldwin's Conservatism. In his memoirs, Harold Nicolson recounts a discussion he had with Harold Macmillan two months after the party's defeat. Macmillan told him: 'Only gradually and with a great effort will the Tory Party recapture its hold on public opinion. But to do this their philosophy must be lucid, consistent and very incessantly formulated; and it must be directed to the ordinary habits of thought of the middle classes.' Nicolson added: 'He shows me the draft of his election address ... It is almost entirely confined to principles.'[74]

After 1945, a large part of the personnel at Ashridge found itself once again leading the party's 'education movement'. Butler had been a member of the education committee at Ashridge and the governing body since 1936. Alport, director of the CPC, had taught at Ashridge for two years; this was the starting-point of his career within the party. Marjorie Maxse, the vice-chair of the party, had been very active at Ashridge and remained true to the ideas of Baldwin and Davidson. Kenneth Pickthorn, master of Corpus Christi College, Cambridge, and a regular lecturer at Ashridge, and Charles Morgan, the writer whom Stanley Baldwin had favoured, were involved in the ACPPE. Lord Tweedsmuir, the son of John Buchan, who had been a central figure at Ashridge, was also a member.

Great similarities in organisation can also be observed. The choice of a residential college, weekend sessions and the choice of a historical site were all features shared with Ashridge. 'Most of the students attending the College will come from the North. It would be of advantage for them to be able to see a well run and beautiful English estate in being.'[75] This was word for word the description of Ashridge. Similarly with the CPC, it intended to have CPC circles in every constituency.

In order to reach a large audience, Butler wanted to create a collection of 'cheap, concise, and readable books', which would be published by Faber and Faber on the model of Arthur Bryant's NBA.[76] Mark Garnett, Alport's biographer, explained: 'The strongest evidence of continuity in the prewar and postwar periods is the new emphasis on political literature. Ashridge could help to ensure that Conservative activists were kept up to date on contemporary issues, but it necessarily catered for a restricted audience. Cub [Alport] and Butler could make a similar effort through the CPC, which they set up to provide weekly lectures, and through regular conferences to inform and encourage party activists.'[77]

The CPC published numerous essays,[78] including 'The Conservative Faith in a Modern Age', 'Essays in Conservatism', etc.;[79] it also managed four 'CPC book shops' and published the work of the One Nation Group,[80] of which Alport was a founding member.

It is worth looking more closely at the One Nation Group, about which much was written in the 1980s. The group was often considered to represent the moderate wing of Conservatism, which was hostile to Margaret Thatcher when she was prime minister. Its origins reveal Baldwin's influence, as well as a more positive attitude to free trade. Alport conceived the One Nation Group as a means of pursuing the work done by Butler before the war,[81] but rejected the idea that the Conservatives had no choice but 'me-tooing Socialist solutions'.[82] The themes that emerged, such as individual responsibility for oneself and one's family and the importance of civil society, would have pleased Baldwin. The main difference arose over economic policy. The One Nation Group campaigned in favour of a policy of full employment, based on the idea that being employed gave one additional duties and responsibilities.[83] Even if it was not prepared to recognise it, the One Nation Group's battle against Socialism and its social security project aimed at creating harmony between the social classes – to 'Give us peace in our time, O Lord',[84] as Baldwin put it – established commonalities between the One Nation Group and Ashridge.

The demise of Ashridge seemed to signal its failure. Yet, if one considers the work undertaken after the war by the CPC, the CRD and Swinton College, one can measure Ashridge's continued influence. Kenneth Clarke, when he spoke of 'the intellectual revival of the Conservative Party after 1945', cited 'Butler, MacLeod, Maudling and Powell'.[85] In his biography of Alport, Garnett wrote:

> By stressing the values of constructive educational work until their voices were drowned in a hubbub of electioneering Butler and Cub had ensured that the next generation of Conservative leaders stayed within a party which was accepted as intellectually respectable by the important minority who paid close attention to policy ideas rather than slogans. They had brought this about in a party which traditionally had no time for the 'intelligentsia', and which was led by a man who was far more interested in action than in thought.[86]

'Butler and Cub' had been at the heart of the Ashridge project.

In 1948, Davidson wrote to Byrant: 'Ashridge will never succeed as it was succeeding before the war unless it can evolve a philosophy of its own.'[87] Ashridge must be financially independent and have control over its teaching programme. These were the objectives when the college was handed back to the trust by the minister for public works on 24 June 1946.[88] Bryant and Davidson sought nothing less than 'A great national regenerative institution'.[89] Bryant wrote: 'The function of Ashridge, and of all political education, as I see it, is to create opinion, and in a country like England this will always be done by letting men hear the facts and thrash them out for themselves.'[90] Developing this subject further, he wrote: 'It is important that average men and women should understand their duties and rights as citizens, but such understanding can only come through conclusions based on established facts. Ashridge aims at supplying the facts and creating an informed and active public opinion.'[91] In a letter to Davidson in June 1949, Bryant summarised Ashridge's objectives: 'Ashridge exists – both in itself and as a potential example – to build foundations: to create confidence and understanding – between classes, callings and points of view. We must not let it die.'[92] The new mission Ashridge was given after the war seemed to be conflated with that which was set by the college before the war. Bryant recognised this when he wrote to Davidson: 'the real enduring object of Ashridge is the restoration of Christian faith and values to England in a revolutionary age', and that Ashridge 'is the justification of all you and SB [Stanley Baldwin] believed in and stood for'.[93]

Ashridge demands its autonomy

Ashridge became the refuge for the Baldwinian old guard. After 1946, the quarrels with the party were unceasing and lasted until 1954, when a formal break was announced. For some, the college should be apolitical. Lord Fairhaven, the son of Urban Broughton, the principal benefactor of the college, declared that 'his father did not want the College to be tied to any one Party, and that his sole idea was that Ashridge should be used as a place for training in citizenship'.[94] He recalled that his father was a Liberal and that Ashridge should in no case be handed over to the Conservative party.[95] He seemed to forget that his own peerage had been the reward for his father's donations to the Conservative party. Another example of history being rewritten can be seen in a memorandum of September 1951 by L. H. Sutton, then director of studies at Ashridge. 'Ashridge,' Sutton wrote,

> was founded in 1929, at a time when the whole education system appeared to be involved in a landslide to the left, particularly University and Adult Education. The Founder, Urban Broughton, wished to found a College which would teach the ordinary citizen the plain facts without party or other sectional propaganda, but in the conditions then prevailing, in order to save his College from any future risk of joining this drift to the left, he gave the Conservative Party certain rights of representation on the Governing Body. This resulted in Ashridge becoming very largely a Party-College, and being

popularly considered as such. This development was not in accord with the wishes of the Founder, whose intention was that Ashridge should not follow the narrow path of training the party worker or provide propaganda ammunition for the converted.[96]

Although not completely false, this account of the origins of Ashridge fails to acknowledge that the college was called the BLMC in honour of the leader of the Conservative party from 1911 to 1921 and prime minister from 1922 to 1923. Nor did it acknowledge that it had been created by Davidson, who was chairman of the Conservative party at the time, for a political purpose, and that all sessions were supposed to end with the presentation of the Conservative perspective.

In July 1946, Graham wrote to Bryant: 'The rank and file of the Conservative Party for all the years which you and I have lived have never been encouraged to think for themselves, for the very obvious reason that so long as thought was submerged docility was secured.'[97] The following month, he declared: 'I am a Conservative, Arthur, but through forty long years of political effort, I have tried to build up an intelligent rank and file behind the Party, always to be thwarted by Party H.Q. who did not really want an educated rank and file.... The Conservative Party know nothing about education and care less. If the rank and file of the Party begin to think for themselves then Central Office dictation will end.'[98]

Graham's opinion was shared by the staff of Ashridge, who favoured education to propaganda. In 1951, at the reopening of Ashridge, Sutton explained: 'This did not mean any fundamental change in basic policy, it meant only that the College was shaking itself free of the restrictions of the Party connections which had grown up around it, and which were preventing it from reaching the most valuable of its potential students.'[99]

The BLMT was still, according to Davidson in 1947: 'a "Tory" Trust'.[100] Davidson intended to demonstrate that Ashridge had not changed, and that instead it was the Conservative party under Churchill that had changed. Davidson wrote to Butler in August 1947:

> It is my belief as a life-long Conservative – and it is in this belief that I have worked since its inception for Ashridge – that an honest, unbiassed and factual search for truth by men of goodwill, even when they seem at first in political disagreement, can do more at the present time than anything else to defeat the threat to that individual freedom of conscience, judgment and action on which the greatness of our country depends and has always depended.... The Governing Body now feels it would be defeating its own objects if it were to restrict students to the ranks of convinced Conservatives, and would be failing in its mission if it did not throw open its doors to all men and women in this country who desire to understand the true principles of democratic Government from a traditional angle.[101]

The continuity between the pre-war and post-war years is also apparent in a letter from Bryant to Joan Davidson in February 1948: 'We must constantly remember that unless those who do not share *our* views are genuinely convinced that the factual teaching of Ashridge is impartial, Ashridge's capacity to change *theirs* is nil.... *Au fond* that has always been our ideal at Ashridge, though for reasons at that time unavoidable we failed to make this clear to those who could see only the Party label.'[102]

Recounting his quarrel with the Conservative party, Davidson wrote: 'I was somewhat alarmed at the beginning by the strength of their [the party's] forces, but I think we out-gunned them; we certainly shook them a bit. I am quite certain that there are any number of first class men in the educational world, who, *though not partisan politicians are anti-totalitarian and lean towards traditionalism* and who could be safely trusted with the direction of adult education colleges.'[103] For Davidson, 'non-partisan', 'anti-totalitarian' and 'traditionalist' were all synonymous with 'Conservative'. 'An Ashridge free from Party domination and concerned simply with factual teaching'[104] meant an Ashridge that was engaged in serving the Conservative cause. In 1946, Davidson explained to Woolton: 'I am ... sure that our weakness in the past has been that the Chairman has relied on the standing army and paid far too little attention to the importance of the reserves during political lulls; but he badly needs these reserves to throw in when the campaign opens and the final polling day battle comes.'[105]

It was also necessary to train these reserves, if one wanted to be able to throw them into the electoral battle. Davidson further explained to Woolton: 'I can conceive of the time when in co-operation with industry and with many of the more moderate of the Trades Union leaders, we will be able to put into the field at an election thousands of men and women who are not necessarily active party supporters, but who will be able to support on the platform the philosophy of the progressive Right against the Left.'[106] Ashridge should emphasise 'the work of popular conversion to political sanity and maturity [i.e. Conservatism!] which was our founders' objective'.[107] In a letter to Bryant dated 1946, Davidson insisted upon this point:

> I think Pierssene [the CCO director] is a very sound, sane fellow. Naturally he must think in terms of Party organization and propaganda, but is a big enough man to realise that unless we go all out to counteract left wing totalitarian propaganda in the educational field by keeping adult education free from propaganda not only the Party but the nation will be sunk.[108]

The sense of being endangered, the defensive form of cultural antagonism and the identification with the nation were familiar themes.

The Baldwinian legacy in debate

Bryant and the principal of Ashridge, Bernard Paget, were both determined to ensure that Ashridge was truly free from any political affiliation. When, in 1946, Ashridge invited General Paget to become the principal, the governing body reported that 'General Paget in accepting the appointment said that he believed the education which Ashridge could provide would be one of the best ways of winning the Peace, and he did not see that education could be run except on non-Party lines and that if it were clearly understood that the work of Ashridge was to be on a strictly non-Party basis he was prepared to take up the appointment.'[109]

In insisting upon the political neutrality of the college, General Paget was referring to ideas expressed by Bryant in his memorandum on the future of Ashridge, drafted in the autumn of 1946. In December 1946, Paget wrote to Bryant: 'As far as I am concerned there can be no compromise on the non-Party issue here ... It would undoubtedly help, if the 7 vacancies on the Governing Body could be filled as soon as possible by others than Conservatives.'[110] The following month, Paget once again set out his vision for Ashridge. He explained that the objective of the new education committee was to ensure that 'the work of the College will be free from any political bias'.[111] During the summer of 1947, Paget and Bryant seemed to have convinced the governing body of the merits of their position. When Butler wrote to ask 'if the use of Ashridge could be granted for a weekend Conference for Conservative candidates', he was told: 'In view of the decision of the Governing Body not to allow Ashridge to be used for Party courses it was regretted that the request could not be granted.'[112]

Between 1946 and 1954, two conflicting projects emerged. The first, supported by Bryant and Paget, proposed to make Ashridge a centre for reflection on 'Christian democracy'. The second, which was eventually adopted, involved turning Ashridge into a school of management. The idea of turning it into a centre for reflection on Christian democracy did not signify the abandonment of the fight against Socialism. In 1948, Bryant explained that: 'Just as SB did, it [Ashridge] goes back to the roots of democracy – to Christianity because it opposes to Communism (which is a religion) a faith as strong as its own and far nobler.'[113] The reference to Communism was perhaps due to the recent appearance of the Iron Curtain. One can also see here fear of an alliance between Christian and Socialist movements, for whom only Socialism was truly inspired by Christianity. The idea of 'Christian Socialism' had grown during the war. In 1942, William Temple, known to be partial to the Labour party, had become archbishop of Canterbury. In 1945, Stafford

Cripps, the future chancellor of the exchequer in the Attlee government and the representative of the Left wing of the Labour party, wrote a book entitled *Towards Christian Democracy* in which he claimed: 'As Christian democrats, we should form an active army fighting injustice and poverty, unemployment and inequality, with as much vigour as we now show in our fight against those same evils in the garb of aggressive Nazism.'[114] Christian democracy did not mean the same thing to Ashridge as it did to Cripps. In 1948, Bryant explained that: 'We should always aim, in my view, at being an inspirational rather than a teaching institution. Ashridge's long-term aim has been to regenerate Britain by inspiring men and women to be missionaries.... Ashridge should be known as a College of Service, but the sense of service and dedication should be woven through everything it sends out.'[115] Cripps, without abandoning the idea of duty, insisted upon the justice and necessity of redistributing wealth: 'We must employ them [Christianity and Democracy] ruthlessly to create a physical human environment of justice and of decency',[116] and to do this, one had 'to sacrifice all ... certainly our personal wealth or privilege, for the sake of the principles in which we believe'.[117]

For Ashridge, these proposals had the smell of class struggle. Christian democracy pointed towards social harmony. In 1948, the college sought, according to Bryant, 'to be something wider, wholly transcending class and politics − a common denominator, on Christian and traditional lines, for the reconstruction of England'.[118] At the start of the 1950s, Enoch Powell, a future minister in the Macmillan government and member of the One Nation Group, wrote the first draft of a book on 'The Church'. There he noted that the nineteenth and twentieth centuries shared with the sixteenth and seventeenth centuries 'the disruption of the natural and organic unity of the nation's life', the symptoms of which were Communism, class conflict and Socialism. Powell explained that, after the Reformation and the English revolution, 'the individual has lost his place in a community which should need him as he needs it'. For Powell, the solution was the revival of Christianity, making the Church the central force in the life of society. He added: 'It may appear an unpractical assertion, but it is an arresting and undeniable one, that if everyone were a full member of the Church, the class war and that mutual envy and fear which is socialism would instantly be inconceivable.'[119] Powell's book was never published. Although the One Nation Group was composed of practising Anglicans, in its publications it only developed a secular vision for society.

The Conservative party, like the Labour party, set aside the idea of Christian democracy. In 1947, Macmillan briefly considered changing the name of the Conservative party to that of 'Democratic party', though he never imagined calling it the 'Christian-Democratic party'. In view of the number and diversity of churches in Britain, it is difficult to imagine uniting the country behind the Christian democrat banner.[120] Besides, the term Christian democrat was commonly associated with the politics of Italy and Germany, which implied an essentially Catholic understanding of the term.[121]

Paget and Bryant agreed upon the importance of a moral and spiritual dimension to the education at Ashridge. Paget declared that 'Every aspect of British life is based on the importance and dignity of the individual, which in turn is based on Christian philosophy', and that Christianity was the source of the British way of life.[122] But in March 1948, a year after Ashridge reopened, the disagreement between Davidson, Bryant and Paget became open. Davidson wrote to Bryant:

> I believe that we shall have to turn Ashridge over to the fight against Communism, in which we should have the support of all Democrats, both from the Left and the Right, and let long-term factual, academic discussion go by the board. Then we should get out of our financial difficulties, and be turning away people, if we get the right Director and staff, who will have to be militant (rather than military) Christian Democrats – and even with a Tory prefix, for they I believe are the kernel of the movement.[123]

From the end of 1947, a gulf had grown between Davidson, Paget, the principal of Ashridge, and Bryant, chair of Ashridge's education committee. Davidson was worried about a lack of cohesion in the teaching programme and concerned that the college might drift to the Left. He found the teaching too theoretical and did not approve of the creation of courses for the clergy. Clergymen were too 'inward-looking', focusing on theological study, biblical exegesis, the study of dogma and Christian ethics rather than a more secular form of training. Davidson, a practising Anglican, was interested in the 'external life' and the fight against Socialism. In this struggle, Christian faith was important but not sufficient. Davidson could have employed the phrase coined by George Orwell: 'The Anglican church is the Tory party at prayer', but he rejected the idea that the Conservatives were simply the political counterpart of the Anglican church. Davidson feared that the expression 'non-party' encouraged the belief that Ashridge was a Left-leaning college. He believed Ashridge should be 'without political affiliations', but 'openly Tory'. Many misunderstandings arose from differing interpretations of what was meant by unpolitical politics. It seemed that 'rightly or wrongly Ashridge on a non-party basis was considered as going left'.[124] The expression 'factual education' was suggested but failed to appeal. Finally, they fell back on 'without political bias' and 'an open forum for the study and discussion of public affairs'.[125] 'Without political bias' was considered a more neutral term than 'non-party' because it was, in many ways, how the Conservatives saw themselves and claimed to be.

In early December 1946, T. N. Graham wrote to Bryant to express his objection to the list of lecturers at Ashridge. He explained: 'When the two of them [Paget and Harper] talk glibly about securing [C. E. M.] Joad and [J. B.] Priestley and people of that ilk then my breadth of mind does not extend to quite that distance. We can quite easily damn Ashridge with the Left blanket as well as the Right, and I am not prepared to argue that either Joad or Priestley is best qualified to supply factual teaching.'[126]

That same month, Davidson similarly complained about the Leftward drift of the college. He wrote to Bryant that '[Paget's] trouble is that he really knows absolutely nothing about politics, which after all in the widest sense Ashridge will teach.'[127] Like Graham, he criticised the choice of some of the lecturers and declared that 'the Victor Gollanczs, the D. N. Pritts, even the Bishop of Chichester, whom I personally do not object to terribly, are not in one sense experts. And they are the wrong type of lecturer to give to our students the kind of inspiration we want them to have.'[128]

A new crisis erupted in the summer of 1949. The immediate cause was the planned opening of a new department, to be called 'the house of citizenship'. It was supposed to be an institute for young women, the headmistress of which wished to move from London. Ashridge's interest in the 'house of citizenship' was financial. The students in this school were boarders and paid substantial fees each term. A part of the college would thus be permanently occupied, guaranteeing a stable source of income. In view of the college's catastrophic financial situation, the directors favoured this arrangement.[129] However, Paget and Bryant criticised Davidson for taking the decision alone, without consulting the education committee. Writing to Lord Woolton in August 1949, Bryant complained: 'the proposal to introduce a girl's finishing school called the House of Citizenship' was brought up at the governing body on 15 July and a final decision was made shortly after at a meeting between Davidson, the two representatives of NUCA, who were ex officio members of the governing body, and two others, against the advice of Bryant, Lord Fairhaven and Lord Wardington.[130] Davidson sought to limit the role played by the education committee in order to rid himself of Paget. Davidson defended himself by saying: 'It is finance which governs everything at the moment.... If Miss Rolfe's fifty girls produce one-third of the annual revenue, and the other students, week-end and mid-week, produce two-thirds, the allocation of accommodation will be broadly in those proportions.'[131]

The Conservative party was not worried about this crisis. In September, Woolton wrote to Bryant, hypocritically perhaps, that while he regretted 'this deplorable controversy', he 'felt unable to take any part in it because

[he] ha[d] no other standing than that of Chairman of the party, and since the whole of your operations have been so strictly and wisely put on to a non-party basis it would be inappropriate for a person who only sits on the Board of Governors by right of party office to join in the discussion'.[132] By the same token, the chairman of the 1922 Committee explained to Bryant that he could not intervene because he had resigned from the governing body of Ashridge in April. 'When the College was a political one I had hopes of being of some assistance, but I had no claims to being an educationalist.'[133] After four years of incessant quarrels, the bridges had been definitively burned. In September 1949, shortly after his resignation, Bryant wrote to Woolton: 'I feel rather like a ship whose anchor has been cut or a balloon whose cable has been cut.'[134] Ashridge's cable had been cut and it was seeking a new anchor.

Ashridge, a school of management

After the crisis in September 1949, a new principal, Admiral Denis Boyd, was appointed. A new education committee was also put into place under the authority of the governing body. The terms of reference for the education committee echoed those of 1930: 'It was decided that the Education Committee be empowered to act for and on behalf of the Governing Body in all matters connected with Education.'[135]

Lord Davidson and the governing body thus reaffirmed their authority. It was also an opportunity to redefine their relationship with the party:

It was essential to be entirely honest on that point and to avoid window-dressing or any suspicion of false colours. The Trust was founded in memory of a great Statesman who was a Conservative. It is however as a Statesman and not as a party politician that he is to be honoured. Thus while the Trust as an educational body must stand for those principles of historic tradition which are among the tenets of the Conservative party of which Bonar Law was a leader, the teaching of the College must be strictly without party or other bias. Lecturers must be chosen purely for their ability and knowledge, irrespective of their political affiliations, except that Communists shall be excluded.[136]

It was then decided to revive the name Bonar Law College, which had been omitted at the reopening of the college in January 1947. In April 1952, in a report to the education committee, the principal explained: 'About the middle of last year we appeared to have allayed the suspicions that the departure of my predecessor meant the introduction of party politics. There is now a marked absence of any query about the politics of the College. Students recognise that there is a bias to the Right, in the sense that our approach is traditional and constitutional, but there is a definite appreciation of the fact that our lecturers are governed by no "party line", and that the students are subjected to no propaganda.'[137]

This tension between 'a right-wing commitment' and being 'non-partisan', which was what gave Ashridge its originality and force in the 1930s, was now its source of weakness. In an article for the *Birmingham Post* entitled 'Ashridge: Its Ideals, Aims and Achievement', Admiral Boyd explained: 'Ashridge could still be called the Conservative and equally justly the Liberal or Labour training college, that is, if your political faith is able to stand the strain of hearing facts and the opinions of those who hold other points of view.... Who comes to Ashridge?... They are of all types and, in the three Services, of all ranks. In accordance with the ideal of the College there is no such thing as class consciousness. Some firms send teams such as a manager, a shop steward and two or three workmen.'[138] Although the principal, shortly after his appointment, declared: 'That is humbly my task: to "extirpate that ignorancy" which prevents us achieving a full satisfying life and being of service to God and Man,'[139] these objectives remained vague. Ashridge moved closer to the business world, which alone could provide a new source of funding. Its financial situation was in fact critical. L. H. Sutton, the director of studies, explained: 'An innovation in 1951 was that of industrial Courses of 12 days duration. The idea of these Courses is that it is essential that all those engaged in industry should appreciate the effect upon their industry of existing economic conditions, of proposed governmental policy at home, and of events abroad.'[140] The business world offered a platform for experimentation, which was important for the teaching of citizenship. Industrial development had become the driving force behind economic recovery and prosperity. Thus began extensive study into social organisation and human relationships within firms. Business was considered not only the driving force of the economy, but also a laboratory for new social relations.

British industry, which until then had failed to engage with Taylorism as practised in the United States, henceforth became interested in management. In 1948, the Anglo-American Council on Productivity was established in order to make Britain aware of this newly arrived American discipline. In 1949, it was followed by the creation of the British Productivity Council, which sought to bring together – independent of government – managers and trade unionists in order to create a climate for co-operation within British industry.[141] These new initiatives were often greeted with scepticism. Most business leaders believed that management training made sense only after several years' experience. Practical experience remained the key to success. In 1951, the magazine *Future* expressed the widely held view that 'practical' knowledge was more important than 'bookish' knowledge.[142] At the start of the 1950s, the tradition of learning on the job was favoured by the economic world. The very idea of a management school seemed as alien to business leaders as it did to academics, as shown by the failed attempt to institute a department of business studies at Cambridge.[143] In the 1960s, some universities opened departments like this, but it was only in the 1990s that the universities of Cambridge and Oxford created their first departments of business studies. Although the British Institute of Management (BIM) was created in 1948, it 'remained largely isolated, essentially ignored by those in business'.[144] In 1955, the *Economist* noted that 'many directors continued to believe that "a manager was born and not made"'.[145] Thus, in 1955, A. Bonham-Carter, director of the BIM, suggested that Ashridge should revive its courses for business leaders, since the BIM was also experiencing financial difficulties.[146] Ashridge seized the opportunity, seeing in it confirmation that the future of the college lay in closer ties with the business world.

In November 1947, the governing body asked Davidson 'to take up without delay the question of approaching industry, explaining the financial position of the Trust and outlining the work of the College, and assuring those to whom he spoke that the Educational Council would be willing to adapt the syllabuses to meet the needs of industry'.[147] In February 1949, Davidson reported that he was in touch with a company which was prepared to offer financial support, 'if its Board could be persuaded that Ashridge was giving the lead that was needed in Industry to-day'.[148]

To the question of what lead industry was prepared to follow, Davidson replied: 'No effort must be relaxed to educate, not only the leaders, but the rank and file, in the economics of Industry, and in their responsibility towards their particular undertaking. There is too much talk of the Two Sides in Industry, and too little of the team which all industry might be.' If Ashridge pursued its efforts, 'there may grow up a new generation which will not be prepared to allow party politics and the class war to poison the spirit of co-operation towards a common achievement without which no industry can succeed'.[149] Davidson was sketching out the broad lines of a new project for Ashridge. As for Admiral Boyd, he was interested in the practical side of this new kind of training. At the end of 1950, he explained: 'It has become apparent that the idea that the apprentice-training should form the main basis of industrial courses must be revised. Such support as has been forthcoming is for the training of junior managers and the pre-entry training of graduates.'[150] The idea of training for industrial managers by short two-week or nine-week courses started to develop. The principal declared: 'I am thinking of Ashridge as a centre of leadership and inspiration in influencing the fast-moving development of our economic structure.'[151] These claims echoed the objectives of Ashridge as originally set out in 1929. In his memorandum of September 1951, Sutton insisted upon the fact that Ashridge must be a 'leaven of public opinion'[152] in business and for society as a whole. In 1951, Ashridge launched its first management courses.

Sutton observed that 'these industrial Courses are *barely out of the experimental stage*, and at present cater for middle and junior management'.[153] But, he added, 'those successes have shown that our net can now be spread more widely. Week-end industrial students are of all grades from the shop floor to the Board Room, and our longer Courses must be expanded to cover the same field.'[154] For Sutton, these courses were the future of Ashridge. In May 1952, Admiral Boyd wrote to Davidson to describe a proposed presentation on the college at the Hendon Chamber of Commerce and Industry: 'I look on this as so important ... [as] we are getting nobody from the smaller industries which surround us.'[155] Ashridge's ambition was to become a centre for the teaching and research for the industrial world in all its guises.

A report of 21 May 1952 indicates that with thirty-six registered students, the first session of economics and management courses had exceeded expectations. At the request of several firms, two further sessions were proposed, one aimed at apprentices and interns, the other at administrative staff. The first attracted only sixteen students and the second seventeen. The principal concluded that: 'Our Industrial Courses as originally planned are the ones that really appeal to Industry, since any departure from the normal has resulted in a serious fall in enrolments. These then must form the basis of our contribution to industrial education. We are however gradually expanding our work in this field.... At the suggestion of Viscount Caldecote we arranged in March a long week-end for undergraduates who were contemplating entering industry. As an experiment this was very successful.'[156]

Ashridge's financial situation nonetheless failed to improve. Reports from Mr Pike, the college's financial director, were pessimistic: 'Income is disappointing',[157] and in December 1952: 'The existing type of programme cannot achieve a financial balance on current account.... The most likely field for the necessary support is industry and commerce.'[158] Developing relationships with businesses, however, required that all ties with the Conservative party be severed. In 1952, the first steps towards changing the trust deed were undertaken. Lord Davidson pointed out: 'A change in the Trust Deed will not affect in any way the present policy in Ashridge education, but it will enable us to demonstrate that the education is factual and not party-propaganda, and is controlled by an educational Trust recognised as a charity.'[159]

As Ashridge was a trust, the governing body was required to present to parliament a proposal for any changes to the statutes. Members of parliament, and in particular members of the Labour party, had to be persuaded to act. In fact, the Conservative party – Swinton College, the CPC and the CRD having taken over Ashridge – would not contest any changes. Lord Davidson wrote:

> Lord Oaksey and I came to the definite conclusion that the reason we failed was because in spite of everything Ashridge is still regarded as a Conservative Party College. The Finance Committee thereupon recommended to the Governors that we should endeavour to rid ourselves of the political liabilities arising from the terms of the Trust Deed; and the Governors, while not having taken any decision yet, have authorised a sub-committee to take Counsel's opinion on the possibility of varying the Trust Deed, and establishing the trust as a charity with no political strings ... Lord Fairhaven, the only other Founder Governor besides myself, is entirely in favour of our going ahead on these lines ... we shall never get the money and the right kind of students unless we break down the belief that Ashridge is a Party College.[160]

Newsom, director of the Hertfordshire County Council Education Committee and member of the education committee at Ashridge, commented: 'I absolutely agree with your contention that Ashridge suffers from the fact that there is dubiety about its relationship with the Conservative Party. I have thought for some time that you ought either to sail openly under the Conservative colours and make it a de facto Conservative College, or do what you are now suggesting.'[161] The private member's Bill, drafted between 1952 and 1953, was presented to parliament in February 1954. It was debated over the course of three sessions without being challenged. The only criticism came from Labour party members who took the opportunity to make some sarcastic comments about the Conservative party. For example, Colonel George Wigg, a Labour MP, said: 'The House is asked today to take this bankrupt Conservative concern which has now exhausted its usefulness as a piece of propaganda machinery for the Tory Party, and to turn it into an educational Trust.'[162] Similarly, Michael Stewart, a young Labour MP who went on to become foreign secretary in the 1960s, commented: 'It is a profound mistake for them [the Conservatives] to start any imitation of other parties' educational ventures among their members. Their history is littered with the failure of attempts of that kind, and for the very good reason that, fundamentally, the attachment of a Conservative to his Party is not based on intellectual conviction.'[163] The Bill was passed without a vote in April 1954, after, apparently, an agreement had been negotiated between Davidson and the Labour party. In March 1954, Davidson wrote to Boyd: 'I had a long talk yesterday with Colonel Wigg and Mr. Chuter Ede, and we were able to set at rest some of their doubts, and to adopt several of the amendments which they proposed, none of which in any way affects the substance of the Bill.'[164] The 1954 Bill made no mention of links between Ashridge and the Conservative party, and thus transformed the college into a foundation with a favourable fiscal status; henceforth it could look for new sources of finance. The Bill set out the public role of Ashridge as follows:

1. To carry out at Ashridge a college for the education of persons in economics political and social science political history with special reference to the development of the British constitution and the growth and expansion of the Commonwealth and Empire and in such other subjects as the governors may from time to time determine calculated generally to enable the students to become useful intelligent and active members of the nation and the Commonwealth;

2. To found and carry on another college or other colleges or similar institutions for such education as aforesaid in any part of the world;

3. To preserve Ashridge for the benefit of the nation.[165]

This was the beginning of a new era for Ashridge. In June 1955, a memorandum sent to the governing body noted that 'over two years ago the Director of Studies submitted a Memorandum on the future of Ashridge which among other recommendations expressed the view that the main hope for the future lay in the expansion of our courses for industrial management'. It continued: 'We are more than ever convinced that the best hope for the future lies in the development of management training... we feel also that in the present state of the nation such a policy, with the further opportunity of improving industrial relations, is one that would be fully in accord with the purposes of the founder.'[166] Ashridge received hundreds of letters of approval from firms which had followed these developments. Company employees acknowledged the difference its courses had made. Throughout the country, company directors publicly praised Boyd.

Although Ashridge was transformed into a school of management, it did not give up teaching some of the courses it was known for. Once again, the continuity is striking. As before, courses were divided into two categories. The weekend courses tended to be on more general subjects, whereas the week-long courses were devoted to management. The weekend courses, on which the college's reputation was built, remained its core activity. Twenty-five weekend sessions were arranged every year, and five subjects were addressed in these sessions: foreign policy, Commonwealth policy, the economy, social problems and the arts. The courses dealt with basics, and it was by them that Ashridge hoped to reach the widest public. Proposals were made for longer courses during the school holidays: 'Ashridge should educate as large a cross-section of the nation as possible in current national and international problems and in responsibilities of citizenship.'[167] Reference to international affairs was important, and Davidson was keen to strengthen ties with the United States. A number of American students came to study at Ashridge, including some fifty students from Western Michigan College and Iowa State Teachers College, who took summer courses of five weeks. The idea was also to develop ties with universities of the Commonwealth and to revive the trips abroad that had existed before the war, 'to enable the ordinary working man to meet his counterpart in continental countries and amongst other things, to learn of the different outlook towards productivity and the standard of living which prevails in many of them'.[168]

However, compared to other business schools established later, Ashridge remained an exception. Its mission was still to train citizens who were engaged with society and conscious of their responsibilities. The business world was the centre of its attention only because it was the focus of social issues after the war. Emphasis was placed on the fact that 'the Industrial Courses are not concerned with technical problems, but with the relations of the partners in industry to each other and their mutual interest in economic conditions affecting this country's prosperity and peace. Ashridge brings together in a friendly and stimulating atmosphere students from many walks of life, who learn much from each other'.[169] Ashridge as a management college conceived and presented businesses as organic enterprises, which had the role of intermediary institutions in society. Management science was to educate and train employers and employees with regard to their duties and responsibilities towards one another, their business and their fellow citizens.

Notes

1 G. Ellis to Lord Baldwin, 7 Aug. 1940, Baldwin papers, SB174, fos 28–29.
2 *Ibid.*
3 P. Hennessy, *Never Again, Britain 1945–1951* (London: Jonathan Cape, 1992).
4 The report set out a series of recommendations for establishing a social security system open to all. The welfare state was one of the suggestions that came into existence after the war.
5 The Butler Education Act was passed in August 1944.

6 He titled one of the volumes of his memoirs *The Adventure of Reconstruction* (London: Cassell, 1945).

7 Minutes of the Governing Body, 4 Nov. 1946, Ashridge papers.

8 Many Conservative party chiefs found themselves in a difficult position within the party after the electoral defeat and consequently many resigned from their positions.

9 J. C. C. Davidson to S. Baldwin, 14 May 1940, Baldwin papers, SB174, fos 275–277. 'Glamour Boys' was an expression that was applied to Conservatives such as Anthony Eden and Duff Cooper. Kingsley Wood became chancellor of the exchequer in 1941. Geoffrey Lloyd was considered to be loyal to Baldwin.

10 For the general public's reaction to Churchill's rise to power, see M. Gilbert, *Finest Hour: Winston S. Churchill, 1939–41* (London: Heinemann, 1983) and A. Calder, *The People's War: Britain 1939–45* (London: Cape, 1969).

11 On the cult surrounding Chamberlain on his death, see A. Roberts 'The Tories versus Churchill during the "Finest Hour"', in *Eminent Churchillians* (London: Weidenfeld & Nicolson, 1994).

12 R. R. James, *A Study in Failure*, 1900–1939 (London: Weidenfeld & Nicolson, 1970).

13 Crookshank Diary, 1 Mar. 1944, Viscount Crookshank papers, Bodleian Library, Oxford, (hereafter Crookshank papers) MS Eng. Hist. D 361.

14 A. Roberts, *Eminent Churchillians* (London: Weidenfeld & Nicolson, 1994), p. 186.

15 J. Barnes and J. Nicholson, *The Empire at Bay: The Leo Amery Diaries*, vol. 2: *1929–1945* (London: Hutchinson, 1988).

16 In P. Addison, *Churchill on the Home Front, 1900–1955* (London: Jonathan Cape, 1992), p. 361.

17 Lord Woolton to R. A. Butler, quoted in Ramsden, *The Age of Churchill and Eden*, p. 18.

18 H. Willink, unpublished autobiography, p. 74, Willink papers, quoted in Ramsden, *The Age of Churchill and Eden*, p. 46.

19 Ramsden, *The Making of Conservative Party Policy*, pp. 97–8.

20 Quoted in Roberts, *Eminent Churchillians*, pp. 203.

21 Quoted in S. Kelly, The Myth of Mr Butskell. The Politics of British Economic Policy, 1950–1955 (Aldershot: Ashgate Publishers, 2002).

22 On the discord between the Conservative party and the government, see Ramsden, *The Age of Churchill and Eden*, pp. 17–31.

23 Harold Crookshank was one of the leading Conservative ministers without portfolio and a member of the 1922 Committee. Crookshank Diary, 16 July 1945, Crookshank papers, MS Eng. Hist. D 361.

24 T. N. Graham to A. Bryant, 10 Aug. 1945, Bryant papers, D11.

25 A. Bryant to Colonel George Filligham, Aug. 1945, in Street, *Arthur Bryant*, p. 132.

26 Bryant to Lord Davidson, 3 June 1947, Bryant papers, D11.

27 On Churchill and the lack of organisation within the party at the time of the election, see Ramsden, *The Age of Churchill and Eden*, pp. 4–5.

28 Cato, *Guilty Men* (London: Gollancz, 1940). 'Cato' was the pseudonym used by Michael Foot, Frank Owen and Peter Howard when attacking the 'guilty men', that is to say, the fifteen politicians whom they considered responsible for the Munich agreement.

29 P. Smithers to R. D. Milne, 19 Oct. 1947, CPA, CRD 2/53/68.

30 M. Fraser 'The CRD and Conservative Recovery after 1945', Aug. 1961, Butler papers, H46, fos 42–56.

31 Cato, *Guilty Men*.

32 W. Churchill, *The Second World War*, vol. I: *The Gathering Storm* (London: Chiswick Press, 1948), p. 697.

33 For example, J. Charmley, *Chamberlain and the Lost Peace* (London: Curtis, 1989); J. Charmley, *Churchill and the End of Glory* (London: Hodder and Stoughton, 1993). A. Roberts, *The Holy Fox. The Life of Lord Halifax* (London: Weidenfeld & Nicolson, 1991). P. Williamson, *National Crisis and National Government: British Politics, the Economy and the Empire, 1926–32* (Cambridge: Cambridge University Press, 1992), and also Schmidt, *The Politics and Economics of Appeasement*.

34 R. Skidelsky, *Politicians and the Slump. The Labour Government of 1929–31* (London: Macmillan, 1967). M. Stewart, *Keynes and After* (Harmondsworth: Penguin, 1972). The opinions of historians from the 1970s who attempted to rehabilitate Baldwin's reputation are still nuanced, amongst them Keith Middlemas and John Barnes, Stuart Ball, John Ramsden and Michael Bentley.

35 Williamson, *Stanley Baldwin*.

36 R. Assheton to Lord Beaverbrook, 25 Jan. 1946, Beaverbrook papers, C96. Michael Foot and Frank Owen, authors of *Guilty Men*, both worked at the *Evening Standard*, which was owned by Beaverbrook.

37 Minutes of the Governing Body, 4 Nov. 1946, Ashridge papers.

38 The party's chief whip is responsible for the party's discipline in the House of Commons.

39 Interview with Churchill described by T. N. Graham, 1 Aug. 1946, Bryant papers, D11.

40 Lord Davidson to General Paget, 18 June 1947, Bryant papers, D14.

41 T. N. Graham to Arthur Bryant, 22 Dec. 1947, Bryant papers, D9.

42 A. Bryant to T. N. Graham, 19 Dec. 1947, Bryant papers, D9.

43 A. Bryant to General Paget, 6 May 1947, Bryant papers, D14.

44 Sir David Maxwell Fyfe, Minutes from the annual Conservative Party Conference at Blackpool, Oct. 1946, CPA, NUA 2/1/55.

45 From various memoranda on the need for political education, dated Feb. 1945, see CPA, CCO 4/2/145.

46 Memorandum by Miss Maxse to the chairman of the Conservative party, Political Education, 27 July 1945, CPA, CCO 4/2/145.

47 *Ibid.*

48 Butler, *The Art of the Possible*, pp. 136–7.

49 Black, 'Tories and Hunters'.

50 The CRD was closed at the beginning of 2003.

51 Butler had created the Conservative Political Circle in 1938, but its existence was cut short because of the war.

52 Two Way Movement of Ideas/Contact Programme. Minutes from the annual Conservative Party Conference at Blackpool, Oct. 1946. CPA, NUA 2/1/55.

53 Minutes from the annual Conservative Party Conference, Blackpool, Oct. 1946, CPA, NUA 2/1/55.

54 Miss Maxse to A. Butler, 20 Sep. 1945, CPA, CCO 4/2/125.

55 Memorandum on the interview between Lord Davidson and Winston Churchill, 30 July 1946, Bryant papers, C61.

56 There was a striking similarity between the programmes at Swinton and Ashridge.

57 Reginald Northam to the constituency officials, 20 Nov. 1950, CPA, CCO 4/4/309.

58 ACPPE, Draft Report, 5 July 1949, For Inclusion in Conference Handbook, CPA, S 13.

59 13 May 1947, CPA, X.Films 65/1 British Conservative Party Committee Minutes, 1909–1964. Reel 1, Policy and Political Education, 1946–1964.

60 13 Apr. 1948, CPA, X.Films 65/1 British Conservative Party Committee Minutes, 1909–1964. Reel 1, Policy and Political Education, 1946–1964.

61 Miss Maxse, Political Education Department, 22 Nov. 1945, CPA, CCO 4/3/145.

62 Quoted in P. Norton 'The Conservative Political Centre, 1945–98', in S. Ball and I. Holliday (eds), Mass Conservatism. The Conservatives and the Public since the 1880s (London: Frank Cass Publishers, 2002), p. 184.

63 This report marked, symbolically at least, some social democratisation of the Conservative party. It reduced the financial dependence of MPs at a local level.

64 Lord Woolton, Memoirs (London: Cassell, 1959), p. 331.

65 Memorandum sent by the General Director, Sir Stephen Piersenne to Heads of CCO Departments, Central Office Agents, and Area Education Organisers 26 May 1950, CPA, CCO, 4/3/48.

66 Memorandum by Miss Maxse to the Chairman of the Conservative Party, Political Education, 27 July 1945, CPA, CCO 4/2/145.

67 Quoted in Garnett, Alport: a Study in Loyalty, p. 73.

68 Minutes 28 Oct., 1947, CPA, X.Films 65/1 British Conservative Party Committee Minutes, 1909–1964, Reel 1, Policy and Political Education, 1946–1964.

69 Garnett, Alport: a Study in Loyalty, p. 82.

70 'CPC National Membership', undated, Minutes and Papers of the National Advisory Committee on Political Education, July 1948–Oct. 1952 CPA, CTC/s/13/3. My italics.

71 CPC Prospectus, Central Lecturers' & Tutors Panel, 21 June 1946, CPA, CRD, 2/53/68.

72 On the continuity between the Conservative party under Baldwin and Chamberlain and under Churchill, see J. Ramsden, 'A Party for Owners or a Party for Earners? How Far Did the British Conservative Party Really Change after 1945?', *The Transactions of the Royal Historical Society*, 37, 1987, pp. 49–63.

73 The Ashridge trust statutes stipulated that the college had to teach British political and social history 'with special reference to the constitutional development of Britain and the Empire'. Special attention was to be placed on the development of British institutions and the power and growth of the British Empire.

74 H. Nicolson, *Diaries and Letters, 1945–62* (London: Collins, 1968), p. 35. My italics.

75 Memorandum on Swinton, Apr. 1946, CPA, CCO 4/2/181.

76 See Chapter 10.

77 Garnett, Alport: a Study in Loyalty, p. 36.

78 In October 1948, the CPC produced more than 50 publications with a total print run of 750,000 copies. 1948, Conservative Party Conference Report, quoted in Garnett, *Alport: a Study in Loyalty*, p. 74.

79 D. Clarke, *The Conservative Faith in a Modern Age* (London: CPC, 1947). T. E. Utley, *Essays in Conservatism* (London: CPC, 1949).

80 The One Nation Group was established in 1950 by a group of Conservative MPs, the majority of whom went on to hold ministerial positions (Iain MacLeod, Enoch Powell, Robert Carr, Edward Heath …). Their aim was to define a Conservative approach to economic and social problems.

81 Garnett, Alport: a Study in Loyalty, p. 104.

82 I. MacLeod to R. A. Butler, 6 Aug. 1950, Butler papers, H34, fos 30–33.

83 On the One Nation Group and its ties with Thatcher and Baldwin, see R. Walsha, 'The One Nation Group: A Tory Approach to Backbench Politics and Organization, 1950–55', *Twentieth Century British History*, 11 (2), 2000, pp. 183–214; and above all, Green, *Ideologies of Conservatism*, as well as E. H. H. Green, 'The Conservative Party, the State and the Electorate, 1945–64', in J. Lawrence and M. Taylor (eds), *Party, State and Society; Electoral Behaviour in Britain since 1820* (Aldershot: Scolar Press, 1997), pp. 176–200.

84 S. Baldwin to Parliament, 6 Mar. 1925, 'Peace in Industry', in *On England*, p. 52.

85 Quoted in Garnett, *Alport: a Study in Loyalty*, p. xi.

86 Garnett, Alport: a Study in Loyalty, p. 89.

87 Lord Davidson to A. Bryant, 22 Apr. 1948, Bryant papers, D11.

88 Minutes of the Governing Body, 24 July 1946, Ashridge papers.

89 A. Bryant to Lord Davidson, 28 Dec. 1948, Bryant papers, D11.

90 Memorandum by A. Bryant, undated, Bryant papers, C61.

91 Presentation by the BLMC, Bryant papers, C22.

92 A. Bryant to Lord Davidson, 24 June 1949, Bryant papers, D19.

93 A. Bryant to Lord Davidson, 7 Jan. 1948, Bryant papers, D11.

94 Minutes of the Governing Body, 4 Nov. 1946, Ashridge papers.

95 *Ibid.* Broughton was not a Liberal but Conservative MP for Preston.

96 Undated memorandum by L. H. Sutton, Sep. 1951, Ashridge papers.

97 T. N. Graham to A. Bryant, 13 Nov. 1945, Bryant papers, D11.

98 T. N. Graham to A. Bryant, 8 Aug. 1946, Bryant papers, D11.

99 Memorandum by L. H. Sutton, undated (?Sep. 1951) Finance and General Purposes Committee, Ashridge papers.

100 Lord Davidson to A. Bryant, 14 Aug. 1947, Bryant papers, D11.

101 Lord Davidson to R. A. Butler, 12 Aug. 1947, Bryant papers, D11.

102 A. Bryant to J. Davidson, 15 Feb. 1948, Bryant papers, D11.

103 Lord Davidson to A. Bryant, 7 Feb. 1946, Bryant papers, D19 and C61.

104 Lord Davidson to A. Bryant, 12 Feb. 1946, Bryant papers, D11.

105 Lord Davidson to Lord Woolton, 1 Aug. 1946, Bryant papers, C61.

106 *Ibid.*

107 Memorandum on the Future of Ashridge, Arthur Bryant, undated, Bryant papers, C61.

108 Lord Davidson to A. Bryant, 7 Feb. 1946, Bryant papers, D19 and C61.

109 Minutes of the Governing Body, 4 Nov. 1946, Ashridge papers.

110 General Paget to A. Bryant, 20 Dec. 1946, Bryant papers, D14.

111 B. Paget to Brigadier Anderson, undated, Jan. 1947, Education Committee Minutes, 1947–49, Ashridge papers.

112 Minutes of the Governing Body, 8 May 1947, Finance and General Purposes Committee, 1945–51, Ashridge papers.

113 A Bryant to Lord Davidson, 12 Mar. 1948, Bryant papers, D11.

114 S. Cripps, *Towards Christian Democracy. A Challenge to the Faithless* (New York: Philosophical Library, 1946), p. 89.

115 A. Bryant to Lord Davidson, 28 Dec. 1948, Bryant papers, D11.

116 Cripps, Towards Christian Democracy, p. 89.

117 *Ibid.*

118 A. Bryant to Lord Davidson, 12 Mar. 1948, Bryant papers, D11.

119 J. E. Powell, 'The Church', undated 1954, J. E. Powell Papers, Churchill College, Cambridge, POLL 3/2/11.

120 One of the reasons Britain had so much trouble establishing a national education system can be linked to religious tensions. It was only in 1944 that these problems were overcome, with the Butler Act that implemented a free and obligatory secondary school system available to all.

121 P. Clarke explained that Cripps was 'sensitive about the appropriation of religion by the right-wing Christian Democrats of Catholic Europe, which he regarded as "a complete misuse of the term Christian"'. P. Clarke, *The Cripps Version: the Life of Sir Stafford Cripps* (London: Allen Lane, 2002), p. 529.

122 General Paget's notes, undated, Finance and General Purposes Committee 1947–1951, Ashridge papers.

123 Lord Davidson to A. Bryant, 2 Mar. 1948, Bryant papers, D11.

124 Memorandum from T. N. Graham, Dec. 1947, Bryant papers, D9.

125 From a debate that was recounted in a letter from T. N. Graham to A. Bryant, 14 July 1947, Bryant papers, D9.

126 J. B. Priestley was a Left-wing writer. He had been a popular radio commentator during the war. C. E. M. Joad was also a Left-wing writer. T. N. Graham to A. Bryant, 3 Dec. 1946, Bryant papers, C61.

127 Lord Davidson to A. Bryant, 30 Dec. 1946, Bryant papers, D11.

128 Victor Gollancz founded the Left Book Club in the early 1930s. D. N. Pritt was a writer and member of the Communist party. Lord Davidson to A. Bryant, 30 Dec. 1946, Bryant papers, D11.

129 The House of Citizenship was established in October 1936 in London. *The Citizen* in October 1936 described it as 'providing an education in citizenship for girls from the age of eighteen who do not need to earn their own living, and who, by their very circumstances, have as a rule had little opportunity of understanding their lives outside their own limited circle'. In 1949, it was integrated into Ashridge.

130 A. Bryant to Lord Woolton, 14 Aug. 1949, Bryant papers, D12.

131 Lord Davidson to A. Bryant, 11 Aug. 1949, Bryant papers, D19.

132 Lord Woolton to A. Bryant, 8 Sep. 1949, Bryant papers, D12.

133 W. S. Morrison to A. Bryant, 9 Sep. 1949, Bryant papers, D13.

134 A. Bryant to Lord Woolton, 9 Sep. 1949, Bryant papers, D12.

135 First meeting of the Ashridge Education Committee, 7 Mar. 1950, Ashridge papers.

136 *Ibid.*

137 Principal's report, 9 Apr. 1951, Ashridge papers.

138 Admiral Sir D. Boyd, 'Ashridge: Its Ideals, Aims and Achievements', *Birmingham Post*, 20 Apr. 1950, Bryant papers, D19.

139 *Ibid.*

140 Memorandum by L. H. Sutton, undated (?Sep. 1951), Finance and General Purpose Committee, Ashridge papers.

141 N. Tiratsoo and J. Tomlinson, *The Conservatives and Industrial Efficiency, 1951–64: Thirteen Wasted Years?* (London: Routledge, 1998), pp. 35–41.

142 'Managers of Tomorrow', *Future. The Magazine for Businessmen*, 6 (4), 1951, p. 53.

143 *Ibid.*, pp. 70–1.

144 *Ibid.*, p. 68.

145 *The Economist*, 17 Dec. 1955, p. 72.

146 J. Stevens to Lord Davidson, 13 Oct. 1955, Governing Body General Correspondence, 1954–55, Ashridge papers.

147 Minutes, 5 Nov. 1947, Governing Body Minutes 1947–1949, Ashridge papers.

148 Minutes, 23 Feb. 1949, Governing Body Minutes 1947–1949, Ashridge papers.

149 Lord Davidson to the Chairman of Lloyds Bank, 20 Nov. 1950, Governing Body General Correspondence, 1947–51, Ashridge papers.

150 Principal's report, 12 Oct. 1950, Governing Body General Correspondence, 1947–51, Ashridge papers.

151 *Ibid.*
152 Memorandum by L. H. Sutton, undated, Sep. 1951, Finance and General Purpose Committee, Ashridge papers.
153 *Ibid.* My italics.
154 *Ibid.*
155 Admiral Boyd to Lord Davidson, 2 May 1952, Governing Body General Correspondence, 1952–3, Ashridge papers.
156 Meeting of the Governing Body, 21 May 1952, Ashridge papers.
157 Memorandum, 9 May 1950, Minutes of the Governing Body, Ashridge papers.
158 Memorandum, 23 Dec. 1952, Governing Body Minutes, Ashridge papers.
159 Lord Davidson to John Newsom, Esq., 16 Mar. 1951, Governing Body Minutes, Ashridge papers.
160 Lord Davidson to John Newsom, Esq., 16 Mar. 1951, Governing Body General Correspondence, Ashridge papers.
161 J. Newsom to Lord Davidson, 19 Mar. 1951, Governing Body General Correspondence, Ashridge papers.
162 *Hansard*, Parliamentary debates, DXXIV, 23 Feb. 1954.
163 *Hansard*, Parliamentary debates, DXXIII, 16 Feb. 1954.
164 Lord Davidson to Admiral Boyd, 31 Mar. 1954, Governing Body General Correspondence 1954–55, Ashridge papers.
165 Unsigned memorandum to the Board of Governors, 'The Future of Ashridge', 21 June 1955, Governing Body General Correspondence, 1954–55, Ashridge papers.
166 *Ibid.*
167 Memorandum on the 1954 Private Member's Bill, Governing Body General Correspondence, 1954–55, Ashridge papers.
168 Undated memorandum, Governing Body General Correspondence, 1954–55, Ashridge papers.
169 Memorandum 1954 Private Member's bill, Governing Body General Correspondence, 1954–55, Ashridge papers.

Conclusion

There is an irony of course in the metamorphosis of Ashridge from its initial purpose to train 'Conservative Fabians', to its rebirth as a school of management. However, the first Fabians sought to create a 'science' of government and transform the civil service into an administration of 'experts'. In this respect, the Conservatives' desire after the war to create a 'science of business' could be interpreted as an extension of the Fabian model. The new middle class trained at Ashridge was indeed what Lewis and Maude[1] had described, or what was referred to as the knowledge middle class, and seemed to represent a new stratum[2] more clearly and self-consciously than had the Fabians at the end of the nineteenth century. In the 1950s, Thomas Balogh, economic advisor to Harold Wilson, saw in Britain's public service 'the apotheosis of the dilettante'.[3] Ashridge sought to introduce 'the apotheosis of the expert'. The 'new Conservatism' aimed to construct constituencies of support by proposing a meritocratic value system which placed qualifications and expertise at the heart of its creed. The accumulation and gradual professionalisation of skills, and the social diversity of people involved in the party – as officers, activists and voters – contributed to giving form and substance to the notion of middle class and led the Conservative party to form its new identity as the 'party of the middle class'.

At first sight, it seems that Ashridge succeeded in none of the three objectives set at the time of its establishment. From a doctrinal point of view, it faded from memory because of its loyalty to Baldwin and Chamberlain. From the electoral point of view, the crushing defeat of 1945 seemed to confirm the failure of institutions like Ashridge which were unable to renew their thinking or the image of the Conservative party. Third, from the structural point of view, Ashridge failed to establish an enduring relationship between the Conservative party and what should have been its intellectual community. Nonetheless, ideas debated there were revived after the war by different organisations such as the CPC, the One Nation Group and Swinton College, and their role in the Conservatives' return to power in 1951 was far from negligible. Ashridge, after a period of trial and error, found its feet in the post-war years by becoming the first private school of management in Britain. Thereafter the priority was less to teach political democracy than to teach 'industrial democracy', that is to say, to create a dialogue between managers and workers. Ashridge opposed the policy of nationalisation favoured by the Labour party and advocated the idea of shared interests between managers and workers within the firm. The college attempted to reconcile 'folk wisdom'[4] with the demands of modern management. True to the college's mission statement of 1929, Ashridge sought to train citizens and to pass on the Conservative heritage, which it equated with the heritage of England.

Within the party, when Ashridge had just reopened its doors, history seemed to repeat itself. R. A. Butler sought to create a Conservative equivalent to the Fabian Society. 'Cuthbert Alport and I have discussed the matter with Tweedsmuir who is very enthusiastic about it.'[5] In 1950, a group of young Conservatives founded the Bow Group. Geoffrey Howe, one of the founders, spoke of being 'strikingly short of intellectual ammunition … [and] our first … proclaimed objective [was] to combat the influence of the Fabian Society'.[6] In 1968, Howe[7] acknowledged that it was because he was an intellectual that he established the Bow Group, adding: 'One of our aims was to make it respectable for an intellectual to be seen in Conservative company.'[8] Similarly in 1992, Keith Joseph, one of Margaret Thatcher's closest advisors, observed in an interview with Brian Harrison: '"We never got an LSE – far from it – and we never got a *New Statesman*". There remained only the Conservative variant of the Fabian Society: the Centre for Policy Studies, using Fabian methods to subvert the Fabian legacy.'[9] Created by Joseph in 1974, the Centre for Policy Studies was also supposed to be a Conservative Fabian Society. Margaret Thatcher shared Joseph's preoccupation. Five months after her election as party leader, she wrote to him: 'I am anxious that we should develop closer links with the universities.'[10]

The anxiety of the Conservatives that they would not be able to obtain the support of a wide electorate if they did not dominate the cultural and intellectual sphere can be interpreted of course as the need to build an enemy and exaggerate its power in order to muster up a sense of purpose and a rallying cry. Anti-Socialism was a very efficient unifying element for the inter-war Conservative party. In parallel, fighting 'the highbrow' helped Conservatives at Ashridge to define themselves in relation to a certain type of intellectualism and articulate plausible representations of intellectual identity. The deliberate choice of the identity of 'the middlebrow' polarised the debate into two distinct camps and the Conservatives saw themselves as proposing an alternative to what they claimed was the dominant cultural norm at the same time as they felt they were expressing values and languages identified as essentially English.

Their defensive position and the wilful choice of the identity of the 'middlebrow' were the result of the ongoing tension between education and propaganda. The cross-fertilisation between propaganda for the voters and academic or expert literature for their own supporters led to the emergence of a middlebrow paradigm which could take a variety of forms and speak to different social groups. The 'middlebrow' was a weapon that offered an alternative to political discourses wherein membership of a social class determined the aspirations of citizens. It was not a matter of denying the existence of different social classes – in many ways, it reinforced it – but a way of imagining a society in which 'peace' reigned between different classes. Frederic Lee, the industrialist and a lecturer at Ashridge, summarised Conservative thinking thus: 'We most of us take exception to the Socialist efforts to create what they call class consciousness. Decent-minded people detest their efforts to foster hatred between the different sections of the people and to bring about a class war.'[11] Because it existed only in relation to the 'highbrow', which it stigmatised and repudiated, the 'middlebrow' was a unique weapon to demonstrate how condescending the Left was to the working class. It offered a powerful cultural model of being down to earth, which was essentially an ideological position. In that respect, Ashridge's success was perhaps more cultural than political: the Conservatives did not win the elections thanks to Ashridge, but they succeeded in constructing an electoral language with a wide cultural purchase and equating Conservatism with sensible, 'no nonsense' and 'middlebrow' by pinning the idea that the 'highbrow' was a Left-wing position. The Conservatives' rhetorical equipment was not affected, not extreme and, above all perhaps, not foreign. At the heart of Ashridge's project was the paradox that the Conservatives developed ideas and theories to show that they had no theories. This was central to their success, in the same way that Stanley Baldwin's denunciation of class conflict and appeal to the 'public' made him a formidable class warrior. The 'middlebrow' was a most efficient weapon because it offered a language that enabled the party to embrace mass democracy and construct broad constituencies of support which transcended class and gender boundaries.

This was of course very different in the war years, with the challenge posed by the perceived 'leftward shift' in public opinion. The inter-war emphasis on education and the need for training was not simply reinforced, it was also altered by fears of the damage supposedly done by the Left in general. The army education classes were seen as particularly Left-wing and the Conservatives were deemed to have lost an educational battle and provided room for 'the future of Socialism'.[12]

Yet, the experience of the war, when Britain alone resisted while the Continent committed suicide, also modified and increased the traditional emphasis on British exceptionalism and national character. It reinvigorated the down-to-earth, common-sense, middlebrow category as representative of the nation and its history of defending liberties.[13] Herbert Butterfield, who had been a staunch critic of the Whig interpretation of history, famously revisited his argument in 1944.[14] It also gave new and powerful ground to the contrast between the abstract-minded European intellectual and the practical Englishman. One striking example of this was the case of Harold Laski, who became a scapegoat and was stigmatised by the Beaverbrook press in a much publicised trial as an 'un-English', unpatriotic, 'over-educated' intellectual who despised 'ordinary people'.[15] Interestingly enough, as Collini points out, in the late 1940s, those who engaged in the most powerful criticism of society and what they thought of as a 'collectivist' age, were T. S. Eliot and Michael Oakeshott, embodying in many respects the model of intellectual *à la française* that the Conservatives had denounced.[16]

The debates that took place at Ashridge in the 1930s foreshadowed the Conservatives' contradictory criticism of Attlee's government. In some respects, the similarities between the 1930s and 1940s were more important than the differences. The Conservative party's apparent inertia under Baldwin, like Butler's innovative spirit and his 'thinking machine', both seem exaggerated.[17] Although the criticism of historians in the 1960s and 1970s of the economic policies of the Baldwin and Chamberlain governments drew upon Keynesianism, the experience of Ashridge showed that the Conservative party, far from being 'inert', actively participated in economic debate. Baldwin's National government, or rather high-ranking treasury officials, started to use new methods of economic analysis in the 1930s.[18] During and after the war, these new methods were used to control inflation and achieve a 'high and stable level of employment'.[19] This mixture of innovation and tradition can be found in the Conservative party's industrial charter of 1947 and in Butler's budgetary strategies in the 1950s. The differences between the Conservatives' economic policies before and after the war were chiefly in the degree of state intervention and the areas of state intervention.

The Conservative anxieties around the Fabian Society and the perceived domination of the Left on the cultural and intellectual scene, and the debates around the category of 'the intellectual' seem to have lasted until the late 1970s. From the 1970s onwards, Conservative party policy was aimed at an 'imagined "Middle Britain"' of 'hard-working families' and promoted values associated with work and entrepreneurial spirit.[20] The professional backgrounds of Conservative members of parliament similarly changed.[21] Although most still belonged to the liberal professions and the private sector, a growing number of them, with backgrounds in consulting firms, think-tanks and research groups, had become professional politicians. With them, fear of Socialist intellectuals dominating British society seemed to have faded away. The Centre for Economic Studies, the Adam Smith Institute, the Institute of Economic Affairs and the Social Market Foundation nowadays occupy a more important place than does the Fabian Society in Britain's intellectual and political landscape.[22]

Notes

1 R. Lewis and A. Maude, *The English Middle Classes* (London: Pelican Books, 1949).
2 Hobsbawm, 'The Fabians Reconsidered'.
3 T. Balogh, 'The Apotheosis of the Dilettante: Government by Mandarins', in H. Thomas (ed.), *The Establishment* (London: Anthony Blond, 1959), pp. 83–126.
4 American industrialists, when visiting Great Britain in the 1950s, criticised the British for depending too much on 'folk wisdom'. Quoted in Tiratsoo and Tomlinson, *The Conservatives and Industrial Efficiency*.
5 R. A. Butler to D. Clarke, 25 July 1947, CPA, CRD, 2/50/11.
6 G. Howe, preface to J. A. Barr, *The Bow Group, A History* (London: British Film Institute, 2001), pp. vii–viii.
7 Geoffrey Howe was chancellor of the exchequer and later secretary of state for foreign affairs as well as assistant to Margaret Thatcher. He resigned in 1990 in response to Thatcher's policies on Europe. See Barr, *The Bow Group*.
8 G. Howe's contribution to 'Intellectuals and Conservatives: a Symposium', *Swinton College Journal*, XIV, 1968, p. 13.
9 B. Harrison, 'Mrs Thatcher and the Intellectuals', *Twentieth Century British History*, 5, 1994, p. 214.
10 M. Thatcher to K. Joseph, 16 July 1975, CPA, CCO 20/8/19.
11 F. Lee, *Manufacturer* (London: Hutchinson & Co., for the National Book Association, 1938), p. 218.
12 A. Crosland, *The Future of Socialism* (London: Jonathan Cape, 1956).
13 Stapleton, *Political Intellectuals and Public Identities*, part III.
14 Butterfield, *The Englishman and His History*.
15 Collini, *Absent Minds*, pp. 130–3. Collini explains that Laski had 'become an issue in the British general election campaign of 1945 in his own right.' (p. 131). The Beaverbrook press was running stories about the 'red professor' behind Attlee and the Tories were trying to portray him as the 'real dictator of future policy should Labour win' (p. 131). On 20 June 1945, the *Daily Express* published a headline stating 'New Laski sensation: socialism even if it means violence' and Laski issued writs for libel against the Beaverbrook

press (p. 131). The trial took place in November 1946. Sir Patrick Hastings led the case for defence and insisted on the difference between the 'unpatriotic intellectual' and 'ordinary people' (p. 132). Laski lost his libel case.

16 *Ibid.*, p. 137.

17 On the inertia of Baldwin's government, see in particular Skidelsky, *Politicians and the Slump*. On the Baldwin's innovative spirit, see A. Howard, *RAB: The Life of R. A. Butler* (London: Jonathan Cape, 1987). Kelly, *The Myth of Mr. Butskell.*

18 R. Middleton, *Towards Managed Economy* (London: Methuen, 1985).

19 G. C. Peden, 'Old Dogs and New Tricks: the Treasury and Economic Management, 1945–1955', in M. Furner and B. Supple (eds), *The State and Economic Knowledge* (Cambridge: Cambridge University Press, 1992), pp. 208–38.

20 J. Lawrence and F. Sutcliffe-Braithwaite, 'Margaret Thatcher and the Decline of Class Politics', in B. Jackson and R. Saunders (eds), *Making Thatcher's Britain* (Cambridge: Cambridge University Press, 2012), p. 147.

21 A. Adonis and T. Hames (eds), *A Conservative Revolution? The Thatcher-Reagan Decade in Perspective* (Manchester: Manchester University Press, 1994).

22 The Centre for Policy Studies was established in 1974 by Sir Keith Joseph. The Adam Smith Institute was founded in 1978 by Madson Pirie. The Institute of Economic Affairs was set up in 1957 by Ralph Harris and Arthur Seldon. The Social Market Foundation was created in 1989 by, amongst others, Robert Skidelsky. All four functioned as political, economic, social and cultural research centres. See R. Cockett, *Thinking the Unthinkable: Think Tank and the Economic Counter-Revolution, 1931–84* (London: Harper Collins, 1995).

Select bibliography

Manuscript sources

Ashridge Papers, Ashridge College, Berkhamsted. The collection has been transferred to the Conservative Party Archive and is in the process of being scanned. Acquisition reference ACCN/2011/002.

1st Earl Baldwin of Bewdley Papers, Cambridge University Library, Cambridge.

Baron Beaverbrook Papers, Parliamentary Archives, House of Lords Record Office, London.

Arthur Bryant Papers, Liddell Hart Centre for Military Archives, King's College, London.

R. A. Butler Papers, Trinity College, Cambridge.

Neville Chamberlain MSS, Cadbury Research Library: Special Collections, University of Birmingham, Birmingham.

Winston Churchill Papers, Churchill Archives Centre, Churchill College, Cambridge.

Conservative Party Archive, Bodleian Library, Oxford.

Viscount Crookshank Papers, Bodleian Library, Oxford.

1st Viscount Davidson Papers, Parliamentary Archives, House of Lords Record Office, London.

Albert Mansbridge Papers, British Library, London.

J. E. Powell Papers, Churchill Archives Centre, Churchill College, Cambridge.

Published contemporary sources

Alport C., *Kingdoms in Partnership* (London: Lovat Dickson for National Book Association, 1937).

Amery L. S., *Union and Strength* (n.p.: Arnold, 1912).

Baldwin S., *On England and other Addresses* (London: Philip Allen & Co., 1926).

Baldwin S., *Service of Our Lives: Last Speeches as Prime Minister* (London: Hodder & Stoughton, 1937).

Ball S. (ed.), *Parliament and Politics in the Age of Baldwin and MacDonald. The Headlam Diaries, 1923–35* (London: The Historians' Press, 1992).

Barker E. (ed.), *The Character of England* (Oxford: Clarendon Press, 1947).

Barnes J. and Nicholson D., *The Leo Amery Diaries*, vol. 1: *1896–1929* (London: Hutchinson, 1980).

Barnes J. and Nicholson D. (eds), *The Empire at Bay: The Leo Amery Diaries*, vol. 2: *1929–45* (London: Hutchinson, 1988).

Benson E. F., *Mapp and Lucia* (London: Hodder & Stoughton, 1931).

Bryant A., *The Spirit of Conservatism* (London: Methuen & Co., 1929).

Bryant A., *The National Character* (London: Longmans, Green & Co., 1934).

Bryant A., *Stanley Baldwin: A Tribute* (London: Hamish Hamilton, 1937).

Bryant A., *Unfinished Victory* (London: Macmillan, 1940).

Bryant A., *English Saga, 1840–1940* (London: The Reprint Society, 1942).

Bryant A., *Protestant Island* (London: Collins, 1967).

Bryant A. (ed.), *The Man and the Hour. Studies of Six Great Men of Our Time* (London: Philip Allan, 1934).

Buchan J., *The Thirty-Nine Steps* (London and Edinburgh: Blackwood & Sons, 1915).

Buchan J., *Greenmantle* (London: Nelson, 1916).

Buchan J., *Huntingtower* (London: Nelson, 1924).

Buchan J., *Montrose* (London: Nelson, 1928).

Buchan J., *Oliver Cromwell* (London: Hodder & Stoughton, 1934).

Buchan J., *Men and Deeds* (n.p.: John Murray, 1935).

Burke E., *Reflections on the Revolution in France* (London: J. Dodsley, 1790, Penguin Books, 1978).

Butterfield H., *The Englishman and His History* (Cambridge: Cambridge University Press, 1944).

Butterfield H., *The Whig Interpretation of History* (London: G. Bells & Sons Ltd, 1931, Penguin, 1973).

Cato (Foot M., Owen F. and Howard P.), *Guilty Men* (London: Gollancz, 1940).

Cecil H., *Conservatism* (London: Home University Library, 1912).

Churchill W. S., *The Second World War*, vol. 1: *The Gathering Storm* (London: Chiswick Press, 1948).

Clarke D., *The Conservative Faith in a Modern Age* (London: Conservative Political Centre, 1947).

Cripps S., *Towards Christian Democracy. A Challenge to the Faithless*, 1945 (New York: Philosophical Library, 1946).

Cronin A. J., *The Stars Look Down* (London: Gollancz, 1935).

Cronin A. J., *The Citadel* (London: Gollancz, 1937).

Crosland A., *The Future of Socialism* (London: Jonathan Cape, 1956).

De La Mare W., *At First Sight: a Romance* (New York: C. Gaige, 1928).

De La Mare W., *On The Edge* (London: Faber & Faber, 1930).

De La Mare W., *Memory: and other poems* (London: Constable, 1938).

Disraeli B., *Sybil or The Two Nations* (London: Henry Colburn, 1845, Wordsworth Classics, 1995).

Dugdale B. E. C., *Arthur James Balfour. First Earl of Balfour, 1848–1930*, vol. 1 (London: Hutchinson, 1936).

Eden A., *Freedom and Order: Selected Speeches, 1939–1946* (London: Faber & Faber, 1947).

Edwards H. W. J., *The Good Patch* (London: National Book Association, 1938).

Eliot T. S., *The Idea of a Christian Society* (London: Faber & Faber, 1939).

Elliot W., *Toryism and the Twentieth Century* (London: Philip Allen, 1927).

Feiling K., *A History of the Tory Party, 1640–1714* (Oxford: Oxford University Press, 1924).

Feiling K., *What is Conservatism?* (London: Faber & Faber, 1930).

Feiling K., *The Second Tory Party, 1714–1832* (London: Macmillan, 1938).

Feiling K., *Sketches in Nineteenth Century Biography* (London: Longmans, Green & Co., 1930, New York: Books for Libraries Press, 1970).

Fisher H. A. L., *The Whig Historians* (n.p.: Humphrey Milford, 1928).

Gooch G. P., *History and Historians of the XIXth Century* (London: Longmans Green, 1952).

Graves R. and Hodge A., *The Long Weekend: A Social History of Great Britain, 1918–1940* (London: Faber & Faber, 1940).

Grossmith G. and Grossmith W., *The Diary of A Nobody* (Bristol: Arrowsmith, 1892).

Haxey S., *Tory M.P.* (London: Gollancz, 1939).

Hearnshaw F. J. C., *Conservatism in England: An Analytical, Historical and Political Survey* (London: Macmillan, 1933, New York: H. Fertig, 1967).

Hill C., 'A Whig Historian', *The Modern Quarterly*, 3 (1), 1938, pp. 276–84.

Hobhouse L. T., *Liberalism* (London: Oxford University Press, 1911, Project Gütenberg Ebook, 2009).

Hobson J. A., *Imperialism: A Study* (New York: J. Pott & Company, 1902).

Hogg Q., *The Case for Conservatism* (West Drayton: Penguin Books, 1947).

Huxley T. H., 'Administrative Nihilism', in *Methods and Results* (New York: Appleton & Company, 1896), pp. 251–89.

James R. R. (ed.), *Memoirs of a Conservative: J. C. C. Davidson's Memoirs and Papers 1910–1937* (London: Weidenfeld & Nicolson, 1969).

Jefferys K. (ed.), *Labour and the Wartime Coalition: From the Diary and Letters of James Chuter Ede, 1941–1945* (London: The Historians' Press, 1987).

Keynes J. M., *The General Theory of Employment, Interest and Money* (London: Macmillan, 1936, 1973).

Kitson Clark G., *Peel and the Conservative Party* (London: Bell, 1929).

Kitson Clark G., *Peel* (London: Duckworth, 1936).

Kitson Clark G., *The English Inheritance* (London: SCM Press Ltd, 1950).

Laski H., *A Grammar of Politics* (Allen & Unwin Ltd, 1930).

Lee F., *Manufacturer* (London: Hutchinson & Co., for the National Book Association, 1938).

Lewis R. and Maude A., *The English Middle Classes* (London: Pelican Books, 1949).

Macleod I. and Maude A. (eds), *One Nation: A Tory Approach to Social Problems, by a group of MPs (C. J. M. Alport, R. Carr, R. Fort [and others])* (n.p.: Conservative Political Centre, 1950).

Macmillan H., *The Next Step* (London: E. T. Heron, 1932).

Macmillan H., *The Middle Way* (London: Macmillan, 1938).

Macmillan H., *Winds of Change, 1914–1939* (London: Macmillan, 1966).

Macmillan H., Boothby R., Loder J. and Stanley O., *Industry and the State* (London: Macmillan, 1927).

McNeile H. C. ('Sapper'), *Bull-Dog Drummond* (London: Hodder & Stoughton, 1920).

McNeile H. C. ('Sapper'), *The Female of the Species* (London: Hodder & Stoughton, 1928).

McNeile H. C. ('Sapper'), *The Finger of Fate: Stories* (London: Hodder & Stoughton, 1930).

Maugham W. S., *Ashenden: or, the British Agent* (London: W. G. Heinemann, 1928).

Maugham W. S., *Cakes and Ale, or the Skeleton in the Cupboard* (London: W. G. Heinemann, 1930).

Maugham W. S., *For Services Rendered*, in *The Collected Plays*, vol. 3 (London: Heinemann, 1931).

Maugham W. S., *Altogether: Being the Collected Stories of W. Somerset Maugham* (London: W. G. Heinemann, 1934).

Mill J. S., 'Autobiography', in *Collected Works*, vol. 1 (Toronto: University of Toronto Press, 1981), pp. 1–290.

Milner A., *Questions of the Hour* (London: Hodder & Stoughton, 1923).

Morgan C., *Portrait in a Mirror* (London: Macmillan, 1929).

Morgan C., *The Fountain* (London: Macmillan, 1932).

Morgan C., *The Liberty of Thought and the Separation of Powers, a Modern Problem Considered in the Context of Montesquieu* (Oxford: Clarendon Press, 1948).

Nicolson H., *Diaries and Letters 1945–62*, 3 vols (London: Collins, 1968).

Northam R., *Conservatism the Only Way* (London: John Gifford for The Right Book Club, 1939).

Ortega Y Gasset J., *La Rebelion de las masas*, Madrid, 1930, trad. *The Revolt of the Masses* (London: Allen & Unwin Ltd, 1932).

Orwell G., *The Road to Wigan Pier* (London: Gollancz, 1937).

Orwell G., *The Lion and the Unicorn: Socialism and the English Genius* (London: Secker & Warburg, 1941).

Orwell G., *Essays* (London: Penguin Books, 2000).

Page Croft H., *The Path of Empire* (London: Routledge, 1912, Thoemmes Press, 1999).

Percy E., *Some Memories* (London: Eyre & Spottiswoode, 1958).

Petrie C., *The Chamberlain Tradition* (n.p.: Lovat Dickson Ltd, 1938).

Petrie C., *Chapters of Life* (London: Eyre & Spottiswoode, 1950).

Petrie C., *The Powers behind the Prime Ministers* (London: MacGibbon & Kee, 1958).

Priestley J. B., *The Good Companions* (London: Heinemann Ltd, 1929).

Priestley J. B., *English Journey* (London: Heinemann Ltd, 1934).

Scanlon J., *Cast of all Fooling* (London: Hutchinson & Co., 1938).

Self R. C., *The Neville Chamberlain Diary Letters*, vol. 3: *The Heir Apparent, 1928–1933* (Aldershot: Ashgate Press, 2002).

Sellar W. C. and Yeatman R. J., *1066 and All That* (London: Methuen & Co., 1930).

Serge V., *Destiny of a Revolution* (London: Hutchinson, 1937).

Simon Sir E. and Hubback E. M., *Training For Citizenship* (Oxford: Oxford University Press, 1935).

Simon Sir E. *et al.*, *Constructive Democracy* (London: Allen & Unwin Ltd, 1938).

Skelton N., *Constructive Conservatism* (London: Macmillan, 1924).

Spencer H., *The Man versus the State* (London: Williams & Norgate, 1884).

Steel-Maitland A., *The New America* (London: Macmillan, 1934).

Strachey L., *Eminent Victorians* (London: Chatto & Windus, 1918).

Strachey L., *Queen Victoria* (London: Chatto & Windus, 1959).

Sutton L. H., *The Nation Keeps House: an Introductory Study of Money and Trade* (London: Hutchinson & Co., 1938).

Teeling W., *Why Britain Prospers* (London: Right Book Club, 1938).

The Industrial Charter (London: Conservative Political Centre, 1947).

The New Conservatism, An Anthology of Post-War Thought (London: Conservative Political Centre, 1955).

The Next Five Years: An Essay in Political Agreement (London: Macmillan, 1935).

Trevelyan G. M., *English Social History* (London: Longmans Green, 1944).

Trevelyan G. M., *The Social History of England* (London: Longmans Green, 1952).

Tweedsmuir S., *John Buchan by his Wife and Friends*, preface by G. M. Trevelyan (London: Hodder & Stoughton, 1947).

Utley T. E., *Essays in Conservatism* (London: Conservative Political Centre, 1949).

Wallace E., *The Square Emerald* (London: Hodder & Stoughton, 1926).

Wallace E., *Again the Three Just Men* (London: Hodder & Stoughton, 1928).

Wallace E., *Sanders of the River* (London: Ward, Lock & Co., 1928).

Walpole H., *Above the Dark Circus: an Adventure* (London: Macmillan, 1931).

Walpole H., *Fortitude: a Romance* (London: Macmillan, 1934).

Walpole H., *The Cathedral* (London: Macmillan, 1936).

Williams-Ellis C., *Britain and the Beast* (London: J. M. Dent & Sons Ltd, 1937).

Wilson Sir A., *Thoughts and Talks* (London: Right Book Club, 1934).

Wodehouse P. G., *The Inimitable Jeeves* (London: Herbert Jenkins, 1923).

Wodehouse P. G., *Carry On Jeeves* (London: Herbert Jenkins, 1925).

Wodehouse P. G., *Hot Water* (London: Herbert Jenkins, 1932).

Wodehouse P. G., *Heavy Weather* (London: Herbert Jenkins, 1933).

Woolf L., *Hunting the Highbrow* (London: Hogarth Press, 1927).

Woolf V., 'Middlebrow', in V. Woolf, *The Death of the Moth* (London: Hogarth Press, 1942), pp. 113–19.

Woolton Lord, *The Adventure of Reconstruction* (London: Cassell, 1945).

Woolton Lord, *Memoirs* (London: Cassell, 1959).
Wyatt W., *The Journals of Woodrow Wyatt*, vol. 2, ed. S. Curtis (Basingtsoke: Macmillan, 1999).
Yates D., *Safe Custody* (London: Ward & Lock, 1924).
Yates D., *Blind Corner* (London: Hodder & Stoughton, 1927).
Yates D., *Blood Royal* (London: Hodder & Stoughton, 1929).
Yeats-Brown F., *The European Jungle* (London: Right Book Club, 1939).

Periodicals

The Ashridge Journal (1930–39).
The Ashridge Quarterly (1947–49).
The Citizen (1936–).
Gleanings and Memoranda

Secondary sources

Ball S., *Baldwin and the Conservative Party. The Crisis of 1921–1931* (New Haven, CT: Yale University Press, 1988).
Ball S., *Portrait of a Party: the Conservative Party in Britain 1918–1945* (Oxford: Oxford University Press, 2013).
Ball S. and Holliday I. (eds), *Mass Conservatism. The Conservatives and the Public since the 1880s* (London: Frank Cass Publishers, 2002).
Barr J., *The Bow Group. A History* (London: British Films Institute, 2001).
Baxendale J. and Pawling C., *Narrating The Thirties* (London: Macmillan, 1996).
Beer L. and Thomas G. (eds), *Brave New World. Imperial and Democratic Nation-Building in Britain between the Wars* (London: Institute of Historical Research, 2011).
Behlmer G. K. and Leventhal F. M., *Singular Continuities: Tradition, Nostalgia and Identity in Modern British Culture* (Stanford, CA: Stanford University Press, 2000).
Bell P., 'A Historical Cast of Mind. Some Eminent English Historians and Attitudes to Continental Europe in the Middle of the Twentieth Century', *Journal of European Integration History*, 2 (2), 1996, pp. 5–17.
Bentley M., *Public and Private Doctrine; Essays in British History Presented to Maurice Cowling* (Cambridge: Cambridge University Press, 1993).
Berthezène C., 'Creating Conservative Fabians: the Conservative Party, Political Education and the Founding of Ashridge College, 1929–1931', *Past & Present*, 182, 2004, pp. 211–40.
Berthezène C., 'Ashridge College, 1929–1954: a Glimpse at the Archive of a Conservative Intellectual Project', *Contemporary British History*, 19 (1), 2005, pp. 79–83.
Bingham, A., *Family Newspapers? Sex, Private Life and the British Popular Press, 1918–78* (Oxford: Oxford University Press, 2004).

Bingham, A., *Gender, Modernity and the Popular Press in Interwar Britain* (Oxford: Oxford University Press, 2004).

Blaas P. B. M., *Continuity and Anachronism: Parliamentary and Constitutional Development in Whig Historiography and in the Anti-Whig Reaction between 1890 and 1930* (London: M. Nijhoff, 1978).

Black L., 'The Lost World of Young Conservatism', *The Historical Journal*, 51 (4), 2008, pp. 991–1024.

Black L., 'Tories and Hunters: Swinton College and the Landscape of Modern Conservatism', *History Workshop Journal*, 77 (1), 2014, pp. 187–214.

Blake R., *Disraeli* (London: Macmillan, 1969).

Blake R., *The Conservative Party from Peel to Major* (London: Arrow Books, 1998).

Bonham J., *The Middle Class Vote* (London: Faber & Faber, 1954).

Booth A., *British Economic Policy, 1931–1949, Was There A Keynesian Revolution?* (London: Methuen & Co., 1989).

Booth A., *The British Economy in the Twentieth Century* (Basingstoke: Palgrave, 2001).

Booth A. and Glynn S. (eds), *The Road to Full Employment* (London: Allen & Unwin, 1987).

Boyce R. W. D., *British Capitalism at the Crossroads* (Cambridge: Cambridge University Press, 1985).

Boyce R. W. D., *The Great Interwar Crisis and the Collapse of Globalization* (New York: Palgrave Macmillan, 2009).

Bracco R. M., *Merchants of Hope: British Middlebrow Writers and the First World War, 1919–1939* (Oxford: Berg Publishers Ltd, 1993).

Briggs A., *The History of Broadcasting in the United Kingdom*, vol. II (Oxford: Oxford University Press, 1965).

Broadberry S., *The British Economy between the Wars: a Macroeconomic Survey* (Oxford: Blackwell, 1986).

Burrow J. W., *A Liberal Descent: Victorian Historians and the English Past* (Cambridge: Cambridge University Press, 1981).

Butler R. A., *The Art of the Possible* (London: Hamish Hamilton, 1971, 1982).

Cain P. J., *Hobson and Imperialism: Radicalism, New Liberalism and Finance, 1887–1938* (Oxford: Oxford University Press, 2002).

Cain P. J. and Hopkins A. G., *British Imperialism: Crisis and Deconstruction, 1914–1990* (London: Longman, 1993).

Cairncross A., *Years of Recovery: British Economic Policy, 1945–51* (London: Methuen & Co., 1985).

Cannadine D., *Lords and Landlords; the Aristocracy and the Towns, 1774–1967*, Leicester: Leicester University Press, 1980).

Cannadine D., *The Decline and Fall of the British Aristocracy* (New Haven, CT: Yale University Press, 1990).

Cannadine D., *G. M. Trevelyan: A Life in History* (London: Harper Collins Publisher, 1992).

Carey J., *The Intellectuals and the Masses. Pride and Prejudice among Literary Intelligentsia 1880–1939* (London: Faber & Faber, 1992).

Chapman J., *The British at War: Cinema, State and Propaganda, 1939–1945* (London: I. B. Tauris, 1998).

Charmley J., *Chamberlain and the Lost Peace* (London: Curtis, 1989).

Charmley J., *Churchill and the End of Glory* (London: Hodder & Stoughton, 1993).

Charmley J., *A History of Conservative Politics, 1900–1996* (London: Macmillan Press Ltd, 1996).

Chester L., Fay S. and Young H., *The Zinoviev Letter* (London: Heinemann, 1967).

Clark A., *The Tories: Conservatives and the Nation State, 1922–1997* (London: Weidenfeld & Nicolson, 1998).

Clarke P., *Liberals and Social Democrats* (Cambridge: Cambridge University Press, 1979).

Clarke P., *Hope and Glory, Britain 1900–1990* (London: Allen Lane, 1996).

Clarke P., *A Question of Leadership: Gladstone to Blair* (London: Hamish Hamilton, 1999).

Clarke P., *The Cripps Version: the Life of Sir Stafford Cripps* (London: Allen Lane, 2002).

Clements R. V., *Managers: a Study of Their Careers in Industry* (London: Allen & Unwin, 1958).

Cockett R., 'Ball, Chamberlain and Truth', *Historical Journal*, 33, 1990, pp. 131–42.

Cockett R., 'The Party, Publicity, and the Media', in A. Seldon and S. Ball (eds), *Conservative Century: The Conservative Party since 1900* (Oxford: Oxford University Press, 1994), pp. 547–77.

Cockett R., *Thinking the Unthinkable: Think-Tanks and the Economic Counter-Revolution, 1931–84* (London: Harper Collins, 1995).

Coleman D. C., 'Gentlemen and Players', *Economic History Review*, 26, 1973, pp. 92–116.

Collini S., 'What Is Intellectual History?', *History Today*, Oct. 1985, pp. 46–9.

Collini S., *Public Moralists: Political Thought and Intellectual Life in Britain 1850–1930* (Oxford: Oxford University Press, 1991).

Collini S., *English Pasts. Essays in History and Culture* (Oxford: Oxford University Press, 1999).

Collini S., 'The European Modernist as Anglican Moralist: the Later Social Criticism of T. S. Eliot', in M. S. Micale and R. L. Dietle (eds), *Enlightenment, Passion, Modernity: Historical Essays in European Thought and Culture* (Stanford: Stanford University Press, 2000), pp. 207–29.

Collini S., *Absent Minds: Intellectuals in Britain* (Oxford: Oxford University Press, 2006).

Collini S., *Common Reading. Critics, Historians, Publics* (Oxford: Oxford University Press, 2008).

Collini S., Whatmore R. and Young B. (eds), *Essays in British Intellectual History, 1750–1950*, 2 vols (Cambridge: Cambridge University Press, 2000).

Corrigan P. and Sayer D., *The Great Arch: English State Formation as Cultural Revolution* (Oxford: Basil Blackwell, 1985).

Coult D., *A Prospect of Ashridge* (London: Phillimore & Co., 1980).

Cowling M., *The Impact of Labour, 1920–1924, the Beginning of Modern British Politics* (Cambridge: Cambridge University Press, 1971).

Cowling M., *The Impact of Hitler, British Politics and British Policy, 1933–1940* (Cambridge: Cambridge University Press, 1975).

Dahrendorf R., *LSE: a History of the London School of Economics and Political Science, 1895–1995* (Oxford: Oxford University Press, 1995).

Daunton M., *Wealth and Welfare: an Economic and Social History of Britain, 1851–1951* (Oxford: Oxford University Press, 2007).

Daunton M. and Rieger B. (eds), *Meanings of Modernity: Britain from the Late-Victorian Era to World War Two* (Oxford: Berg Publishers, 2001).

Davies A. J., *We, the Nation. The Conservative Party and the Pursuit of Power* (London: Little, Brown & Co., 1995).

Dickinson M. and Street S., *Cinema and State: the Film Industry and the British Government, 1927–1984* (London: British Film Institute, 1985).

Durbin E., *New Jerusalems: the Labour Party and the Economics of Democratic Socialism* (London: Routledge & Kegan Paul, 1987).

Eastwood D., *Governing Rural England. Tradition and Transformation in Local Government, 1780–1840* (Oxford: Oxford University Press, 1994).

Eccleshall R., 'Ideology as Common Sense: the Case of British Conservatism', *Radical Philosophy* 025, 1980, pp. 2–8.

Eccleshall R., *English Conservatism since the Restoration* (London: Macmillan, 1990).

Evans B. and Taylor A., *From Salisbury to Major. Continuity and Change in Conservative Politics* (Manchester: Manchester University Press, 1996).

Eyerman R., *Between Culture and Politics, Intellectuals in Modern Society* (Cambridge: Polity Press, 1994).

Eyerman R., Svensson Lennart G. and Söderqvist T. (eds), *Intellectuals, Universities and the State in Western Modern Societies* (Berkeley, CA: University of California Press, 1987).

Faber R., *Young England* (London: Faber & Faber, 1987).

Fair J. D. and Hutcheson Jr. J. A., 'British Conservatism in the Twentieth Century: an Emerging Ideological Tradition', *Albion*, 19, 1987, pp. 549–78.

Feske V., *From Belloc to Churchill, Private Scholars, Public Culture, and the Crisis of British Liberalism, 1900–1939* (Chapel Hill, NC: University of North Carolina, 1996).

Fielding S., Thompson P. and Tiratsoo N., *'England Arise': the Labour Party and Popular Politics in 1940s Britain* (Manchester: Manchester University Press, 1995).

Francis M. and Zweiniger-Bargielowska I., *The Conservatives and British Society, 1880–1990* (Cardiff: University of Wales Press, 1996).

Fraser D., *The Evolution of the Welfare State: a History of Social Policy since the Industrial Revolution* (Basingstoke: Palgrave, 2003).

Fraser D. (ed.), *Municipal Reform and the Industrial City* (Leicester: Leicester University Press, 1982).

Freeden M., *The New Liberalism: an Ideology of Social Reform* (Oxford: Oxford University Press, 1977).

Freeden M., *Liberalism Divided; a Study in British Political Thought, 1914–1939* (Oxford: Oxford University Press, 1986).

Freeden M., *Ideologies and Political Theory: a Conceptual Approach* (Oxford: Clarendon Press, 1996).

Fussell P., *The Great War and Modern Memory* (Oxford: Oxford University Press, 1975).

Fyvel T. R., *Intellectuals Today: Problems in a Changing Society* (London: Chatto & Windus, 1968).

Gamble A., *The Conservative Nation* (London: Macmillan, 1974).

Gamble A., *The Free Economy and the Strong State* (London: Macmillan, 2nd edn, 1994).

Garnett M., *Alport, A Study in Loyalty* (Teddington: Acumen, 1999).

Garside W. R., *British Unemployment 1919–1939: a Study in Public Policy* (Cambridge: Cambridge University Press, 1990).

Ghosh P. R., 'Disraelian Conservatism: a Financial Approach', *English Historical Review*, 98, 1984, pp. 268–96.

Gilbert M., *Finest Hour: Winston S. Churchill, 1939–41* (London: Heinemann, 1983).

Gilmour I. and Garnett M., *Whatever Happened to the Tories? The Conservative Party since 1945* (Basingstoke: Macmillan, 1997).

Girouard M., *The Return to Camelot: Chivalry and the English Gentleman* (New Haven, CT: Yale University Press, 1981).

Glynn S. and Oxborrow J., *Inter-War Britain: a Social and Economic History* (London: Allen & Unwin, 1975).

Goldman L., 'A Peculiarity of the English? The Social Science Association and the Absence of Sociology in Nineteenth Century Britain', *Past & Present*, 114, 1987, pp. 133–71.

Goldman L., *Dons and Workers, Oxford and Adult Education since 1850* (Oxford: Clarendon Press, 1995).

Gottlieb J., *Feminine Fascism: Women in Britain's Fascism Movement, 1923–45* (London: I. B. Tauris, 2000).

Gottlieb J., *The Culture of Fascism: Visions of the Far Right in Britain* (London: I. B. Tauris, 2004).

Gottlieb J. (ed.), *The Aftermath of Suffrage: Women, Gender and Politics in Britain, 1918–45* (Basingstoke: Palgrave, 2013).

Green E. H. H., *The Crisis of Conservatism: the Politics, Economics and Ideology of the British Conservative Party, 1880–1914* (London: Routledge, 1995).

Green E. H. H., 'The Conservative Party, the State and the Electorate, 1945–64', in J. Lawrence and M. Taylor (eds), *Party, State and Society: Electoral*

Behaviour in Modern Britain since 1820 (Aldershot: Scolar Press, 1996), pp. 176–200.

Green E. H. H., *Ideologies of Conservatism: Conservative Political Ideas in the Twentieth Century* (Oxford: Oxford University Press, 2002).

Green E. H. H., 'The Conservative Party and the City in the Twentieth Century: a Troubled Relationship', in P. Williamson and R. Michie (eds), *The British Government and the City of London in the Twentieth Century* (Cambridge: Cambridge University Press, 2004), pp. 153–73.

Green E. H. H. and Tanner D., *The Strange Survival of Liberal England. Political Leaders, Moral Values and the Reception of Economic Debate* (Cambridge: Cambridge University Press, 2007).

Greenleaf W. H., *The British Political Tradition*, vol. 2: *The Ideological Heritage* (London: Methuen & Co., 1983–87).

Griffiths R., *Fellow Travellers of the Right, British Enthusiasts for Nazi Germany, 1933–39* (Oxford: Oxford University Press, 1983).

Griffiths R., *Patriotism Perverted: Captain Ramsay, The Right Club and British Anti-Semitism, 1939–40* (London: Constable & Co. Ltd, 1998).

Griffiths R., 'The Reception of Bryant's *Unfinished Victory*: Insights into British Public Opinion in Early 1940', *Patterns of Prejudice*, 38 (1), 2004, pp. 18–36.

Grimley M., *Citizenship, Community, and the Church of England. Liberal Anglican Theories of the State between the Wars* (Oxford: Oxford University Press, 2004).

Grimley M., 'The Religion of Englishness: Puritanism, Providentialism and "English National Character", 1918–1945', *Journal of British Studies*, 46 (4), 2007, pp. 884–906.

Gross J., *The Rise and Fall of the Man of Letters* (London: Weidenfeld & Nicolson, 1969).

Guttsman W. L., *The British Political Elite* (London: MacGibbon & Kee, 1963).

Guttsman W. L., *The English Ruling Class* (London: Weidenfeld & Nicolson, 1969).

Hall J. A., 'The Curious Case of the English Intelligentsia', *British Journal of Sociology*, 30 (3), 1979, pp. 290–306.

Hamburger J., *Macaulay and the Whig Tradition* (Chicago, IL: Chicago University Press, 1976).

Harper S., *Picturing the Past* (London: British Film Institute, 1994).

Harris J., *Unemployement and Politics: A Study in English Social Policy, 1886–1914* (Oxford: Oxford University Press, 1972).

Harris J., 'Political Thought and the Welfare State, 1870–1940: an Intellectual Framework for British Social Policy', *Past & Present*, 135, 1992, pp. 116–41.

Harris J., *William Beveridge. A Biography* (Oxford: Oxford University Press, 2nd edn, 1997).

Harris J. (ed.), *Civil Society in British History. Ideas, Identities, Institutions* (Oxford: Oxford University Press, 2003).

Harrison B., 'Mrs Thatcher and the Intellectuals', *Twentieth Century British History*, 5, 1994, pp. 206–45.

Harrison B., *The Transformation of British Politics, 1860–1995* (Oxford: Oxford University Press, 1996).

Hattersley R., *Borrowed Time: the Story of Britain between the Wars* (London: Little, Brown & Co., 2007).

Hennessy P., *Never Again, Britain 1945–1951* (London: Jonathan Cape, 1992).

Heyck T. W., *The Transformation of Intellectual Life in Victorian England* (London: Croom Helm, 1982).

Hickox M. S., 'Has there Been a British Intelligentsia?', *British Journal of Sociology*, 37 (2), 1986, pp. 260–8.

Higson A., 'Britain's "Outstanding Contribution" to the Film: the Documentary-Realist Tradition', in C. Barr (ed.), *All Our Yesterdays: 90 Years of British Cinema* (London: British Film Institute, 1986), pp. 72–97.

Higson A., *Waving the Flag: Constructing a National Cinema in Britain* (Oxford: Oxford University Press, 1995).

Hirschman A. O., *The Rhetoric of Reaction. Perversity, Futility, Jeopardy* (Cambridge, MA: Harvard University Press, 1991).

Hobsbawm E., 'The Fabians Reconsidered', in *Labouring Men: Studies in the History of Labour* (London: Weidenfeld & Nicolson, 1964, 1968), pp. 250–71.

Hobsbawm E. and Ranger T., *The Invention of Tradition* (Cambridge: Cambridge University Press, 1992).

Holroyd-Doveton J. O., *Young Conservatives* (Durham: The Pentland Press Ltd, 1996).

Honderich T., *Conservatism* (London: Hamish Hamilton, 1990).

Howard A., *RAB: the Life of R. A. Butler* (London: Jonathan Cape, 1987).

Hynes S. L., *A War Imagined: the First World War and English Culture* (London: Bodley Head, 1990).

Ingham G., *Capitalism Divided: the City and Industry in British Social Development* (London: Macmillan, 1984).

Jackson A. A., *The Middle Classes, 1900–1950* (London: Routledge, 1991).

James R. R., *A Study in Failure, 1900–1939* (London: Weidenfeld & Nicolson, 1970).

Jarausch K. H. (ed.), *The Transformation of Higher Learning 1860–1930* (Chicago, IL: University of Chicago Press, 1983).

Jarvis D., 'Stanley Baldwin and the Ideology of the Conservative Response to Socialism, 1918–31' (PhD dissertation, Lancaster University, 1991).

Jarvis D., '"Mrs. Maggs and Betty"; the Conservative Appeal to Women Voters in the 1920s', *Twentieth Century British History*, 5, 1994, pp. 129–52.

Jarvis D., 'British Conservatism and Class Politics in the 1920s', *English Historical Review*, 110, 1996, pp. 59–84.

Jarvis D., 'The Conservative Party and the Politics of Gender, 1900–1939', in M. Francis and I. Zweiniger-Bargielowska (eds), *The Conservatives and British Society, 1880–1990* (Cardiff: University of Wales Press, 1996), pp. 172–93.

Jarvis D., 'The Shaping of the Conservative Electoral Hegemony, 1918–39', in J. Lawrence and M. Taylor (eds), *Party, State and Society: Electoral*

Behaviour in Modern Britain since 1820 (Aldershot: Scolar Press, 1996), pp. 131–51.

Jefferys K., 'British Politics and Social Policy during the Second World War', *Historical Journal*, 30, 1987, pp. 123–44.

Jefferys K., *The Churchill Coalition and Wartime Politics, 1940–45* (Manchester: Manchester University Press, 1991).

Johnson P., *Intellectuals* (London: Weidenfeld & Nicolson, 1988).

Johnson P. (ed.), *Twentieth Century Britain: Economic, Social and Cultural Change* (Harlow: Longman/Pearson Education Ltd, 1994).

Joll J., *Intellectuals in Politics. Three Biographical Essays* (London: Weidenfeld & Nicolson, 1960).

Jones H., 'The Conservative Party and the Welfare State, 1942–1955' (PhD dissertation, University of London, 1992).

Jones H. and Kandiah M. (eds), *The Myth of Consensus: New Views on British History, 1945–64* (Basingstoke: Macmillan, 1996).

Kavanagh D. and Morris P., *Consensus Politics from Attlee to Major* (Oxford: Blackwell, 2nd edn, 1994).

Kelly S., *The Myth of Mr. Butskell. The Politics of British Economic Policy, 1950–1955* (Aldershot: Ashgate, 2002).

Kidd A. and Nicholls D., *Gender, Culture and Consumerism: Middle Class Identity in Britain, 1800–1940* (Manchester: Manchester University Press, 1999).

Kidd A. and Nicholls D. (eds), *The Making of the British Middle Class? Studies of Regional and Cultural Diversity* (Stroud: Sutton, 1998).

Landy M., *British Genres: Cinema and Society, 1930–1960* (Oxford: Princeton University Press, 1991).

Langford P., *Englishness Identified* (Oxford: Oxford University Press, 2000).

Lawrence J., *Speaking for the People: Party, Language and Popular Politics in England, 1867–1914* (Cambridge: Cambridge University Press, 1998, [pbk, 2002]).

Lawrence J., 'Forging a Peaceable Kingdom: War, Violence and Fear of Brutalization in Post-First World War Britain', *The Journal of Modern History*, 75 (3), 2003, pp. 557–89.

Lawrence J., *Electing Our Masters: the Hustings in British Politics from Hogarth to Blair* (Oxford: Oxford University Press, 2009).

Lawrence J. and Taylor M. (eds), *Party, State and Society: Electoral Behaviour in Britain since 1820* (Aldershot: Scolar Press, 1997).

LeMahieu D. L., *A Culture for Democracy. Mass Communication and the Cultivated Mind in Britain between the Wars* (Oxford: Clarendon Press, 1988).

Levine L. W., *Highbrow/Lowbrow. The Emergence of Cultural Hierarchy in America* (Cambridge, MA: Harvard University Press, 1988).

Lewis J., *The Voluntary Sector, the State and Social Work in Britain* (Aldershot: Sage, 1995).

Light A., *Forever England; Femininity, Literature and Conservatism between the Wars* (London: Routledge, 1991).

Lockwood D., *The Blackcoated Worker* (Oxford: Oxford University Press, 1958).

Lunn K. and Thurlow R. (eds), *British Fascism* (London: Croom Helm, 1980).

McAleer J., *Popular Reading and Publishing in Britain, 1914–1950* (Oxford: Clarendon Press, 1992).

McBriar A., *Fabian Socialism and English Politics, 1884–1918* (Cambridge: Cambridge University Press, 1962).

McBriar A., *An Edwardian Mixed Doubles: the Bosanquets versus the Webbs: a Study in Social Policy, 1890–1929* (Oxford: Oxford University Press, 1986).

McCarthy H., *The British People and the League of Nations. Democracy, Citizenship and Internationalism, c. 1918–48* (Manchester: Manchester University Press, 2011).

McCarthy H., 'Whose Democracy? Histories of British Political Culture between the Wars', *Historical Journal*, 55, 2012, pp. 221–38.

McCloskey D. N. and Floud R. (eds), *An Economic History of Britain since 1700*, 3 vols (Cambridge: Cambridge University Press, 1981, 1994).

McCrillis N., *The British Conservative Party in the Age of Universal Suffrage: Popular Conservatism, 1918–1929* (Columbus, OH: Ohio State University Press, 1998).

Macintyre S., *A Proletarian Science: Marxism in Britain, 1917–1933* (Cambridge: Cambridge University Press, 1980).

MacKenzie N. and MacKenzie J., *The First Fabians* (London: Weidenfeld & Nicolson, 1977).

McKibbin R., '"Class and Conventional Wisdom": the Conservative Party and the "Public" in Inter-war Britain', in *The Ideologies of Class: Social Relations in Britain, 1880–1950* (Oxford: Oxford University Press, 1990), pp. 259–93.

McKibbin R., *Classes and Cultures: England, 1918–1951* (Oxford: Oxford University Press, 1998).

McKibbin R., *Parties and People, England, 1914–1951* (Oxford: Oxford University Press, 2010).

Maclean I., Montefiore A and Winch P. (ed.), *The Political Responsibility of Intellectuals* (Cambridge: Cambridge University Press, 1990).

Mandler P., '"Against Englishness": English Culture and the Limits to Rural Nostalgia, 1850–1940', *The Transactions of the Royal Historical Society*, 7, 1997, pp. 155–75.

Mandler P., *The Fall and Rise of the Stately Home* (New Haven, CT: Yale University Press, 1997).

Mann G., 'The Intellectuals', *Encounter*, 4, June 1955, pp. 42–9.

Mannheim K., *Conservatism: A Contribution to the Sociology of Knowledge* (London: Routledge & Kegan Paul, 1986).

Marlow J. D., *Questioning the Post-War Consensus Thesis* (Aldershot: Dartmouth, 1996).

Marrison A. J., *British Business and Protection, 1903–1932* (Oxford: Clarendon Press, 1996).

Marwick A., 'Middle Opinion in the Thirties: Planning, Progress and Political "Agreement"', *English Historical Review*, 79, 1964, pp. 285–98.

Middlemas K. and Barnes J., *Baldwin. A Biography* (London: Macmillan, 1969).

Middleton R., *Towards the Managed Economy* (London: Methuen & Co., 1985).

Moggridge D. (ed.), *The Collected Writings of John Maynard Keynes*, vol. XIX: *Activities 1922–1929, the Return to Gold and Industrial Policy* (Cambridge: Macmillan/Cambridge University Press, 1981).

Morris R., *Class, Sect, and Party: the Making of the British Middle Class; Leeds, 1820–1850* (Manchester: Manchester University Press, 1990).

Morton H. V., *In Search of England* (London: Methuen & Co., 1927).

Neill, E., *Michael Oakeshott* (London: Continuum International Publishing, 2011).

O'Sullivan N., *Conservatism* (London: J. M. Dent, 1976).

Oakeshott M., 'Political Education', in P. Laslett (ed.), *Philosophy, Politics and Society* (Oxford: Basil Blackwell, 1956), pp. 1–20.

Oakeshott M., 'On Being Conservative', in *Rationalism in Politics and Other Essays* (London: Methuen & Co., 1962, Indianapolis, Liberty Press, 1991), pp. 407–37.

Offer A., *Property and Politics, 1870–1914: Landownership, Law, Ideology and Urban Development in England* (Cambridge: Cambridge University Press, 1981).

Overy R., *The Morbid Age. Britain between the Wars* (London: Allen Lane, 2009).

Parker R. A. C., *Chamberlain and Appeasement: British Policy and the Coming of the Second World War* (Basingstoke: Macmillan, 1993).

Parker R. A. C., *Churchill and Appeasement* (Basingstoke: Macmillan, 2000).

Perkin H., *The Rise of Professional Society: England since 1880* (London: Routledge, 1991).

Phillips G. A., *The General Strike: the Politics of Industrial Conflict* (London: Weidenfeld & Nicolson, 1976).

Phillips G. D., *The Diehards: Aristocratic Politics and Society in Edwardian England* (Cambridge, MA: Harvard University Press, 1978).

Pimlott B., *Labour and the Left in the 1930s* (Cambridge: Cambridge University Press, 1977).

Pollard S., *The Development of the British Economy* (London: Edward Arnold, 4th edn, 1992).

Potts, A., '"Constable Country" between the Wars', in R. Samuel (ed.), *Patriotism: The Making and Unmaking of British National Identity*, vol. 3, *National Fictions* (London: Routledge, 1989), pp. 160–86.

Pugh M., *The Tories and the People, 1880–1935* (Oxford: Basil Blackwell, 1985).

Pugh M., *State and Society: A Social and Political History of Britain, 1870–1997* (London: Edward Arnold, 1999).

Pugh M., *The Making of Modern British Politics, 1867–1945* (Oxford: Blackwell, 3rd edn, 2002).

Pugh M., *We Danced All Night: a Social History of Britain between the Wars* (London: Vintage Books, 2009).

Pugh P., *Agitate, Educate, Organize: 100 Years of Fabian Socialism* (London: Methuen & Co., 1984).

Quinton A., *The Politics of Imperfection. The Religious and Secular Traditions of Conservative Thought in England from Hooker to Oakeshott* (London: Faber & Faber, 1978).

Ramsden J., *The Age of Balfour and Baldwin, 1902–1940* (London: Longmans, 1978).

Ramsden J., *The Making of Conservative Party Policy: the Conservative Research Department since 1929* (London: Longmans, 1980).

Ramsden J., 'A Party for Owners or a Party for Earners? How Far Did the British Conservative Party Really Change after 1945?', *The Transactions of the Royal Historical Society*, 37, 1987, pp. 49–63.

Ramsden J., *The Age of Churchill and Eden, 1940–1957* (Harlow: Longmans, 1995).

Ramsden J., *An Appetite for Power. A History of the Conservative Party since 1830* (London: Harper Collins, 1998).

Ritschel D., 'A Corporatist Economy in Britain? Capitalist Planning for Industrial Self-Government in the 1930s', *English Historical Review*, 106 (418), 1991, pp. 41–65.

Ritschel D., *The Politics of Planning: the Debate on Economic Planning in Britain in the 1930s* (Oxford: Oxford University Press, 1997).

Roberts A., *The Holy Fox. The Life of Lord Halifax* (London: Weidenfeld & Nicolson, 1991).

Roberts A., *Eminent Churchillians* (London: Weidenfeld & Nicolson, 1994).

Samuels S., 'English Intellectuals and Politics in the 1930s', in P. Rieff (ed.), *On Intellectuals: Theoretical Studies, Case Studies* (New York: Doubleday, 1969), pp. 196–247.

Savage M., Barlow J., Dickens P. and Fielding T., *Property, Bureaucracy and Culture: Middle Class Formation in Contemporary Britain* (London: Routledge, 1992).

Schmidt G., *The Politics and Economics of Appeasement: British Foreign Policy in the 1930s* (Leamington Spa: Berg Press, 1984).

Scruton R., *The Meaning of Conservatism* (London: Macmillan, 1980).

Searle G. R., *Corruption in British Politics, 1895–1930* (Oxford: Clarendon Press, 1987).

Seawright D., *The British Conservative Party and One Nation Politics* (New York: Continuum, 2010).

Seldon A. and Ball S. (eds), *Conservative Century: the Conservative Party since 1900* (Oxford: Oxford University Press, 1994).

Self R. C., *Tariffs and Tories: the Conservative Party and the Politics of Tariff Reform, 1922–1932* (London: Garland Publishers, 1986).

Seliger M., *Ideology and Politics* (London: Allen & Unwin, 1976).

Shepherd R., *A Class Divided: Appeasement and the Road to Munich, 1938* (London: Macmillan, 1988).

Shils E., 'The Intellectuals: Great Britain', *Encounter*, 4, 1955, pp. 5–16.

Shils E., 'British Intellectuals in the Mid-Twentieth Century', in *The Intellectuals and the Powers: and other Essays* (Chicago, IL: University of Chicago Press, 1972), pp. 135–53.

Short M. E., 'The Politics of Personal Taxation; Budget-Making in Britain, 1917–31' (PhD dissertation, University of Cambridge, 1984).

Skidelsky R., *Politicians and the Slump. The Labour Government of 1929–31* (London: Macmillan, 1967).

Smart N., *The National Government, 1931–40* (London: Longmans, 1999).

Smith H. L. (ed.), *War and Social Change: British Society in the Second World War* (Manchester: Manchester University Press, 1986).

Soffer R. N., *Discipline and Power: the University, History, and the Making of an English Elite, 1870–1930* (Stanford, CA: Stanford University Press, 1994).

Soffer R. N., *History, Historians, and Conservatism in Britain and America: From the Great War to Thatcher and Reagan* (Oxford: Oxford University Press, 2008).

Stannage T., *Baldwin Thwarts the Opposition: the British General Election of 1935* (London: Croom Helm, 1980).

Stapleton J., *Englishness and the Study of Politics: the Social and Political Thought of Ernest Barker* (Cambridge: Cambridge University Press, 1994).

Stapleton J., 'Resisting the Centre at the Extremes: "English" Liberalism in the Political Thought of Interwar Britain', *British Journal of Politics & International Relations*, 1 (3), 1999, pp. 270–92.

Stapleton J., *Political Intellectuals and Public Identities in Britain since 1850* (Manchester: Manchester University Press, 2001).

Stapleton J., *Sir Arthur Bryant and National History in Twentieth-Century Britain* (Lanham, MD: Lexington Books, 2006).

Stedman Jones G., 'The Pathology of English History', *New Left Review*, 46, 1967, pp. 29–44.

Stevenson J., *British Society, 1914–45* (Harmondsworth: Penguin Books, 3rd edn, 1990).

Stewart G., *Burying Caesar: Churchill, Chamberlain and the Battle for the Tory Party* (London: Phoenix, 2000).

Stone D., *Breeding Superman: Nietzsche, Race and Eugenics in Edwardian and Interwar Britain* (Liverpool: Liverpool University Press, 2002).

Stone D., 'The English Mistery, the BUF and the Dilemmas of British Fascism', *Journal of Modern History*, 75 (2), 2003, pp. 336–58.

Stone D., *Responses to Nazism in Britain 1933–1939: Before War and Holocaust* (Basingstoke/New York: Palgrave Macmillan, 2003).

Stone D., The Far Right and the Back-to-the-Land Movement, in J. V. Gottlieb and T. P. Linehan (eds), *The Culture of Fascism: Visions of the Far Right in Britain* (London: I. B. Tauris, 2004), pp. 182–98.

Stone R. and Rowe D. A., *The Measurement of Consumers Expenditure and Behaviour in the United Kingdom, 1920–38* (Cambridge: Cambridge University Press, 1954).

Street P., *Arthur Bryant. Portrait of a Historian* (London: Collins, 1979).

Swinton College, '"Intellectuals and Conservatives": a Symposium', *Swinton College Journal*, 14, 1968.

Szamuely T., 'Intellectuals and Conservatism', *Swinton Journal*, 14 (1), 1968, pp. 5–15.

Taylor A. J. P., 'Tory History', in *Essays in English History* (London: Hamish Hamilton, 1976), pp. 17–22.

Taylor D. J., *Bright Young People: the Rise and Fall of a Generation, 1918–1940* (London: Chatto & Windus, 2007).

Thackeray D., *Conservatism for the Democratic Age: Conservative Cultures and the Challenge of Mass Politics in Early Twentieth Century England* (Manchester: Manchester University Press, 2013).

Thompson E. P., 'The Peculiarities of the English', in *The Poverty of Theory* (London: Merlin Press, 1978), pp. 245–301.

Thompson F. M. L., *Gentrification and the Enterprise Culture, 1780–1980* (Oxford: Oxford University Press, 2001).

Thompson N., *The Anti-Appeasers: Conservative Opposition to Appeasement in the 1930s* (Oxford: Oxford University Press, 1971).

Thorpe A., *The British General Election of 1931* (Oxford: Clarendon Press, 1991).

Thurlow R., *Fascism in Britain: a History, 1918–1945* (Oxford: Basil Blackwell Ltd, 1987).

Tomlinson J., *Employment Policy: the Crucial Years* (Oxford: Clarendon Press, 1988).

Tomlinson J., *Public Policy and the Economy since 1900* (Oxford: Clarendon Press, 1990).

Toye, R., *The Labour Party and the Planned Economy, 1931–1951* (London: Royal Historical Society, 2003).

Toye, R., *Lloyd George and Churchill: Rivals for Greatness* (London: Macmillan, 2007).

Toye, R., *Churchill's Empire: The World that Made Him and the World He Made* (London: Macmillan, 2010).

Toye, R., *The Roar of the Lion: The Untold Story of Churchill's World War II Speeches* (Oxford: Oxford University Press, 2013).

Turner B. S., 'The Absent English Intelligentsia', *Comenius*, 38, 1990, pp. 138–51.

Turner B. S., 'Ideology and Utopia in the Formation of an Intelligentsia: Reflections on the English Cultural Conduit', *Theory, Culture and Society*, 9 (1), 1992, pp. 183–210.

Turner J., 'A Land Fit for Tories to Live in: the Political Ecology of the British Conservative Party, 1944–94', *Contemporary European History*, 4, 1995, pp. 189–208.

Waites B., *A Class Society at War: England, 1914–18* (Leamington Spa: Berg, 1987).

Walsha R., 'The One Nation Group: a Tory Approach to Backbench Politics and Organization, 1950–55', *Twentieth Century British History*, 11, 2000, pp. 183–214.

Webber G. C., *The Ideology of the British Right, 1918–1939* (London: Croom Helm, 1986).

Webster C., 'Conservatives and Consensus: the Politics of the National Health Service, 1951–1964', in A. Oakley (ed.), *The Politics of the Welfare State* (London: UCL Press, 1994), pp. 54–74.

Wiener M. J., *English Culture and the Decline of the Industrial Spirit, 1850–1980* (Cambridge: Cambridge University Press, 1981).

Williamson P., *National Crisis and National Government: British Politics, the Economy and the Empire, 1926–32* (Cambridge: Cambridge University Press, 1992).

Williamson P., 'The Doctrinal Politics of Stanley Baldwin', in M. Bentley (ed.), *Public and Private Doctrine: Essays in British History Presented to Maurice Cowling* (Cambridge: Cambridge University Press, 1993), pp. 181–208.

Williamson P., *Stanley Baldwin: Conservative Leadership and National Values* (Cambridge: Cambridge University Press, 1999).

Williamson P., 'Baldwin's Reputation: Politics and History, 1937–1967', *Historical Journal*, 47 (1), 2004, pp. 127–68.

Williamson P. and Michie R. C. (eds), *The British Governement and the City of London in the Twentieth Century* (Cambridge: Cambridge University Press, 2004).

Witherell L., *Rebel on the Right: Henry Page Croft and the Crisis of British Conservatism, 1903–14* (Newark: University of Delaware Press, 1997).

Wolfe W., *From Radicalism to Socialism: Men and Ideas in the Formation of Fabian Socialist Doctrines, 1881–1889* (New Haven, CT: Yale University Press, 1975).

Worley M., *Labour inside the Gate: a History of the British Labour Party between the Wars* (London: I. B. Tauris, 2005).

Worley M. (ed.), *The Foundations of the British Labour Party: Identities, Cultures and Perspectives, 1900–1939* (Farnham: Ashgate, 2009).

Young H., *One of Us* (London: Macmillan, 1991).

Zweiniger-Bargielowska I., 'Rationing, Austerity and the Conservative Electoral Recovery after 1945', *Historical Journal*, 37, 1993, pp. 173–97.

Zweiniger-Bargielowska I., *Austerity in Britain: Rationing, Controls, and Consumption, 1939–1955* (Oxford: Oxford University Press, 2000).

Index